HOMOSEXUALITY

Review and Comments

"A comparative study of the origins, development, and potential treatability of the male homosexual. The authors of this work base their findings on clinical work with 106 male homosexuals and 100 male heterosexuals in psychoanalytic treatment. . . . This book is therefore a welcome contribution . . . to social responsibility and enlightenment."

Scientific American

"It is a rare pleasure to find a well-grounded statistical study in which the subjects emerge as real people, recognizable, and seen in depth through the sensitive eyes of skilled clinicians. . . . The bulk of the book confirms or rebuts the generalizations from which we work."

Sheldon B. Kopp, Ph.D.
American Journal of Psychotherapy

"The book is a notable contribution to the literature on homosexuality. It clarifies muddy concepts, gives us data instead of speculations, and leaves us with many ideas for future research."

Harold I. Lief, M.D.
Archives of General Psychiatry

"The conclusions reached are of great interest. . . . The authors' views are supported by evidence . . . collected in such a way that subjective bias is excluded as far as possible, and, until further equally careful studies have either supplemented or disproved this work, it must be allowed to stand. . . . It is a pleasure to welcome a book from a group of psychoanalysts which is both self-critical and constructive.

Times Literary Supplement

"It is encouraging to see such a complex clinical topic handled with such scholarly and dispassionate objectivity. . . . The reader will find himself better informed on the subject when he puts the book down, and will have enjoyed the process of his enlightenment."

James C. Miller
Director of the Mental Health Research Institute
University of Michigan

HOMOSEXUALITY

A Psychoanalytic Study

IRVING BIEBER

Toby B. Bieber
Harvey J. Dain
Paul R. Dince
Marvin G. Drellich
Henry G. Grand
Ralph H. Gundlach
Malvina W. Kremer
Alfred H. Rifkin
Cornelia B. Wilbur

ARONSON
Jason Aronson Inc.
Northvale, New Jersey
London

10 9 8 7 6 5 4 3 2 1

The authors gratefully acknowledge permission to reprint portions of Irving Bieber's article, "Male Homosexuality," © 1979, *The Canadian Journal of Psychiatry*, Vol. 14, pp. 402-403.

Library of Congress Cataloging-in-Publication Data

Homosexuality : a psychoanalytic study / Irving Bieber . . . [et al.].
p. cm.

Bibliography: p.
Includes index.
ISBN 0-87668-989-6
1. Homosexuality, Male. 2. Psychoanalysis. I. Bieber, Irving, 1908– .
[DNLM: 1. Homosexuality. 2. Psychoanalysis. WM 615 H7665]
RC558.3.H65 1988 616.85'834—dc 19
DNLM/DLC for Library of Congress 88-14560 CIP

Manufactured in the United States of America.

Jason Aronson Inc. offers books and cassettes. For information and catalog write to Jason Aronson, Inc., 230 Livingston St., Northvale, NJ 07647

For Ralph H. Gundlach, Malvina W. Kremer, Alfred H. Rifkin, and Paul Zimmering

Contents

Foreword

THE LAST TWENTY-FIVE YEARS have marked a period of social, behavioral, and ideological change in male homosexuality. Homosexuality before then was hardly a topic of casual conversation, nor was it an issue claiming the attention of activists, politicians, and health workers, nor was it ever openly dealt with in the mass media. When in 1963 the *New York Times* broke the silence and ran a front-page feature story on male homosexuality, other major publications and television programs in quick succession followed suit. The sexual revolution was already under way, but gay liberation as an organized entity did not take off until the end of the sixties when it joined the mainstream of the ongoing minority and women's protest movements against discriminatory practices.

The loosening of uptight sexual attitudes and the significant lessening of social taboos against homosexuals are now part of everyday life. Increasingly, however, there has been a blurring of lines between the broader social, political, economic, and discriminatory issues—especially since the tragic onslaught of AIDS—and the study and evaluation of the psychological processes that determine an individual's capability of being sexually turned on by another of the same sex. As psychoanalysts, our scientific interest has been and continues to be centered on the psychosocial development of homosexuality, its cognitive dynamics, family dynamics, interpersonal processes, adaptive techniques, and the results of psychoanalytic therapy. The republication of this book deals with those same aspects exactly as written twenty-five years ago. Since then, there has been a burgeoning of contributions, many with viewpoints disparate to our own. With this foreword we aim to revisit some of the original research, review salient aspects, and familiarize the reader with at least a few of our ideas and observations formulated since the book was originally published (Bieber et al. 1962).*

When we began that project, the Society of Medical Psychoanalysts had 100 members from whom a group of analysts and two psychoanalytically trained psychologists were recruited—a research team that co-authored this book. Of the Society's roster, seventy-seven analysts volunteered as respondents; each filled out a detailed questionnaire that tapped information from two patient samples consisting of 106 male homosexuals and a comparison group of 100 male heterosexuals.

When the book first appeared, critics questioned the methodology on two major points: first, how reliable were data obtained not directly from patients but from their analysts (data concerning not only the patients, but their families whom the analysts had never met); second, could the findings obtained from a white, middle- and upper-class patient sample be generalized to the homosexual population at large? In the intervening years we have personally seen well over 1,000 homosexual men in psychoanalytically focused interviews where we obtained information from them directly. We also have examined many parents. A substantial number were interviewed at a municipal hospital; others were seen in private practice. The clinic patients came from a socioeconomic stratum lower than those seen in private practice and were made up of three ethnic groups: black, Puerto Rican, and white, distributed about evenly. The data obtained were in accord with the findings first reported. In those areas where we tapped similar items, the findings were in agreement with a study done in England by Westwood (1960) of 127 working-class male homosexuals, only 5 percent of whom had ever been in psychiatric treatment. Another study of nonpatient homosexuals by Snortum and co-workers (1969) and one by Evans (1969), each using our questionnaire, also reported findings similar to ours, although there were some differences in interpretation of data. The consistency of information on nonpatients and patients coming from lower socioeconomic

*The book was given the Hofheimer Award, Honorable Mention, by the American Psychiatric Association, 1964.

strata supports the appropriateness of generalizing from our patient sample to the homosexual population at large.

Over the years more than a few critics in and out of the psychiatric field have misquoted our work, abstracted it simplistically, or assigned erroneous meanings. One frequently occurring error cites a dominating mother and a weak or absent father as the modal combination we supposedly said influences a homosexual outcome. Although more mothers of homosexual sons than comparison mothers were dominating, what distinguished the two groups was the difference in frequency and intensity of an overly close attachment. The mothers and homosexual sons who were significantly more often closely attached to each other than heterosexuals and their mothers comprised three-fourths of that sample. We tagged this relationship "close-binding-intimate" (CBI). A singular type of defective father-son relationship was described in the background of homosexual subjects and corroborated by our observations since then. The research questionnaire did not include as a single item, "weak" father, nor did we find as causative an "absent" father as an item in itself. If the time spent with a son is positive, paternal absence need not be deleterious. Fathers who are home infrequently may still be excellent fathers and role models. The study examined through many items and clusters of items the relationships among members of the nuclear family, tapping attitudes and behavior between the parents and the patient, and between the patient and his siblings, as will be noted in a perusal of the questionnaire.

The interparental relationships in the homosexual sample were, in general, unsatisfactory. These parents spent little time together, shared few interests, were usually hostile to each other, and often, one was contemptuous of the other. Where there were other children, the homosexual son was clearly the mother's favorite, and in many cases she openly preferred him to her husband. She spent a great deal of time with this son, shared confidences with him, was overly concerned about his health and the possibility of injury to him, and tended to be overcontrolling. A sexual quality was noted in the relationship between a CBI mother and her homosexual son in 85 percent of that group. This was a key variable. The son became a close partner with whom the mother lived out a nongenital, but nonetheless sexualized bond in which the son was sexually overstimulated within the context of overintimacy with the mother; yet at the same time these women induced heterosexual inhibition through sexually restrictive prohibitions. In some instances the erotic component was overt. Seductive maternal behavior was expressed in inappropriate physical exposure, disregard for the son's privacy, sensuous kissing, and various other kinds of unwarranted physical contact. As a general trend within the family system, the CBI mother-son bond constituted a closely attached dyad while the father and other siblings remained relatively peripheral.

A son so patterned tends to be submissive to his mother and overly dependent upon her. He develops profound love for her, and she becomes and usually remains the most important figure in his emotional life. Although such a son may become angry at his mother, his basic attitude is most often one of devotion and love, not hostility and fear. Other mother–son patterns were also noted; for example, six mothers seemed detached and disinterested. As young boys their sons had been farmed out to institutions or foster homes where the mothers rarely visited. This small subsample is exceptional but illustrative of types of mothers other than those who formed a close binding intimacy with their homosexual son.

The father-son relationship was strikingly different. The fathers were at best ambivalent, oscillating between affectionate behavior and rejection; at worst, they were unremittingly hostile. In some cases, the rejection was covert but more often it was overt. Covert hostility may be screened behind detachment and apparent disinterest. As children, sons sense the hostility; as they grow older, they may repress their perceptions and by the time they are adults remember only that the father was detached and disinterested. Fathers who are constructive and affectionately related to their son and not submissive to a CBI wife will protect against deleterious maternal influences. A good illustration is a family we followed from the time the son was born. The mother had had several previous miscarriages followed by two stillbirths. When she finally carried through and bore an extraordinarily beautiful, healthy boy, the father responded to the newborn with as much joy and caring as did the mother who, however, soon fitted the CBI pattern. The father, an unsophisticated but sensible man, did not enter into a competitive struggle with his wife, but out of love for his son was able to protect him against becoming a "sissy," which surely would have happened had the mother been given free rein with the child. When the boy sometimes engaged in a prank that ordinarily would deserve a reprimand or dirtied the expensive clothing his mother had bought for him, the father would speak of it with pride, a reinforcement of assertiveness this boy needed.

The father would enter into playful conspiracies with his son such as, "We won't tell mother, but you and I are going fishing on Sunday." The youngster grew to heterosexual manhood seemingly unbeset by dislocating childhood problems. He married and had a loving relationship with his wife and several children.

In the initial phase of interviews, ambivalent fathers not infrequently talk about their love for their sons. They seem genuinely puzzled that their boys turned out to be homosexual. One such consultation brought in a professional couple. The father was a dignified man with charming manners. He declared that he was completely at sea as to why his 21-year-old son was having so many problems. On probe, the parents recalled that when their son was about 13, he acquired a close friend. He was otherwise isolated from close peer relationships, a situation commonly noted in homosexual childhood history. The father objected to the friendship and tried to break it up. He called the chum a "son of a bitch," whereupon the boy retaliated by calling his father a "son of a bitch." Enraged, the father wrestled the boy to the ground and began to choke him. The mother heard the struggle and rushed in to separate them. The boy ran out of the house and after she searched anxiously for him for several hours, she finally found him wandering the neighborhood. When she coaxed him to return home, he resisted, saying he knew his father hated him and wanted to kill him.

One recent patient observed that when his mother was away, his father was friendly, even affectionate. With the mother's return, the father would revert to his usual hostile, abusive behavior. Such men enter into a sexually competitive struggle with the son against whom they act out a gamut of destructive attitudes and behaviors.

Another father, although obviously psychotic, offers a caricature and therefore an enlarged view of the psychopathology inherent in the father-homosexual son relationship. When the patient was born, the father left declaring he would not share his home with another male. A sister, three years older, had not had the same repelling effect. The family lived in a small town, and the patient often saw his father, who never greeted or otherwise acknowledged him. The patient, a schizophrenic and exclusively homosexual, was 37 years old when he was interviewed. Despite the utter rejection, he still called his father on Christmas to wish him well. When asked how he responded, the patient said, "He just hangs up."

Most boys who become homosexual leave childhood with a profound fear and hatred of the father, usually consciously felt. At the same time there is an overweening desire for paternal affection and acceptance. The same father who is detached from or critical of his homosexual son may "light up" for another son or possibly a nephew or a friend's son. We have repeatedly stated and written that a boy who has an affectionately related, constructive father will not become homosexual; however, one must not get trapped into the fallacy of the converse, that is, that a hostile destructive father produces a homosexual son.

It sometimes happens during the course of analysis that the mother of a homosexual patient dies. The reaction we have observed is usually one of profound grief and a sense of deep loss. Neurotic hostility and guilt are generally not in evidence. Not so when the father dies. Reactions vary from bitter regret that there will never again be a chance to redeem paternal love and rectify old hurts, to icy disregard.

Relationships with siblings also tend to be disturbed. A central factor is the mother's overt favoritism to the homosexual son, which creates sharp rivalry and hostility toward mother's pet. Intense jealousy is usually much more pronounced in brothers than in sisters. There are occasional exceptions, such as when an older brother takes on a paternal role and, to a greater or lesser extent, helps repair or prevent paternal damage. More often, brothers are hostile, and most homosexuals who have siblings of either sex have more positive relationships with their sisters.

The study of the family, family therapy, and group therapy are increasingly important in therapeutic programs. In assessing family adaptation, we have found it productive to compare the older and younger children in terms of work, sexual effectiveness, and interpersonal effectiveness. Where the older children have fared better than the younger ones, we usually find that the parental relationship has deteriorated over time, adversely affecting the younger children. Where the younger ones are more successful, the parental relationship has improved and the family strengthened. In large families, the son who becomes homosexual tends to be a younger member. By the time he is born, the marital relationship has become sorely strained.

Closely similar to sibling relationships are the peer group associations with members of the same sex, particularly before adolescence. Between the ages of 5 and 13 most prehomosexual boys integrate poorly into same-sex peer groups. They are either isolates or have one or two friends very much like themselves, or play predominantly with girls. They fail to integrate into a peer group essentially because they fear the combativeness they see in other boys. There are heated disagreements among sex researchers as to the determinants of homosexuality and its place in a diagnostic category, but there is general agreement that as children, homosexuals as a rule do not fare well with same-sex peer groups. Characteristically, prehomosexual boys are excessively fearful of physical injury. The scrambling and aggression that go on in games and activities frighten them and they withdraw. The all-boy peer group is an important, probably essential association that provides an opportunity for a desensitization of the fear of male combativeness, and it gives boys easily assimilated models for positive masculine identification. If a boy cannot enter into situations that might help overcome fears of male combativeness and that would strengthen the identification with other males, he is not only deprived of a reparative experience but is further traumatized by boys who could have been of enormous help, but instead become antagonists. They identify him as a "sissy" or "oddball" and make him the butt of verbal and physical abuse. If there is any single factor that stands out in homosexual development, it is the consistency of negative relationships with other males.

The pathogenic mother-son relationship as an explanatory theory has achieved primacy in current psychoanalytic literature. The fear of the castrating father as part of the oedipal dynamic is, of course, accorded significance, but in explicating homosexuality it has become secondary to the mother-son hypothesis. The two currently dominant themes are that homosexual men fear the castrating power of women—an idea emphasized by Melanie Klein (1932)—and that defective separation and individuation in the symbiotic relationship with the mother promote a context for a feminine identification with her (Stoller 1987). Our data have not supported either of these formulations. We have found that the large majority of homosexual men are not afraid of women. They do fear a sexual or romantic relationship but if such a possibility is excluded, most feel comfortable with women, enjoy their company, and often trust them more than they trust men. T. Bieber (1971) has observed that the attitudes of male patients toward her are fondness, trust, and at times covert sexuality; the transference is essentially maternal. Since the therapeutic situation precludes sexual acting-out, a private relationship may still be had with a woman, but without anxiety. In contrast, the relationship of male homosexual patients with I. Bieber (1980) is often dominated by ambivalence—the wish for acceptance and affection on the one hand and competitive hostility and mistrust on the other.

As for the hypothesis that men primarily fear castration by women and, as formulated in the concept of the "dentate vagina," are therefore sexually inhibited by such fear, an analytic patient offered a dream that illuminated the meaning of that concept. The patient, a dentist, dreamed that he was looking at his wife's vagina when, to his horror, he saw that it had teeth. In associating to the dream he stated that the teeth were not hers and described them in detail. They were wide, spatulate, and yellow-stained; he was sure they were his uncle's, whose own teeth were yellow-stained from his habit of smoking cigars. Thus, the castrating teeth belonged to a man, obviously an oedipal figure. We view the "dentate vagina" as a composite symbol that incorporates the erotic stimulus of the vagina with the threat of castration by a feared male.

It is our view that difficulties in separation and individuation are not the primary determinants of psychopathology but are the consequences of faulty parenting. Children with separation-individuation difficulties are those whose maturation had previously been interfered with. This concept is basically synonymous with earlier ideas developed by Kardiner (1939) on dependence and independence. The only feasible connection between incomplete or defective separation-individuation and homosexuality is that the mothers tend to promote pathologic dependency, a characteristic that indeed may be discerned among many homosexuals. It does not account, however, for a homosexual choice as the object for gratifying neurotic dependency wishes and the exclusion of a dependent heterosexual relationship.

Theorists who ascribe the dominant psychopathology of homosexuality to the mother-son relationship place its origins in the preoedipal phase, an assumption that also rests upon the separation-individuation paradigm. It is unlikely that meaningful productions can be recovered from adults concerning a period of life before the age of 2. Undoubtedly, profound psychopathology established in the first two years of life can have deleterious effects upon the sexual as well as other biosocial systems; however, psychoanalytic formulations dealing with the preoedipal period, no matter how imaginative, must be viewed as speculative unless they rest upon observational data. The oral phase of sexuality, for example, is a speculative theory that has no support in clinical observation, unlike the later Oedipus complex, which can be observed in the behavior of children. How preoedipal pathology specifically distorts oedipal development has yet to be demonstrated. We cannot accept at face value a theoretical construct as an operational process. One may document a father's hostility to his son from birth on and even demonstrate disturbances in father-son contact before the oedipal period. Similarly, a mother's inappropriate attachment to a son from birth on may be observed in various kinds of pathogenic behaviors. Such very early influences may well dislocate heterosexual development, but that is quite different from interpreting adult psychopathology as having evolved from defects in separation-individuation in the preoedipal relationship with either parent.

Three categories of homosexually arousing stimuli have been delineated by I. Bieber (1975). First, there is a displacement of the heterosexual stimulus to a homosexual object. One patient became aware that he was aroused by men who had eyebrows resembling his mother's. Displacing the stimulus to a homosexual partner conceals the nature of the heterosexual stimulus. Feminine characteristics in skin texture, body build, absence of body hair, and so forth, may constitute heterosexual stimuli, which are then displaced to men. Freud was aware of a somewhat similar mechanism. He observed that sexual arousal by a woman could be acted out with a man. "We have frequently seen that inverts have by no means been unsusceptible to the charms of women but have continually transferred the excitation aroused by women onto a male object."

Second, there is an eroticization of the feared object. One patient was attracted to men with hands similar to his father's. Often beaten and pummeled as a child, he was consciously aware that he feared his father and his hands. By converting the threatening hands into an erotic object, the patient was able to neutralize the perceived danger. In another case a young man revealed that he was sexually aroused by hairy men. He reported a dream of himself in bed with an attractive woman; then from under the bed came a brawny, hairy arm with a knife in hand, poised to kill him. In the dream, hair is linked to lethal attack; yet consciously, this man was sexually excited by hairy men. A basic mechanism in sexual masochism is the eroticization of feared objects.

Third, arousal is associated with affection shown by men. A man who offers warmth and acceptance may have a sexually arousing effect even when he does not conform to his partner's physical standards of sexual preference. The need for physical contact and the wish to be held may also stir a sexual response. In many instances, the act or even the fantasy of being held tenderly by a man is erotically stimulating.

The process of identification as explicating, at least in part, certain homosexual behaviors and the choice of partners is well accepted, but there is a lack of clarity about whom homosexuals identity with, a problem that seems to have originated in contradictory statements made by Freud (1953). He initially believed that homosexuals identified with women because, like women, they were erotically responsive to other men. Later, Freud introduced the idea that the homosexual identified with his mother. "In all cases we have examined, we have established the fact that . . . in the earlier years of their childhood (they) pass through a phase of very intense but short-lived fixation to a woman (usually their mother) and that after leaving this behind, they identify themselves with a woman." In the same paper, however, he also stated: "There can be no doubt that a large proportion of male inverts retain the mental quality of masculinity, that they possess relatively few of the secondary characters of the opposite sex and what they look for in their sexual object are, in fact, feminine mental traits." Thus, Freud advanced the idea that homosexuals identify with both men and women. This seeming contradiction was consistent with the bisexual theory postulating a male and female potential on a linear continuum of masculinity and femininity; men were closest to one end of the line and women were closest to the other end, whereas homosexuals were placed at various points on the centinuum.

Gender role behavior has become a criterion for judging a feminine or masculine identification. If a male child or adult acts effeminately, the identification is said to be with a woman—mother and sisters first; later on, other women. Green (1987) gives detailed criteria for assessing feminine role behavior, such as playing with dolls, choosing toys girls usually prefer, playing with girls, and so forth. But can female role behavior be used reliably as a pathognomic criterion for feminine identification? The fetishistic transvestite who cross-dresses from childhood on is a useful example. He dons the clothes of his mother or sister and is clearly role-behaving as a woman in a literal sense, comparable to male actors of old who took female roles in theatrical presentations; however, the fetishistic transvestite reacts as a male to the woman he is role-playing and with the characteristic sexual excitement, erection, and masturbation. Although such men engage in feminine role behavior, they react as a male to a female. Another example is that of a man who chooses a look-alike partner and, as the insertee in sexual intercourse, enacts the role of a woman. The classical explanation is that a self-similar choice reflects an individual's narcissism, that such a person can only love another like himself. Yet, the dynamics may be viewed quite differently: the insertee acts out a feminine role but identifies himself with the look-alike insertor who is taking a male role. The homosexuals we have examined or treated are generally identified with men, although a sense of impaired masculinity is felt by all of them. In describing their preadolescent boyhood, most recall pained feelings of fragility and being unlike other boys, because they felt physically inferior. Convinced that they were incapable of athletic performance, especially in baseball and football, they often describe themselves as having been poorly coordinated even though self-descriptions in other activities indicate they were far from clumsy. As adults, they are not less physically adept than the average, and many are agile and graceful on the dance floor; oddly enough, they tend not to consider social dancing as an athletic enterprise that requires coordination.

In a comparison study of male homosexuals and heterosexuals, Bell and colleagues (1981) found that only 18 percent of the homosexual sample felt "very masculine" compared to 67 percent of the heterosexuals. In our clinical experience we have not encountered a male homosexual who had a "very masculine" self-concept. In an informal meeting with a man referred by a colleague as representing a well-adjusted homosexual, his current adaptation was discussed. He was successful, urbane, an intelligent conversationalist, and enjoyed his social life. He was of strapping build, well over 6 feet tall, and weighed over 200 pounds. Asked how he felt about his size, he said he did not think of himself as a big man, that no homosexual sees himself that way—a reference to an impaired sense of masculinity despite his apparently good adjustment.

One of the fallacies of the bisexual theory places masculinity as an opposite of femininity. The opposite of masculinity is nonmasculinity. A feeling of effeminacy is not comparable to a sense of masculine inadequacy. A biological basis for effeminacy has been proposed that links homosexuality to insufficient masculinization of the brain due to low androgen levels pre- and perinatally, an idea extrapolated from experiments on rats but one that remains unsupported as a condition affecting man. In a study of twelve males who had a 47 XXY chromosome syndrome and whose median age was 16.7, Bancroft and colleagues

(1982) found that on a masculinity sex inventory scale these young men scored below average, but they also scored below average on a femininity scale.

The determinants we find salient in men who are effeminate or state a wish to be a woman consist of: submissive compliance with parental wishes to have a girl, seen particularly in transsexuals; a son's belief that femininity evokes paternal affection as expressed to the mother and sisters; the belief that women can much more easily acquire a dependable benefactor; a usually unconscious fear of exposing masculinity lest it evoke hostile behavior in other men, especially father and brothers. I. Bieber (1977) has described preferential parental behavior that is dramatically corroborated by Green (1987), who followed the development of a pair of identical twins, one homosexual (Paul), the other heterosexual (Frank, named after his father). Asked, "How different are the two boys (aged 8) in regard to masculinity?" the mother replied, "Very. First of all, Frank walks like a clodhopper. Paul, on the other hand, walks femininely. He is on the pretty side. He has a feminine ring to his voice. He is like a female when he gets upset. He thoroughly enjoys playing with dolls. He and his sister can play day upon day. His brother will deliberately go out and get into a football game or anything with the older boys in the neighborhood. Paul will still dress in woman's clothes, but he is getting out of the habit because he knows it really aggravates us. He will put hair clips in his hair. When they play house Frank is always the father and Paul is always the mother and sister." Green also cites a report of four other sets of identical twins; in each pair one was homosexual, the other, heterosexual. The four heterosexuals had been named after the father, a phenomenon we observed in one other case.

The growing emphasis on biological factors in the etiology of male homosexuality has centered mainly on hormonal function, a focus that, in our view, leads up a blind alley; however, the interest in biological aspects does have merit. All animals whose reproduction depends on heterosexual mating have inborn mechanisms guaranteeing heterosexual arousal. There is no evidence in any species of a built-in biological guarantee for homosexuality. In mammals this mechanism is olfaction. I. Bieber (1959) presented evidence of the role of olfaction in human sexuality and its importance in the early triggering of sexual response to the opposite sex and ushering in of the Oedipus complex. Kalogerakis (1963) described the olfactory reactions of a child between the ages of 2 and 5. Never a witness to parental sexual activity, the boy's reaction after they had intercourse was distinctly negative. He complained about the smell even after they had showered. After some time, his olfactory reactions became positive to the mother but aversive to the father. He also developed an olfactory foot fetish to women, a fetish that ultimately disappeared. All children go through a heterosexual phase, including those who later become homosexual. Freud referred to this in his well-known letter to the mother of a homosexual, in which he said that the seeds of heterosexuality can be noted in all homosexuals.

That there is a biological heterosexual imperative is demonstrated in an unusual clinical syndrome reported by Peterson and co-authors (1977) with a group of pseudohermaphrodites from several small villages in the Dominican Republic. These young men were born with a deficiency of the enzyme steroid 5-alpha reductase, which is necessary for the production of dihydrotestosterone from testosterone. Dihydrotestosterone is required for testes descent and for normal formation of the external genitalia. Designated as female at birth, these boys were brought up as girls until adolescence. "At puberty virilization occurred in the affected male with a deepening of the voice, an increase of muscle mass and considerable growth of external genitalia. . . . They have a libido directed toward females and all but two of thirty-three have assumed the male gender role. They have male gender identity." Thus, despite having been raised as girls, the biological heritage of these young men steered them toward heterosexuality.

All comparison studies find similar behavioral patterns among prehomosexual boys. As emphasized, they are excessively afraid of physical injury, avoid rough play and competitive sports, and play predominantly with girls. If there is a biological underpinning for this kind of behavior, it can be summarized as related to timidity. Suggestive evidence appears in a study by Jacklin and colleagues (1983) of the relationship between neonatal sex steroid hormones and timidity in 6- to 18-month-old boys and girls. The study found a lower testosterone level in the umbilical cord blood of boys judged to be timid compared with nontimid babies. This condition was found in two of their three samples. In the study of the adolescent 47-XXY-chromosome boys, timidity was one of the significant differences between them and the comparison group. "The common theme in their personality was timidity and lack of assertiveness which showed itself most strikingly as problems in peer group relations. Evidence of gender identity disturbances was less common." None of the twelve subjects was homosexual at the time of examination. Of the 100 comparison patients in the study, forty-six were rated as excessively fearful of physical injury, and they were not homosexual.

Timidity may predispose to homosexuality by obstructing integration into a male peer group and by evoking contempt and disappointment in parents, particularly fathers. If parents of a timid boy are sensitive and do not humiliate him, nor indicate dissatisfaction with him but encourage positive assets, they are not likely to undermine his self-esteem or damage his sense of masculinity; hence, they are not likely to promote homosexuality. There may indeed be a biological factor associated with timidity, but there is no evidence that there are specific biological determinants for homosexuality.

The psychodynamics we have noted in adult homosexuals revolve mainly around their problems with men, most especially the fear of male aggression. The fear of competing with men arouses anxiety and inhibition, prominently in the area of sexuality. The intolerable fear of having a romantic heterosexual relationship with a valued woman has a profoundly inhibiting effect, with the result that women are relinquished as lovers. The patients are seldom conscious of their fears but express them in a typical dream trilogy that *begins* with a heterosexual theme: He is lying in bed with a woman; he is attacked by a man; he is engaged in homosexual activity. The fear of competing may be observed in other areas such as sports, but notably in work and achievement resulting in the fear-of-success syndrome (Bieber 1980), which, of course, is not limited to homosexuals. Feelings of inferiority and a sense of impaired masculinity and self-esteem accompany these difficulties contributing further to the fear of having a meaningful sexual relationship with a woman. Failure in sexual performance with a man, e.g., impotence or prematurity, is not especially disturbing, but the anticipation of failure with a woman is extremely threatening. The belief that even if a woman is initially receptive she will ultimately prefer a more masculine heterosexual man is another deterrent. *Pari passu* with their fears of competing and the hidden but intense rivalry with men, there is a profound wish for acceptance, affection, and respect. Homosexuality not only replaces a male for a female who is psychologically beyond reach, but it offers a series of complex defenses and reparative mechanisms for coping with the fear of men and the pain of rejection from them.

The aim of psychoanalysis is to resolve as much psychopathology as is possible. The homosexual patient may have in mind discrete goals, including change in sexual orientation, but personal goals do not necessarily articulate with therapeutic possibilities. Most do not become heterosexual, but most resolve many other problems in their lives such as those related to self-esteem, assertiveness, work effectiveness, and social relationships. A substantial number do become and remain heterosexual. This shift does not mean that the potential for homosexual arousal has been totally extinguished. Total extinction sometimes but not usually occurs. Should homosexual interests reappear, patients learn that they do not have to act out their impulses; that it is to their benefit not to if their preferred adaptation is heterosexual; that they should search out and work out the problems that have increased their anxiety about heterosexuality. The circumstances that tend to increase such fears are plans to have a child, the wife's actual pregnancy, and the birth of a child. One patient who had been exclusively homosexual and had become exclusively heterosexual before treatment experienced a return of homosexual impulses, which he acted out, after the birth of a daughter. He soon lost interest in homosexuality and continued his life at home as before. Two years later a son was born. Homosexual interest returned and he came for psychoanalytic therapy, but he remained exclusively homosexual and his marriage ended in divorce.

Five years after publishing our study, a follow-up of patients showed that one-third whose adaptation had shifted to heterosexuality remained so, and we have personally followed some patients for as long as twenty years who remained exclusively heterosexual. Our clinical studies over the years have corroborated the original data, confirmed the conclusions, and, we trust, sharpened our insights.

Irving Bieber, M.D.
Toby B. Bieber, Ph.D.

Preface

THIS VOLUME PRESENTS a systematic study of 106 male homosexuals and 100 male heterosexuals in psychoanalytic treatment with members of the Society of Medical Psychoanalysts. It is the first time that voluminous and detailed data obtained in individual psychoanalyses have been collected for such a large number of homosexuals and subjected to clinical and statistical analysis. This is also the first published study in which a group of full-time psychoanalysts have participated in such an extensive, long-term research program. The work began in 1952 with the forming of a Research Committee under the chairmanship of Irving Bieber. The Committee was composed of members of the Society of Medical Psychoanalysts who were eager to start investigative work with a group of colleagues. The subject of male homosexuality was chosen as the initial study because it was considered to be a key problem in psychoanalytic theory and a clearly defined behavioral pattern which would not present any diagnostic difficulties.

In 1955, Ralph H. Gundlach, a clinical psychologist with many years of academic experience and a practicing psychoanalyst, accepted an invitation to join the Research Committee. This interdisciplinary enrichment gave us new impetus and perspective.

In the fall of 1956, the Committee suffered a sad loss in the death of

Paul Zimmering, one of the original members of the group and an important creative contributor. Shortly thereafter, Paul Dince joined the Committee, bringing it to its current composition of eight medical psychoanalysts and one clinical psychologist.

The nine years of research and study of findings entered its final and crucial phase in a review of older formulations and in the construction of new ones. Toby B. Bieber, a social psychologist and practicing psychoanalyst, was called upon to join us in this challenging task and in the writing of this book.

Thus, the volume is the end product of an interdisciplinary effort.

The research was carried out on an incredibly small budget—five thousand dollars. Between the years 1952 and 1957 nine hundred dollars were contributed; we wish to thank the members of the Society of Medical Psychoanalysts for their confidence and support with an appropriation of four hundred dollars, and the Women's Auxiliary of the Society of Medical Psychoanalysts for graciously contributing five hundred dollars. In 1957, we were fortunate enough to receive a grant of two thousand three hundred dollars from the National Institute of Mental Health (US Public Health Grant M2125), which was of great help to us. We wish to thank the Alexander Gralnick Foundation for its generous financial contribution of one thousand dollars. The members of the Research Committee personally contributed eight hundred dollars.

We wish to thank Robert S. Lee of IBM for his advice and assistance on the application of statistical techniques and Robert Meister for his editorial help and advice.

Our special thanks go to the members of the Society of Medical Psychoanalysts who contributed directly to the study by filling out the questionnaires and by generously co-operating with the Research Committee throughout the study.

HOMOSEXUALITY

I

Concepts of Male Homosexuality

THIS IS A STUDY of male homosexuals in psychoanalysis. It is only fitting that such a study should begin with Freud's contribution since Freud was the first to question the concept that homosexuality was a degenerative disease—a concept that was a pseudoscientific reformulation of a moralistic attitude which considered homosexuality synonymous with degeneracy.

Freud's formulation of the etiology of homosexuality postulated a continuum between constitutional and experiential elements. As a consequence, he regarded homosexuality as resulting in some cases solely from constitutional predisposition and in other cases from exclusively experiential factors, although he cited no clinical or experimental proof for either contention. He regarded the vast majority of cases as products of the interaction of both inherent and extrinsic factors, the relative dominance of each varying in different cases.

One of Freud's basic premises was that all individuals differed in their hereditary biologic endowment. He felt that the physical differences among people which distinguished them as individuals must be reflected not only in underlying physiologic, metabolic, and other characteristics of the biologic organism but also in terms of needs, drives, action potentials, and activity-passivity tendencies. He offered the concept of the inherent nature of the individual's tendencies toward activity or passivity which, he felt, must influence the way in which drives and experiences were dealt with. In terms of sexuality, he saw the child as reacting to sexual needs according to the intensity of its active or passive tendencies without any initial conceptualization of masculine or feminine roles. Only after the child becomes aware of gender does it identify itself with the sex that represents the active or passive tendency in its own constitution. If the child tends to be active, it identifies with masculinity, and if passive, with femininity. Freud, therefore, regarded the form of the homosexual activity as determined, in part and independent of experience, by the relative intensities of innate active or passive tendencies. While he did not imply that experiential factors could not accentuate these components, he did postulate that inherited action potentials *must* be influential in determining the outcome.

The concept of bisexuality was another fundamental idea emphasized by Freud as essential to the understanding of neuroses and perversions. He viewed the sexual impulse as initially nonspecific concerning the sex of the object from whom satisfaction is sought and even as indifferent to the species of the object. Consequently, the homosexual object-choice was not regarded as biologically abhorrent. Only later developments channelize the sexual impulse into heterosexuality or homosexuality.

Freud believed that the homosexual component can be sufficiently strong to be dominant in some cases, and that in others its intensity can be hypertrophied by specific experiences. However, in terms of his concept of libidinal development, he maintained that *the existence of homosexual tendencies is permanent* since a portion of the libido is assigned to this component of the sexual constitution.

The innate strength of the various components of sexuality was seen by Freud as the source of additional constitutional determinants of homosexuality. For example, he viewed congenitally intense libidinization of the anal zone in certain individuals as favoring a homosexual propensity; or, some individuals might fail to master the Oedipus phase because of an inherent weakness of the phallic organization. It is, of course, impossible to assess clinically or experimentally the congenital intensity of any of the constitutional components enumerated by Freud, so that this concept must remain conjectural.

The manner in which the sexual instinct and the mental apparatus evolve and affect personality structure was regarded by Freud as most explanatory of the homosexual adaptation. He viewed the sexual instinct as arising from somatic sources and as being continuously operative, although predominantly expressed at different stages through different erogenous zones; the experiences occurring during the various phases result in various personality precipitates, as well as in accentuations or inhibitions of the partial impulses contributed by the various erogenous zones. These zones continue to make libidinal demands which are either gratified, repressed, or sublimated.

Freud correlated the development of object relationships with libidinal phases of development. He saw the child as evolving from autoerotic and narcissistic phases to object love. The particular quality of the libido which is cathected determines the nature of the object relationship; and, in turn, once cathected the object then directs the development, expression, and vicissitudes of that particular phase of libidinal development. He thus regarded homosexuality as resulting from this development in the following principal ways:

The autoerotic phase partially persists and object cathexis is partially accomplished, but on a narcissistic level. As a consequence, the individual seeks a love object representing himself and, therefore, necessarily having to possess the male genital. The individual is thus sexually involved with himself and his own genital in the form of another male who symbolizes himself.

Mental attitudes that exist during the phallic phase; here the male child reaches a stage where sexual impulses formerly expressed through other zones and instincts now become organized, so that the penis becomes the principal organ of discharge and pleasure. The boy begins to place enormous value on the male organ as the chief executor of the sexual function. As a result of earlier experiences with deprivation of other sources of pleasure (breast, feces, etc.), there develops during this (phallic) phase an unconscious fear of the loss of the prized organ. And, when the male child discovers the absence of the penis in the female this knowledge confirms the fear that the penis can be lost or removed. Females are consequently avoided to prevent the arousal of castration anxiety, and are devaluated because of their lack of the narcissistically overvalued male genital.

Difficulties associated with the Oedipus phase. A second type of castration anxiety fostering homosexuality is associated with unconscious incestuous feelings for the mother, later transferred to all women. The castration anxiety in this context derives from fear of retaliation for wishes to castrate the father who is perceived as a sexual rival for the mother.

Freud believed that the sexual practices in the homosexual relationship symbolize regressions to developmental fixation points. For instance, if there is an anal fixation, the individual may identify with his mother and then attempt to play the mother's role through the symbolic equation of the anus with the vagina. On the other hand, if there is stronger identification with the father, the homosexual might subject other males to a passive role in the sodomitic act, which symbolically transforms these men into females and at the same time covertly expresses hostility toward them as males. Homosexuality, therefore becomes one way of coping with rivalry with the father while at the same time gratifying sexual wishes.

Neither Freud nor his followers assumed that only one mechanism underlies homosexuality in any given case. In most cases, various kinds of feelings toward the mother and the father are acted-out through many homosexual symbolizations. Thus, there is a more frequent alternation of roles and a greater variety of sexual practices and identifications between homosexual partners than between heterosexual partners. The multiple roles enacted in homosexual relationships are related to the three basic phases in the development of object relations described above.

Adherents of the libido theory have laid stress on still other mechanisms. Abraham,[1] for instance, described homosexuality as an attempt to compensate for the failure to achieve the Oedipus goal by substituting the father as the love object. Ernest Jones emphasized two features: an unusually strong oral eroticism, and an unusually intense sadism. Anna Freud stressed the conflict between desires for active and passive roles as the major determinant for identification mechanisms.

Melanie Klein, whose viewpoint on homosexuality is shared by Bergler, regarded the oral phase as most determining of a homosexual outcome. In her analyses of children she found that oral fixation affects all post-oral phases of psychosexual development, not in the sense of merely contributing elements to the genital phase but in determining the very nature of genital organization. For example, oral frustrations in the infant result in cannibalistic fantasies toward the mother's breast and her total person. Because the child projects its feelings and fantasies, it also views the external world as cannibalistic and develops fears of objects in it. This results in an unconscious fear of being devoured by the love object. The vagina, which is unconsciously equated with the mouth, comes to represent the castrating, devouring organ.

[1] All sources referred to in this volume will be found alphabetically listed in the Bibliography.

Such anticipations result in avoidance of the heterosexual object, and only a relationship with a male—in whom the male genital, symbolizing the breast, is reassuringly present—becomes suitable as a sexual object. The determinants of homosexuality were thus extended by Klein to earlier levels than Freud had conceptualized.

Harry Stack Sullivan held a similar viewpoint. He wrote: "The oral zone is involved in such varied functions that it is perhaps the central trunk, the main stem for evolution of the self." Sullivan elsewhere discussed the dream of a boy in which he cannibalistically incorporated a girl's nipple. However, Sullivan interpreted this as an expression of genital tendencies.

According to Jules Masserman, sexuality is engrafted on primitive oral incorporative patterns. He views sexuality as a derivative rather than as a primary form of libidinal activity. The polymorphous perverse sexuality, regarded by Freud as basic, is described as "our mammalian heritage" by Masserman, but the subsequent vicissitudes of the sex instinct are attributed by him to the fate of orality rather than to Oedipus complex displacements or to castration threats. He finds that sexual patterns vary with oral conflicts and with the resolution of such conflicts, but the reverse does not obtain. As he writes: "Genital conflicts are, therefore, not essential to etiology of neurosis." In his experience, the more basic difficulties of patients, including homosexuals, lie at the far deeper levels of oral dependencies, primal anxieties, reactive aggressions, neurotic object cathexes, and autistic withdrawals. It is the solution of these deeper problems that restores genitality rather than the directing of attention to secondarily derived sexual maladjustments.

Kolb and Johnson regard homosexuality as deriving from the unconscious sources described by Freud, but state that the impetus for the transformation of latent homosexuality to an overt form often results from parental suggestion. This may consist of parental encouragement of acting-out by the child of unconscious parental wishes or forbidden impulses, unconscious permissiveness by one parent, with the other parent more or less condoning, or the parents' conscious or unconscious image of the child. Parental fears, hopes, wishes, frustrations, and interests may be perceived by the child in their gestures, intonations, body movements, provocative smiles, and maneuvers. This attitudinal network stimulates the child to act-out homosexually, because his unconscious tendencies are now reinforced by suggestions derived from the parents. These findings are emphasized again by Litten, Griffin, and Johnson: "Perversion and antisocial sexual behavior in children and adolescents result from adaptation of the child's ego to subtle attitudes of its parents which distort the instinctual development of the child. The parental influences operate reciprocally with the needs of the child so that eventually each participant stimulates the other. Many patients have strong latent homosexual, exhibitionistic, and transvestite trends, but do not act-out these impulses until there is unconscious permission and subtle coercion by the parents."

Bychowsky regards homosexuality as the outcome not only of sexual development as outlined in the libido theory but of ego and superego development which represents the individual's experiences with reality and with the parents on nonsexual levels.

Sullivan regarded homosexuality as resulting from experiences which have "erected a barrier to integration with persons of the other sex." He found one of the important sources of homosexuality in the preadolescent period, since it is during this era that the child first develops an intimate relationship with a "chum." He viewed the "chum" relationship as prognostically favorable and believed it to be an important counterinfluence against the development of a permanent homosexual adaptation. Sullivan cited a group of preadolescents in which two members who had failed to become somewhat homosexually involved with other members of the group were the only ones to become homosexual as adults. Homosexuality may also result, in Sullivan's view, if the preadolescent is driven to form a relationship with an older boy or adult. He saw another possible source of homosexuality in maturational retardation which separates the boy from his chronologic peers. When this occurs, the immature individual may become fixated at the preadolescent level. The failure to fulfill the need for a "chum" in preadolescence while the lust dynamism undergoes biologic maturation may, in some cases, result in a homosexual orientation. During the adolescent period, homosexuality may result from "collisions of lust, security, and the intimacy need." The collision between lust and security, for instance, may occur when the adolescent is burdened with culturally prohibitive attitudes towards heterosexuality, so that a "primary genital phobia" may develop and homosexuality may be resorted to. Homosexuality may also result if there is parental prohibition of heterosexual interests during the adolescent period. A collision between lust and the need for intimacy may occur if there is an underlying fear of intimacy with a heterosexual object, or if sexual guilt results in the division of females into "good" girls with whom emotional intimacy without sex is possible, and "bad" or "sexy" girls with whom genital contact but not an emotional relationship is conceivable—a mechanism also described by Freud. Sullivan recognized that the fear of female genitals may exist in men even when they regard women as pleasurable sexual objects—"a fear amounting to a feeling which is literally uncanny, which is quite paralyzing," and which is able to force the male to escape from this "uncanny feeling" into homosexuality. The origin of this fear, he believed, may derive from the "not me," indicating a serious dissociation in the personality.

Karen Horney focused attention on the importance of nonsexual needs in sexual activity. Her remarks on homosexuality were based on observations of bisexuals in whom she found needs to conquer and subdue, or needs to please, of such intensity that the sex of the partner became a matter of indifference. These elements, then, became part of a homosexual personality. In addition, she thought, the homosexual has such a fear of injury to his neurotic pride that he withdraws from competition with his equals and inhibits heterosexual attraction.

Clara Thompson, who shared Sullivan's views, regarded the term "homosexual" as "a wastebasket to which all friendly and hostile feelings toward members of one's sex are applied." She considered homosexuality not as a specific entity having characteristic determinants but only as a symptom of a character problem. She agreed with Freud that all people are biologically polysexual and bisexual, and that uncritical enjoyment of body stimulation exists in childhood. Consequently, she asserted, sexual pleasure in childhood may be derived from either sex. In a permissive culture this basic biologic tendency would result in recourse to homosexual relationships whenever heterosexuality was not available. On a biologic level, therefore, human beings resort to the best type of interpersonal relationship available to them: when heterosexual objects are accessible there is a biologic tendency towards heterosexuality since it is the most "satisfactory." Thompson did not regard the biologic polysexual and polymorphous tendencies as having any influence in personality development, and maintained that these tendencies did not demand that defenses be in constant readiness against their expression. Her conclusion was that homosexuality is a consequence of dependency, hostility, attitudes towards familial or other figures, security operations, and so forth, all covertly expressed in the homosexual relationship. She found that homosexuality disappears as general character problems are solved.

Rado discarded the concept of bisexuality and attributed homosexuality to the following factors:

"Hidden but incapacitating fears of the opposite sex which result in a homosexual adaptation, which through symbolic processes is in fantasy a heterosexual one, or in which problems of rivalry with isophilic partners who represent father are solved"; temporary expedience when heterosexual partners are not available; a consequence of "a desire for surplus variation." The latter, Rado believes, stems from the fact that in humans the sex drive has ceased to be a mechanism related exclusively to procreative purposes and has become autonomously pleasure striving. The "healthy" individual, therefore, may even under ordinary circumstances yield to a desire for "variation in performance because of the latter's pleasure value." This occurs because such a desire is either culturally sanctioned or represents "an individual enterprise."

Ovesey, following Rado's adaptational theory, classified homosexuality as a neurosis divisible into true and pseudohomosexual types. He attributed the first type to early and excessive sexual discipline; homosexuality is resorted to with the objective of achieving orgastic satisfaction. The pseudohomosexual type is equated with "latent" or "unconscious" homosexuality. He regards this form as motivationally determined by the wish for dependency, or as the consequence of inhibited assertiveness which the individual unconsciously equates with castration—therefore with femininity and homosexuality.

Kardiner, in reviewing Kinsey's findings as well as the evidence obtained from the study of various animal species and many primitive cultures, arrived at a different conclusion. He regarded neurosis and perversion as deriving from social efforts to institute sexual control in adolescents and preadolescents who are unable to assume mature responsibility for procreation. To prevent sexual irresponsibility in the immature, social efforts "terrorize the child out of its sexual interests, so that the sexual drive is deflected into channels other than heterosexual." This produces neuroses and perversions and is the indirect consequence of social efforts to limit population growth. As for societies in which homosexuality exists despite the lack of sexual restrictions, Kardiner held that biogenetic factors may possibly be responsible.

Silverberg distinguished between homosexual *behavior* and true or neurotic homosexuality. He regarded the former as deriving from disciplinary problems with the father or, more commonly, from attempts to substitute the father for the mother as a source of oral gratification. This dependency upon the father, he believed, may account for the high incidence of "homosexual outlets" reported by Kinsey (37 per cent of American adult males) in individuals whose homosexuality was transient or sporadic.

Silverberg's concept of "true" homosexuality is identical with Freud's to the extent that it is regarded as an outcome of the Oedipus complex. Homosexuality is viewed as an unconscious maneuver to separate the parents and bind the father symbolically in the homosexual relationship, thereby making him unavailable to the mother. This sexual solution is attempted because of the unconscious idea that parental sexuality is determined by the father's insistence on phallic satisfaction. The homosexual, therefore, offers himself to the symbolic father as a substitute for the mother and thereby interferes with the parental sexual relationship. The oral factors emphasized by Klein and Bergler are regarded by Silverberg as consequences of regression rather than as primary determinants. He concurs with Freud in according psychogenetic importance to an unconscious view of women as genitally castrated.

Various other writers who have attempted to ascertain the etiology of homosexuality have found other determining causes. The factors held to be responsible are often unidimensional and oversimplified. Some of the unitary causes adduced are: strong attachment to a man; immaturity with lack of comprehension of sex drives; lack of virility in the fathers; excessive defeat in assertiveness; feminization by being dressed as a female; incidents, such as venereal diseases, which render heterosexuality unpleasant; disillusionment in marriage; being treated by homosexuals as an equal; inherent or acquired timidity; persistence of childhood concepts that heterosexual coital activity is degrading, humiliating, dirty, prohibited, painful, mutilating, etc. Mantegazza suggested that in certain cases homosexuality represents an attempt to achieve sexual satisfaction by means of homosexual sodomy as a consequence of a lack of adequate stimulation by the female genital organ, owing to the latter's expansiveness ("la desolante larghezza").

Another line of inquiry raises the fundamental question as to whether homosexuality is a disease, or simply a natural form of human behavior which becomes categorized as a disease only in specific cultures. The view that homosexuality is a disease originated in the organic approach characteristic of the nineteenth century. Krafft-Ebing attributed it to "hereditary neuropathic degeneration," without demonstrable degenerative pathology in the central nervous system. He also postulated that excessive masturbation acted as the stress which uncovered the latent neuropathic taint. Others attributed the neuropathic state to other varieties of somatic disease in the parents. Some suggested that homosexuality resulted from the presence of a female soul in a masculine body while others conceptualized it as the occurrence of a female brain combined with masculine sex glands. Another hypothesis of Krafft-Ebing's was that male and female sex centers existed in the brain, with the female center predominating in the homosexual. Mantegazza, writing as recently as 1932, ascribed homosexuality to either psychic or organic causes. The latter, he rather ingeniously postulated, consisted of a reversal of nerve supply to the genitals and rectum, so that sexual satisfaction could only be obtained perversely. Ellis and Hirschfeld regarded homosexuality as of congenital origin and even Freud and Glover assumed that at least some cases were congenitally determined. Lombroso concluded that homosexuality, like criminality, resulted from the persistence of an atavistic sexual instinct. Carpenter viewed homosexuality as representing another sex, intermediate between the male and female. He did not regard this intermediate type as possessing specific somatic characteristics, but only mental attributes indicative of a contrasexual temperament. In the male pervert this expressed itself, he wrote, in "a rather gentle emotional disposition with defects, if such exist, in the direction of subtlety, evasiveness, timidity, vanity, etc.; the mind is generally intuitive and instinctive in its perceptions, with more or less artistic feeling." He also considered this intermediate sex to be a "sport or variation" which had the important functions of acting "as reconcilors and interpreters of each sex to each other."—"The homogenic affection," he stated, "is a valuable social force and in some cases a necessary element of noble human character."

The theory of the organic etiology of homosexuality can be tested in the following research areas: Hereditary transmission of potentialities for homosexuality; physiologic, anatomic, and endocrine dysfunction in homosexuals; response of homosexuals to endocrine therapy; the effects of rearing upon sexual identity.

Studies of a possible hereditary factor to account for homosexual proclivities have been, at best, only suggestive. Kallman investigated 40 monozygotic pairs of homosexuals and found only one father of a homosexual pair who was homosexual. In all cases of twins "concordance as to overt practices and quantitative behavior after adolescence" was found. "All denied any history of mutuality in overt sexual relations" and many "claimed to have developed their often very similar sexual pattern independently and far apart from each other." Kallman also asserted that the individuals of each pair had so marked a sexual taboo between them that each disclaimed knowledge of any intimate details of his co-twin's sex life. However, in 45 dizygotic twin pairs the co-twin of each of the homosexual subjects did not generally show overt homosexuality, and the incidence of homosexuals among these was only slightly in excess of Kinsey's rate for the total male population. Kallman, therefore, regarded it as clearly evident that only the uniovular twins developed identical patterns of overt practice, and these genetic studies strikingly indicated to him that homosexuality was determined basically by hereditary factors.

In support of Kallman's findings, Mayer-Gross quotes Saunders' report of seven uniovular pairs. In six pairs both members were homosexual; in one pair, one member was homosexual and the other was not. Despite Kallman's tremendous emphasis on a genetic basis for homosexuality he nevertheless states that there is "multiple causation of homosexual behavior in the adult male," and that personality and sexual function are "easily dislocated" by experiential factors.

Witschli and Mengart postulated a sex-linked hereditary factor. They quoted Lang's statistical studies based upon German police records. They demonstrated that there is a higher incidence of male siblings among homosexual men than might be expected statistically. This finding was explained by assuming a "sex-reversal" factor which is carried by a gene transmissible by females to offspring born anatomically male but potentially homosexual. Kallman, however, questioned the statistical adequacy of such studies on the siblings of homosexuals.

Bauer concluded that homosexuality is a genetic problem including psychologic as well as hormonal factors. "The basic underlying cause of homosexuality," he stated, "is an abnormality of the chromosomal structure with a subsequent sexual differentiation of certain cerebral portions extending, however, to other functions and structures of the body in a variable degree. Only the genetic conception of homosexuality can explain the fact that different kinds of intersexuality, both physical and mental, occur as a hereditary trait in certain families." Kallman pointed out that if homosexual men are assumed to be genetically female but phenotypically male intersexes without a Y-chromosome, their children must all be female, and cytologic examinations must show the absence of Y-chromosomes. No such conclusive data are available.

In a chromosomal study of 50 male homosexuals Paré found that they had a normal male chromosomal pattern, which he cited as evidence against Lang's theory that male homosexuals are female genotypes. Raboch and Nidoma studied 36 men with a female type sex-chromatin. Thirty-two of the 36 were heterosexual and the remaining four eunuchoid. They also studied 194 adult exclusive or almost exclusive male homosexuals. Of the 194 only 9 were found to have hypoplastic testes, and of these 6 had masculine sex chromatin. Thirty-two of the total, selected at random, showed the male chromosomal pattern in each case. They concluded that "the finding of a female type of sex chromatin in a homosexual man would amount to pure coincidence."

Further doubt is cast on the simple assumption that sexual identity is definitely determined by genetic constitution in studies of the effect of rearing upon sexual orientation. Money, Hampson, and Hampson, in a study of the sexual development and life of 76 pseudohermaphrodites and individuals with gonadal agenesis, found that in 19 cases there was a contradiction between chromosomal sex and sex assignment and rearing. In every case, however, the person established a gender role and orientation consistent with the assigned sex and rearing, and inconsistent with the chromosomal sex. This strongly indicates that sexual identity is not determined by the chromosomal factor exclusively, and illustrates the high importance of experiential elements in modifying, and even reversing, genetic constituents.

A review of the endocrinological aspects of homosexuality was made by Sawyer, from which the following summary is quoted:

"The development of sexual responsiveness in the two sexes is dependent more upon psychological conditioning and availability of sexual outlets than upon levels of circulating sex hormones. From the fact that most individuals showing predominantly or exclusively homosexually directed libido undergo a normal puberty at a normal time, it may be inferred that the detection of significant hormonal abnormalities would be most unlikely. A homosexual cannot be diagnosed by physical examination. No convincing demonstrations of endocrine imbalance in homosexuals have been forthcoming. In patients suffering from the male climacteric, eunuchism and eunuchoidism, there is absolutely no increased incidence of homosexuality as compared with that in the general population. The one possible variety of homosexuality which may be causally related to androgen deficiency in eunuchoidal patients is the passive type. This, moreover, is the only type in which male hormone treatment may prove of some therapeutic value. In the majority of cases, the hermaphrodite assumes a heterosexual libido and sex role that accord primarily not with his or her internal and external somatic characteristics, but rather with his or her masculine or feminine upbringing."

In reviewing the sex hormone treatment of homosexuality Sawyer stated that failure "is indeed now the generally accepted conclusion." He quoted Sand and Okkels who had treated 100 cases of perversion and homosexuality by castration, which merely reduced the libido without in any way altering its direction. As for androgen treatment, it "serves merely to increase the libido which still remains homosexual in outlet." He concludes: "There is no convincing evidence that human homosexuality is dependent upon hormonal aberrations," and, "The use of sex hormones in the treatment of homosexuality is mainly disappointing."

The view that homosexuality is not a disease was the position taken in the so-called Wolfenden Report. There is no legal definition of "disease" or of "disease of the mind"; and "health" and "ill health" as well as "normal" and "abnormal" are relative terms. The Report pointed out that a particular type of aberrant behavior cannot be regarded as a manifestation of disease, if there are no other associated symptoms and if the existence of deviant behavior is compatible with "full mental health" in other respects. In those cases of homosexuality which are now associated with distressing symptoms, the latter may be determined not by the homosexuality itself but as a consequence of social attitudes. In addition, there is a lack of proof for the presence of a pathologic physical condition accompanying homosexuality, so that the designation of the latter as a "disease" necessitates a revision of the generally accepted view of the nature of a diseased state. Furthermore, the Report emphasized, none of the various theories formulated to explain the perversion is conclusive or specific to it, since the postulated etiologic factors are also found in other psychopathologic states.

The publications of Kinsey *et al.*, also supported the concept that homosexuality is not a disease. Aberrant behavior such as homosexuality was viewed as a general capacity of all human beings, originating in an inherent capacity for indiscriminate sexual responsiveness. As a result of conditioning and social pressure, the sexual potential becomes channelized in the direction of accepted social behavior. Sporadic homosexual behavior in the general population prior to maturity was found to be the rule rather than the exception. Kinsey's statistics indicated that about 4 per cent of adult white males are exclusively homosexual after adolescence, and that about 10 per cent of the total male population is to a greater or lesser degree exclusively homosexual for at least three years some time between the ages of sixteen and sixty-five. An even more remarkable finding was that at least 37 per cent of the total male population has had some overt homosexual experience, with or without orgastic culmination, some time between puberty and old age. In preadolescent boys Kinsey found an incidence of 48 per cent homosexual genital play, and this percentage increased if non-genital activity was included. Since preadolescent heterosexual play occurred in 40 per cent of his sample, it appears that, among many males, homosexuality in some form exceeds heterosexuality during the preadolescent period.

In view of Kinsey's statistics, many social scientists and psychiatrists maintain that it is difficult to uphold on rational grounds legal, social, and individual attitudes which imply that homosexuality is exceptional and therefore should be regarded as a crime against nature. As Kinsey has written, "In all the criminal law there is practically no other behavior which is forbidden on the ground that Nature may be offended and that Nature must be protected against such offense. This is the unique aspect of our sex codes." Thus, by Kinsey's standards homosexuality should not be regarded as a disease. He speculated that only a small number of those customarily involved in perverse behavior are ever particularly disturbed by their experiences, and that personality disturbances associated with homosexuality derive from the expectation of adverse social reactions.

Anthropological data in Ford and Beach also support the concept that homosexuality is not a disease. These data show that "100 per cent of the males in certain societies engage in homosexual as well as heterosexual alliances." They state that "one cannot classify homosexual and heterosexual tendencies as being mutually exclusive or even opposed to each other. Human sexual behavior is controlled and directed primarily by learning and experience. It is possible, by a process of cultural and individual conditioning, to make a person an exclusive homosexual, and this can be done precisely because human sexuality is so labile, so dependent upon individual experience."—"Some homosexual behavior occurs in a great many human societies. It tends to be practiced more frequently by men than by women. The basic mammalian capacity for sexual inversion tends to be obscured in societies like our own which forbid such behavior and classify it as unnatural."

Two studies are oriented to the conclusion that adult male homosexuals may fall within the ranges of psychologic normality. Hooker has reported a group of 30 homosexuals and 30 heterosexual controls, matched for age, I.Q., and education. The homosexuals were carefully chosen on the basis of good adjustment and function in the community. Subjects who were in therapy and any who showed "evidence of considerable disturbance" in the preliminary screening were eliminated. The investigation "consisted of a battery of projective techniques, attitude scales, and intensive life history interviews." Hooker's hypothesis was that homosexuality is not necessarily a symptom of pathology. The report is based on analysis of the test materials by different, independent judges who did not know whether the record was that of a homosexual or a heterosexual. The general outcome of the study was that the judges could not reliably identify whether the records were from a homosexual or a heterosexual subject. Various ratings of the subjects' "adjustment" were made based on the test results. There was no significant difference between the homosexuals and the heterosexuals. Hooker's conclusion, which is expressly presented as tentative, is that "homosexuality may be a deviation in sexual pattern which is within the normal range psychologically."

Chang and Block also could not show differences between samples of homosexuals and a control group. Their study utilized a comparison of self-ratings with ideal self-ratings; and the degree of correspondence was interpreted as a measure of "self-acceptance." Their sample consisted of 20 male homosexuals (only 1 of whom had ever been in therapy) whose homosexual pattern involved a homosexual "marriage." The "self-acceptance scores" for these homosexuals were not significantly different from the scores for the control group. Their conclusion was that the members of this homosexual group were not psychiatrically disturbed. The findings of several other studies, which will be reported in Chapter II, are not in accord with those of Hooker and Chang and Block.

The theories that have been presented fall into two major categories: those which are based on the assumption that adult homosexuality is a psychopathologic state and those which are not.

All *psychoanalytic* theories assume that adult homosexuality is psychopathologic and assign differing weights to constitutional and experiential determinants. All agree that the experiential determinants are in the main rooted in childhood and are primarily related to the family. Theories which do not assume psychopathology hold homosexuality to be one type of expression of a polymorphous sexuality which appears pathologic only in cultures holding it to be so.

II

Chronology and Methodology

Psychoanalysis is oriented toward the study and treatment of the individual. Consequently, the original case history method of investigating and presenting psychoanalytic findings, such as Freud's accounts of "Dora," the "Wolfman," "Little Hans," and others, is still the most prevalent. Individual case reports have continued to provide a richness and depth of insight into personality and the dynamics of behavior. Based on the proposition that psychodynamic principles have broad applicability, the case history method has made it possible to formulate generalizations from given case studies to other patients.

The basis for deciding that certain principles are applicable to one patient but not to another rests upon clinical acumen, experience and diagnostic judgment in the treatment of individual patients. Nevertheless, a clinician may be led to impute general theoretical significance to some factors important only in the limited number of cases available to him at any one time, and he may be led to make erroneous generalizations by some chance run of cases that suggests an association among variables where none exists.

The developments in statistical techniques in scientific research provide a methodology for estimating the probable significance of any findings, and these techniques are applicable to clinical research. Based on this premise, we have collected clinical data according to procedures that enabled us to make statistical analyses of the information gathered.

Our first objective was to collect information about a large enough number of cases to permit statistical handling of the data—and at the same time to collect information rich enough in detail to permit us to make our own clinical evaluations of the cases under study. The research was not designed as an experiment to test the association of controlled variables. The problems we have approached do not lend themselves to study at that level. We have sought to delineate those variables that have the *most probable* relevance or are most central to the problem of male homosexuality. The design of the research has also permitted us to test some of the current psychoanalytic hypotheses.

It seems worth while to present a short chronology of our progress. It will outline the apparently circuitous route we have followed, and may make more understandable our slowness in digesting the material and bringing our findings to publication.

When the Research Committee of the Society of Medical Psychoanalysts was formed in 1952, the members of the Committee had a total of 20 male homosexuals in treatment. We decided to utilize these 20 patients as the basis of a pilot study since the data were immediately accessible to the members of the Committee.

An extensive and complex pilot questionnaire was constructed, based upon the psychodynamics of homosexuality as conceptualized by the members of the research group. The Committee decided to begin with a questionnaire study, a method that seemed to offer the best possibility for collecting data, and that would elicit meaningful information in sufficient detail to permit comparison and statistical analysis. The document covered 26 legal-sized pages, and took about two and a half hours to fill out. It was divided into seven sections: relationship *between parents of the homosexual patient;* relationship *between mother and patient;* relationship *between father and patient; developmental items,* particularly as they affected sexual development; *adaptational responses; psychosomatic reactions and trends; socioeconomic background.*

The Committee was unanimous about certain theoretical aspects. Our conception of the genesis of homosexuality gave minimal attention to hereditary, chemical, or organic-genetic theories. We assumed that the dominant sexual pattern of the adult is the adaptive consequence of life experiences interpenetrating with a basic biological tendency toward heterosexuality.

Each member of the Committee filled out the pilot questionnaires on the homosexual patients he had in treatment, and some members of the Society who were not on the Committee also contributed cases. The data for each case were divided into the above seven sections for processing, and each section was assigned for analysis to one or two Committee members. After discussion, the sections were reassembled and studied as individual cases by the entire Committee. Questions that elicited high percentages of affirmative answers were selected from the pilot questionnaire. The questions on socioeconomic background seemed unrewarding since almost all patients were white middle class. These data revealed such uniform information that it was decided to eliminate the socioeconomic parameter as unprofitable. The topics ultimately included in the First Questionnaire were as follows:

Relations between parents
Relations between mother and patient
Relations between father and patient
Relations between siblings and patient and siblings and parents
Sexual development and functioning
Social development
Choice of homosexual partner and homosexual practices
Relations to women
Adaptational responses
Psychosomatic disorders

Three copies of the First Questionnaire were then distributed to each member of the Society of Medical Psychoanalysts together with a covering letter, requesting each to fill out the questionnaire on every male homosexual presently in treatment. The members were further requested to fill out additional questionnaires if they were treating more than three male homosexuals. In the event they were treating fewer than three, or none, they were asked to fill out the unused questionnaires for heterosexual male patients. These heterosexual patients formed the comparison sample. No formal instructions for the selection of comparison patients were given. Unrestricted choice elicited cases with which the responding psychoanalysts were well familiar, as shown by the fact that few comparison patients had been in therapy for less than 100 hours when the First Questionnaire was answered. A more detailed discussion of the selection of the sample will be found on pages 25-29.

We found, as we proceeded, that we had to construct a succession of questionnaires. In order to encourage the maximum response from the psychoanalysts, the First Questionnaire was necessarily brief; therefore, certain questions required more precise definition and elaboration, and some new areas needed to be tapped. Furthermore, as the study progressed, we had to shift our methods of handling the data in order to accommodate the vast increases in the amount of data collected.

The First Questionnaire required about half an hour to fill out. The response was gratifying; 70 of the 100 members of the Society responded, and we obtained completed questionnaires for 69 homosexual and 60 comparison cases. The names of the responding psychoanalysts and their theoretical orientation (see pages 34-36) were then listed and their cases divided among the members of the Committee. Each member was assigned to a number of psychoanalysts. In this way, further contacts between the Committee and the responding psychoanalysts were facilitated when additional data for any particular case were required.

The plan of study, as outlined thus far, defined the area of inquiry as an evaluation of comparisons between a group of male homosexuals and a group of male heterosexuals in psychoanalytic treatment. Such an inquiry was expected to bring out features associated with homosexuality distinct from other aspects of psychopathology common to both homosexuals and heterosexuals. The aim of the investigation was to reveal information on the following: The general characteristics of a large group of homosexual patients; the degree of uniformity or variation among the homosexual sample with respect to specific attributes; the extent to which findings in individual cases were present in the group as a whole; relationships not apparent from the study of single cases or small groups of cases; and, tangentially, viewing both samples as a whole, the psychogenetic features in the backgrounds of males in psychoanalysis.

A progress report was presented to the membership of the Society of Medical Psychoanalysts at a meeting on April 28, 1955. As a result of discussion, suggestions, and criticisms offered at this meeting, and of subsequent discussions of the Committee, a supplementary questionnaire was developed.

In the First Supplementary Questionnaire (also referred to as the Second Questionnaire) we extended the search for data in the following directions: In terms of interparent and child-parent relations, we sought more evidence of intimacy, hostility, rivalry, and differences in attitudes toward the patient and other male siblings; the area of sexual attitudes and development was extended by questions on sexual fantasies, dreams, and childhood identifications; additional questions focused on details of homosexual practices; a set of questions was added about diagnosis, duration and frequency of treatment, and changes in sexual and other functions during treatment, or at termination.

The First Supplementary Questionnaire was sent out to all the originally responding psychoanalysts and to others who had notified us that they were treating homosexuals. These newly acquired respondents were provided with copies of the First and Second Questionnaires. This added 31 homosexuals and 40 comparisons, thus enlarging the study population to 100 in each group.

The simple calculations, sufficient for the study of the First Questionnaire, were inadequate to handle the now enlarged mass of data. We decided to put the data on Keysort cards which facilitated the analysis of the data.

The findings derived from study of the first two questionnaires were presented at a Round Table at the annual meeting of the American Psychiatric Association in Chicago, May, 1956. In preparation of this report, the Committee developed from several related questionnaire items a number of "Cumulative Scores," in order to obtain meaningful index numbers of salient aspects of parent-son relationships and developmental characteristics. A number of charts were prepared displaying cross-tallies between different variables. Tentative interpretations were formulated. The suggestions made during the discussion at the Round Table raised new questions for exploration, and as a result of this exchange of ideas the Research Committee, after several months of lengthy discussion, formulated the Second Supplementary Questionnaire (also referred to as the Third Questionnaire). It was designed to accomplish the following essential tasks: To distinguish more clearly between parental attitudes which could be overlapping (for example, overprotectiveness as contrasted with close-binding intimacy or dominating attitudes); to distinguish beween parental affection and psychopathologic attitudes simulating affection, and to define "seductive" behavior; to probe the relationship between parental attitudes toward the patient and his physical make-up in childhood, such as the relationship of maternal overprotectiveness and the child's frailty, robustness, co-ordination, etc.; to explore the notion of "latent homosexuality"; to clarify and elaborate data regarding the patients' early sexual experiences.

The data derived from the first two questionnaires on the items probing early sexual experiences had given striking but somewhat imprecise data. For example, different psychoanalysts had different types of early sexual experiences in mind when answering the general questions, so that one might list a "necking date" as a "first sexual experience" whereas another would designate the first intercourse. Furthermore, so many more homosexuals than comparisons were reported to have had sexual experiences before the age of twelve that the information had to be corroborated.

The Second Supplementary Questionnaire was forwarded to members who had completed the preceding two questionnaires.[1] In this manner, a final group of completed questionnaires was assembled, containing in all about 450 items. Of the 106 homosexuals there were 10 cases with no Second Supplement, and of the 100 heterosexuals who constituted the comparison group there were 4 cases with no Second Supplementary Questionnaire.

At this point the extensive amount of data could no longer be handled by the Keysort punch cards, and preparations were made to punch the data on IBM cards for processing.[2]

In order to facilitate the IBM card punching, the Committee undertook two important tasks: the formulation of a number of revised Cumulative Scores, and the over-all clinical evaluation of the mother-son relationship and the father-son relationship of every case in terms of different categories. These were distinguished by calling them "Inferential Assessments."

The establishment of an Inferential Assessment was a complex

---

[1] Some time between the filling out of the First Supplementary Questionnaire and returns on the Second Supplementary Questionnaire six additional homosexual patients were acquired for a total of 106.

[2] A procedural question arose at this time regarding the disposition of (a) those cases for which we were unable to obtain answers on the Second Supplementary Questionnaire from the psychoanalysts; (b) those few cases where a patient had lost a parent early in life (through death, divorce, or separation); (c) cases where the responding psychoanalyst had seen the patient for only a few weeks or months and hence had incomplete information; or (d) cases already discharged by the time the responding psychoanalyst had received the Second Supplementary Questionnaire and thus had to depend on notes or memory for answers.

Also, the responding psychoanalysts did not always answer each question; certain questions did not apply to each patient as, for example, questions regarding siblings.

It was our decision that every case be included, however incomplete or inconsistent, in order to avoid selective treatment of the cases. This decision explains the varying number of cases in certain sections of the data.

process. The task was to determine the various assessment categories to be employed, and to agree upon the pertinent questions throughout the three questionnaires that related to each inferential category. These procedures are described in Appendix B.

We were now ready for the IBM program of analysis. Although the IBM machines made possible the handling of our voluminous data, this by no means simplified the project. The Committee was still responsible for programing the machines, for evaluating the complex data that emerged, and for sorting and evaluating the cases in terms of individual clinical material. All items from the three questionnaires were punched, requiring five cards for each individual case. For reasons of economy, a short "work deck" of a selected list of important items was prepared and punched out on two additional cards for each case. This selected list included, in addition to the identification data, about 180 items; 38 for the mother, 30 for the father, 20 developmental, 36 for sexual development and choice of partner, Cumulative Indices, 3 Inferentials, and others.

The sample

All patients resided in or near metropolitan New York City during the period of the study. They were referred for treatment through a wide variety of channels. Many had come to seek psychoanalytic assistance independently. Others were advised by friends, physicians, clinics, or agencies. Thus it seems unlikely that the patients were drawn from any particular segment of the psychoanalytic population.

Certain general features characterized both groups. The patients were not, of course, random samples of all the males of their respective types in the area. The samples were, in a sense, self-selected, in that they were composed of patients who had sought psychoanalytic treatment. They had to be aware that such treatment was available; they must have had sufficient motivation to seek treatment; they were able to sustain the cost of treatment over an extended period of time. In most cases, the members of both groups were persons with above average education and with adequate income to pay for treatment.

Table II-1 presents the data on date of birth, education, income level, and occupation, for both groups.

In terms of age the two groups are quite similar, but in terms of education there are some differences although these are not statistically significant. More homosexuals completed high school only, but also more homosexuals reported postgraduate college work. In contrast, a larger number of comparisons had completed college. Both groups had a higher proportion of college and postgraduate work than prevails in the general population. The income of the two groups showed rough comparability, with a third of each group reporting incomes over $10,000. Since less than a fifth of the total sample had incomes under $5,000, higher than average socioeconomic status appears to

TABLE II-1 *Date of Birth, Education, Income, and Occupation (in per cent)*

	Homosexual	Comparison
N =	106	100
1. Date of birth:		
1910 or before	7	11
1911-1920	26	24
1921-1930	49	48
1931-1940	18	17
2. Education:		
Did not complete high school	3	5
High school graduate	29	19
Some college	6	5
College graduate (no postgraduate education	25	41
Postgraduate education	37	30
3. Income:		
Under $5,000	19	11
$5,000 to $10,000	30	36
Over $10,000	40	46
Unemployed	4.5	0
Students	6.5	7
4. Occupation[a]:		
Professional,[b] technical and kindred workers	60	57
Management, officials, and kindred workers	12	16
Sales	8	8
Clerical and kindred workers	5	6
Craftsmen	2	3
Service workers	1	2
Laborers	0	1
Unemployed	5	0
Students	7	7

[a] *Occupational Classifications,* published in *Statistical Abstract of the United States,* served as a guide in ordering these data.

[b] Of 64 H-patients who were professionals, 37 were in the arts; of 57 C-patients who were professionals, 16 were in the arts.

be a frequent characteristic of those in private psychoanalytic treatment in the New York area.

Item 4 in Table II-1 presents data regarding the reported occupation of the patients. The two groups, combined, obviously do not reflect the occupational distribution of the general population in the United States, or even the distribution of employment in an urban center. Nearly 60 per cent of each group was composed of persons in the "arts" and other professions. The occupational distribution in terms of broad categories was almost identical; however, the tabular breakdown shows the differing occupational choices; e.g., among the homosexual patients the largest professional sub-group (35 per cent) was in the "arts," as compared to 16 per cent of the comparisons who were in the "arts" (significant at the .01 level), while business enterprises and the sciences, including social and political, tended to occur somewhat more frequently among the comparisons.

On the basis of socioeconomic data, presented in Table II-1, the homosexuals and the heterosexuals are comparable. Let us turn, then to a comparison of the two groups in terms of religion and place of residence during childhood, Table II-2.

The percentages for the various religions show many more Protestants among the homosexuals than among the comparisons, and many

TABLE II-2 *Religion and Place of Residence during Childhood (in per cent)*

	Homosexual	Comparison
N =	106	100
1. Religion†:		
Catholic	18	10
Jewish	41	67
Protestant	40	16
Other	1	7
2. Place of residence during childhood**:		
New York	50	74
Other Atlantic States	27	13
Midwest	6	7
South	8	0
Far West	6	3
Foreign	3	3

* .05 level of significance
** .01 level of significance
† .001 level of significance
NOTE: These designations (*, **, †) will be used throughout this volume to denote statistical significances of .05, .01, and .001, respectively.

more Jews among the comparisons than among the homosexuals. Catholics, who make up a considerable proportion of the population of New York City, are clearly underrepresented whereas a much higher percentage of Jews occurs in the total patient sample than is represented in the population of New York City.

The data for place of residence during childhood reveal that half of the homosexuals and over three-quarters of the comparisons were native New Yorkers. More homosexuals than comparisons came from other regions. (The fact that half of the homosexuals were brought up outside of New York City points to a sociological phenomenon: homosexuals seem to have a tendency to migrate to large urban centers where sexual contacts are more readily available and where it is easier to avoid exposure of homosexual behavior.)

Another basis for the estimation of the comparability of our two groups was derived from data regarding the psychiatric diagnoses.

The diagnoses summarized in Table II-3 were made by the psychoanalysts, and it is assumed that the terminology used was in accordance with standard diagnostic criteria. Many psychoanalysts routinely classify homosexuality as a character disorder yet this diagnosis was made with almost equal frequency in each group. Schizophrenia was diagnosed more frequently for the homosexual cases, and psychoneurosis more frequently for the comparisons; however, no significant differences between the two groups were noted diagnostically, homosexuality aside. Over-all, the psychiatric picture was similar for both groups. The initial complaints of the homosexual patients were similar to those of the heterosexuals, and included sexual difficulties, anxiety, various neurotic symptoms, work inhibitions, and so forth.

TABLE II-3 *Diagnostic Distribution (in per cent)*

		Homosexual	Comparison
	N =	106	100
Psychiatric diagnosis:	Schizophrenia	27	18
	Psychoneurosis	29	42
	Character Disorder	42	36
	Manic-Depressive	0	2
	Other	2	2

The two groups studied were thus comparable diagnostically, and in distribution of age, income, education, and *level* of occupation. Among the homosexual patients, 50 per cent were reared out of town while among the heterosexuals 74 per cent were native New Yorkers. More Protestants and fewer Jews were homosexuals.

Certain attitudes among the homosexuals toward treatment are listed in Table II-4. At the outset of treatment only half the group had stated that they were undertaking psychoanalysis because of sexual problems. The great majority (90) were eager to conceal their homosexuality and even more were concerned about its exposure. Over two-thirds were exclusively homosexual, and about one-third had had sexual experiences with both males and females.

TABLE II-4 *Some Attitudes of Homosexuals Regarding Treatment*

N =	106
1. What was the patient's stated reason for coming into treatment:	
Did he name a sexual problem?	51
Other than sexual problem?	52
2. Is the patient eager to conceal his homosexuality? Yes.	90
3. Is the patient concerned about exposure of his homosexuality? Yes.	96
4. Patterns of sexual behavior:	
Exclusively homosexual	72
Homosexual and heterosexual (bisexual)	30
Inactive at this time	4
Married	8
5. Did the patient want his homosexuality "cured"?	
Yes.	64
No.	32
No answer.	10

A pitfall awaiting all who venture into research is the love of one's own theories and beliefs. In a satirically critical article, N. R. F. Maier formulated the following law: Maier's Law states, in effect, that if one has a theory but there are facts standing against it, one disposes of the facts. A corollary holds that one can always find some evidence to support any theory. Another corollary states that given any set of facts one can always invent a theory to explain it.

Maier's Law calls attention to the fact that techniques of science provide no guarantee against the universal human tendency to collect and present data that tend to make one's own theories emerge favorably.

Some of our attempts to guard against biases and to bring precision into our study are elaborated in the next section.

Questionnaire items

The questionnaires (see Appendix A) used in this study were unique in two respects. First, the actual "respondents" (the patients) had never seen the questionnaires: they were represented, as it were, by their psychoanalysts. (This will be discussed in the next section.) Second, the questions were designed to be answered by persons who had very intimate long-range knowledge and insight about the patients. In many respects, then, the questions were quite unlike those found in opinion and attitude studies or personality inventories and scales. The questions were not the conventional "objective" ones, and they did not seek to eliminate the observer by pinpointing some specific bit of behavior.

Inspection of the questionnaires will show that the questioning ranged from factual information to clinical inferences. Questions probing for "facts" were: Did specific conditions prevail in the patient's life, such as being deprived of girl playmates for a period of years? Or: At what age did his first heterosexual experience involving sexual intercourse take place? Other questions referred to parental attitudes or attitudes of the patient during childhood or adolescence: Was mother dominant in the family? Was the patient the father's favorite? Did patient respect his father? Still other questions requested the psychoanalyst's observations and appraisal of the patient. All responses represented those of the psychoanalyst.

What is the validity of such responses? To what extent do they correctly report the "true" state of affairs, subject as they may be to distortion by the patient, to interpretation by the psychoanalyst, and presented in a brief answer on a questionnaire?

It must be recognized that the questionnaires were not filled out by naïve observers but by the patients' own psychoanalysts—well-trained psychiatrists with experience in making value judgments based on clinical impressions and interpretations. Furthermore, the questionnaires were carefully designed to be specific enough to elicit a particular answer, yet broad enough to provide us with material for our own clinical evaluations. Thus, the general question about interparental relations was phrased as: Can the relations between the parents be described as good, fair, poor? It was then explored in detail by specific questions: Were there open demonstrations of affection? Was contempt by one parent for the other shown? Did they share similar interests? etc.

By this method the attention of the responding psychoanalyst was directed to those specific items that might confirm or refute his earlier response to the general question. This provided the responding psychoanalyst with a final check on possible inconsistencies in his responses to the various questions.

Problems of bias in the distribution and selection of cases among the responding psychoanalysts

A total of 77 psychoanalysts co-operated in this study. Twenty-six contributed cases in both the homosexual and comparison group, for a total of 47 homosexual patients and 55 comparisons. Thirty-two contributed the remaining homosexual cases, and 19 contributed the remaining heterosexual cases. Two psychoanalysts contributed 4 homosexual cases each, and 1 contributed 5. There were 26 psychoanalysts who reported only 1 homosexual case each, and 20 who reported 2; 18 who contributed only 1 comparison and 14 who reported 2.

A series of cases were contributed by the members of the Research Committee. A total of 58 psychoanalysts contributed to the total of 106 homosexual cases, which is at the rate of about 2 cases for each member. The 10 Committee members contributed a total of 18 homosexual cases, which is at about the same rate. A different situation obtains for the comparison sample. A total of 45 psychoanalysts contributed the total of 100 cases. The 10 Committee members contributed 33 cases representing an overload of about 14 cases.

Since the selection of comparison cases was unrestricted for all responding psychoanalysts, the question of selective bias arose. Had they selected a representative sample of the heterosexuals from their patient load or did they choose their most effective heterosexuals? Table II-5 shows the length of time that both homosexual and comparison patients had been in treatment at the time the First Questionnaire was answered. We found that the comparison patients had been in treatment for a significantly longer time (.01 level) than had the homosexual patients, indicating that the comparisons were selected on the basis of longer contact with the psychoanalyst who had greater familiarity with the details of the patient's life history. There were 13 psychoanalysts who each contributed 3 or more comparison cases. These cases were carefully reviewed by members of the Committee to ascertain whether a similar pattern of responses was discernible for each psychoanalyst. No such trends could be identified. Variations in response were clearly related to the nature of the case; e.g., on the item, Was the patient excessively fearful of injury in childhood? the same psychoanalysts varied their responses in different cases; "latent" homosexual problems were reported for one patient and no homosexual problems for another, regardless of theoretical orientation, thus providing strong evidence that a representative sample had been selected.

TABLE II-5 *Number of Treatment Hours Preceding First Questionnaire*

No. of Sessions	H	C
0-25	3	1
26-50	11	5
51-100	18	7
101-150	14	10
151-200	14	17
201-250	7	10
251-300	17	14
301-450	8	22
Over 450	8	13
No answer	6	1
	106	100

Summary of Table II-5

	Under 200 Treatment Hours	Over 200 Treatment Hours
H	60	46
C	40	60

Significance: .01

Similarly, the overload noted for the Committee members was not viewed as a source of distortion in the study. In this regard, one might suggest that the members, influenced by the trends in the pilot questionnaire may have had an unconscious bias in their choice of comparison cases in the direction of a "good" heterosexual adaptation.

As a check of this possibility, the Keysort cards for the 100 comparisons were divided into two groups: the 33 cases processed by members of the Committee, and the 67 cases provided by other members of the Society of Medical Psychoanalysts. Twenty questions were tallied, sampling questionnaire sections of mother-son, father-son, childhood, and sexual development and behavior. In no case was there a significant difference between the two groups, and in only two were the differences even close to the .10 level of statistical significance. The major differences found between heterosexuals and homosexuals in this study would be about the same had no members of the Research Committee contributed comparison cases.

The sex of the psychoanalyst

Of the 77 responding psychoanalysts 12 (16 per cent) were females. In the Directory of the Society of Medical Psychoanalysts for 1961 there are 16 per cent female members listed. The female psychoanalysts are thus proportionately represented in our study, according to their distribution in the Society. There were 19 homosexuals who were treated by 9 female psychoanalysts (2.1 per psychoanalyst) as compared with 87 homosexuals who were treated by 49 male psychoanalysts (1.8). Thus, responding female psychoanalysts were treating proportionately slightly more homosexuals than were the male respondents. In the comparison sample, 18 patients were treated by female psychoanalysts. While this represents a small number of cases, it is sufficient to point to any strong tendencies or distortions attributable primarily to the sex of the psychoanalyst.

Answers to the first two questionnaires were tabulated according to the sex of the psychoanalyst. Examination of these answers was oriented to a search for statistically significant differences between patients who had female psychoanalysts and patients who had male psychoanalysts, for both the homosexual and comparison groups.

We expected that of about 200 tabulations, a number of significant differences should have appeared by chance alone. Yet only two items had statistical significance: the first item, Was the patient the father's favorite? was answered affirmatively for only 1 patient of a total of 37 patients in treatment with female psychoanalysts. The number of male psychoanalysts who reported patients as the father's favorite differentiated these answers at the .05 level of significance. The second item, Was the father dominating? was answered affirmatively by a female psychoanalyst for 1 of 18 comparison patients, in contrast to a 50:50 split among the male psychoanalysts for the comparison cases, a difference significant at the .01 level. The female psychoanalysts also reported proportionately fewer instances of dominating fathers among homosexual patients though the difference did not achieve statistical significance.

Over-all, it seemed to us that the sex of the psychoanalyst had negligible bearing upon the questionnaire responses.

The theoretical orientation of the responding psychoanalysts and of the members of the Research Committee

Although there are basic agreements among members of the Society of Medical Psychoanalysts regarding certain fundamental assumptions in psychoanalysis, substantial differences which are particularly pertinent to the subject of homosexuality *are* extant. These differences permit a division between those psychoanalysts who assume that disturbances in sexual maturational processes play a particularly important role in psychopathologic processes and those who regard disturbances and aberrations in sexual development to be but one consequence of a more general disturbance in interpersonal relationships. The first group we will designate as "Freudian" and the second as "Culturalist." Both groups recognize the determining influences of life experience. The "Freudians" view the Oedipus Complex to be an integral part of psychosexual development operant in all cultures with a nuclear family structure; the "Culturalists" view the Oedipus Complex as occurring only in a highly psychopathologic family matrix and as usually associated with schizophrenia.

Approximately 70 per cent of the membership of the Society of Medical Psychoanalysts were "Freudians"; 30 per cent were "Culturalists." Seven members of the Research Committee were "Freudians," 3 were "Culturalists." In all, 18 "Culturalists" and 59 "Freudians" filled out questionnaires for this study. Eleven "Culturalists" treated 25 of the comparison patients; 9 "Culturalists" treated 14 of the homosexuals. Forty-nine "Freudians" treated 92 homosexuals; 33 "Freudians" treated 75 comparisons.

An IBM sort was made on all questionnaire items, in order to determine differences in response between "Freudians" and "Culturalists." Few significant differences between them were noted. Their responses to only one item revealed a significant difference in both the homosexual and comparison cases: The item, Did the patient feel his father liked women? was affirmatively answered by significantly more "Freudians" (.01 level). Other significant differences in responses were noted for three items but applied only to the homosexual sample: (a) Mother allied with the patient against her husband (.01 level); (b) Patient was the mother's confidant (.05 level); (c) in the judgment of significantly more "Freudians" the patient identified his homosexual partner with a family member (.01 level).

Now if the differences between "Freudians" and "Culturalists" on items (a) and (b) reflect a tendency among the latter to overlook the phenomena being tapped, then similar response differences between the two groups of psychoanalysts should have emerged for the same items in the comparison as well as the homosexual sample. Such was not the case. Affirmative responses by "Culturalists" and "Freudians" to these two items were in about equal proportions for the comparison sample. For example, among the "Freudians" 39 per cent of the responses (29 of 75) were affirmative on item (a) to 44 per cent of affirmative "Culturalist" responses (11 of 25). Yet, for the homosexual sample "Culturalists" responded affirmatively on this item in only 21 per cent of the cases (3 of 14). However, since this number of cases is quite small, we are led to conclude that the difference represented a chance run in "Culturalist" responses.

There were 9 items where differences occurred only in the comparison sample. In all these instances "Freudians" answered affirmatively more frequently than did "Culturalists":

Was mother regarded as puritanical? (.05 level)

Was mother affectionate to the patient in childhood? (.02)

Did the father admire the patient? (.02)

Was there heterosexual activity in the manifest content of dreams? (.01)

Was there homosexual activity in the manifest content of dreams? (.01)

Was there incestuous activity in the manifest content of dreams? (.02).

Were there fantasies during sexual intercourse? (.01)

Were there fantasies during masturbation? (.01)

What was the patient's earliest memory of arousal involving a female? State age. ("Culturalists" reported significantly fewer comparison cases who were aroused by a female before the age of 11 than did "Freudians" [.05].)

Inasmuch as by chance alone 20 significant differences in 450 items can be anticipated, the occurrence of only 9 differences between "Freudians" and "Culturalists" in item responses for the comparison sample is within expected limits. Since 7 of the 9 items concern sexual data, this may indicate a trend among the "Culturalists" to underestimate sexual factors—or, among the "Freudians" to overestimate them. However, since there were about 100 items probing sexual attitudes and behavior in which significant differences were not found, the over-all concordance between "Freudians" and "Culturalists" indicates that their theoretical orientation played no major role in biasing responses to the questions of this study.

Computational methods

The significant differences between the homosexual and comparison groups could have been evaluated by a variety of methods. We minimized computations in our study by the use of the tables published by Mainland *et al.* These tables permitted the rapid determination of differences significant at .05 and .01 levels where sub-groups being compared were approximately of equal size. Differences at the .001 levels of significance were made by the use of Trites's graphs, though in some instances this level of significance was calculated. Where subgroups were unequal, and for all contingency tables, chi squares (including Yates's correction) were computed.

Reliability of answers

How reliably did the psychoanalysts answer the questions? Will the same question be answered in the same way about a patient six months or a year later?

In order to provide for a measure of variations (at the time the Second Questionnaire was formulated), two questions tapping different levels of abstraction and inference were duplicated from the First Questionnaire, and in one instance the same question was duplicated in a different context on the same questionnaire.

One of the questions repeated on the Second Questionnaire was, What was the amount of contact (time spent) between mother and patient? Great deal—average—little—very little—absent. The judgments in 63 homosexual cases on this item showed no variation in responses on the First and Second Questionnaires, while in 36 homosexual cases judgments shifted by only one position; in 7 cases shifts in two positions were noted, and in 1 case in three positions.

For the simpler "yes-no" type of response represented by the item, Did the patient feel he was accepted by his father? in 91 homosexual cases the responses had not shifted on both questionnaires, while in 12 cases they did; three psychoanalysts failed to answer one of the two questionnaires.

The item, Did the patient respect his father? was repeated on the same questionnaire and only 3 shifts in response were noted in 106 homosexual cases and 4 shifts in 94 comparison cases; in 2 cases there were no answers.

Assuming these three items to be representative of responses on repeated items, the degree of reliability appears to be satisfactory. Moreover, the variation of response by individual psychoanalysts tends to balance out on any item involving 100 or more judgments. For example, on the item tapping the amount of time the mother spent with the patient, "great deal'" was reported by 46 psychoanalysts affirmatively on the First Questionnaire and by 49 psychoanalysts on the Second Questionnaire though the latter group of psychoanalysts did not include all members of the former. Since we were dealing with totals, however, the individual differences balanced out.

Even more important than the question of reliability and validation of the responses to any single item is the nature of the evidence for conclusions of the study as a whole. Although it can be presumed that there was a certain amount of unreliability and lack of validity for any given item, all conclusions were based on a concatenation of evidence derived from many items on the questionnaires. Thus, no one item bore the weight of any major finding or conclusion.

Applicability of the study

Several sources of evidence indicate that our findings are in accord with those of other studies of homosexuals, and that our generalizations have wider application.

One member of the Research Committee was Chief of Psychiatric Services at a hospital in an overseas theatre during World War II, and had the opportunity to examine many male homosexuals who had been apprehended for homosexual activity by the Criminal Investigation Department. Repeated interviews were conducted with about 50 such patients. Sexual history, sexual practices and dreams were studied though the findings were not published Anecdotal reports revealed no major differences between the sexual symptomatology, practices, and dream content of homosexuals within that group and those of the present study.

Two members of the Research Committee conducted an independent investigation at Bellevue Hospital, New York City. This descriptive study of adolescent homosexuals and their mothers appears for the first time in this volume (Chapter VIII). The general findings parallel those of the present research. The marked differences between the samples and between the methodology of the two studies add material strength to our assumption that our findings have wider applicability. The adolescent patients represented a group not usually found in private psychoanalytic practice, and differed from the subjects of our study in that, as adolescents, they were much closer to the family situation; they were more seriously disturbed, requiring hospitalization during adolescence; they were of much lower income, education, and social status.

Another source of evidence is a questionnaire study of male and female homosexuals conducted by a committee of a society of female homosexuals published in *The Ladder*. The questionnaires were filled out anonymously and voluntarily by over 100 male homosexuals. Sociological information about this group revealed them to have striking similarities to the homosexuals in this study, although only 35 per cent had had any psychotherapy and 7 per cent had required hospitalization for psychiatric reasons. As in our sample, many had completed college (49 per cent), and 25 per cent had done postgraduate college work. Over 50 per cent were engaged in some profession. Ninety per cent reported that they were concerned about exposure of their homosexuality, and 57 per cent admitted to difficulties in adjusting to the life of a homosexual, although 75 per cent claimed to be "well adjusted" on the whole. Their early sexual experiences were in concordance with our findings, described in Chapter VII.

Further evidence supporting our findings is the report by Westwood on the lives of male homosexuals in England. This researcher, a psychologist, conducted extensive personal interviews of several hours' duration with 127 male homosexuals. Many similarities and some differences between the two studies emerged. The British group included more older men, many more with only grammar school education; considerably fewer of Westwood's subjects had completed college. There were many more tradesmen, skilled and unskilled workers, and fewer professionals. As in our study, a large number had migrated to urban centers.

Few in Westwood's group had had any psychoanalytic treatment. Although 19 per cent reported having attempted some form of treatment, only 12 per cent had consulted a psychiatrist, and half of those withdrew from therapy before the end of three months. The vast majority resented the idea that they might need treatment and were convinced that homosexuality was inborn.

Our findings and those of Westwood support each other since the data concerning attitudes and practices of homosexuals are similar in both studies, even though the samples and sources of information differ markedly: Westwood interviewed all subjects directly while we obtained information through the responding psychoanalysts; Westwood's sample was a non-patient population; the socioeconomic and educational levels of the two samples differed; Westwood's study was conducted in England.

A number of items in Westwood's study were quite similar to our own, especially with regard to parental relations, to siblings, sexual development, and homosexual practices. Westwood reported "defective relations between parents" in 40 per cent of his sample—we found "poor relationships" in 57 per cent. He found that the mother was considered dominant in 57 per cent, and the father in 29 per cent of the families—we found the mother dominant in 58 per cent and the father in 40 per cent of the families. Ten per cent of his cases and 8 per cent of ours were married. In these and other respects the homosexuals in each study displayed a range of similarities.

The remaining sources of evidence are the results and conclusions from a sample of research publications by American psychologists. In four studies, evidence of pervasive disturbances was found among homosexuals not in psychoanalytic treatment.

Davids, Joelson, and McArthur investigated Rorschach responses and Thematic Apperception Test responses, in an effort to find some indices or signs of homosexuality. The males studied were attending eastern colleges. Three groups of 20 cases each were employed: one group of homosexuals, one of "neurotics," and one of "normals." The authors concluded that no clear-cut sign or other definite indicator of homosexuality could be found, but they did find that the homosexual group could be described as having certain definite tendencies: A preoccupation with sex, its content characterized by lack of satisfaction and derogation; derogatory attitudes toward women as well as some identification with them; an "unnatural" love for and an over-close relationship with their mothers which, at the same time, was deprecated, as though they were trying desperately to break from the tightness of the relationship; bonds to another man were usually idealized ("an older man who was *really* interested in him"); the test response images and concepts were often at an extreme, ranging between "most romantic and unrealistic to most lurid," implying a lack of realism in thinking.

Doidge and Holtzman studied a group of Air Force trainees. They compared four groups of 20 each: one "markedly homosexual"; one composed of men who were predominantly heterosexual but had some limited homosexual experiences; one composed exclusively of heterosexuals who had been charged with some offense; and one composed of heterosexuals neither charged with any offense nor under disciplinary survey. As in the previously reported study, the most striking finding was the difference between the "markedly homosexual" group and the other three groups. They found that "severe pathology is likely to accompany the markedly homosexual individual." They concluded that "the homosexual individuals are likely to be suffering from an emotional disorder which is relatively pervasive, severe, and disqualifying from military service."

Miller reported on 50 homosexual males from the Federal Prison System. His sample consisted entirely of markedly effeminate homosexuals, a type which constituted less than 2 per cent of our own sample. Parents were classified as: absent, active-negative, passive-negative, and over-positive. The largest single group in Miller's study consisted of subjects who had an over-positive mother and a negative father. Forty-six fathers were classified as either negative or absent. All of Miller's subjects were criminally antisocial. Twenty-eight per cent were also drug addicts and 40 per cent were either preschizophrenic, latent, or actively schizophrenic. Despite the marked differences between the type of subjects in Miller's sample and the patients represented in this study, there are notable similarities between the characteristics of parent-child relationships in his group and those to be described in the following chapters.

West assembled histories on 50 homosexuals and 50 control cases from the files of Maudsley Hospital in England. Abstracts of the case histories were rated by two independent judges. The criteria were: "Paternal relationships to be judged according to the degree of deviation from the ideal of a competent father who likes and takes an interest in his child and who makes a good model for masculine identification . . . according to degree of unsatisfactoriness . . . assessed by such manifestations as absence from home, emotional aloofness, ineptitude, inability to assert himself in the home, or any other deficiencies tending to interfere with a son's ability to identify with and hero-worship his father . . . maternal relationships to be judged according to the intensity of the mother-son relationship . . . ambivalent feelings to a domineering mother to rate equally with a strong, dependent attachment to a quiet, affectionate mother."

West concluded: "The homosexual case histories show, significantly more frequently than the controls, the presence of a typical parental constellation; over-intense mother and unsatisfactory father relationship . . . it is the *combination* (West's italics) of parental relationships that characterized the homosexual groups . . . exclusive emphasis on the mother figure in the male homosexual is misplaced." These conclusions are in remarkable agreement with our findings on the child-parent relationship based on more detailed and extensive psychoanalytic material.

Summary

A brief history of this study and details of the methodology have been presented in this chapter. The composition of the sample and how it was obtained have been described. The safeguards employed against a variety of potential pitfalls in our research were discussed. Related studies were cited to substantiate our findings as applicable to homosexuals outside our sample.

Prefatory Note to Chapters III-VI

THE ADJUSTMENTS within a family represent the nature of the interrelationships and reciprocal interactions of its members. Within the family system, the personality development of the child is influenced by each member and, in turn, influences every other. The flow of interchange within a family will vary, change its course from time to time, and fluctuate with the give-and-take of daily life. But at any particular point in time, the family has coherence, role assignment, and a system of relationships characterized by subtle but well-defined interpersonal alignments. Shifts in pattern occur as new members come and old ones leave. These rearrangements may create revolutionary shifts in family relationships or they may be smoothly integrated into the forward movement of growth and change.

The parents are the architects of family structure and fundamentally determine the ongoing interactive processes. Personality maladaptation is the objective manifestation of dysfunction in the family and the development of personality disorders in a child is almost always evidence of the pervasive effects of parental psychopathology.* The extent of pathogenic influence varies depending on the parental interaction with each specific child. In some families one child may bear the brunt; in others, most or all children may be seriously affected. Psychopathologic responses differ in each child depending upon how a multiplicity of factors—sex, rank order, physical and intellectual endowment—articulate with parental needs, attitudes, and values.

* Nathan Ackerman has developed the thesis that personality disorders and disturbances in social adaptation can be understood only if examined within the context of family interaction.

In the chapters ahead, we shall locate parameters of intrafamilial disturbances by examining major sub-systems within the family, e.g., marital pair, parent-child, parent-sibling, child-sibling. Dividing the family into its component sub-systems is inevitably an arbitrary technique justified, however, by the complex operations of the totality. An integrated view will become apparent; the study of each sub-system necessarily cuts across arbitrary system boundaries since each interpenetrates with others.

In an attempt to come up with a more complete understanding of homosexuality, we have conducted a systematic inquiry into the nature of certain intrafamilial interactions, behaviors, and attitudes, always keeping the patient in the foreground.

III

Mother-Son Relationship

AT THE TIME the questionnaire items were originally formulated the Research Committee had no a priori convictions on the nature of findings to be derived from the data. While it was known that the fathers of homosexuals (H-fathers) were usually hostile to their sons, there was less certainty about the mothers (H-mothers),[1] aside from the general assumption that these mothers were often unusually close to their sons.

Seventy questions explored the relationship between mother and son, and 27 of these 70 questions were found to be the most sensitive indicators of differences between the homosexual and nonhomosexual groups.

Table III-1 lists the 27 questions, the percentage of affirmative responses, and the statistical differences between answers that reached levels of significance varying from .05 to .001.

The responses to the First Questionnaire indicated that an intimate H-mother-son dyad occurred frequently, and that this intimate pairing was often associated with restrictive and binding maternal behavior. at statistically significant levels turned out to reflect close-binding-Nearly all answers that differentiated the H-mothers from the C-mothers

[1] In order to avoid repetition and awkwardness of designations, an abbreviated way of referring to patients, parents, and categories will be used throughout. Homosexual patients will be referred to as H-patients or H-sons; comparison patients as C-patients or C-sons; parents of homosexual patients as H-mothers, H-fathers, or H-parents; parents of comparison patients as C-mothers, C-fathers, or C-parents; the homosexual sample as H-group, H-sample, or H-category; and the comparison sample as C-group, C-sample, or C-category.

TABLE III-1 *Significant Items Regarding Mother-Son Relationships Which Distinguish Homosexuals from Comparisons (in per cent)*

		Answered Yes	
		H	C
	N =	106	100
1.	Sibling preference: Was patient mother's favorite[a]?	66	50*
2.	Did mother demand to be the prime center of the patient's attentions?	61	36†
3.	Was she dominating?	81	65*
4.	Was she seductive	57	34*
5.	Amount of contact (time spent between mother and patient):		
	(a) Great deal	56	27†
	(b) Average	20	53
	(c) Little	15	11
	(d) Very little	7	9
	(e) Absent	2	0
6.	Did mother encourage masculine activities and attitudes?	17	47†
7.	Did mother discourage masculine activities and attitudes?	37	16**
8.	Did mother encourage feminine activities and attitudes?	35	11†
9.	Was mother considered to be puritanical?	62	48*
10.	Was mother considered to be sexually frigid?	64	47**
11.	Did mother try to ally with son against husband?	62	40**
12.	Did mother openly prefer patient to husband?	58	38**
13.	Did mother want patient to grow up to be like some particular individual?	26	27
	(a) Like mother?	6	0*
	(b) If male, was he a virile male?	9	21*
14.	Were there families with other male siblings?	64	63
15.	If yes, was mother, as compared to other siblings[b]:		
	(a) More intimate with patient?	56	29*
16.	Does analyst believe mother interfered with patient's heterosexual activity?	58	35**
17.	Was patient the mother's confidant?	52	36*
18.	Was mother the patient's confidante?	39	23*
	Cases	96	96

TABLE III-1 *Significant Items Regarding Mother-Son Relationships Which Distinguish Homosexuals from Comparisons (in per cent)* (Cont'd.)

	H	C
N =	106	100
19[c]. Was mother *unduly* concerned about protecting the patient from physical injury?	58	39*
20. Did mother's concern about health or injury cause her to interfere with or restrict his play, social or other activities?	49	26†
21. Does the patient consider his mother to have been overprotective?	61	46*
22. Does analyst consider patient's mother to have been overprotective?	67	43**
23. In childhood, was the patient *excessively* dependent on his mother for advice or direction in making decisions?	64	42**
24. Does patient feel his mother "babied" him?	61	41**
25. Did mother administer frequent enemas?	15	4*
26. Which parent does the patient feel he could cope with more easily? Mother?	64	48**
27. Did patient use the technique of rebellion to cope with mother?	9	23*

[a] Based on number of families in which patient had siblings (see Chapter V).

[b] Based on number of families in which patient had male siblings (see Chapter V).

[c] Questions 19-27 were derived from equal samples of 96 homosexuals and comparisons. These questions were on the Third (Second Supplementary) Questionnaire and there was no Third Questionnaire for 10 homosexual cases (106 − 10 = 96) and 4 comparison cases (100 − 4 = 96).

* .05 level of significance

** .01 level of significance

† .001 level of significance

intimate (CBI) qualities. Consequently, when responses to questionnaire items, comments included by the responding psychoanalysts, and inferences had been evaluated (see Appendix B), 73 of the 106 H-mothers were assigned to a CBI category. Of the remaining 33 homosexual cases, 8 mothers who were classified as hostile and rejecting were also found to be CBI. (The ambivalence expressed by these mothers was the justification for grouping them separately.) In 11 cases detachment was the salient maternal feature, and in 9 cases domination and exploitativeness were the outstanding maternal characteristics justifying independent categorization. All but 2 were the biological mothers;

mother surrogates were grouped separately. In 3 homosexual cases the mother-son relationship precluded classification; the pattern was either erratic or without clear definition. These cases were grouped as "unclassifiable."

The criteria for classifying H-mothers were also applied to the comparison sample. In 19 comparison cases, however, maternal attitudes appeared neither exceptional nor pathological. These mothers were grouped independently as "not remarkable."

Table III-2 presents the number of mothers in the various categories. A separate descriptive section will be devoted to each category, with the exception of the "Not Remarkable" group.

TABLE III-2 *Number of Mothers in Each Category*

	Mother Categories:	H	C
I.	Close-binding-intimate (CBI)	73	32
II.	Rejecting-minimizing-hostile but not detached	8	6
III.	Detached mothers:		
	(a) poorly related	7	6
	(b) hostile-detached	4	3
IV.	Controlling-dominating	9	27
V.	Mother surrogates	2	1
VI.	Not remarkable	0	19
VII.	Unclassifiable	3	6
		106	100

I. Close-binding-intimate (CBI) mothers

Homosexual group

As shown in Table III-2, by far the greatest number of H-mothers (73, or 69 per cent of the total sample) were CBI. The outstanding characteristic of these mothers was an extraordinary intimacy with their H-sons. Pathological sexual attitudes and behavior were frequently expressed, covertly or subtly, and constituted central aspects of the relationship. The CBI H-mother exerted a binding influence on her son through preferential treatment and seductiveness on the one hand, and inhibiting, over-controlling attitudes on the other. In many instances, the son was the most significant individual in her life and the husband was usually replaced by the son as her love object.

Table III-3 shows the percentage distribution of affirmative answers to 18 questions (which had significantly differentiated the total homosexual group from the total comparison group, see Table III-1) for the CBI and non-CBI maternal categories in both H- and C-samples.

TABLE III-3 *Comparison of CBI and Non-CBI Mothers (in per cent)*

	CBI		Non-CBI	
	H	C	H	C
N =	73	32	33	68
1. Patient mother's favorite[a]	85	77	27	39
2. Mother more intimate with patient than with other male siblings[b]	87	82	8	12
3. Patient mother's confidant	71	84	9	13
4. Mother patient's confidante	51	50	12	10
5. Mother spent great deal of time with patient	78	63	6	10
6. Mother demanded center of attention	73	66	36	22
7. Mother dominating	79	69	85	63
8. Mother allied with son against husband	73	75	39	24
9. Mother openly preferred son to husband	75	88	21	15
10. Mother overprotective	73	59	33	32
11. Mother interfered with heterosexuality	68	44	36	31
12. Mother interfered with other activities[c]	62	38	6	19
13. Patient believed mother babied him[c]	74	72	33	24
14. Mother seductive	73	69	21	18
15. Mother encouraged masculinity	12	38*	27	51
16. Mother discouraged masculinity	45	34	18	7
17. Mother encouraged femininity	45	28	12	3
18. Mother puritanical and/or frigid	79	66	73	50

[a] Based on number of patients with siblings
[b] Based on number of patients with male siblings
[c] N for H — CBI = 66
N for H — non-CBI = 30
N for C — CBI = 30
N for C — non-CBI = 66

The CBI characteristics of the H-mothers become evident in the following data from Table III-3:

The CBI mothers favored their homosexual sons over other siblings in 85 per cent of the cases. These mothers were more intimate with their homosexual sons than with other sons in 87 per cent of the families where there were male siblings. Yet, in *no instance* was a CBI mother more encouraging of masculinity in her homosexual son than in her other son(s).[2] In fact, half of these mothers were *less* encouraging of masculinity in the homosexual sons than in other sons in the family.

The mothers made confidants of the homosexual sons in 71 per cent of the cases in the CBI category. Ordinarily, women confide in their husbands or perhaps in one or several female friends. The H-mothers, however, not only made confidants of their sons by divulging highly personal matters to them, but in some cases revealed intimate details of marital sexual relationships. A few mothers even confided details of extramarital affairs. The seductive quality inherent in the confidant relationship is borne out by the interaction of the items on "Confidant Relationship and Maternal Seductiveness" in Table III-4.

TABLE III-4 *Mothers' Seductiveness Associated with Confidant Relationship*

	H		C	
	Confidant	Not confidant	Confidant	Not confidant
Seductive	40	20	20	14
Nonseductive	15	31	17	49

Significance: H .001; C .01

Half of the homosexual sons in the CBI category made confidantes of their mothers and in 47 per cent of the cases this type of relationship was reciprocal.[3]

Further attesting to the unusually close H-mother-son relationship was the amount of time each spent with the other. In only 2 of the 73 CBI cases (3 per cent) did mothers spend "little" or "very little" time with their sons; 14 (19 per cent) spent an "average" amount of time, while 57[4] (78 per cent) spent "a great deal" of time with their sons.

One might infer from these data that the homosexual patients required extraordinary attention in their childhood, to which the mothers responded by devoting much time to them. Yet other material in the study indicates that the excessive time they spent together, and their

[2] See Appendix A: II Q 4.

[3] See Table III-7.

[4] There were 59 H-cases for whom a "great deal" of time spent with patient was answered on either the First or Second Questionnaire. Because this was an extreme on a 5-point scale, it was assumed that when the responding psychoanalysts chose an extreme point, there was unusual amount of time spent with the mother.

unusual closeness, were initiated by the mother in order to fulfill a range of conscious and unconscious wishes.

Many mothers encouraged reciprocal alienation between father and son, thus leading the son to concentrate upon his mother for parental support, resulting in even greater binding closeness between the two: 73 per cent of the CBI H-mothers demanded to be the center of the son's attention; 79 per cent exercised a dominating control over the son and 48 per cent did both; 73 per cent drew the son into an alliance against the father; 75 per cent openly preferred the son to the husband.

Among CBI mothers, 73 per cent were overprotective. Overprotectiveness is a psychiatric euphemism indicating a type of parental behavior, usually ascribed to the mother, which is characterized by interference with normal childhood activities by overdirective, controlling, overanxious attitudes. Two questions were designed to tap maternal interference with activity:

Did the mother's concern about health or injury cause her to interfere with or restrict her son's play—social or otherwise? This question was answered affirmatively in 62 per cent of the CBI H-cases, in sharp contrast to 19 per cent of the comparison cases where the mothers were *not* CBI, a difference which is significant at the .001 level.

The parental restriction of childhood activities seriously impairs personality development, often reflected in areas of social relationships (particularly with peers), self-esteem, effectiveness, and independence. One might argue that the restricting mother is responding appropriately to the needs of a biologically weak or impaired child. It must be pointed out, however, that these mothers had restricted not only physical activity but sexual activity as well. In 29 of the 41 restrictive CBI H-mothers (Table III-5), there were affirmative responses to the question: Did the mother interfere with heterosexual activity during adolescence?

TABLE III-5 *H-CBI Mother Interferes with Heterosexuality—Restricts Physical-Social Activities*

	Restricts activity	Does not
Interferes with heterosexuality	29	10
Does not	12	13

Significance: .05

Mothers may often rationalize interference with physical activities in the interests of health, and one might be persuaded that such restrictions may occur for that reason; but it is obvious that gross interference with heterosexual relationships is not in the child's best interests from any point of view. We infer from the association between maternal restriction of sexual activity and the restriction of other activities (.05 level of significance) that the H-mothers did not restrict their sons for realistic reasons. This inference is further supported by the significant association between CBI characteristics and maternal interference with heterosexuality, shown in Table III-6.

TABLE III-6 *CBI Mother and Non-CBI Mother—Interferes with Heterosexuality*

	H		C	
	Interferes	Does not	Interferes	Does not
CBI	50	23	14	18
Non-CBI	13	20	21	47

Significance: H .01; C not significant

Additional evidence of maternal interference with normal masculine development was brought out by the question: Did the mother baby her son? In 74 per cent of the CBI cases affirmative answers were elicited. It is universally acknowledged and accepted that infantilizing a child is an expression of parental psychopathology.

In 53 (73 per cent) of 73 cases, the CBI H-mothers were reported as "seductive" toward their sons. When a great deal of time is spent by mother and son in an unusually close, intimate relationship, the situation in itself becomes sexually stimulating for the son. The sexual bond is further strengthened and reinforced by maternal seductiveness. Each responding psychoanalyst was asked to make a judgment as to whether or not the mother was seductive. A list of criteria for seductiveness was itemized into eight questions and the responding psychoanalyst was asked to underline any of the eight items that were pertinent in his case. (See Appendix A, II F3.)

The CBI-seductive-H-mother is easily distinguishable from the "normal" warmly affectionate mother of the developing male child. We consider the "normal" mother to be openly affectionate to all her children and to her husband. She will feel free to express her own feelings openly and spontaneously and to accept the sexual expressiveness of her children without guilt or anxiety. She will either be relatively free of anxiety about her own sexual responsiveness (conscious or unconscious) to a male child, which occurs normally in every mother, or will not be inhibited or inhibiting of a reciprocal affectionate relatedness by any anxiety she may have about this. In fact, a feeling of constraint in overt affection toward a male child tends to have deleterious effects in that the child's demonstrativeness may, in turn, be inhibited.

In contrast, the seductive H-mother *covertly* indulges in frequent and intense stimulation of her son's sexual feelings which she exploits and manipulates within a range of self-interest. The motivation to evoke specifically sexual responses in a son, on either a conscious or unconscious level, may be considered as seductive behavior. If, on the other hand, a mother is warmly affectionate and demonstrative, but is not motivated to elicit specifically sexual responses, she is not seductive.

In most cases, the mothers' seductive and sexually stimulating behavior was masked by overt antisexual attitudes and demasculinizing tendencies. Seventy-seven per cent of the seductive CBI H-mothers (Table III-7) were reported by the responding psychoanalysts to have

TABLE III-7 *Comparison of Seductive and Nonseductive CBI H-Mothers (in per cent)*

		Seductive	Nonseductive
	N =	53	20
1.	Mother's favorite[a]	96	75
2.	Mother demanded center of attention	81	45*
3.	Mother dominating	79	80
4.	Mother spent great deal of time with patient	79	75
5.	Mother discouraged masculinity	49	35
6.	Mother encouraged femininity	49	35
7.	Mother puritanical and/or frigid	83	70
8.	Mother allied with son against husband	72	75
9.	Mother openly preferred patient to husband	75	75
10.	Mother interfered with heterosexual activity	77	45*
11.	Patient mother's confidant	75	60
12.	Mother patient's confidante	53	45
13.	Reciprocal confidant relationship	51	35
14.	Mother overprotective	75	65
15.	Mother either discouraged masculinity or encouraged femininity	64	50
16.	Mother did both	34	15

[a] Based on number of families in which patient had siblings

TABLE III-8 *Sexual Relations Involving Patient's or Partner's Genitals Before Patient Was 14 Years of Age*

	Homosexual activity	Heterosexual activity	Total†
Homosexual (N = 106)	58	4	62
Comparisons (N = 100)	19	7	26

actively interfered with their sons' heterosexual activities during adolescence and early adult life. Eighty-three per cent of the seductive mothers were reported as puritanical and/or frigid, further indicating restrictive sexual attitudes. Among seductive mothers, 8 discouraged masculine attitudes and 8 encouraged feminine attitudes, while 18 both discouraged masculine attitudes and encouraged feminine attitudes. Thus, 34 of 53 (64 per cent) seductive mothers were demasculinizing and/or feminizing.

A seductive CBI maternal configuration emerges from these data. Such mothers overstimulated their sons sexually within the context of an overclose, overintimate relationship, and, at the same time, through antisexual attitudes, prohibitions, and demasculinizing behavior toward their sons, compelled them to conceal all manifestations of sexuality. Thus, the sons were caught in a double-bind: *maternal seductiveness—maternal sexual restriction.*[5]

The psychoanalysis of adult male homosexuals discloses that in many cases disguised heterosexual impulses are expressed in the homosexual act. Psychoanalysts who treat homosexuals frequently observe an anxiety reaction to a heterosexual stimulus followed by flight into homosexual activity. This pattern may obtain during the childhood of homosexuals when they are faced with the maternal double-bind. The occurrence of homosexual behavior in the preadolescence of many cases in our study appears to be an acting-out, at least in part, in response to maternal sexual stimulation on the one hand, and sexual overrestriction on the other. The data in Table III-8 indicate that 62 homosexuals had engaged in sexual activity (involving partners' genitals) before the age of fourteen, as compared to 26 of the comparison patients. Among the homosexuals the majority (58) participated in homosexual relationships.

[5] We are indebted to Bateson *et al.* for the concept of "double-bind." See Bibliography.

As shown in Table III-7, most of the questions which tapped the H-mother-son relationship for both the seductive and nonseductive groups drew similar answers from the responding psychoanalysts. However, *a trend toward consistently higher percentages of affirmative answers* concerning the seductive mothers was noted.

Thus, when the mother's seductiveness toward her son was included as a variable, it appeared that 53 CBI mothers acted-out tendencies toward directly stimulating their sons sexually while 20 CBI mothers did not. The item response configuration for nonseductive mothers indicates that although they were close-binding-intimate, the seductive CBI mothers were more so. Maternal seductiveness did not significantly differentiate the mothers so reported from those who were presumably nonseductive except on the following two items: Did the mother demand to be the center of her son's attention? and Did the mother interfere with heterosexual activity? Responses to both questions significantly differentiated the seductive from the nonseductive CBI mothers at the .05 level.

The Committee's judgment as to whether or not a mother was to be classified as CBI was not based on the item tapping maternal seductiveness. Since the majority of seductive mothers (53 of 60) fall within the CBI classification, the combination of seductiveness with close-binding-intimacy further attests to the association between the two variables. As Table III-4 showed, there is a positive association between maternal seductiveness and the use of the son as a confidant in both the H- and C-samples.

Two case histories illustrating CBI H-mothers follow:

CASE NO. 129

The patient, thirty years old, came from a fairly well-to-do background.

The patient's mother was extremely possessive and overprotective. She supervised the play of both the patient and his older sister and chose their playmates. Neither was allowed to play rowdy games, and the boy in particular was constantly cautioned against "rough" boys and "rough" play.

When the patient was six years old, he and his sister were enrolled in a private school close to their home. Since the daughter was excessively shy, the mother decided that something had to be done to ameliorate the child's social backwardness, and she hired an elocution and voice teacher for both children who were tutored after school hours. When the patient was eight years old, the school closed and the children were sent to separate private schools within commuting distance. At the same time, they continued with their elocution and voice lessons and the patient showed unusual vocal ability. Shortly after he was settled at the new school, his mother decided that his talent was of professional caliber and she arranged for him to try out for a singing engagement. He soon made his professional debut and received good critical notices. By the time he was nine years old his career was well launched. His mother became deeply involved in all matters affecting his voice and his performance. People who had to deal with her considered her a prime example of the "difficult" mother of a child performer. She was intent on fighting her son's way to the top. She tempered her aggressiveness and singlemindedness with a tendency to be seductive with the men she met in the course of managing her son's career, and some even admired her in a grudging way.

The patient's father was a moderately successful business man before World War II. When the war broke out, he joined the Navy and, except for one short leave, was away from home for almost seven years. Even before this prolonged absence the father had been a shadowy figure who was away on frequent business trips. When home, he was completely dominated and intimidated by his wife, who showed open preference for her son. When the father rejoined the family late in 1945, he did not return to the business world. The mother, in fact, seemed to discourage him from doing so. The patient's career was running successfully and the financial returns were more than substantial. His father tended to while away his time. "My father was there and there was nothing for him to do; it made me feel guilty." The patient had a vague feeling he had usurped his father's position and felt guilty and uncomfortable with him. He never got to know his father very well. He seemed nice enough, but was no match for his wife. Whenever it appeared that she might not get her way with her husband or with others, as a final resort she would take to her bed. On one occasion she developed hysterical paralysis. The physician who attended her coolly informed her that she was a "hysterical" woman with delusions of grandeur.

The mother was the most important influence in the patient's life. Except for the few hours a day he spent at school during childhood, he was with his mother almost constantly. She accompanied him everywhere. When on tour or on a trip, they shared the same hotel room. While his father was away during the war the patient slept in his mother's room.

The patient began to earn a great deal of money, and soon his mother bought a beautiful home. He was assigned a bedroom and bath on the first floor. She frequently entertained people, and the boy, because he needed rest, would retire before all the guests had left. Afterwards, his mother would go to his room, rouse him, and take him to her room on the next floor to sleep the rest of the night. The patient reported the clandestine flavor of these occasions to his psychoanalyst and detailed the hushed, conspiratorial air she would assume. The mother's rationalization was her dread of kidnapers. She repeatedly alluded to her fear of kidnapers when she accompanied him on tours, trips, the theater, and everywhere else he went.

The mother's open seductiveness to her son ran parallel with her prudish attitudes concerning heterosexuality, which "disgusted" her. Although she permitted some socialization with girls during the patient's adolescence, he was strictly supervised and, in a sexual sense, warned repeatedly against women. Whenever the patient liked a girl, the mother immediately found fault. She encouraged his relationship with a boy with whom the patient had his first homosexual affair.

During the war years the mother often entertained servicemen. She invited many young men to stay overnight. If there was only one guest the patient would share his room, otherwise he would sleep in the master bedroom with his mother. He started his homosexual practices when he was twelve years old. Since his mother enjoyed inviting young men to her home, the patient had a number of homosexual partners supplied by his mother. On one occasion she discovered her son in bed with a guest, but she raised no objection and made no comment. The patient concluded that his mother did not object to, or at least could overlook, homosexual activity.

The mother was often coy and seductive with the young men she entertained and the patient had conscious, incestuous fantasies about her. After noticing her flirtatiousness he had fantasies of his mother having a sexual relationship with one of the young men.

The patient's sister was somewhat neglected, especially after the boy became a successful singer. All the mother's plans revolved around him. The brother and sister, however, maintained a fine relationship. He deeply admired his sister and always kept in touch with her. He spoke of her as "a wonderful girl, but she needs analysis." During childhood they were playmates and allies. He usually took the lead in mischief, but his sister loyally joined him and never "tattled." The patient enjoyed being with her. They were able to discuss everything together, even the problems each had with the other. Interestingly, the only subject the patient did not discuss with her was his homosexuality.

When the patient was nineteen years old he informed his parents that he wanted to be on his own and away from home. This led to a prolonged family quarrel, but the patient was able to break away even though he continued to send most of his earnings home.

At one point in his career the patient found it difficult to find employment and was unable to continue to send money home. His mother had spent all his earnings. A series of financial rearrangements were made which permitted him an independent life. However, his mother was constantly after him to return home and "with her help" get back into a high-income bracket. He refused, partly because he valued his newly found freedom away from his ubiquitous mother, and partly because of his current homosexual partner.

The patient's mother continued to believe that she could win him back to her side. One evening he appeared on a television program and at the end of a tender love song to a beautiful young actress he kissed her passionately. The next morning he received a phone call from his sister warning, "Be careful, Mother is trying to seduce you." In the next mail he received a recorded message from his mother in lieu of a letter. The patient brought the disc to his psychoanalyst who reported that the mother's seductiveness more than matched the patient's previous description. The message was filled with endearments, coy blandishments, intimacy of voice, intimate recollections, sighs and suggestiveness.

The patient was twenty-eight years old when he undertook psychoanalysis with a female analyst. He had been referred by his homosexual partner's psychoanalyst. The partner was not particularly interested in the patient but stated that he hesitated to terminate the relationship lest the patient "collapse" in the face of rejection. The patient wanted help with two problems: how to free himself of all ties, including financial ones, from his family—especially his mother; and how to cope with his homosexual partner. He did not believe he could give up homosexuality nor did he wish to be "cured" of it.

The relationship between the two men was a difficult, unstable one. The partner drank heavily and during his drinking periods he teased and acted rejectingly. The patient felt devoted to him yet became involved in other homosexual affairs. The partner, too, was promiscuous. On occasion, he invited men to his home and sent the patient away. The partner also carried on an affair with an older woman. He kept his friends worried about his excessive drinking and erratic behavior. The patient felt protective but was excessively dependent upon him.

During the course of analysis sexual contacts between the pair diminished and all but disappeared, yet the patient felt guilt-ridden about the other homosexual affairs he had from time to time. Soon he began to have a few heterosexual experiences. He was concerned about his partner's approval and there were indications that he was trying to keep up with or outdo his partner in a heterosexual adjustment.

The relationship between the pair contained many elements suggestive of transference phenomena stemming from the patient's parents. The patient was many years younger than the partner, who was titillating, seductive, exploitative, egocentric, advisory, demanding. In short, he had all the salient characteristics of the patient's mother. At the same time the partner's coolness, detachment, frequent absences out of town, as well as his liaison with a *dominating* older woman, were characteristic of the patient's father.

Treatment was often interrupted by the exigencies of the patient's career and his analysis did not fully develop. When he last saw the responding psychoanalyst he was still concerned about his partner's difficulties, though more as a friend than a lover. He had not given up homosexuality but he was bisexual. He was potent with women, attractive to them, and attracted by them.

CASE NO. 153

The patient entered psychoanalysis with a female analyst at age thirty-five, after he was retired from the army on neuropsychiatric grounds toward the end of World War II. His homosexual practices began with mutual masturbation at the age of seventeen with a partner of the same age. During the following years he participated in homoerotic activities of all types, with mutual fellatio predominating. The patient went through long periods without homosexual activity and during the war he was sexually inactive. He achieved a distinguished war record.

The patient described his mother as an extremely nervous woman who was overprotective, seductive, and close-binding-intimate. "She is a bundle of nerves and terror. . . . She considers my father a villain—she has accused him of playing God, being unhelpful, and all sorts of things."

When the patient was four years old his parents quarreled bitterly; he did not know why. At that time the mother stated that she would raise the child without the father's help. The father, indeed, remained an outsider. He was of German extraction and this created difficulties for his son during World War I. He was frequently chased off the street by other children and called "Heinie," whereupon his mother would say, "Never mind, come into the house with me—I will teach you how to knit." He learned to knit well.

Between the ages of four and seven the patient had a minor intestinal condition and his mother kept him in bed most of the time. Her daily ritual was to rub his back, then pat his buttocks and kiss them. When he was seven years old he had an erection while his mother was thus engaged. He was completely terrified and was desperately frightened that she would notice it. His immediate thoughts were that he must hide it from her and that it must never happen again. He referred to "the back-rub business" many times during the analysis, and stated that it had made him so afraid of sexual activity that he had divided himself in half—from the waist down he was numb.

The patient had no playmates during childhood although the family lived in the same house for a long time. Beginning at an early age and continuing through his later life, his mother would criticize him as soon as he "opened up" with others. She arranged to cut him off from any outside relationships. "It was as if she demanded that I give her all my attention. She criticized my friends and did it so nicely that it hurt more."

The mother was a "vitamin-conscious" hypochondriac who expressed a great deal of concern for the patient's health. She created in her son a marked tendency to worry excessively about health. At the age of eight and nine he had asthma. "My asthma is the story of my attachment and dependency on my mother." Along with her emphasis on nutrition she considered any waste of food a cardinal sin. All leftovers were saved. Although the father earned a fair living, the mother behaved as though they were very poor people, and the patient resented the feeling of great poverty this gave him.

The patient detailed how his mother constantly "babied" him and continued to do so into his adult life. He frequently received gifts from her "on the sly." During his analysis he went to a store to buy her a birthday present. While there, he had an attack of numbness, feelings of chest congestion, and believed that his eyesight had suddenly become defective. He never overcame intense feelings of anxiety associated with his mother; even during his adult years, a call or visit from her made him feel "morbid."

The patient was an outstandingly handsome man, of imposing height and muscular development. When on vacation he would avoid homosexual gathering places; instead, he would go to Miami where he enjoyed exposing his magnificent physique on the beach for the ladies to admire. He attempted heterosexual intercourse for the first time at age twenty-eight, and failed. He lived with a woman for about a year although no sexual relationship existed between them. He attempted intercourse with another woman and failed again. Following his three failures he gave up heterosexuality entirely.

The patient maintained occasional contact with his psychoanalyst after his analysis was terminated. At the last contact he had given up homosexual activities, did not become heterosexual, and remained sexually inactive.

Comparison group

Of the 100 mothers in the comparison group, 32 were classified as CBI, in contrast to 73 (69 per cent) in the homosexual group. Table III-3 compares data derived from the CBI H-mother group; the CBI C-mother group; the non-CBI H-mother group; the non-CBI C-mother group.

As expected, the 32 CBI C-mothers closely resemble the 73 CBI H-mothers. Comparing columns 2 and 3 of Table III-3, we find that in the CBI C-category, slightly less than one-third of the comparison sample, the responses differ significantly (and in the same direction as the homosexual sample) from the responses elicited for the non-CBI H-mothers, who comprise about one-third of the H-sample.

It was also expected that those patients in the comparison sample who resembled homosexuals most closely would be found in the CBI category. The patterns of answers for 9 comparison patients were indistinguishable from those found in the majority of the homosexual group, and these 9 cases received special attention: the responding psychoanalysts were personally interviewed in order to define possible determinants in the life history of each patient which differentiated him from homosexuals. It was found that all 9 cases had had CBI mothers and each case had revealed so-called "latent" homosexual problems.[6]

Close-binding-intimacy and maternal seductiveness were closely related to the son's sexual problems in general, and specifically to the homosexual aspects of his problems. As was the case with the CBI H-mothers, a positive association between *seductiveness* and a *confidant* relationship was established for the CBI C-mothers (Table III-4).

All items, with two exceptions, which distinguished the CBI H-mothers from the non-CBI H-mothers (Columns 1 and 3, Table III-3) also distinguished the CBI C-mothers from the non-CBI C-mothers (Columns 2 and 4, Table III-3). The exceptions were:

Mother interfered with heterosexuality (*Item 11*). In the CBI category, H-mothers interfered in 68 per cent of the cases, as contrasted to 36 per cent of the non-CBI H-mothers, whereas in the C-mother category the percentages were 44 per cent to 31 per cent respectively.

Mother interfered with other activities (*Item 12*). The CBI H-mothers interfered in 62 per cent of the cases, as contrasted to 20 per cent of the non-CBI H-mothers; in the CBI C-category mothers interfered in 37 per cent of cases, as contrasted to 21 per cent in the non-CBI C-category.

Despite the similarities noted between the CBI H- and CBI C-mothers, there were several items which differentiated the groups in respect to psychopathology of mother-son relations: *Mother encouraged masculinity* (12 per cent of H-mothers, and 38 per cent of C-mothers—.05 level of significance). Two other items approached but did not reach the .05 level of significance: *Mother interfered with heterosexual activities in adolescence* (68 per cent of H-mothers and 44 per cent of C-mothers); *Mother interfered with other activities* (62 per cent of H-mothers and 37 per cent of C-mothers). These three items reflect maternal interference with the son's development of self-assertiveness, independence, self-esteem, and appropriate sexual identification.

[6] Five of these cases will be discussed in detail in Chapter X, "Latent" Homosexuality.

Relationship of patients to the CBI mothers

Table III-9 demonstrates certain patient reactions to CBI H- and C-mothers and to non-CBI H- and C-mothers.

TABLE III-9 *Patients' Relations to CBI and Non-CBI Mothers (in per cent)*

	CBI		Non-CBI	
	H	C	H	C
N =	73	32	33	68
1. Patient felt accepted by mother	81	72	45	56
2. Patient felt admired by mother	64	66	15	35
3. Patient respected mother	64	66	52	51
4. Patient thought mother admirable	72	50	27	40
5. Patient feared physical injury from mother	8	16	21	16
6. Patient knowingly hated mother	26	31	36	31
7. Patient knowingly feared mother	36	50	58	41
8. Patient was a clinging child	48	31	39	22
9. Patient sided with mother in parental arguments during childhood	67	67	45	44
10. Patient turned to mother for protection, not to father; or to neither	67	50	26	21
11. Patient coped with mother more easily than with father	64	63	42	38
12. Patient felt mother protected him from father	49	60	18	17
13. Patient coped with mother by:				
(a) submission	53	50	61	57
(b) rebellion	0	13	27	27
14. Patient feared his assertiveness might:				
(a) disappoint mother	36	34	27	25
(b) anger mother	51	38	52	62
(c) hurt mother	41	44	12	28
(d) lose her love	47	53	45	34
(e) make her sick	23	43	18	21

Questionnaire items tapping the patient's attitudes toward his mother are presented in Table III-9. Columns 1 and 2 give the percentages achieved by the CBI H- and CBI C-groups on each item; columns 3 and 4 give the percentages achieved by the non-CBI H- and C-groups. In general, with a few exceptions, the two CBI groups show concordance on every question; similarly, there is concordance between the two non-CBI groups. This finding is noteworthy since none of the 14 items listed in Table III-9 were used as criteria in establishing the CBI maternal category.

Items 1-4, taken as a cluster, reflect certain reciprocal positive aspects of the mother-son relationship: about two-thirds of the CBI mothers in both groups accepted and admired their sons; in turn, most sons respected and admired their mothers. The non-CBI H-mothers achieved lower percentages on each item which tapped closeness and intimacy and their sons achieved somewhat higher percentages than did CBI H-sons on items tapping hatred and fear of the mother.

Items 5-7 tap negative aspects of the mother-son relationship. Few patients consciously feared physical injury from their mothers in either group; approximately one-third hated their mothers.

Items 8-12 tap pathologic dependency upon the mother. On Item 8, all homosexuals achieved higher percentages than did all comparison patients, significant at the .01 level. On the remaining items in this cluster, the two CBI groups achieved significantly higher percentages than did the two non-CBI groups.

Item 13 lists two ways the patient coped with his mother. Whereas about the same percentage of cases in the 4 categories coped with their mothers by submission, *not one* of the 73 CBI H-sons showed rebellion.

The various alternatives for Item 14 do not indicate marked trends, although the CBI H-sons were significantly more fearful that self-assertiveness would hurt their mothers than were non-CBI H-sons.

In summary, we infer that the CBI patients felt reasonably certain of their ability to maintain a stable relationship with their mothers, although this stability appeared to be contingent upon compliance with the maternally prescribed pattern of behavior.

II. Rejecting-Minimizing-Hostile but Not-Detached H-Mothers

In this group there were 8 mothers of the total sample of 106 H-mothers. Each was closely attached to her son and exerted a strong, binding influence. Each concealed intimacy with her son and his importance to her by openly expressing rejection and hostility. These mothers were similar to the CBI mothers and might have been classified with them but for these marked differences in *overt* attitudes and behavior toward their sons.

Seven of the 8 mothers were reported to be contemptuous of their sons and/or humiliated them. None of the 8 patients believed himself to be his mother's favorite; none felt accepted by her; 5 of 8 consciously hated their mothers; 6 of 8 feared their mothers, including 3 who consciously feared physical injury from them; 5 of 8 consciously hated *and* feared their mothers.

Despite this picture of hatred and fear, 6 of 8 patients reported that their mothers "babied" them; 7 mothers were rated as "overprotective"; 5 demanded to be the center of their sons' attention; 7 were reported as dominating. In 3 cases the mother allied with their sons against husbands and 3 mothers were explicitly seductive to their sons. In one case the mother made the patient her confidant. As in the CBI group, these 8 mothers were sexually restrictive; 7 were puritanical and/or frigid; 3 interfered with adolescent heterosexuality; 3 discouraged masculine attitudes in their sons. Despite overt maternal destructiveness, 3 of 8 sons in this group respected their mothers, and 4 believed them to be admirable women. Two case summaries which follow are representative of this group.

CASE NO. 128

The patient was a twenty-two-year-old middle child. He had one sister nine years older, and another sister fourteen years younger. The parents had a disturbed, stormy relationship, characterized by frequent arguments and rare demonstrations of affection. The mother made the decisions in the family and was contemptuous of her husband whom she regarded as her inferior. When the patient was seven years old his mother discovered her husband had engaged in extramarital affairs. Her discovery precipitated violent arguments which the patient witnessed. He was aware that his father was going out with other women yet he responded to the scenes between his parents with fear and anger toward his mother for her displays of hostility.

Although the patient was her only male child, the mother openly preferred her older daughter to whom she was affectionate and attentive. She never expressed affection for him; she did not caress, kiss, or hug him, but would nag and dominate him, using the familiar phrase, "You do what I tell you to."

The patient slept in a crib in his parents' bedroom until he was five years old. After crying for a larger bed for some time he was transferred from the crib, but he slept in his new bed in the parental bedroom until he was 14 years of age. He clearly remembers witnessing his parents having intercourse; he believes his mother enjoyed it.

It became his regular practice to get into bed with his mother after his father left for work. He reported that he would "lie close to her backside" and felt at times that she was aware of it and liked it. The patient enjoyed it, too. He would expose his genitals and pretend to be asleep; he wanted his mother to see his genitals. In early adolescence, when he began to have emissions, he wanted his mother to see the stained sheets, to prove to her that he was a man.

The patient's mother exposed him to a great deal of sexual stimulation. In view of her psychopathic sexual behavior toward him one would expect her to permit him a measure of freedom in his own heterosexual activities, but this was not the case. At the age of thirteen he became interested in a little girl his own age. The mother discovered it and would not allow him to continue his relationship with the girl on the ground that he was too young to go steady. When he was twenty-one he became interested in a woman who was several years older. The mother learned about it and prevailed upon her older daughter to talk him out of the relationship.

The patient admired his older sister and was not hostile to her, although he envied her close relationship with the mother. His envy was expressed in a wish to be a woman so that he could experience the same type of warmth and affection. He had his first homosexual experience at the age of ten. His partner was forty. As he performed fellatio he fantasied he was a woman.

When the patient was fourteen his younger sister was born. The mother did not respond to this sister as she had to the older one. The patient undertook most of the care and responsibility for his younger sister. His psychoanalyst interpreted his behavior as being multimotivated: in part, it was an unconscious maneuver to replace his mother and become mother to his younger sister who was perceived to be as rejected as he was, and who needed his love; in part, it was an attempt to prevent his sister from having the same kind of attachment to the mother as had been formed by his older sister; in part, it was an attempt to please his mother and to show her what a good boy he was, thus hoping to win the maternal affection and interest for which he so yearned.

Although the patient would become angry with his mother for her towering rages at his father, he nonetheless sided with her in parental arguments. The mother, in turn, encouraged this alliance by openly preferring the patient to her husband. The patient constantly attempted to get close to his mother: he confided in her, made her his confidante, submitted to her, and tried to be charming with her. He was careful never to hurt her. He was afraid to assert himself lest he anger her and lose what little affection he thought he might get from her. He was quite dependent upon her and would seek her advice in any decision-making.

When the patient was a child his father showed him some affection and interest. As the patient entered preadolescence—coinciding with the period when the father embarked on his extramarital liaisons—attempts to communicate were met with a growing paternal detachment. The patient was afraid of his father, yet persisted in trying to win his attention and affection, without success. He felt totally unaccepted by his father and eventually lost all interest in him.

The patient was sickly in early childhood. He suffered from frequent colds and often stayed home from school. His frequent colds and absences from school suggest that he used his ailments as attention-getting devices, since his mother would be attentive when he was sick. He was excessively fearful of physical injury, avoided fights, but had contact with his peers and played with them. He was a clinging child who started his schooling reluctantly. He was a poor student. He was dropped from college during his first year because of inferior scholarship. When he was ten or eleven he was overweight and somewhat small for his age, but at thirteen or fourteen he tried to develop muscularly. At present, he is short, slight, and has a somewhat effeminate appearance.

SUMMARY: In this case the mother bound her son to her by seductiveness, sexual displays, domination, allying him with her against her husband, and showing him openly that she preferred him to his father. At the same time, she rejected him, was contemptuous and unaffectionate, and demonstrated her preference for the older sister. For all this the patient always respected and deeply admired his mother. (When the patient terminated his analysis he was exclusively heterosexual.)

CASE NO. 137

The patient was the younger of two children. His parents separated when he was three years old. The father never returned and had no further contact with the family.

The mother made no attempt to conceal her marked preference for the patient's older brother. The patient received little or no affection. He was afraid of his mother, feared asserting himself to her, and feared angering her. In turn, his mother underestimated and humiliated him, and was often physically cruel to him. She interfered with his childhood activities, and when he was an adolescent she would persist in preventing him from participating in peer group activities. She told him explicitly that he might get sick or hurt, and pointed out that this would be a burden to her since it was she who would have to take care of him.

Concurrent with her rejecting attitudes was an undue concern about the patient's health. She was particularly preoccupied with his gastrointestinal functions and gave him frequent enemas. She manifested anxiety about his being physically injured. When he was inducted into the army in World War II she told him of her fear that he would get killed.

The patient was overweight and clumsy as a child. He was unduly fearful of physical injury and assiduously avoided fights or rough activities with his peers. He was pretty much a lone wolf who did not play with other children, did not play ball, and had no interest in sports.

The mother remarried when the patient was ten. Her relationship with her second husband was unsatisfactory, though it was better than that with her first husband. There were frequent arguments. She was dominating, showed contempt for her husband, and considered him her inferior. The patient got along very well with his stepfather who showed affection for him and protected him from his mother. They developed a close relationship.

At the time of his mother's remarriage the patient had his first homosexual experience; he performed fellatio on a fourteen-year-old boy. Shortly afterward he had another episode in which an older man was involved.

The patient's first conscious awareness of his sexual feelings for his mother occurred when he was twelve years old. It was her habit to undress before him. On this particular day he became sexually aware of her nudity and of his response to her. She also used the bathroom in his presence until he was well along in adolescence.

The mother openly preferred the older brother while the stepfather preferred the patient; he took over the father role with him in a way he did not with the older brother and thus filled a great emotional need. He played a constructive role in repairing in important ways some of the psychological damage that had occurred before he entered the patient's life.

SUMMARY: The patient had a rejecting, hostile, physically cruel mother who openly preferred his older brother. At the same time, she was closely binding and overprotective, and interfered with childhood activities and peer relationships. She infantilized him, interfered with his sexual activities and, finally, disapproved of his wife when he married. (During the course of psychoanalytic treatment this patient became exclusively heterosexual.)

As practicing psychoanalysts we have directly observed many women patients who—like the mothers in this sample—are rejecting, minimizing, and hostile, yet not detached from their sons. These mothers tend to identify specific sons with their own fathers or older brothers, thus acting-out with a selected son sexual transferences stemming from relationships with important male figures in their lives. Unconscious guilt feelings observed in such mothers are, in the main, connected with incestuous impulses toward their own fathers and/or brothers, and hostile impulses arising from rejecting or competitive reactions which they extend to include all men. Feelings of personal unacceptability are invariably discernible in these mothers. The son who is the object of her transference reactions comes to represent her own unacceptable self. Her hypercritical, harsh, rejecting behavior is, in part, an expression of the self-hatred she projects to her son. The preoccupation with the son attests to the closeness and meaningfulness of his relationship to her. Such mothers make close contact, but it consists of continuous and carping criticism and disapproval. Their sons do not necessarily become homosexuals, but tend to have psychiatric problems.

III. Detached H-mothers

In 11 of the 106 H-cases, the mother-son relationships were characterized by detachment. They differed sharply from the 73 CBI mothers and from the 8 rejecting-minimizing-hostile but not-detached mothers. Although some of these detached mothers showed affection, they were only superficially related to their sons. They were rejecting mothers.

This group was divided into two sub-groups: 7 poorly related, detached mothers whose rejection was concealed by superficial affability and affection (informally referred to by the Committee members as the "dearie" type), and 4 hostile-detached mothers whose rejection was openly expressed and accompanied by hostility (the "get-away-you-bother-me" type).

Poorly related, detached mothers

Of the 7 cases in this group, 5 mothers were described as spending "very little time" with their sons and 2 as spending "little time." None was regarded by the patient or by the responding psychoanalyst as overprotective. What is particularly interesting about this group is the degree to which the son distorted his perception of his mother. Despite obvious rejection, 4 of these 7 sons regarded themselves as the mother's favorite; 2 tried to make confidantes of her; 5 felt accepted by her; none consciously hated the mother though 2 consciously feared her; 5 respected her, and 2 admired her. The case histories that follow illustrate this sub-group and underscore the sons' perceptual distortions.

CASE NO. 107

The patient's parents were divorced when he was seven years old. Shortly afterward, two older sisters, a younger brother, and the patient were placed in separate foster homes. He lived with various foster parents until he was old enough to be on his own. During these years his mother would visit him about once every six months. At these times she fussed over him and put on displays of solicitude and affection. She would then disappear into her world of marginal prostitution and promiscuity. The father was a benign alcoholic who visited his son more frequently. He would, on occasion, make rather limp and unrealistic plans for reconstituting the family but nothing ever came of them.

SUMMARY: The patient regarded himself as his mother's favorite and felt accepted by her, though he believed she resented other men. He respected her, thought that she was concerned about his welfare, and felt no hostility toward her. As an adult he kept in touch with her, although it was he who initiated the contact. She died when the patient was twenty-nine. (He was exclusively homosexual at the beginning of psychoanalytic treatment and became bisexual during the course of analysis.)

CASE NO. 136

The patient was the only son of wealthy, socially prominent parents. He had one younger and two older sisters. Child care and child rearing were assigned to nurses, one of whom encouraged feminine attitudes. During World War I the mother occupied an important position in the American Red Cross and scarcely saw her children during that period. The father rejected the patient but exhibited guilt-laden reaction formations of oversolicitude and overprotectiveness. He was apprehensive about his son's riding a bicycle, horses, or even using roller skates, although he encouraged these activities for his daughters who were active and athletic. They were excellent horsewomen. The mother favored her only son but rarely spent time with him. When she was with him she was dominating and controlling, but she hid her "iron fist under a velvet glove." She was the "grande dame" who took obeisance for granted. As a preadolescent the patient was seduced by the butler. At the age of fifteen he was sent away to an exclusive boarding school for boys. After that, he seldom saw either parent.

SUMMARY: The patient respected and admired his mother whom he viewed as a great woman; as for himself, he felt unworthy of her and undeserving of her concern. He could never bring himself to defy his mother, although he had no conscious awareness of his fear of her. (When this patient terminated his analysis he was still exclusively homosexual.)

Hostile-detached mothers

The 4 hostile-detached mothers showed a range of consistently negative attitudes toward their sons. These women showed no affection to their sons, spent little time with them, were openly hostile, contemptuous, critical, and derogatory. None of the patients in this group was a favorite; none felt accepted by his mother. In 3 of 4 cases the sons consciously hated their mothers; all 4 feared them, and 2 also feared physical injury from them. All were afraid of arousing their mothers' anger and were either submissive or tried to stay out of the way. None of the mothers had a confidant-confidante relationship with her son; none was overprotective. In two of these cases the sons had fathers who, although leaving much to be desired as parents, did nonetheless offer some modicum of protection against these mothers.

The following case is illustrative of the mothers in this group.

CASE NO. 141

The patient was a thirty-year-old middle child with an older brother and a younger sister. The mother preferred the older brother and the patient was the least favored child. She showed him no affection, humiliated him, and was physically cruel. The patient had a realistic fear of physical injury from her. He behaved submissively and tried to avoid provoking her wrath. The father, too, was rejecting. He openly favored the other siblings. The attention he did show was hostile and deprecatory. On several occasions, the father threatened to cut off the patient's hand or penis if he touched his genitals. In adolescence, the patient renounced the possibiiity of ever achieving love or acceptance from either parent. He oriented himself to his peer group where he won affection and respect. (The patient became exclusively heterosexual during psychoanalytic treatment with a warm, emotionally expressive female psychoanalyst.)

IV. Controlling-dominating H-mothers

The salient feature of the 9 H-mothers in the controlling-dominating group was *egocentricity*. Since they were oriented to the fulfillment of their own narcissistic wishes, they exploited, dominated, and manipulated their sons. These mothers implemented maternal control by a variety of techniques, including explicit insistence on obedience, guilt provocation, and expressions of displeasure when their excessive demands were not met. The responding psychoanalysts rated the entire group as dominating. There were 6 out of 9 "yes" answers to the question, Did the patient feel that he was used by his mother to satisfy her needs? To the question, Which needs? the following answers were recorded.

Case No. 119: "Need for affection and ego-satisfaction (exhibitionism)."
Case No. 133: "A need to dominate and control."
Case No. 139: "A need to control."
Case No. 162: "A need for emotional and financial support."
Case No. 163: "Aggrandizement—mother excessively proud of her sons; required them to be gentlemen from infancy."
Case No. 169: "Companionship."

The controlling and exploitative devices of these mothers did not include sexual techniques. Only one mother was seductive; all were puritanical and frigid. In fact, their attitudes and behavior can be described as antisexual. In the main, if sex was discussed at all, it was in negative terms. These mothers had an inhibiting effect on their sons' heterosexual development. None of these mothers discouraged masculine attitudes directly, and only one encouraged feminine attitudes. They tended to create the good, clean, gentlemanly "mother's boy" types. Six out of 9 patients were submissive to their mothers and none was rebellious. Six felt accepted by their mothers, and probably were—so long as they fulfilled maternal demands.

Although all spent an "average" amount of time with their sons, the contact and relatedness were somewhat defective. The mothers were self-preoccupied and did not seem to have the capacity to appreciate their sons as individuals or as males. These mothers were considered insensitive to the patients' needs in all cases. In 3 cases, conscious hatred of the mother was reported, 5 feared their mothers but respected them, and 4 felt their mothers to be admirable people. Corresponding to behavior frequently observed clinically among exploitative mothers, most in this group tended to encourage effective performance. Such encouragement did not apply to sexual effectiveness, where inhibition was fostered by restrictive, antisexual attitudes. In general, the encouragement of effective performance tends to promote masculine attitudes and masculine identification despite the deleterious influence of sexual restrictiveness. It was of interest to us that within the context of aberrant sexuality all 9 patients were "insertors" in their homosexual activity, though 4 were occasional "insertees." (See Chapter IX.)

CASE NO. 139

The mother of this homosexual patient was an extremely masochistic, hypochondriacal, anxiety-ridden woman, and a compulsive housecleaner who needlessly overworked, and frequently complained of fatigue. She often quarreled with the patient's father, yet appeared to be rather dependent upon him. Although the family had never been in any special financial straits, the mother was penurious and reacted with anxiety whenever money had to be spent for any purpose other than bare subsistence needs. There was no display of affection between the parents, and they appeared to be rather distant from each other. The father was generally the dominant parent who made family decisions.

Until the patient was six years old, the mother dressed him as though he were a girl, kept his hair in a "Buster Brown" bob (similar to her own hairstyle during her childhood), and encouraged him to play with dolls. The mother had wanted a girl when the patient was born.

She would react with worry and anxiety whenever her son did not feel well or sustained some injury. When he was ill, she would take repeated rectal temperatures, administer frequent enemas (to "clean out" the body) and give him oral medications, all of which she had to force on the patient since he strongly resisted. As a result, the patient developed a dread of doctors and dentists. In adulthood he tended to avoid medications or ministrations of any kind. His terror of dental treatment resulted in seriously neglected teeth. Whenever the mother became ill, she would worry but neglect herself, while insisting that the rest of the family cater to her needs. She demanded attention whenever she was upset or anxious. Thus, this mother did not dominate by direct demand, but by guilt and fear provocations. For example, she would become upset when her son was enjoying himself or spending money on a luxury. Her behavior generated feelings of guilt, anxiety and self-reproach in the patient whenever he experienced a desire for pleasure of any kind.

The patient would side with his mother in her quarrels with his father. He felt that his father was in the wrong and was needlessly cruel to his mother (who seemed "a model saint"), but when he joined the argument on his mother's side, both parents turned on him in anger and frightened him away. The mother also displayed inconsistent behavior in other situations: she always assumed a charming and socially gracious demeanor in the company of friends, in contrast to her anxious, complaining, cheerless self in the privacy of her immediate family. She seemed to have a psychopathological attachment to her brother, for whom she showed more affection and more concern than for her own husband. She hated her sister-in-law intensely.

The patient felt that any self-assertion on his part would upset his mother (i.e., make her sick, anger her, and so forth). He had no close friends prior to puberty, and would spend much time in solitary pursuits such as reading, stamp-collecting, and cooking. He would avoid sports, not only because he feared injury, but because he expected to fail in his attempts. He lavished much time, attention, and affection on his female dog, whom he regarded as pitiable—like himself. Although he admired his mother during childhood, he was unaware of feeling affection for her—or for his father. His brother (six years his senior) was a somewhat distant figure whom he admired and envied for being favored by the mother.

The patient viewed his mother as puritanical and sexually frigid. When he became aware of the sexual aspect of marriage, he felt that his mother disliked sexual intercourse—he had the idea that marriage was a businesslike agreement under which the wife agreed to submit to the husband's sexual wishes in exchange for material benefits. In order to gain acceptance by his mother, he felt he had to be the "clean-cut young man" (a favorite phrase his mother used)—meaning a compliant, neatly dressed individual who showed no interest in pleasure, sexual or otherwise. Another important maternal standard was utter "unselfishness." However, his constant attempts to please his mother—a disagreeable effort—failed to bring the acceptance he yearned for. He would often become depressed and moody when his mother's frenetic and angry dissatisfaction could not be dissipated through his compliant and placating maneuvers. At the same time that she demanded self-denial from the patient, she was tolerant of the father's and brother's pursuit of "selfish" pleasure.

After puberty, the patient shifted his admiration and respect for his mother to his brother, who seemed strong, masculine, heterosexual, and much more successful in coping with the parents. Nevertheless, he continued to try to please his mother. She did not encourage self-assertiveness, independence, or his association with girls. After she had learned that her son was a homosexual, she appeared to want him "cured," but not because she wanted him to be heterosexual. She wanted social conformity. Her ambitions for her son were restricted to vocational and financial success.

The patient was bisexual but predominantly homosexual when he entered treatment. After four years, he left psychoanalysis essentially unchanged except that he had begun to engage in more frequent heterosexual experiences. He went to another psychoanalyst for a time but finally abandoned treatment and left New York.

V. Mother surrogates

In 2 homosexual cases and in 1 comparison case the patients were brought up by mother surrogates. Both these H-patients suffered the loss of their mothers before the age of one year. Their case summaries follow:

CASE NO. 154

The patient was twenty-eight years of age. He had a sister who was seven years older. The mother had died in childbirth with the patient, and both children were sent to foster homes. He remembered nothing about these early years. When he was four his father remarried, and the children returned to the new family unit. The stepmother was hostile and rejecting, particularly to the patient. When he was eight, she had a son by the father and showed open partiality toward her own son. The father was killed during a hold-up when the patient was fifteen years old. He remained with his antagonistic, resentful, hostile stepmother. She is classifiable with hostile-detached mothers. (The patient remained exclusively homosexual.)

CASE NO. 116

The patient was twenty-seven years old and the youngest of five siblings. When he was eleven months old his mother died and he was sent to live with an uncle and aunt. His aunt was affectionate but she infantilized and feminized him. When the patient was five years old, his father reconstituted the family. A sixteen-year-old sister took over the mother role. She was affectionate, oversolicitous, overprotective, and somewhat seductive. She behaved in a manner descriptive of the close-binding-intimate mothers. (The patient was exclusively heterosexual when he terminated psychoanalysis.)

CASE NO. 295

This comparison patient was orphaned when five years of age and he was raised in an institution for parentless children. We have scant information about his early years and therefore he was listed as "unclassifiable." The patient is married and has no homosexual problems.

We are in no position to draw conclusions about the effects on the son of the absence of a biological mother, since we did not study this problem. We may say, however, that when foster children are exposed to types of mothering such as we found among mothers of homosexuals, a similar sexual adaptation may ensue.

Comparison of H-mother categories

Table III-10 compares the five categories of H-mothers for eleven items.

Table III-10 compares a relatively large group (73 CBI H-mothers) with small groups of mothers in other categories. The differentiated maternal attitudes noted justified their separation into the various maternal classifications. The reader may rapidly survey the outstanding similarities and differences among these groupings. In Rows I and II of this table, we compare the CBI H-group with the Rejecting-minimizing-hostile but not-detached H-group (8 mothers). These two groups are similar in three items which reflect close-binding maternal qualities: Item 4—sided with mother in parental arguments; Item 5—mother overprotective; Item 8—mother interfered with outside activities. They differ in six items: Item 1—mother's favorite (significant at .01 level); Item 2—felt accepted by mother (significant at .01 level); Item 6—mother was seductive; Item 7—mother interfered with heterosexuality; Item 10—patient hated mother; Item 11—patient feared mother.

The responses for the CBI mothers differ markedly from those for the hostile-detached mothers in all items (Rows I and III) and these CBI mothers also reveal differences from the detached, poorly related group (Rows I and IV). The CBI mothers differ from the dominating mothers on all items associated with close-binding qualities (Rows I and V).

The Rejecting-minimizing-hostile but not-detached class (Row II) resembles the Hostile-detached group (Row III) in overt expressions

TABLE III-10 *Comparison of Five H-Mother Categories (in per cent)*

		1	2	3	4
		Mother's favorite	Felt accepted by mother	Thought mother admirable	Sided with mother in parental arguments
I.	CBI	85	81	72	67
II.	Hostile-Not-Detached	0	0	50	75
III.	Hostile-Detached	0	0	0	25
IV.	Detached, Poorly Related	57	71	29	71
V.	Dominating-Controlling	22	67	44	44

of maternal hostility and absence of affectionate behavior. These two maternal groups are differentiated, however, in overprotectiveness in which the Rejecting-minimizing-hostile but not-detached mothers score 88 per cent—the highest percentage of all five groups—and the Hostile-detached group scores 0. The patient reactions are similar in that none felt accepted by his mother, and conscious fear and hatred of the mother was prominent. Yet half the patients of the Hostile but not-detached class admired their mothers and most sided with them in parental arguments, thus indicating some positive relatedness with the mother.

The Hostile-detached mothers and Poorly related mothers (Rows III and IV) indicate emotional distance from their H-sons. Both maternal groups score 0 for overprotectiveness and achieve low percentages in maternal seductiveness. Taken together with the other data for these two groups the low scores on overprotectiveness reflect maternal detachment rather than an absence of psychopathology. The two groups differ in maternal expressions of hostility: none of the poorly related mothers showed open hostility to their H-sons. In the Hostile-detached category the patients reacted to their mothers with hatred and fear; they did not admire them. Most patients who had Poorly related detached mothers felt accepted and sided with their mothers; none consciously hated their mothers and few feared them.

The Controlling-dominating mothers bear no clear resemblances to any of the other four groups. The scores are low for seductiveness, for interference with activities (sexual and other), and for expressions of contempt. These mothers did not behave seductively nor did they interfere with outside activities as techniques for control. Case studies

5	6	7	8	9	10	11
Mother over-protective	Mother seductive	Mother interfered with hetero-sexuality	Mother interfered with other activities	Mother showed contempt/ humilia-tion	Patient hated mother	Patient feared mother
73	73	68	62	38	26	36
88	38	38	63	88	63	75
0	0	25	25	100	75	100
0	14	42	0	14	0	29
33	11	33	33	11	33	55

revealed that maternal domination was achieved through establishing in the son a belief that maternal requirements superseded his own. Guilt provocations were used to reinforce this belief. Although these mothers were not openly threatening, as were the hostile mothers, they were nevertheless consciously feared in more than half the cases.

Comparison of C-Mother Categories

The CBI category of C-mothers has already been described. Limitations of space and the primary orientation of this volume to male homosexuality preclude extensive discussion of the other categories of C-mothers. Table III-11 summarizes the data.

Table III-11 compares the responses to the same eleven items in Table III-10, for six categories of C-mothers. In five of the six categories the differences and similarities described for the H-sample hold for the C-sample. The sixth group of "Not Remarkable" mothers, which according to our data represents the least psychopathologic maternal group in the entire study, scored consistently low in all items reflecting psychopathology in the mother-son interrelationship; consistently high scores point to affectionate and positive mother-son relationships.

When the corresponding categories in Table III-11 for the C-mothers and in Table III-10 for the H-mothers are compared, there is an over-all trend in the H-sample toward higher scores for items that reflect psychopathology.

To highlight the psychopathologic aspects of the H-mother-son

TABLE III-11 *Comparison of Six C-Mother Categories* (*in per cent*)

		1	2	3	4
		Mother's favorite	Felt accepted by mother	Felt mother admirable	Sided with mother in parental arguments
I.	CBI	77	72	50	67
II.	Hostile-Not-Detached	0	0	33	50
III.	Hostile-Detached	0	0	0	33
IV.	Detached, Poorly Related	0	33	33	50
V.	Dominating-Controlling	52	52	26	48
VI.	Not Remarkable	53	95	84	42

relationship we present in Table III-12 a comparison between a group of 53 seductive CBI mothers (representing the most highly psychopathologic relationships) and 19 comparison mothers classed as "Not Remarkable" (representing the least psychopathologic group in the entire patient population).

Despite the small number (19 in the "Not Remarkable" group), there are 13 items differentiating these two maternal groups at levels of statistical significance from .05 to .001. The percentages of affirmative responses are uniformly lower for the C-group. The highly significant differences between these two groups on many items tapping desirable and undesirable maternal attributes point to the H-mothers as singularly deficient in fulfilling the mother role.

SUMMARY AND CONCLUSIONS

I. CBI H-mothers

A preponderant number of H-mothers fell into the CBI category —69 per cent, as contrasted with 32 per cent of comparison cases. The nature of the intimate closeness had the effect of binding sons to mothers. We conclude from our data that mothers in this group promoted homosexuality in the following ways:

Interference with heterosexual development

(a) These mothers sexually overstimulated their sons through seductiveness (73 per cent were seductive), or through sexual overstimulation implicit in overclose intimacy.

5 Mother over-protective	6 Mother seductive	7 Mother interfered with hetero-sexuality	8 Mother interfered with other activities	9 Mother showed contempt/ humilia-tion	10 Patient hated mother	11 Patient feared mother
59	69	44	38	31	31	50
67	17	67	50	100	33	100
0	0	67	0	67	100	67
17	33	0	17	0	33	17
41	26	44	37	52	41	59
21	11	16	5	16	0	11

TABLE III-12 *Comparison of CBI Seductive H-mothers and "Not Remarkable" C-mothers (in per cent)*

	Seductive H-CBI	Not remarkable C
N =	53	19
1. Patient was mother's favorite	96	53**
2. Mother demanded center of attention	81	0†
3. Mother dominating	79	32
4. Time spent—great deal	79	5†
5. Mother discouraged masculinity	49	5**
6. Mother encouraged femininity	49	0**
7. Mother puritanical/frigid	83	37*
8. Mother allied with son against husband	72	11**
9. Mother openly preferred son to husband	75	0†
10. Mother interfered with heterosexuality	77	16**
11. Patient was mother's confidant	75	5†
12. Mother was patient's confidante	53	21
13. Confidant relationship reciprocal	51	0**
14. Mother overprotective	75	21*
15. Patient knowingly hated mother	30	0*
16. Patient knowingly feared mother	40	11
17. Patient afraid assertiveness:		
(a) would anger mother	51	26
(b) would lose her love	38	11
18. Mother both hated and feared	15	0

(b) They sexually inhibited their sons and indicated a need to suppress all overt manifestations of filial heterosexual responsiveness. Such suppression seems to have served as a defensive means of concealing from themselves and others their own sexual feelings toward their sons. Most CBI H-mothers implemented sexual restrictiveness with explicit antisexual attitudes, reflected in a marked tendency to endow sexuality, particularly masculine sexuality, with an aura of unacceptability, aggressiveness, and brutishness.

(c) Demasculinizing and/or feminizing maternal attitudes and behavior had both the intention and effect of discouraging masculine attitudes and behavior patterns.

(d) These mothers interfered with their sons' peer group participation and thus minimized opportunities for masculine identification with other boys and with the heterosexual interests usually encouraged through group support.

Interference with the father-son relationship

(a) The CBI H-mothers, by openly preferring the H-son to his father, fostered the wish in the child for exclusive maternal possession.

(b) They fostered father-son competitiveness by pitting each against the other for maternal favor.

(c) They acted-out a "romance" with the son as a substitute to compensate for the deficiencies and disturbances in their marital relationship.

(d) They included the son in inappropriate situations, e.g., sleeping arrangements, parental arguments, and so forth.

Interference with peer relations

(a) The CBI H-mothers interfered with boyhood friendships and activities under the guise of protectiveness, solicitude, and so forth. They prohibited relationships with spirited "regular" boys whom these mothers considered as "roughnecks."

(b) They fostered adult relationships (particularly that of mother and son), and derogated participation with peers who, in general, were regarded with condescension and as intruders.

(c) They selected a particular child for preferential treatment, most usually the H-son, thus fostering competitive relationships among siblings and setting the stage for rivalrous peer relationships.

Interference with development of independence

(a) The CBI H-mothers preëmpted decision-making and then "took over."

(b) They encouraged timidity by interdicting self-assertiveness.

(c) They infantilized by "babying," overindulging, and showing undue concern for health and safety.

(d) They isolated the H-son from father, siblings, and peers, and by so doing restricted social choices; consequently, extreme dependency upon the mother was fostered.

II. Rejecting-minimizing-hostile but not-detached H-mothers

A small but distinctive group of 8 mothers was located in the homosexual population. Although these mothers were rejecting-minimizing-hostile, they were also close-binding and often overintimate with their sons. They were overtly rejecting but covertly seductive. Homosexuality was promoted in all the determinants detailed for the CBI mothers.

Maternal derogation and apparent rejection accentuated a sense of inadequacy in the son. The patients appeared to have no way of accurately assessing the true nature of their mothers' attitudes and came to regard themselves as individuals of little worth. As a result, they developed a lack of confidence in their ability to evoke affection and respect, especially from females.

The data of our study strongly suggest that closeness and over-intimacy combined with hostility, minimizing attitudes, and apparent rejection have the effect of inhibiting genitally oriented heterosexuality among these men, at the same time creating a persistent and strong yearning and need for women. All of the patients in this group sought out relationships with women, and it is of particular interest that of the total of 29 in the homosexual sample who became exclusively heterosexual 5 came from this group of 8. In contrast, only 2 of the 7 patients who had superficially "affectionate" but detached and basically rejecting mothers, sought out female social contact; none became exclusively heterosexual.

III. Detached H-mothers

Mothers who had a detached relationship with their homosexual sons were characterized by rejecting and/or casual maternal attitudes. In the "affectionate" group the detachment was obscured by a surface affability and by evanescent demonstrations of affection, whereas in the detached-hostile group detachment and hostility were explicit.

Poorly related, detached ("affectionate") H-mothers

The dynamics believed to have influenced a homosexual adaptation in this group were:

Neither parent provided the support and protectiveness required both psychologically and physiologically for normal growth and development.

These patients were exposed to a range of traumatic experiences that go along with a hostile, affectionless milieu. Several of these children were seduced in boarding schools to which they had been sent in preadolescence.

Maternal detachment combined with paternal absence and detachment (5 of 7 fathers spent "very little time" with their sons) emphasized the extent of affect impoverishment suffered by these patients.

Refuge and surcease were sought in pathologic pursuit of warmth and support in homosexual relationships.

None of these patients became heterosexual in psychoanalytic treatment.

Hostile-detached H-mothers

Although this sub-group included only 4 cases, nonetheless, there were suggestive trends. The detached-hostile mothers made no attempt to conceal rejection, hostility, and indifference. They made it quite clear to their sons that they felt no affection for them, nor could any be expected, thus impelling the sons to seek more tolerable human relationships elsewhere.

Despite the very small number of cases from which these data were drawn, it appears that where there is no possibility of an affectionate or supportive relationship with the mother, and where the child is himself aware of this, he may, as it were, attempt to burn his bridges behind him and seek out healthier relationships. In this group of 4 patients, 2 became exclusively heterosexual.

IV. Controlling-dominating H-mothers

Each mother in this group was characterized by egocentricity and dominantly exploitative attitudes toward her H-son. Her own needs were primary, and, although she usually convinced herself that her motives were in the best interests of her son, there was little evidence that she was at all considerate of him or sensitive to his needs. Each of the 9 mothers was reported as either puritanical and/or frigid, suggesting that the son's sexuality probably provoked her own sexual anxieties and antisexual defenses.

The exploitative attitudes of these mothers tended to foster wariness and distrust in their sons since they anticipated, and were oversensitive to, exploitative behavior in others. Yet, impulses to defy unreasonable demands stimulated such profound guilt feelings as to override suspicion and mistrust, thus impelling them toward submissive compliance, since guilt provocation was the major dynamic through which these mothers controlled and dominated their sons.

V. C-mothers

The C-mothers were divided into the same categories as the H-mothers, except for the addition of a group classified as "Not Remarkable." There was a parallel profile in the corresponding categories of H- and C-mothers, as detailed for the CBI mothers particularly. The important difference was to be found in the number of cases in the CBI category: 32 CBI C-mothers to 73 CBI H-mothers. In general, responses reflecting psychopathology among the H-mothers achieved higher percentages, whereas responses reflecting more adequate maternal attitudes achieved higher percentages among the C-mothers. The differences between the H-mothers and the C-mothers will become even more apparent when we consider the extent to which the mother-son relationship affects the father-son relationship.

IV

Father-Son Relationship

In the psychoanalytic experience of the Committee members, a uniformity of seriously defective father-son relationships has been observed among male homosexuals. The results of our pilot study confirmed our clinical observations.

To guard against the possibility that certain preconceptions might restrict the kinds of questions asked, the Committee followed the procedure of repeating the 70 questions that have probed the mother-son relationship for probing the father-son relationship. Affirmative answers to 20 of these questions differentiated the homosexual and comparison groups at the .05 level of statistical significance, and better (see Table IV-1). Another group of 7 questions did not reveal significant differences between H- and C-fathers; nevertheless, they revealed a more distinct trend toward psychopathology in the homosexual sample than appeared in the comparison cases (see Table IV-2).

In Table IV-1, the questions that significantly differentiated the father-son relationship in the H- and C-groups tapped detachment, hostility, and rejection by the father, as well as reciprocal hostility between father and son. The characteristics of the father-son relationships in the homosexual group contrasted markedly with those obtaining between mothers and sons, where a close-binding intimacy was outstanding, whereas detachment and hostility emerged as the most conspicuous traits among the H-fathers; therefore, these traits became the two major criteria for classifying fathers (see Table IV-3).

Answers to the question, How much time did father spend with the patient? provided data from which we could make inferences about paternal detachment.

In judging whether a father was detached, the amount of time he spent with his son heavily weighted our decision. In our clinical experience with parents who habitually spend little time with their families or with any one child, we have found the avoidance of continuity of contact to be the result of psychological problems, no matter how convincingly absence is rationalized. There may be unusual circumstances

TABLE IV-1 *Items Distinguishing H- and C-Fathers* (*in per cent*)

	H	C
N =	106	100
1. Patient is father's favorite[a]	7	28†
2. Another sibling is father's favorite[a]	59	36**
3. Patient is least favored child[a]	44	24**
4. Patient felt accepted by father	23	47**
5. Time spent with patient: little, very little, father absent	87	60†
6. Father encouraged masculine attitudes	45	60*
7. Patient knowingly hated father	60	37†
8. Patient both hated and feared father	57	31†
9. Patient respected father	28	48**
10. Patient accepted father	20	50†
11. Father expressed affection for patient	25	51**
12. Father had less respect for patient than for other male siblings[b]	42	19*
13[c]. Patient sided with father in parental arguments:		
in childhood	7	23**
in adolescence	11	25*
14. Patient coped with father more easily than with mother	21	40**
15. Technique for coping with father: rebellion	8	20*
16. Patient feared his assertiveness would:		
anger father	76	55**
hurt father	7	18*
17. Patient feels father considered his needs	6	20**
18. Patient feels currently respected by father	30	50**
19. Patient regards father as admirable	16	47†
20. Patient was excessively dependent on father	7	19*

[a] Based on number of families with siblings
[b] Based on number of families with male siblings
[c] Items 13-20 based on 96 cases
* .05 level of significance
** .01 level of significance
† .001 level of significance

which necessitate long-term absence, as occurs during war, or absence may be required for limited periods of time, but when discontinuous contact becomes part of the father's design for living, it represents a fear of closeness to the family as a group, or to individual members in particular.

TABLE IV-2 *Items Differentiating Homosexuals and Comparisons at Less than Statistical Levels of Significance (in per cent)*

	H	C
N =	106	100
1. Father expressed contempt for patient	40	27
2. Father humiliated patient	44	40
3. Father was physically cruel to patient	19	17
4. Father was feared by patient	66	54
5. Patient feared physical injury from father	56	43
6. Patient felt father protected him from mother[a]	7	15
7. Technique patient used to cope with father:		
Detachment[a]	29	17

[a] Based on 96 cases

We assumed that the effects of paternal attitudes would vary with the amount of time the son spent with his father. For this reason, we used *detached* and *not detached* as criteria for the major categorizations, and then coded the data from the major categories into seven sub-categories to denote patterns of hostility, ambivalence and affection.

Separating the detached, absent,[1] and unclassifiable fathers from the homosexual and comparison samples, a residue of 13 cases of H-fathers and 41 C-fathers remained. Questions arose whether this represented a heterogeneous collection which, for convenience, could be put into a *not-detached* category, or whether these cases reflected for some fathers an active positive relatedness and for others an active negative relatedness which different members of this residue shared with one another. By constructing a *not-detached* category in order to obtain homogeneity and to determine whether positive or negative

[1] In 3 H-cases, the father had left the family in the first year of the patient's life; no information about these fathers was available. These cases will be referred to as "fatherless." In 9 H-cases and 4 C-cases the father left the family by the time the patient was 10 years old. Some information about the father-son relationship was available but in all these cases it was inadequate. For this reason, these fathers were classified as "absent," bringing the totals for the homosexuals to 12 and for the comparisons to 4.

TABLE IV-3 *Classification and Frequency of Kinds of Fathers*

	H	C
I. Detached Fathers		
A. Hostile	44	25
B. Indifferent	18	9
C. Ambivalent	14	20
D. Dominating and exploitative	3	0
	79	54
II. Not-Detached Fathers		
A. Hostile, minimizing	4	11
B. Ambivalent	6	17
C. Affectionate, warmly related	0	8
D. Close-binding and/or overprotective	3	5
	13	41
III. Absent Fathers	12	4
IV. Unclassifiable	2	1
TOTAL	106	100

relatedness was operant among not-detached fathers, we were able to establish that such relatedness did indeed exist and that meaningful sub-groups could be established.

Comparison of Detached and Not-Detached Groups of H- and C-Fathers

Table IV-4 compares the detached and not-detached fathers for 25 items in both H- and C-groups. Only two questionnaire items significantly differentiate the detached H-fathers from the not-detached H-fathers. Did the father show affection? and How much time did he spend with his son? Inasmuch as these two items were used to determine the classifications, it follows that these items would reveal significant differences between the detached and not-detached groups. There were, however, *only 13 not-detached fathers* of the total 106 H-fathers. The small number of not-detached fathers may have kept other differences between them and the 79 detached fathers from reaching statistically significant levels, though certain trends are indicated.

TABLE IV-4 *Comparison of Detached and Not-Detached Groups of Fathers on Father-Son Items (in per cent)*

	H		C	
	De-tached	Not-de-tached	De-tached	Not-de-tached
N=	79	13	54	41
1. Time spent: average, great deal	4*	62	9**	85
2. very little	56	62	46**	2
3. Father showed affection	19*	62	31**	91
4. Patient was father's favorite	3	23	19	41
5. Patient was least favored	48	54	30	17
6. Father showed contempt/humiliation	53	69	57*	29
7. Father interfered with heterosexual behavior	23	31	11	24
8. Father encouraged masculine behavior	48	54	57	68
9. Father demanded center of attention	10	31	4*	22
10. Father dominating	43	46	39	46
11. Patient accepted by father	18	31	33	66
12. Patient respected father	22	38	37	54
13. Patient accepted father	24	8	41*	63
14. Patient thought father admirable	10	46	33	51
15. Patient hated father	67	85	46	24
16. Patient feared father	72	77	56	54
17. Patient hated and feared father	62	69	35	24
18. Patient feared physical injury from father	58	77	48	41
19. Patient sided with father against mother	8	38	30	41
20. Patient coped with father more easily than with mother	18	15	41	37
21. Patient coped with father: by submission	54	85	48	61
22. by detachment	30	23	24	10
23. by rebellion	6	23	28	10
24. Patient feared his assertiveness would anger father	80	92	57	51
25. Patient feared his assertiveness would lose father's love	27	53	19*	46

In the detached H-category, a consistent trend toward less involvement and interaction between father and son is noted in 5 items.

9. Did the father demand to be the center of attention?

14. Did the patient think of his father as admirable?
19. Did the patient side with his father against his mother in parental arguments?
21. How did the patient cope with his father? By submission?
25. Was the patient fearful that his assertiveness would lose his father's love?

Among the C-fathers (Columns 3 and 4) there were 54 who were detached and 41 who were not detached. In contrasting these two groups of fathers, 7 items revealed significant differences: Items 1, 2, 3, 6, 9, 13 and 25. All except Nos. 3, 6 and 13 are listed above; the additional items are:

3. Father showed affection.
6. Father showed contempt/humiliation.
13. Patient accepted father.

Comparison of detached H- and C-fathers
(Columns 1 and 3, Table IV-4)

Although these two groups resemble each other on items that determined the *detached* classification, they also vary in ways which indicate a quite different configuration of father-son relatedness. In 12 items, the differences were significant or approached significant levels. All these differences were in the direction of a more positive father-son relationship in the comparison group. In general, the differences parallel those noted in Tables IV-1 and IV-2 which compared fathers in the total homosexual and comparison samples. When the detached groups were further separated into their sub-categories, subgroups emerged where H- and C-fathers showed a similarity. These will be discussed later in the chapter.

Comparison of not-detached H- and C-fathers
(Columns 2 and 4, Table IV-4)

Although some H-fathers were categorized as *not detached,* they appear to represent a quite different parent population than do the not-detached C-fathers. These C-fathers emerge as the most adequate fathers in the total patient sample. Their scores on almost all items reflect a more consistent pattern of constructive paternal attitudes than do all other father groups. The not-detached H-fathers, however, reveal no such constructiveness. They scored higher than the other 3 father groups on the following 9 items:

5. The patient is least favored.
6. Father showed contempt and humiliation.
15. Patient hated father.
16. Patient feared father.
17. Patient both hated and feared father.
18. Patient feared physical injury from father.
21. Patient coped with father by submission.
24. Patient feared assertiveness would anger father.
25. Patient feared assertiveness would lose father's love.

These H-fathers scored lowest of all groups on the item "Patient accepted father." One might note that this group of fathers did show a consistency—they were consistently destructive toward their sons. Yet, despite the hostile and destructive features revealed by their scores, other items (Column 2) show that, as a group, they still were more frequently affectionate than the detached H- and C-fathers. They also were more often admired; their sons more often feared to lose their love and more often sided with them against the mothers.

Detached-hostile fathers

The detached-hostile fathers comprise the largest sub-group of detached fathers in both the homosexual and comparison samples (Table IV-5, Columns 1 and 4). In regard to numerical superiority this group is similar to the CBI mother category.

The most disturbed father-son relationships noted among the total patient sample are found among the detached-hostile fathers. In the homosexual sub-group (Column 1) none of the sons was his father's favorite, and in 73 per cent of the cases the patient son was the least favored sibling. None felt accepted by his father. Paternal expressions of contempt and humiliation were reported in 82 per cent of the cases. In 84 per cent of cases, the patients were consciously aware of both hating and fearing their fathers, and accepted them in only 9 per cent of cases. Less than 25 per cent respected their fathers, who appear to have provoked fear and hostility by openly expressing rejection and hostility toward their sons. Of the 20 H-fathers who were reported to be physically cruel to their sons, 15 were located in this sub-group of 44 fathers (significant at .01).

The detached-hostile C-fathers (Column 4) achieved similar percentages on all but two items. There were significantly fewer sons in the comparison group who were the least favored siblings and there were more sons in this group who openly rebelled against their fathers. As noted among the H-fathers, most C-fathers who were reported as physically cruel (12 of 17) were found in these 25 cases of hostile-detached fathers (.001).

The H-fathers and C-fathers in the detached-hostile sub-group

TABLE IV-5 *Comparison of the Sub-groups of Detached Fathers (in per cent)*

	H			C		
N=	44[a]	18[b]	14[c]	25[d]	9[e]	20[f]
1. Time spent with father: very little or none	50	83	36	44	78	40
2. Father showed affection	9	6	71	4	11	75
3. Patient was father's favorite	0	0	14	4	0	35
4. Patient was father's least favored	73	28	0	48	22	10
5. Father showed contempt/humiliation	82	22	14	88	33	30
6. Father interfered with heterosexuality	27	11	7	16	11	10
7. Father encouraged masculinity	61	11	57	56	33	70
8. Father was dominating	55	17	29	50	0	20
9. Patient was accepted by father	0	28	64	4	33	70
10. Patient respected father	23	22	43	24	22	65
11. Patient accepted father	9	33	64	20	22	75
12. Patient felt father was admirable	7	6	14	20	22	55
13. Patient knowingly hated father	86	50	36	72	56	10
14. Patient knowingly feared father	91	44	50	80	33	35
15. Patient hated/feared father	84	39	29	64	33	5
16. Patient feared physical injury from father	70	33	43	76	22	25
17. Patient coped with father by: submission	64	28	36	52	22	55
18. detachment	20	44	29	20	33	25
19. rebellion	5	0	7	36	0	25
20. Patient feared his assertiveness would anger father	84	61	50	80	22	45
21. Patient feared his assertiveness would lose father's love	25	11	36	16	22	20

[a] Hostile (H)
[b] Indifferent (H)
[c] Ambivalent (H)
[d] Hostile (C)
[e] Indifferent (C)
[f] Ambivalent (C)

demonstrate a similar configuration of father-son relatedness. In comparing this configuration with that derived from the data on the 8 "warmly related" C-fathers (Table IV-6, Column 2), the contrast between the affectionate C-fathers and the detached-hostile H- and C-fathers serves further to emphasize the deeply disturbed father-son relationships obtaining in the detached-hostile groups. Despite the small number of warmly affectionate C-fathers (8) there are 12 items of the 21 in Table IV-6 which differentiate them from the detached-hostile H-fathers at statistically significant levels. Two case reports of hostile-detached fathers follow.

CASE NO. 153 (The patient's mother is described in a case report in Chapter III.)

Early memories in analysis go back to the age of two, and the patient remembers always having had a feeling of uneasiness with his father. He remembers a violent quarrel between his parents that took place when he was about four years old. He overheard his mother inform his father that she alone would raise the patient, who was an only child. From that time on, his father was like a "boarder" in the house, occupying his own room.

The father was described as always having been assiduously protective of his possessions and immaculate in dress and personal habits. He fastidiously avoided drinking out of a glass that either the patient or the mother had used. He never kissed either one on the lips. The patient was never permitted to wear his father's ties, even ones that had been discarded. In fact, the father did not permit the patient to touch anything belonging to him. One day, the patient was discovered using his father's typewriter. A severe scolding followed. Even later on, when the patient attended high school, the father would not permit his son the use of the typewriter.

When the patient was four, he developed an intestinal condition that kept him in bed for three years. He was cared for solely by his mother. During this time, his diet was controlled and he was not allowed to have candy. One day, when he was up and about again, he bought a five-cent candy bar. His father saw him with it and was "fit to be tied." He grabbed the candy and threw it away, shouting, "I spend hundreds of dollars on doctors and there you are breaking your diet with nickel candy."

The patient resented his parents' inconsiderate economies. "Everything they bought for me, they bought large so I could grow into them. This always created a problem." When the patient was three and a half he was given a tricycle that was too tall for him. His feet did not reach the pedals. "I got on to ride it, but I started to roll down the hill. My father was standing there—tall, still, dressed very correctly. He watched but did nothing to try to stop me. I couldn't reach the pedals to stop the tricycle. I was terrified. I went racing down the hill and fell off. My father just continued to stand there."

The patient believed his father had a snobbish attitude toward labor and would do nothing manual for fear he would "dirty" his hands. Whenever the patient played on the streets and got at all soiled, he feared his father would be contemptuous and think him "grubby." He stated that his father was violently anti-Semitic. In contrast, as the patient matured, he developed great tolerance for minority groups. He also believed that through his father's prudishness he had become imbued with the idea that sex was filthy and revolting.

The patient never had a feeling of moral support for any assertive acts but when he ran away from fights his father would harshly accuse him of cowardice. "My father's voice always sounded rough and harsh to me. Whenever I had a boss who had a harsh voice, I would panic."

The patient recalled only one occasion when his father played with him. This occurred when the mother requested him to play ball with his son. The father complied but his reluctance provoked the mother to anger. He retaliated by saying that the boy couldn't catch. The patient felt extremely humiliated. Since then, he has experienced anxiety when anyone suggest playing "catch."

After the patient graduated from high school, his father advised him to take a job in South America since his godfather had a substantial business there. But the patient felt his father wanted only to get rid of him and he refused to go.

Frequently, the patient had conscious death wishes for his father and often dreamed of his death. He thought of his father as his enemy whom he feared and hated.

(When the patient terminated psychoanalysis, he was sexually inactive.)

CASE NO. 127

A homosexual pattern was established by the age of seventeen when the patient engaged in fellatio with a partner thirty-five years of age.

The patient's father was thirteen years older than the mother toward whom he was soft-spoken and quite timid. The patient remembers his father sneaking out of the house to keep a poker date. The mainstay of the family was the paternal uncle who took the father into business with him.

The patient was an only child. In childhood he was fearful of the dark, of burglars, and of people with knives. He would leave his bedroom door open so that he could see the light from the hall. His father would taunt him and call him "sissy" because of this. One night, he heard his parents arguing. He developed fears that something would happen to him for listening. He reported sleep-walking to his parents' door on several occasions.

The patient saw very little of his father though he remembers sometimes getting into his father's bed early in the morning. The father began to have increasing financial difficulties and eventually was forced out of business. He tried other ventures with no success and subsequently lost most of his money on the stock market. He also lost his pride and retreated even further from the family. The patient felt his father had completely abandoned him.

The patient recalled that his father had always been highly critical of him and nothing he attempted was thought of as satisfactory. When told to cut the lawn, he would do so willingly. But when his father came home, he would yell at his son in a rage because, on close inspection, he had found a tuft of grass here or there that had been missed. The father did not encourage the patient to have friends. If other children came onto the lawn, the father would become agitated. He would rant and loudly complain that the kids were spoiling the lawn. When the patient got involved in arguments with other boys, he would balk at fighting. The father would resort to his favorite epithet, "sissy."

At the time the patient entered college, the mother went into business and made a success of it. The father felt more defeated than ever. He became preoccupied with his health since he had developed Buerger's disease and a heart condition. He finally had a stroke and was incapacitated. He lived his last few years as a remote, solitary invalid.

(At termination, the patient was no longer having either homosexual or heterosexual relations. He was sexually inactive.)

DETACHED-INDIFFERENT FATHERS

In 18 homosexual cases, the fathers appeared to be quite indifferent to their sons. The relatively low percentages scored on most of the items in Table IV-5, Column 2, reflect a low rate of father-son interaction. In 83 per cent of the cases, fathers spent "very little time" with their sons. In no case was the son a favorite child and in only one case was the father affectionate. As contrasted with other sub-groups, the detached-indifferent sub-group comprised the least number of fathers reported as dominating. In about half the cases, sons neither consciously hated nor feared them and only one of these sons thought of his father as an admirable person.

The 9 comparison cases in this category presented a similar pattern of answers to the items listed in Column 5. Most percentages of affirmative answers ranged between 11 per cent and 33 per cent as was the case with the 18 H-fathers in this category.

A detailed discussion of these fathers would not be instructive since they represented distant figures to their patient-sons and, on the whole, had little affirmative meaning to them.

The following case report of a detached-indifferent H-father is illustrative of the emotionally shallow father-son relationship characteristic of this sub-group.

CASE NO. 17

The patient was the third of four sons of a Midwestern family. The mother was the uncontested, dominant parent. She was grandiose, driving, and overambitious. A rather ignorant woman, she had intellectual and social pretensions and she inculcated the feeling in her children that they were above the other working-class people in the neighborhood. It was the mother alone who decided upon the professional choice of each of her sons and she would brook no interference in implementing her ambitions for them. She completely dominated her husband who remained in the background as a nebulous and rather pathetic figure.

The father was a storekeeper who worked long hours. He appeared neither contented nor discontented with his lot in life. He trudged through his daily routine, showing no deep concern for anyone, not even for himself. The only semblance of relatedness to the patient occurred when he would enlist the help of his sons for the store, but only after consulting the mother. The patient co-operated out of a mechanical sense of duty. He neither enjoyed nor resented it. His father neither criticized the patient's work nor praised him; he was neither hostile to the patient, nor manipulating, nor affectionate. In brief, paternal contact was meager, nondescript, barren. The patient and his brothers were contemptuous of their father but they were not hostile to him. The patient could not recall any desire to win his father's approval or affection. These affective needs were sought from his maternal uncle, a successful business man. The patient also greatly respected and admired his oldest brother who achieved considerable distinction in his profession.

When the patient and his brothers were adults, the mother died. Then, for the first time, the father emerged as an individual. He attempted to come into a more meaningful relationship with his sons and even after his remarriage a few years later continued to show affection and generosity, never indicating any discrimination against the patient. The patient responded slightly to his father's overtures but did not develop any real interest or feeling for him. The father rarely appeared in the patient's dreams or associations. When the father died, the patient felt little emotion. It seemed as though an acquaintance had passed away.

The patient's homosexuality was established in late adolescence. He was exclusively homosexual until treatment was well advanced. He had heterosexual intercourse for the first time when he was thirty-three years old. He has not been able to sustain a heterosexual relationship exclusively. He is bisexual.

Detached-Ambivalent Fathers

In 14 H-cases and 20 C-cases, despite the father's detachment, some positive paternal attitudes were expressed to the sons. Detachment was inferred since these fathers in no instance were reported to have spent an "average amount of time" with their sons; in about 40 per cent of the cases, the fathers were reported to have spent "very little time" with them. Nevertheless, 75 per cent of these H- and C-fathers showed affection to the patient-sons; several sons were favorites, and in the H-father group, no son was the least favored sibling. Compared to the other sub-groups, these fathers were infrequently contemptuous or humiliating. The majority of their sons accepted and also felt accepted by them. In addition to detachment, there were other evidences of ambivalent paternal attitudes—more so among the homosexual sub-group than among the comparison cases. In half the homosexual cases, the father was consciously feared and in one-third of the cases consciously hated; half the H-patients were fearful that self-assertiveness would anger their fathers. Though fewer items reflected ambivalence among the C-fathers, there were more among C-fathers (30 per cent) who were contemptuous/humiliating to their sons. One-third of the C-sons feared and over half were submissive to their fathers; almost half the C-sons were afraid that self-assertiveness would anger their fathers. Only one item significantly differentiated the homosexual from the comparison cases in this subcategory (Item 12—"Patient felt father was admirable"). Two case reports illustrating the detached-ambivalent category follow.

CASE NO. 192

The patient is a twenty-five-year-old professional who began to have homosexual experiences at the age of sixteen. He is the older of two sons of a middle-class Protestant family.

The father was conservative and reserved. He was an electrical engineer by profession but a physicist by training. He often said that were it not for economic necessity he would prefer doing basic research in physics rather than practical engineering in industry. He had a broad intellectual background but was not inclined to demonstrate his erudition, except in matters of engineering interest. The mother, on the other hand, made a great display of her artistic and literary knowledge but was totally uninterested in any subject that touched upon science. Despite the father's apparent lack of enthusiasm for his work, he nevertheless worked late hours and took on heavy responsibilities in completing assigned projects. He appeared to be continuously preoccupied with work even while at home. Basically, the father was nonassertive. He was afraid to speak up for a raise when he merited it. He was also reluctant to speak up to his wife. The mother had almost exclusive responsibility for raising the two sons.

The father was a hobbyist who spent much of his time at home tinkering in the basement with electrical inventions and devices. On several occasions he made efforts to include his son. During the patient's early adolescence, his father attempted to instruct him in the fundamentals of electricity. The father would painstakingly explain the mathematics and physics of electrical circuits to him and would try to acquaint him with some of the delicate mechanisms in the workshop. The patient would feel restless and uneasy during these scientific sessions, aware of the contrast to the usual detachment he expected in his father. The patient also had difficulty understanding his father's explanations. This failure to comprehend is of interest since he was an excellent student in mathematics and physics while the father had a reputation as an excellent teacher of these subjects. Gradually, the father began to invite two older nephews, cousins of the patient, into the workshop. The nephews responded much more enthusiastically to his experiments and teaching than did the patient. Soon the workshop contact between father and son dwindled and finally ended.

The patient remembers his father's infrequent attempts to teach him chess. Eventually, he learned to play but their occasional games were overshadowed by what the patient described as his father's intense preoccupation with winning. The father did indeed win every game, and the patient remembers feeling exploited as a chess partner rather than welcomed as a companion in a mutually satisfying experience. Upon his return from college one year, he won a chess game from his father. This turned out to be the last chess game the two ever played together.

On the infrequent occasions when the patient and his father were alone together, an embarrassing silence widened the gulf between them since they had so little to say to each other. The patient felt his father to be something of a stranger to him.

The younger brother was not homosexual. The mother has described him to the patient as having been the more "masculine" of the two. He was a rebellious child whom she found difficult to manage. He appears to have had an impulse-disorder during adolescence. He was addicted to hot-rods and motorcycles, and on one or two occasions had a brush with the police. He settled down as he approached adulthood and married early. Although he did not have a close relationship with the father, he was far closer to him than was the patient.

Family decisions were made at round table meetings, supposedly to stimulate a democratic atmosphere. Although there were discussions involving family members, the patient remembers these discussions as characterized mainly by indirection and avoidance of crucial issues. The meetings were run by the mother who attempted to impose parliamentary procedure. The father barely spoke out, but when he did it was without firmness or conviction. The brother did not participate actively, either.

Apart from the so-called "family discussions," the patient never remembered get-togethers for entertainment, or other activities. Whenever conflict arose involving father and son, the mother would vote for the patient's position as though she were chairman of the board. The father would skulk out of the room defeated, but obviously silently resentful. There were only isolated instances not consistent with this general pattern. Once, before the age of seven, the patient remembers his father disciplining him for some misdeed by hitting him on the hand with a short piece of coaxial electrical cable. The patient remembers one pleasant experience with his father. They built a snow tower together—"We both got a big kick out of it." He does not recall any other pleasant experience.

Open arguments were rare. The patient remembers having had temper tantrums at the dinner table when he was a young child. His father would send him away without his dinner but the mother could always be depended upon to bring food to his room, thereby subverting the father's authority.

The patient never asked his father for anything. The mother would intercede on her son's behalf thus eliminating the need for him to approach his father directly.

In summary, this is an example of a detached-ambivalent father. He was excessively preoccupied with his work, probably because of his obsessive and compulsive traits. Reserved and inhibited, he did not assert himself sufficiently at his employment or at home. Clearly, abortive attempts were made to establish contact with the patient but these attempts were, at least in part, competitively inspired and were neither successful nor satisfying to either one. Open cruelty was rare. The patient felt that his father liked him in some odd way but there were never any open demonstrations of affection. The patient felt that his father's inhibitions and reticence, in concert with the mother's overpowering, dominant position in the household, prevented him from being the kind of constructive and affectionate parent he may have wanted to be and that the patient believed he wanted his father to be.

The patient is still in treatment. Both parents are aware of their son's overt homosexual problem. The father's reaction remains unclear; he is reluctant to discuss the subject but he seems ashamed and helpless about the situation. The mother has insisted he pay for his son's analysis.

In the psychoanalytic transference, the patient has related to the analyst (male) as to a wished-for, strong, effective, masculine father who is at the same time gentle, sensitive, and learned.

CASE NO. 133

The patient began homosexual activity at the age of twenty-two. His partner was a year older. He was often tense in his homosexual relationships and, on occasion, developed attacks of panic.

The patient was an only son, with one older and two younger sisters. His father was a cultured professional man who came from a socially prominent but poor family. The patient's mother was wealthy but came from "the wrong side of the tracks." She dominated the family and kept a firm hand on the purse strings while her husband, a socially active dandy, earned very little in his profession.

The father spent most of his time at his clubs. When he saw his son, he was mildly affectionate and sometimes confided in him. However, when the mother sent the boy to a girls' private day school, the father did nothing to protect the patient against this decision. The boy had no male playmates.

When the patient was about five years old, his father gave him a glove and a bat. The equipment was of excellent quality and had probably been chosen with care. When the gift was handed to the child, the father said, "Now you can play baseball." But he knew no other boys with whom he could play. When the patient was twelve years old, his father brought him a birthday gift of an elaborate set of tools encased in a handsome chest, costing well over two hundred dollars. Once again, the father made no effort at mutual participation with his son. He neither showed the patient how to use the tools nor did he manifest any further interest. The patient resented his father's casual attitude and began to hate the tool outfit. He never used it.

(When the patient terminated treatment, he was still exclusively homosexual.)

DETACHED DOMINATING-EXPLOITATIVE FATHERS

There were 3 H- and 0 C-fathers in this sub-group. All 3 were dominating and all demanded a great deal of attention from their patient sons. All 3 were reported as puritanical and all interfered with the heterosexual activities of their sons in adolescence. None of the sons received affection or felt accepted. All feared physical injury from their fathers, all were submissive and fearful of angering them. The father-son relationship in this sub-group is characterized by clear-cut domination-submission patterns.

THE NOT-DETACHED FATHERS

In 13 H-cases and 41 C-cases the fathers were *not detached* from their sons. The fathers in this category were similar in that the majority were reported to have spent an "average amount of time" with their sons and in several instances "a great deal of time."

TABLE IV-6 *Comparison of Sub-groups of Not-Detached Fathers* (*in per cent*)

	H	C[a]		
		Warmly related	Ambivalent	Hostile
N =	13	8	17	11
1. Time spent with father: very little, or none	23	0	6	0
2. Father showed affection	62	100	88	45
3. Patient was father's favorite	23	38	18	36
4. Patient was father's least favored	54	0	12	18
5. Father showed contempt/humiliation	69	0	12	82
6. Father interfered with heterosexuality	31	25	18	36
7. Father encouraged masculinity	54	88	59	73
8. Father was dominating	46	0	47	82
9. Patient was accepted by father	31	100	82	9
10. Patient respected father	38	88	53	18
11. Patient accepted father	8	100	71	27
12. Patient felt father was admirable	46	50	53	55
13. Patient knowingly hated father	85	0	18	64
14. Patient knowingly feared father	77	25	53	82
15. Patient hated/feared father	69	0	12	64
16. Patient feared physical injury from father	77	0	41	73
17. Patient coped with father by: submission	85	38	59	73
18. detachment	23	0	12	18
19. rebellion	23	25	6	9
20. Patient feared his assertiveness would anger father	92	63	41	73
21. Patient feared his assertiveness would lose father's love	54	38	35	64

[a] 5 C CBI fathers not included

Not-detached H-fathers

Despite the small number of not-detached H-fathers (13), this group was logically separable into three sub-groups:

Not-detached, ambivalent

This sub-group was composed of 6 cases. The following items indicated a positive father-son relatedness: Of the 6 fathers, 4 spent an "average amount of time" or more with their sons, and no father spent "very little time." Affection was expressed by 5 fathers and 1 favored the patient. Three sons respected their fathers, 3 thought them admirable and 3 sided with them in parental arguments. On the other hand, negative attitudes were suggested by the following data: In 3 cases, the sons were the least favored siblings; 5 fathers showed contempt/humiliation; 5 sons consciously both hated and feared their fathers, and 5 feared that assertiveness would anger them. In 4 cases, the patients feared physical injury by the father. Paternal ambivalence appears as the outstanding characteristic of this sub-group. It is of interest that during psychoanalysis 3 of the 6 patients became exclusively heterosexual.

Not-detached, hostile

This sub-group was composed of 4 patients. All were least favored and none felt accepted by their fathers; all feared physical injury from them; none accepted or respected their fathers and 3 sons consciously hated them.

(A case report describing one not-detached, hostile father is presented at the end of the discussion of not-detached fathers.)

Close-binding

In 3 cases, the paternal qualities suggested a marked similarity to the close-binding mothers. In one case, the father spent a "great deal of time" with his son and was reported as "overprotective." All 3 sons sided with these fathers in parental arguments and 2 sons were favorites. Of the 3 patients 2 had male siblings and in both cases the fathers were more intimate with the patient-son than with the other sons. These close-binding fathers differed from the maternal counterpart in that a far greater ambivalence was apparent in the father-son relationship. Of the 3 sons 2 consciously hated their fathers; 2 feared them; 2 feared physical injury from their fathers; 2 feared that self-assertiveness would anger them, and all 3 were submissive to their fathers. Yet, of the 3 patients 2 became exclusively heterosexual.

In the not-detached H-group, not one father could be classified as "warmly related" while in the C-group 8 fathers were so classified. Yet, 7 of the 13 homosexual patients whose fathers were not detached became heterosexual as compared with the 22 other cases who became heterosexual. This difference is significant at the .05 level. These data suggest that despite the ambivalent attitudes which becloud father-son relationships, the absence of paternal detachment is a favorable prognostic indicator in the treatment of homosexuals.

Not-detached C-fathers

The 41 C-fathers in this group have been categorized into 4 subgroups:

Warmly related

In 8 cases, the fathers appeared to be the only ones in the total sample who had a warm and affectionate relationship with their sons (Table IV-6, Column 2). All fathers in this group spent an "average amount of time" with their sons; all showed them affection; all accepted their sons and, in turn, were accepted by them. None was contemptuous of his son and in no case was the patient a least favored child. None of the sons consciously hated their fathers and none feared physical injury from them. Most respected their fathers and half the patients admired them. In 2 cases, however, the sons feared their fathers; 3 were submissive to them, and 5 feared that self-assertiveness would anger them. Nevertheless, a predominantly positive theme characterizes these father-son relationships. Impaired father-son contact as an important determinant of psychopathology in males is reaffirmed by the minimal number of adequate fathers studied—only 8 warmly related fathers appear in a sample of 206 male patients in psychoanalysis.

Not-detached, ambivalent

There were 17 C-fathers in this sub-group (Table IV-6, Column 3). These fathers show a greater similarity to the warmly related fathers than to the not-detached, ambivalent H-fathers. Higher scores were consistently achieved on items reflecting positive father-son relatedness, while on items reflecting negative factors scores were lower than those achieved by not-detached H-fathers. In comparing Columns 2 and 3, there is more evidence of conflicting attitudes among the "ambivalent" fathers than is noted among the "warmly related" group.

Not-detached, hostile

This sub-group is composed of 11 fathers. Although ambivalence runs through the fabric of these father-son relationships, animosity predominated. Almost half the number in this group showed affection and several even favored their sons over their other children, yet the majority were contemptuous of their patient-sons. Only 1 of the 11 sons felt accepted by his father and only 3 accepted and 2 respected their fathers. Of the 11 cases, 9 feared them. More than half the sons consciously hated and feared their fathers and 9 were afraid that self-assertive behavior would provoke paternal anger. On the other hand, 7 sons feared that the consequence of self-assertion would be loss of their father's love. Clearly, despite his hostility, when the father is not detached his love has value to the son who fears losing it. Comparing all the scores for Item 21 ("Fear that assertion will lose father's love") in Tables IV-5 and IV-6, we note that the range of percentages achieved by the detached fathers is 11-36 (mean 22 per cent) while the range for the not-detached fathers is 35-64 (mean 48 per cent).

Close-binding

There were 5 C-fathers in this sub-group. All showed affection to their sons. Of the 5 patients, 2 were "only" children. The three others were the father's favorites. In 2 of these cases, the fathers were more intimate with their patient-sons than with other sons and they also spent a "great deal of time" together. In 3 cases, the sons regarded the father as puritanical. Though none of these fathers was hated, only 1 was respected and admired. Of the 5 sons, 4 were submissive to the father and 4 of the 5 feared that self-assertion would anger the father. This pattern of response closely resembles that appearing in the CBI mother category.

CASE NO. 125

The patient is a thirty-nine-year-old professional man who had his first homosexual experience when he was twenty-seven, though he had decided when he was eighteen years old that he was homosexual. He had recognized in himself a fear of closeness with girls and feelings of sexual stimulation by men. Rigid moral controls had prevented his "acting-out." The patient's father was a successful farmer who also had made a great deal of money in real estate. By the time the patient was five years old, the hatred characterizing the father-son relationship was well defined. Humiliations and beatings were frequent. All through childhood the father threatened his son with images of wild beasts and Indians in pursuit of him. It seemed to him that his father enjoyed watching the frightened reactions to these anxiety provocations. When the patient showed fear, the father always ridiculed him. On one occasion, the patient spied a snake. Panic-stricken, he fled from it. The father shot the snake, picked it up and waved it in front of the frightened child, thus taunting him and humiliating him for his fear in the presence of other people who were at the scene. The father took the attitude that if his son did not act "like a man" he deserved to be ridiculed. As the boy grew, he was given responsibilities around the farm. But should he balk at doing an assigned task, the father would beat him.

In his late childhood and adolescence, the patient spent much of his time with his father not only during the day around the farm but also in the evenings. Their evenings together were spent at local taverns where the patient detested going. He would try to escape these ordeals but the father insisted that it was his paternal duty to "show him the sordid side of life." The patient was often the butt of his father's coarse jokes about the women who frequented the taverns, many of whom were prostitutes. The father did not require his son to drink with him, but he did insist that he stay and listen to coarse talk and vulgarities.

The father made him feel that sex was dirty and unacceptable. Suspecting that his son was masturbating when the boy was about twelve years old, the father confronted him by saying, "If you must play with yourself let me give you a cow and you can screw her." The patient witnessed the hired men on the farm masturbating and engaging in homosexual activities. He was aware that these scenes stimulated him sexually.

The mother's relationship with the patient was contradictory and confusing to him. Publicly she was rejecting. Two younger sisters were openly preferred. Privately, she was close-binding. He slept with her between the ages of five and nineteen and was his mother's confidant. The father held her in contempt and completely dominated her. She did little to protect her son from his father's brutality. The patient felt he hated her.

When the patient was ready to enter college, he tried to avoid accepting financial assistance from his father whom he loathed and feared. Though he had to take some money to see himself through school, when he entered postgraduate training he was able to obtain tuition expenses from sources other than his father.

The patient has lived with his homosexual partner for twelve years. He has reported that his partner treated him cruelly and humiliated him just as his father did, unless he, the patient, appeased the partner sexually.

At termination of treatment, the patient was still exclusively homosexual.

PATIENT-FATHER INTERACTION

Hatred

Among the homosexual patients 63 were consciously aware of hating their fathers, as compared to 37 comparison patients. This difference is significant at the .001 level. Tables IV-7 through IV-10 present data associating specific types of rejecting and hostile paternal behavior with filial hatred.

TABLE IV-7 *Association Between Patient's Hatred of Father and Paternal Contempt/Humiliation*

	H		C	
	Hates father	Does not	Hates father	Does not
Father showed contempt/humiliation	44	8	26	19
Did not	19	32	11	44

Significance: H .001; C .001

TABLE IV-8 *Association Between Patient's Hatred of Father and Lack of Paternal Respect for Patient*

	H		C	
	Hates father	Does not	Hates father	Does not
Father respected son	12	18	9	39
Did not	51	22	28	24

Significance: H .01; C .01

TABLE IV-9 *Association Between Patient's Hatred of Father and Paternal Physical Cruelty*

	H		C	
	Hates father	Does not	Hates father	Does not
Father physically cruel	17	3	15	2
Not cruel	46	37	22	61

Significance: H .01; C .001

TABLE IV-10 *Association Between Patient's Hatred of Father and Lack of Paternal Acceptance of Patient*

	H		C	
	Hates father	Does not	Hates father	Does not
Father accepted patient	7	17	8	39
Did not	56	23	29	24

Significance: H .001; C .001

As expected, rejecting and hostile behavior provoked hatred in the sons. Of interest is the fact that proportionately more homosexuals were consciously aware of hating their fathers than were comparison cases. Where fathers were contemptuous/humiliating, the proportion of hating to not hating among homosexuals is 5.5:1 (Table IV-7) whereas among the comparisons it is only 1.8:1. Where fathers did not respect their sons (Table IV-8) the ratio is 2.3:1 for homosexuals and 1.5:1 for comparisons. Where fathers did not "accept" their sons (Table IV-10) the ratio is 2.8:1 for homosexuals as compared with 1.5:1 for the comparisons. These disproportions seem to reflect the greater intensity and consistency of rejecting and hostile behavior in the fathers of homosexuals than occurred among comparison fathers.

Fear

There were 70 homosexuals who were reported to have consciously feared their fathers, as compared with 54 comparison cases. The following tables contain data from which correlations can be made between fear of the father and other items concerned with the son's fear.

(*a*) *Hatred and Fear*. We note from Table IV-11 that when a son hated his father, in almost all cases he also feared him. There were only

TABLE IV-11 *Association Between Hatred and Fear of Father*

	H		C	
	Hates father	Does not	Hates father	Does not
Fears father	58	12	31	23
Does not	5	28	6	40

Significance: H .001; C. 001

5 H-cases and 6 C-cases where this did not hold. There were, however, 12 H-patients and 23 C-patients who feared their fathers but did not hate them. Dependency upon the father (and we are referring to the realistic dependency of childhood), in a sense, places the son in his father's power. Feelings of hatred toward the parent also inspire fear of him, in that should this filial attitude be discovered the parent is then in a position to retaliate against the child. Thus, filial hatred is a wellspring of filial fear. The data of Table IV-12 suggest that the son's hatred of his father is one determinant of fear of physical injury from the father.

TABLE IV-12 *Association Between Hatred of Father and Fear of Physical Injury from Father*

	H		C	
	Hates father	Does not	Hates father	Does not
Fears physical injury from father	44	15	28	15
Does not	19	25	9	48

Significance: H .01; C .001

(*b*) *Fear of Physical Injury.* A high degree of association between fear of the father and fear of physical injury was expected. Its meaning is self-evident, though the converse is not necessarily true—a child may fear his father without fearing physical injury if he has not been exposed to corporal punishment or brutality. There were 17 C-fathers who were reported as physically cruel; 15 of their patient-sons feared physical injury from them.

The meaning of the association between the patients' fear of physical injury from the father and fear of genital injury is not immediately apparent. In Tables IV-13—IV-16 data are assembled which associate fear of genital injury with fear of physical injury from the father and hatred of him.

Clinical observations make possible several interpretations to explain the significant association between fear of physical injury from the father and patients' fear of genital injury.

TABLE IV-13 *Association Between Fear of Physical Injury from Father and Fear of Genital Injury*

	H		C	
	Fears physical injury from father	Does not	Fears physical injury from father	Does not
Fears genital injury	39	18	25	18
Does not	20	26	18	39

Significance: H .05; C .05

TABLE IV-14 *Association Between Paternal Cruelty and Fear of Genital Injury*

	H		C	
	Father cruel	Not cruel	Father cruel	Not cruel
Fears genital injury	11	46	7	36
Does not	9	37	10	47

Significance: H not significant; C not significant

TABLE IV-15 *Association Between Fear of Physical Injury from Father and Fear of Genital Injury—Minus Cruel Fathers*

	H		C	
	Fears physical injury from father	Does not	Fears physical injury from father	Does not
Fears genital injury	28	18	18	18
Does not	11	26	8	39

Significance: H .05; C .01

Does the fear of physical injury create the fear of genital injury?

One might assume that fear of physical injury from the father stimulates fear of genital injury in the son. Our data on the cruel fathers do not support this view. In 20 H-cases and 17 C-cases (Table IV-14), fathers were physically cruel. In all 20 H-cases and in 15 C-cases, fear of physical injury from the father was reported. Yet, in the H-cases 9 of the 20 did not fear genital injury and in the C-cases 10 of the 17 did not. Thus, we found no association between cruel fathers and fear of genital injury. If a fear of physical injury *per se* created a fear of genital injury, we would expect that in those patients who had cruel fathers genital injury would be feared. As a matter of fact, when these 20 cases were excluded from the statistics testing the association between fear of physical injury and fear of genital injury on the assumption that paternal cruelty masked other possible determinants of fear of physical injury, the Chi squares were even higher. To assume a displacement from a generalized fear of physical injury to any specific anatomical part, though reasonable, is not supportable, judging from our findings.

Does the fear of injury to the genitals create a fear of physical injury from the father?

We have been able to delineate three types of observational data which bear upon the association between the patient's fear of genital injury and his fear of physical injury from the father.

(*a*) *Paternal interference with masturbation.* Male patients in psychoanalysis frequently report that their fathers had manifested prohibitive and punitive attitudes toward masturbation. In some instances, fathers are reported to have told their sons that masturbation would harm their sexual development and interfere with their sexuality as adults. In rare instances, fathers threatened to "cut off" the son's penis.

TABLE IV-16 *Association Between Hatred of Father and Fear of Genital Injury*

	H		C	
	Hates father	Does not	Hates father	Does not
Fears genital injury	43	14	18	25
Does not	20	26	19	38

Significance: H .01; C not significant

Our questionnaire did not probe direct interference with masturbation by either parent. It did, however, contain a question, Did the patient have guilt feelings about masturbation? Much—Some—Little—None. We assumed we would find a high correlation between guilt about masturbation and recollected parental interference. Proceeding on this assumption, we tested for an association between masturbatory guilt and fear of physical injury from father, fear of genital injury, and aversion to female genitalia. No associations were found. We are inclined to believe that paternal interference with masturbation does not account for the association found between fear of genital injury and fear of physical injury from the father.

(*b*) *Sexual competitiveness with father.* In general, psychoanalysts observe in male patients evidences of competitiveness with their fathers. According to classical psychoanalytic theory, this competitiveness is rooted in the unresolved sexual rivalry for the mother (Oedipus complex). The wish to castrate the father, which is almost always unconscious, is one expression of sexual rivalry. This unconscious wish is manifested in dreams and in symbolic forms of thought and behavior. Castration wishes, in turn, evoke retaliatory fears experienced as a fear of genital injury. Thus, the formulation of the castration complex offers one interpretation for the association of fear of genital injury with fear of physical injury from the father. The significant association between hatred of the father and fear of genital injury (Table IV-16) is supportive.

Two assumptions may be made: the closer the mother-son relationship, the more intense is the son's sexual competitiveness with the father; the significant association between fear of genital injury and fear of physical injury from the father is a function of the son's sexual competitiveness with the father. If these assumptions hold, we would expect that this association would reach a higher level of significance among sons who had CBI mothers than among sons who did not have CBI mothers. The data in Tables IV-17 and IV-18 support our assumptions.

Fear of genital injury is significantly associated with fear of physical injury from the father in H cases who had CBI mothers and is not significantly associated in H cases who did not have CBI mothers.

(*c*) *Sexual competitiveness of father with son.* In the course of psychoanalysis of male patients, rivalrous feelings toward their sons are frequently revealed. Many fathers will be competitive with their sons in a way not observable with daughters. Evidence of the sexual nature of the rivalry is observable in dreams and in the free associations of patients who have sons. Dream content will include injury to sons and, occasionally, genital injury. It is not unreasonable to assume that even unconscious hostility is communicated by "unaware" attitudes and behavior. When rivalry is sexually determined, the "message" received by the son serves as a sexually inhibiting influence, which may be symbolically represented as genital injury. Paternal competitiveness, *specifically, sexual competitiveness,* may be one determinant for the association between fear of genital injury and fear of physical injury from the father.

Where we found an association between fear of genital injury and fear of physical injury from the father, sexual competitiveness between son and father (in both directions) appears to underlie the son's fear of genital injury. Murderous wishes frequently accompany intensely hostile sexual competitiveness. Such wishes will be represented in fears of physi-

TABLE IV-17 *Association Between Fear of Physical Injury from Father and Fear of Genital Injury—Patients with CBI Mothers*

	H[a]		C	
	Fears physical injury from father	Does not	Fears physical injury from father	Does not
Fears genital injury	31	10	13	8
Does not	10	19	3	8

Significance: H .01; C not significant
[a] N = 70; see Footnote 1, p. 87

TABLE IV-18 *Association Between Fear of Physical Injury from Father and Fear of Genital Injury—Patients with Non-CBI Mothers*

	H		C	
	Fears physical injury from father	Does not	Fears physical injury from father	Does not
Fears genital injury	8	8	12	10
Does not	10	7	15	31

Significance: H not significant; C not significant

cal attack. We conclude that fear of injury to the genitals does not create a fear of physical injury in any one-to-one relationship; rather, sexual competitiveness accounts for fear of genital injury as well as for fear of physical injury from the father and the association between these fears.

Summary and Conclusions

The most arresting feature of father-son relationships in the entire patient sample is the consistency with which psychopathologic phenomena appear. *Profound interpersonal disturbance is unremitting in the H-father-son relationships.* Not one of the H-fathers and only 8 of the 100 C-fathers could be regarded as reasonably "normal" parents, though the C-fathers, on the whole, presented a far more wholesome picture. The responses to 21 questions tapping psychopathologic factors distinguish the H-fathers from the C-fathers at statistically significant levels (from .05 to .001). As a group, the H-fathers were detached, hostile, minimizing, and openly rejecting. The outstanding attitudes of homosexuals toward their fathers were hatred and fear.

Detached fathers

Of the 106 H-fathers, 79 were classified as detached. Of these, 18 fathers were distant and indifferent to their sons; 44 were hostile and 14 were ambivalent and 3 were dominating-exploitative.

(a) The effects of paternal detachment

A detached pattern of father-son relatedness obviously promotes a defective relationship to which the child may react multifariously. He may develop a cognitive awareness of a lack of paternal affection, warmth, and interest, or he may be unable to formulate the lack and may merely experience a vague hunger or yearning for something he cannot identify. Some children may interpret detachment as rejection, but in any case, no matter how it is experienced, it is always traumatic. The child may attempt a way out by seeking other reparative relationships to fulfill his yearnings—often with other males. Thus, the pathologic seeking of need fulfillment from men has a clear point of origin in fathers who were detached. Our study revealed that sons of detached fathers sought in homosexual partners the qualities they had not known in their own fathers: 45 homosexuals sought warmth, 47 sought friendliness, and 63 sought "contact."[2] *We assume that any circumstances that create pathologic needs in males which can be satisfied only by other males, operate in the direction of promoting homosexuality or homosexual problems.*

(b) The effects of "little time" spent with sons by detached fathers

Only 3 of the 79 H-fathers who were classified as detached spent an "average" amount of time with their sons. In 32 cases (41 per cent) "little time" and in 44 cases (56 per cent) "very little time" was spent together, which contributes to the failure to provide the son with an adequate male model for identification.

(c) The need for a male model for identification

It is a generally accepted psychoanalytic assumption, based on repeated observation, that favorable personality development, particularly in its sexual aspects, depends in large measure on an identification with a parent or parent surrogate of the same sex. The patterning and reinforcement of masculine traits derive largely from paternal encouragement of identification. The father who lives in the family group yet has little contact with his son discourages filial attachment thus blocking identification processes.

(d) Failure to protect the son against destructive maternal influences

As the chapter on mother-son relationships has demonstrated, homosexuals usually have pathogenic mothers. Few homosexuals have fathers who take a firm stand in protecting against destructive maternal behavior. Of the 79 homosexual patients who had detached fathers, 53 (67 per cent) sought masculine traits in their partners. The homosexual's attraction to masculine qualities may represent, at least in part, a reparative and self-protective attempt to relate to a strong male who will be able to defend against the power of the mother—unlike the father who did not.

(e) The effects of paternal hostility

Paternal hostility adds a specific psychopathologic dynamic to the development of a male child. The reasons for this have been widely

[2] We mean by "contact" a need for nearness, closeness—the reassurance of physical presence.

presented and well documented, especially in psychoanalytic literature, and we shall not expand the discussion. A clinical observation was contributed by several members of the Research Committee who had independently observed that whenever some fathers of homosexuals perceived "masculine" behavior in their sons, hostile paternal behavior ensued. The discernment of a connection between sexual and masculine expressiveness and the arousal of paternal hostility set off severe anxiety in the son followed by inhibition of behavior felt to be "masculine." The effeminate gestures and posturing often seen among homosexuals are not necessarily part of a feminine identification. They may represent a concealment of masculinity developed as a defense against paternal competitive hostility.

Since 54 fathers in the comparison group were classified as detached, one may ask why did not their sons become homosexuals? Comparisons of detached H-fathers with C-fathers reveal consistently less detachment and hostility among the C-fathers. The extent of detachment and the intensity of hostility apparently play a determining role in the sexually adaptive outcome.

(f) Paternal seductiveness

In the entire homosexual sample, only 3 fathers were reported as seductive. In one of the cases, the judgment was made by the responding psychoanalyst on the ground that the father frequently slept with his son while the wife worked at night. In the second case, the judgment was made on the basis of an incident where the father had placed the patient's head in his lap, and the patient believed his father had an erection. In the third case, seductiveness appeared to be unequivocal; the father had introduced his son into practicing mutual masturbation. More subtle manifestations of paternal seductiveness were not reported.

Not-detached fathers

Of all fathers, the not-detached H-fathers revealed the greatest range in attitudes. Several were among the most pathogenic fathers studied (Case No. 125 is illustrative). Yet, although no father of a homosexual was classified as "warmly related," there were several in this group who, despite ambivalence and conflict, appeared to have some positive attitudes which were communicated to their sons. The homosexual sons of not-detached fathers achieved higher scores than other H sub-groups on the item, Did patient fear self-assertiveness would lose father's love? The clinical implications are noteworthy. Of these 13 homosexuals, 7 became exclusively heterosexual. This is the highest percentage of change in sexual pattern of any homosexual sub-group.

The not-detached C-fathers, as a group, represented the best father-son relationships. In 8 cases, the fathers were "warmly related" to their sons and these were the only reasonably "normal" fathers in the entire patient sample.

It appears that if a father is not detached from his son—despite a range of undesirable paternal attitudes—he will nonetheless tend to introduce an element into their relationship which, among homosexuals, favors recovery and, among heterosexuals, militates against homosexual problems.

V

Siblings

THUS FAR we have dealt primarily with dyadic aspects of the family system; in this chapter we shall examine the attitudes of the parents toward the patient-sons and other siblings. Our major emphasis will be on comparative parental attitudes toward patients and other siblings, and aspects of the patients' attitudes toward siblings. One must keep in mind, however, that family dynamics have a configurational unity. The interpenetration of family sub-systems with the larger and more complex total family system appears within each chapter, at times tangentially and at others centrally. Though the emphasis is on the sibling sub-system, the contours of the family system become apparent.

General characteristics of the families

Of 106 homosexuals, 11 were "only" children as compared to 22 of 100 comparison patients, significant at the .05 level. Of the 95 H-families with siblings, there were 31 in which the patients had only female siblings and 33 in which there were only male siblings. Hence, as many homosexuals were brought up in a predominantly masculine as in a feminine sibling environment.

The greater percentage of patients in both groups came from small families. About 50 per cent in each group came from families of

TABLE V-1 *Family Make-up of Sample Population*

	Only child	Sisters only	Brothers only	Brothers and sisters	Totals
H	11*	31	33	31	106
C	22	15	32	31	100

* .05 level of significance
** .01 level of significance
† .001 level of significance

TABLE V-2 *Number of Children in Each Family*

	Only child	2	3	4	5	6	Over 6	Total
H	11	42	20	24	4	4	1	106
C	22	33	22	11	9	3	0	100

2 or fewer children and 69 per cent of the H-sample and 77 per cent of the C-sample came from families of 3 or fewer children.

The families in both C- and H-groups had more than twice as many male as female children (209:95 in the H-group; 184:77 in the C-group). Obviously, this does not represent the sex distribution in the population at large but occurred in our study because, by definition, each family had at least one male child. The H-patients have many more older than younger siblings (significant at .001). Although 56 per cent of H-patients and 57 per cent of C-patients were firstborn *male* children, Table V-3 demonstrates that the homosexual is more likely to be one of the younger children in the family.

As seen in Table V-4, significantly fewer homosexuals were first-born. These data indicate that the homosexual is more likely to be a younger than an older child in families with several children.[1]

Parental child preference

In the psychoanalyses of parents we have found that preference for any one child in families with several children is a psychopathologic

[1] The findings of Westwood are in accord with our own. Of the 127 "contacts" in his sample, 102 were either an only child, only son, youngest child, or youngest son (p. 13).

TABLE V-3 *Distribution of Older and Younger Brothers and Sisters of Patients*

	Older brother	Younger brother	Age not given	Total brothers	Older sister
H	54	30	19	103	53
C	41	30	13	84	35

symptom in the parent and is pathogenic for the preferred as well as for the nonpreferred child. Though the present study has no statistics on the prevalence of child preference in the general population, it is possible that this occurs in the majority of American families and even in the majority of families in most cultures. Certainly, in the sample studied, favoritism occurred as a result of parental psychopathology. In our clinical evaluations of parents who chose a favorite, we found that such choices were, for the most part, unrelated to the attributes of the preferred child, except as his traits articulated with parental neurotic needs, discussed more fully in Chapter III. With these comments in mind, let us now review parental preferences in our patient sample.

TABLE V-4 *Number of Children in Family Where Patient is Firstborn*

	2 children	3 children	4 children	5 children	Totals	Expected numbers
H	16	5	1	0	22	36*
C	12	5	0	2	19	29

The following comparisons may be noted in Table V-5:

Of 95 H-mothers who had the opportunity of choosing a favorite, 88 showed child preference. Favoritism occurs significantly more often among H-mothers than among C-mothers (61 of 78), which is significant at the .05 level. Of the favorites chosen among the H-mothers, 63 were the homosexual sons, 18 were other male siblings, while only 7 were daughters. In contrast, 39 C-mothers chose the patient, 15 chose another male child, and 7 chose a daughter.

Of the 95 H-fathers, 63 chose a favorite. Only 7 H-sons were among those chosen. In 25 H-cases another male child was the father's favorite, and in 31 H-cases a daughter was favored. Of the 78 C-fathers who had several children, 50 had favorites, among whom 22

Younger sister	Age not given	Total sisters	Older siblings total	Younger siblings total
28	14	95	107†	58†
27	15	77	76	57

were the patients. In 11 C-cases another male child was chosen, and in 17 C-cases a daughter was favored.

A clear pattern of patient-son favoritism emerges for all mothers. However, the H-mothers preferred their homosexual sons to their other sons at a ratio of 3.5:1 while C-mothers favored their patient sons at a ratio of 2.6:1 (differences are significant at the .05 level). Daughters were infrequently preferred in both groups.

The patterns of child preference among H-fathers differ radically from the favoritism patterns of H-mothers and C-fathers. Among the C-fathers who made choices, they preferred twice as many patient-sons to other sons. H-fathers who made choices preferred more than three times as many other sons to patient-sons, while among H-mothers a reverse pattern was noted.

We are going to analyze data relevant to parental preferences in three different arrangements of sibling distribution: cases with female siblings only; male siblings only; male and female siblings.

In Table V-6, the preference trends are very clear for the H-group.

TABLE V-5 *Parental Preferences in Total Sample*

	Mother prefers				
	Patient	Brother	Sister	Total children preferred	No child preferred
H	63*	18	7	88*	7
C	39	15	7	61	17

	Father prefers					
	Only children	Patient	Brother	Sister	Total children preferred	No child preferred
H	11	7	25	31	63	32
C	22	22	11	17	50	28

TABLE V-6 *Parental Preferences Where Patient Has Female Siblings Only*

	Mother prefers			Father prefers				
	Patient	Sister	No Preference	Patient	Sister	No Preference	No. of families	Total no. of sisters
H	25	4	2	1	19	11	31	40
C	11	3	1	5	7	3	15	18

TABLE V-7 *Parental Preferences Where Patient Has Male Siblings Only*

	Mother prefers			Father prefers		
	Patient	Brother	No preference	Patient	Brother	No preference
H	21	12	0	2	17	14
C	15	6	11	12	8	12

TABLE V-8 *Parental Preferences Where Patient Has Both Male and Female Siblings*

	Mother prefers						Father prefers				
	Patient	Brother	Sister	No preference	Total sisters	Total brothers	Patient	Brother	Sister	No preference	No. of families
H	17	6	3	5	55	49	4	8	12	7	31
C	13	9	4	5	59	45	5	3	10	13	31

The mother preferred her homosexual son and the father preferred a daughter. The C-mother also preferred her patient-son more frequently than she did her daughter, but the C-father preferred his patient-son almost as frequently as he did daughters. The H-father, in striking contrast, preferred 19 daughters to 1 H-son.

In Table V-7, maternal preference trends are also in the direction of preferring patient-sons to other sons. The C-fathers, too, preferred more patient-sons to other sons (12:8) while the H-fathers showed a marked reversal—17 other sons were favored and only 2 patient-sons were preferred.

In Table V-8, where the parents have a choice of favorites among sons and daughters other than the patient, we find that the H-mothers continued the trend of choosing more H-sons than other children. They favored twice as many H-sons over brothers and sisters combined, whereas the C-mother favored patient sons and other siblings in equal numbers. Both groups of mothers, however, significantly preferred their sons to daughters, though the fathers preferred daughters as frequently as they did sons. More H-fathers, however, preferred other sons to patient-sons while more C-fathers preferred patient-sons to other sons. Though these differences are not significant, the trends noted thus far continue.

Table V-6 is significant at the .001 level for the group of 31 homosexuals who have female siblings only, in four directions: mothers prefer sons to daughters; mothers prefer sons more frequently than do fathers; fathers prefer daughters more frequently than do mothers; fathers prefer daughters more frequently than they do sons. Mothers preferred 25 of 31 H-sons, while of 40 daughters only 4 were preferred. They consistently preferred the patient-son to all other siblings. Their preference was *specific* for the homosexual son and would appear to be heterosexually determined. We mean by this that such mothers not only have a heterosexual orientation to the son simply because he is a male, which may be "normal" if unimpeded by other attitudes as described in Chapter III, but *she has a particular kind of orientation.* The sex of her son becomes the nucleus around which her relationship to him develops and it becomes the determining factor in her preferring him to a daughter. The importance of sexually salient components in the mother's relatedness to her son helps explain why incestuous problems appear to be more central among male homosexuals than among heterosexuals.

We found a consistently pathologic maternal relatedness throughout the study, and especially among H-mothers who tended to be close-binding-intimate and frequently seductive toward their highly favored H-sons, who were with few exceptions preferred to daughters. In the 31 families where patients had male and female siblings, H-mothers favored sons to daughters at a ratio of 8:1. Our clinical evaluations of the mothers so favoring their sons, and our firsthand experience in the analyses of mothers who prefer sons to daughters, have consistently revealed that such mothers in almost all cases have difficulties in their relationships with other women. In fact, as a group, H-mothers tend to have defective relationships with both women *and* men. Their interpersonal problems lead to seeking emotional gratification through their children. Their concentration on the homosexual son is intense.

The pattern of child preference among H-fathers takes an opposite course. Where the patient was the only son in the family, of 31 H-sons 1 was preferred while of 40 daughters 19 were preferred. Among the C-fathers, the trends for the same category show notable differences. Of 15 sons, 5 were preferred; of 18 daughters, 7 were favored. The preponderance of daughter preference among the H-fathers has the same psychodynamic implications as son preferences among mothers. Psychoanalytic as well as popular literature have strongly emphasized the covert "romance" mothers act-out with their sons. The "romance" acted-out by fathers with daughters is a contrapuntal theme in many H-families.

In his analysis of the parent-son relationship, Westwood has stated: "This survey indicates that an over-developed relationship between the mother and son is not more important in the aetiology of homosexuality than the lack of relationship between father and son where the father is absent, is a nonentity, or is inadequate in some way." Our data strongly support these findings; in fact, the fathers we studied were more actively and destructively involved with their homosexual sons than is indicated in Westwood's study. The greater degree of aggression against the son apparent in our group of American fathers may be an indication of a national characteristic; or, it may be that our investigation into the relationship between H-fathers and *siblings* delineated the aggression more clearly. Now, why were the homosexual sons in our sample so unpopular with their fathers? Was it because they were inadequate and unattractive as children? Their mothers obviously did not find them undesirable—in 63 of 95 families the patients were their favorite sons (11 were only children). Of the 42 H-sons who were least favored by their fathers, 29 were preferred by their mothers in contrast to only 10 of 19 C-patients who were preferred by their mothers and least favored by their fathers. A child's status of "least preferred" is as pathogenic in personality development as is preference over other siblings—even more so—and is as much an indicator of parental psychopathology. Were the father's antagonism and aversion provoked by the close, intimate, sexually colored relationship between the mother and her preferred son? The close maternal-filial bond may have played an important part in arousing paternal resentment but, where it did, it seems merely to have reinforced pre-existing paternal psychopathology. A reasonably "normal" father protects his child from destructive maternal influences. He will step in as an interceding agent against undue "coddling," overprotectiveness, seductiveness, and so forth. But, as discussed in Chapter IV, these fathers will be either openly hostile, or will detach themselves and leave the "field," permitting the mother to take over the son's demasculinization. The paternal pattern of detachment and hostility is all the more poignant when one considers that in 42 H-cases the son was either the only child or the only son. In 63 of 95 H-families, the father formed preferential attachments to his children—but only in 7 instances was it to the H-son. Were paternal attitudes of rejection and hostility stimulated out of feelings of disappointment and failure because of the son's homosexuality? Although, in the main, H-sons were not athletic as children, neither were they effeminate. Only 18 fathers were *reported* to have been aware of their son's homosexuality.

We are led to the conclusion that the H-father's behavior toward his homosexual son was not simply reactive to the mother-son relationship. We evaluate him as a man who acts-out hostility by projecting onto a particular son a range of rivalry problems with other men. Thus, he enters into a hostile and destructive relationship with his own son. Further, the psychopathology of the father and the mother interlock in a complementary system of psychopathologic relatedness to this son—who becomes a homosexual.

THE PATIENT-SIBLING RELATIONSHIP

A series of questions probed identification mechanisms and admiring, hostile, and fearful attitudes in the patient-sibling relationship. Table V-9 provides data on three items: hatred, fear, and admiration.

TABLE V-9 *Siblings Hated/Feared and Admired in Families Where Patient Has Both Male and Female Siblings*

		Hated/Feared	Admired	No. of families
Brothers	H	18	7	31
	C	9	11	31
Sisters	H	2	13	
	C	7	7	

All responding psychoanalysts reported competitive problems among the total patient sample. The ubiquity of neurotic competition among the patients did not permit us to differentiate one group from another. We found, however, that competitive attitudes were covertly expressed significantly more often among homosexuals than among the comparison group whose aggressive, competitive hostilities were more frequently open and frank. The homosexuals more often used artistic ability while the comparisons used athletic ability as competitive techniques.

Male homosexuals, with few exceptions, report that they prefer men to women not only sexually but socially. One might assume that this masculine preference would be reflected in their relationships with male siblings. Yet, the data in Table V-9 indicate that precisely the opposite situation prevails. The male homosexuals in our study hated their brothers much more frequently than they did their sisters, and they hated brothers more frequently than was noted for C-patients. A reverse pattern is noted for positive attitudes: in the 31 H- and C-families having siblings of both sexes, H-patients admired 13 sisters and only 7 brothers while C-patients admired 11 brothers and 7 sisters. Usually, a male child tends to admire male siblings in preference to female siblings. This tendency is more apparent in the C-patients while a reverse tendency is noted among the H-patients.

Identification with Siblings

In both the homosexual and comparison groups, patients reported a wish to be like a sibling. Tables V-10 and V-11 show the direction of identification.

The wish to be like a sibling was more frequently noted among homosexuals than among comparison patients, though it was not statistically significant. Attempts to identify with a sibling were more frequently directed toward brothers than sisters in both groups, though 6 H-patients and 1 C-patient expressed a wish to be like a sister.

Of 14 H-patients who wished to be like a brother, 8 brothers were identified with the homosexual partner. Of 6 H-patients who wished to be like a sister, 1 sister was identified with the homosexual partner. Of the 14 brothers, 10 were admired, 3 of the 10 were hated/feared (Table V-11); of the 6 sisters, 4 were admired, 1 of the 4 was feared. Where identification is directed toward a sibling, one would expect that an *admired* sibling would be chosen as object, though hatred and fear do not necessarily preclude admiration and identification—as has been observed in individuals who identify with an aggressor. Although more C-patients than H-patients admired brothers, fewer comparisons had the wish to be like their brothers. This may indicate the greater need of the homosexual to find a male model for identification since, in most cases, the H-father does not fulfill such needs. In support of this assumption, we found that there were 28 fathers who were reported as "currently admired," but in no case where H-patients wanted to be like a brother was the father admired (significant at the .05 level).

Homosexual patients who identified the homosexual partners with a sibling

The responding psychoanalysts reported their clinical evaluations of the patients' relationships with homosexual partners. In 23 cases,

TABLE V-10 *Patients' Direction of Identification (A)*

	"Wanted to be like" a sibling	Brothers	Sisters	No. of families
H	20	14	6	95
C	7	6	1	78

TABLE V-11 *Patients' Direction of Identification (B)*

	"Wanted to be like" an admired brother	Admired but hated/feared brother	Total no. of brothers admired	No. of families
H	10	3	24	64
C	4	3	30	63

the impression was that the H-patients identified their homosexual partners with a sibling—17 with a brother and 6 with a sister. These patients may be divided into three groups:

Patients who identified the homosexual partner with a sister

Of the 6 H-patients in this group, 5 admired their sisters and 1 of the 5 hated/feared and admired her. The sister reported as "not admired" was the only one among the 6 where the patient wanted "to be like" a sister. These H-patients' relationships with their sisters appear to be positive. Identifying the homosexual partner with a sister may be an expression of the patient's love for her, including covert sexual feelings disguised in homosexuality.

Patients who identified the partner with a brother whom they "wanted to be like"

Of 8 brothers in this group who were identification objects, 4 were admired and only 1 was reported as hated/feared. In 3 cases, fraternal homosexual activity occurred in childhood and of these cases 1 brother also became a homosexual. Patients in this group may be seeking the idealized brother in the homosexual partner in an attempt to continue the fraternal identification.

Patients who identified the partner with a brother whom they did NOT wish "to be like"

Of 9 brothers in this group, 8 were hated/feared. The relationship between H-patients and these brothers was essentially negative. Where patients identify the homosexual partner with a hated/feared brother, the partner has a profound emotional value in that he may absorb an acting-out of hostile feelings against the brother.

The parents "set the stage," as it were, for the personality development of their children but each sibling may play a prominent role with the other. The following cases will illustrate how parentally induced sibling psychopathology reinforced existing psychologic disturbances in patients who became homosexual. Although it is not possible to assess in what proportion the determining factors in homosexuality were contributed by the siblings or by the parents, our study reveals that it is the parents who are the *prime movers* in the family system.

The following case illustrates female sibling participation in the psychodynamics of a patient, leading to a homosexual adaptation.

CASE NO. 78

The patient entered psychoanalysis two years ago in the hope of resolving his homosexual problem. Nothing in his gestures or posture betrayed him to be homosexual.

He was brought up in a small New England mill town. His father, a foreman in a textile factory, had a somewhat superior attitude toward the workers he supervised. The paternal grandfather had been a well-to-do real estate dealer who, having lost his fortune, suffered a depression and committed suicide when the father was about three or four years old. The grandmother lived in genteel poverty until her death when her sons were adolescents. The father made an adequate living for his family and during lay-off periods would help out at the bar of his older brother's restaurant, a rather elegant establishment close to Boston. When thus employed, the father would come home only one or two afternoons a week. He would often spend the better part of a week end at his brother's. He would enjoy talking to the customers and exchanging jokes with them. On occasion, he would get involved in betting on horses or gambling on a stock market tip. On rare occasions, the patient remembers going along, and this was considered a treat. He was very fond of his uncle and his cousins, twin girls slightly older than himself.

The mother got along poorly with her brother-in-law and even more so with her sister-in-law. She resented her husband's attachment to his brother and was extremely jealous of her sister-in-law's good looks and easy-going poise. The mother was of Pennsylvania Dutch extraction. The maternal grandfather had been a hard-bitten, bigoted, stern man. His wife feared him but went along with all his decisions. Both were strict disciplinarians. They had many children; the mother was among the older ones. When she graduated from high school she decided to enter a nurses' training school, mainly to get away from the cheerless, harsh atmosphere of her home. She met the patient's father, ten years her senior, and after a brief courtship quit nursing school, having completed about six months of her training, and married him. Her daughter was born a year later; the patient was three years younger than his sister.

The mother was apparently attracted to marriage because it promised freedom from the sexual restrictions of her background. But once in the marital situation she was unable to overcome the puritanical attitudes with which she was imbued. She was sexually prohibiting and prudish; she frightened the patient about masturbation. When dissatisfied with something she never complained openly but went about her duties with an air of tragedy and doom. When the father was around, the atmosphere "lifted." When he left, the children tended to cling to each other, partly in an effort to dispel the feeling of gloom generated by the mother. She was quite dependent on the father for her own feeling of well-being and held him responsible for any subjective discomfort. The patient was ten years old when his father died suddenly of coronary thrombosis.

After the initial shock wore off, a new family equilibrium was established. The mother refused financial help from her brother-in-law and decided to get along on the modest insurance funds she now had. More importantly, she decided to take up nursing again and become a practical nurse. The patient and his sister were left alone a good deal of the time. The mother cast the patient into the role of the "man of the family"; when she left on a case, she would leave instructions with him about running the house rather than with his older sister.

When the sister was about fourteen, she began to run around with a "fast" crowd. The patient was caught between feelings of jealousy and fear that his mother would find out. During psychoanalysis, the patient recalled a lively interest in one of his sister's boy friends. Although the patient had no conscious awareness of homosexual desires at the time, in reconstructing the situation psychoanalytically he himself suspected a homosexual attraction.

When the sister was fifteen, she became pregnant. She confided this to the patient before she told her mother. He was ashamed to go to his uncle whom he seldom saw now; he had no one to whom he could turn. From his account, he seemed more upset about the realistic consequences than was the sister. He also described feelings of being "trapped," "guilty," and "irresponsible." The sister had been aware of her pregnancy for about a month when the mother was told. Her reaction was of cataclysmic proportions. She became completely hysterical. The patient cowered in a corner while she berated her daughter, herself, and her life in general. An abortion was finally arranged. After it was over, and the sister had recovered, the mother continued to harp on it. She became obsessed with her daughter's illegitimate pregnancy and never lost an opportunity to refer to it and expand at length on the iniquity of her daughter's behavior. According to the patient, "It was the monkey on my back." The mother's untoward reaction to the sister's unscheduled pregnancy, the extent of the mother's puritanical fury, the weight of feelings of sexual shame, the mechanism of identification with the boy who impregnated the sister and the guilt thus precipitated, the belief that sexuality could create extreme disruption, harm and rejection—all were psychologically scarring, particularly since the incident occurred at puberty. The patient's more immediate reaction was one of withdrawal and depression. He began to avoid his peers and resigned from posts of leadership he had won at school. This almost dissociated state and depression continued for about a year.

The patient had not experienced any homosexual relations in childhood or adolescence. When he was fifteen, while wandering about in a forested area outside of town he met a girl whom he knew from the neighborhood. She participated in sex play with him and was the initiator in genital intercourse. He reacted quite blandly; he recalled no anxiety or guilt. This relationship continued for several years, though it had little emotional meaning to him. He did not consider her to be his "girl friend" nor did he try to strike up a relationship with other girls.

Around the time he was to graduate from high school, the sister married and left to live in New York with her husband, a man the mother disapproved of since he was of another religious faith. The patient had been an unusually good student and won a college scholarship. The mother bewailed her fate about being left alone, and the patient did not take advantage of his educational opportunity. Instead, he went to work in the mills as had his father before him.

When the patient was about twenty-one years old, he decided to break away and come to New York. He got a part-time job several evenings a week, and with his sister's help enrolled in college. He became a lawyer.

He had his first serious affair with an older woman after he graduated from law school. He lived with her for a year or two and gradually lost interest when her demands on him became too insistent. Some time later, he met a younger woman with whom he became more emotionally involved than he has been able to recognize consciously. They lived together for almost four years. He functioned well with her sexually and considered her "sweet and intelligent," but did not feel he loved her. When she began to press for marriage he broke off the relationship. Some months later, a young man about his own age joined his law firm. The patient was immediately attracted to him. "It was like a flash. I was in love for the first time." The partner had always been homosexual. The relationship had great intensity and passion and culminated with the shock of sudden death. The partner, during a depressive episode, committed suicide. The patient had two or three other exclusive relationships since then but was not able to sustain them. He began to have casual homosexual affairs. At the time he entered psychoanalysis his homosexual pattern was not one of exclusive relatedness to one partner. He had begun to frequent "gay" bars and often "cruised" compulsively in known homosexual areas.

The patient has maintained his deep attachment to his sister and has conscious affectionate feelings toward her. His dreams repeatedly demonstrated that she was identified with his mother and that he had sexual feelings toward both, accompanied by anxiety. As an example, one dream was reported in which he was standing at a railroad station with a woman. Two tough-looking sailors approached. The patient thought they looked menacing and he was frightened. In his associations, the patient identified the sailors with homosexuality and the woman with his sister. Also, the mother had come for a visit the day before and had made the trip by train. Three major themes appear: (1) a heterosexual element; (2) threat from aggressive males; (3) a flight into homosexuality. We assume the sailors to be a homosexual protection against sexual feelings for the sister-mother complex. We assume the menacing quality of the sailors to be the projection of the patient's competitive attitudes to males, defended against by homosexuality which, in turn, is a denial and protection against sexual feelings for the mother-sister combination.

As this case illustrates, parents "load" the situation for homosexuality; siblings may add the critical elements. The patient had strong affectional and incestuous ties to his older sister; the aftermath of her sexual activity precipitated a depression in the patient and reinforced guilt feelings about heterosexuality and fears of dire consequences attached to heterosexual fulfillment.

CASE NO. 17

An account of the following case also appears in Chapter IV, giving an indication of the father's role in the family. This brief report will emphasize the sibling relationships.

The patient was the third of four brothers. The eldest was

presumably the mother's favorite—at least she had concentrated most of her ambitions for producing a famous son onto him—yet she was closest and most intimate with the patient. The second son was rejected by both parents, receiving little affection or attention from the mother and none from the father. This boy had a somewhat behavior-disordered childhood and would frequently get into scrapes; he was a very aggressive child, fought a good deal, and often took his hostility out on the patient by beatings, threats and humiliation. The mother did nothing to intercede between the two. This second brother became allied with the youngest, a bright but neurotic individual who never achieved his early potentiality. The oldest brother took the role of the father with the patient—a controlling, dominating, and exploitative father who would order the patient around even when they were adults. Favors would be demanded as though a privilege were being bestowed. The patient submitted to his oldest brother for if he had not he would have been isolated from the fraternal group.

When aggressive male figures appeared in the patient's dreams, as they often did, they were identified with the second oldest, hostile-aggressive, brother. In this case, the fear of an attacking male, which psychodynamically has its roots in the Oedipus complex, is given reality focus as an older sibling acts-out a threatening role. The image of the oldest brother as the authority figure fused with that of the second brother, the attacking male, and became the symbol of all attacking, frightening males.

Parents' Attitudes Toward the Patient and Male Siblings

One group of questions probed the parents' reactions to the patient as compared with their reactions to his male siblings. These questions were divided into four categories: "intimate," "ambitious," "shows respect for," and "encourages masculinity"; and scored as: "more," "less," "none for any male sibling," and "equal." "Equal" was considered to be the answer indicating the most salutary parental attitude, and then in descending order, "more," "none for any," and "less." There were 64 H-families and 63 C-families with male siblings. The relevant data were collected on 56 H-families and 60 C-families.

TABLE V-12 *Contrast of Four Parental Attitudes toward Patient and Male*

	Intimate				Ambitious			
MOT								
	+	−	0	=	+	−	0	=
H[a]	36*	13	5	2**	20	12	7	11*
C[b]	18	16	8	17	19	10	5	24
FAT								
H	5	21	15	11	1*	20	15	17
C	17	16	8	16	8	10	14	23

[a] N = 56
[b] N = 60

On the "intimate" item, statistics for mother and father are approximately the same in the comparison group, while for the H-parents significant differences are noted. The H-mother is more intimate with the patient than she is with his male siblings in 36 of 56 (64 per cent) cases, while the H-father is more intimate with his H-son in only 5 cases. Of 60 C-mothers, 18 (30 per cent) were more intimate with the patient-son. In contrast to the H-father, the C-father was more intimate with the patient-son in 17 cases. Only 2 H-mothers were equally intimate with all sons as compared with 17 C-mothers (29 per cent). We again encounter the recurrent theme of H-parents. The mother stands out as overly close to her H-son and the father recedes into detachment.

On the "ambitious" item, 20 H-mothers (36 per cent) were more aspiring for the homosexual son than for other sons. Only 1 H-father (2 per cent) was more ambitious and 20 H-fathers (36 per cent) were less ambitious for H-sons than for other sons, in contrast to 10 C-fathers (17 per cent) who were less ambitious for their patient-sons. Once again, the oppositional, counteractive attitudes of H-parents toward the homosexual son come into view. The ratio of "equally ambitious" H-mothers to C-mothers was 11:24, significant at the .05 level. The mothers in both groups, however, were more aspiring for their sons than were the fathers, at a ratio of 39:9.

On the item "shows respect for," 17 H-mothers (30 per cent) had more respect for their patient-sons than for other male siblings, in contract to 3 H-fathers (5 per cent). As for having less respect for

Siblings

HER	Shows respect for				Encourages masculinity			
	+	−	0	=	+	−	0	=
	17	15	5	14	0*	20	10	22
	17	16	4	20	6	11	10	28
HER								
	3	27**	10	15	2	17	14	21
	9	12	9	25	8	9	14	18

the patient than for other sons, 27 H-fathers (48 per cent) as against 12 C-fathers (20 per cent) were reported. The minimizing, rejecting attitudes characteristic of H-fathers are well documented by the "respect" item.

Rather striking statistics were gathered on the item "encourages masculinity." While more H-mothers appeared in the plus column on the "intimate," "ambitious" and "shows respect for" items than did either H-fathers or C-mothers and fathers, there were *zero* H-mothers appearing in the plus column for "encourages masculinity" in H-sons more than in other sons. Further, the H-mother appeared more frequently than did any other parent in the minus column (20 of 60 cases), indicating that she was more often less encouraging of masculinity in her H-son than in her other sons. The statistics on the H-father run parallel to those on the H-mother in that he was reported as more encouraging of masculinity in the H-son in only 2 cases while in 17 cases (30 per cent) he was less encouraging. Balancing these gloomy extremes, there were 22 H-mothers (39 per cent) and 21 H-fathers (38 per cent) who were reported as "equally encouraging" of masculinity in their sons.

Over-all, there were consistently more C-parents than H-parents who showed the "equal" attitudes we consider to be most favorable toward sons, with one exception: H-fathers are equally encouraging of masculinity in their H-sons as are C-fathers in their C-sons. In the least favorable minus group, however, H-fathers appear with greater frequency than do C-fathers.

PSYCHOPATHOLOGY IN SIBLINGS

About 25 per cent of the families in both groups had at least 2 children who required psychiatric treatment. Major psychiatric illness was reported in the siblings of 33 H-patients and 26 C-patients. In some families more than one sibling was reported as suffering from a gross psychiatric disorder. A psychotic sibling was reported for 4 H-families and for 7 C-families, while borderline states were reported for 9 H- and 2 C-families.

At some time in childhood or early adolescence, several patients had had homosexual relations with a sibling. In 17 H-cases, 8 patients participated in homosexual activity with older brothers and 9 patients were involved with younger brothers. Early homosexual experience with a sibling in each of 3 comparison cases was had with an older brother. We assume that the older child most frequently initiated sexual play. Among these homosexual patients, more than half had had homosexual experiences with a younger brother, and most likely were the initiators, while among the comparisons they were probably the followers.

Of the 95 homosexual patients with siblings, 9 had siblings who also were homosexuals. This group was composed of 4 older and 4 younger brothers and 1 was a younger sister. In the comparison group of 78, 3 patients had homosexual siblings—1 older brother and 2 older sisters. In 64 H-families where the patient had male siblings, 8 families produced 2 homosexuals, which represented 12 per cent of the sample. Statistics on the prevalence of homosexuality in males are unobtainable, but 12 per cent appears to be an unusually high number. In the comparison group, there was only 1 male homosexual in the 63 families where the patient had male siblings. The difference between H- and C-families is significant at the .05 level.

Our sample of siblings who were homosexual is too small to warrant any conclusions; it points up another problem for further investigation. Most of the homosexual patients did not have homosexual siblings. This supports our assumption that parents form a special relationship with their homosexual son. The capacity to form a special filial relationship does not, of course, preclude the possibility of the parents' exerting similar influences on more than one child. To take two instances of families who produced more than one homosexual, in one case the mother switched child preference from the patient to a younger male sibling, and in the second the mother switched from an older homosexual sibling to the homosexual patient. In both instances, there was a span of seven to eight years between the births of the proximal siblings.

SUMMARY

The sibling data support our assumption stated in previous chapters that at least one H-parent (and usually both H-parents) has special and characteristic attitudes toward the homosexual son. These attitudes are highly pathologic but are not usually directed toward other siblings in the family. The H-mother clearly prefers her homosexual son to her other children. If she has sons only, she is most likely to prefer her homosexual son. In families with male and female children, she seldom prefers a daughter. Therefore, child preference sharply divides according to sex of child. In view of the low frequency of daughter preference, we are led to infer that the H-mother has disturbed relationships not only with her daughters but with women in general. In the differentiated relationship of the H-mother and her homosexual son, she is closer and more intimate with him than with any of her other children. Yet, she never encourages him toward attitudes and behavior associated with the masculine role more than she will her other sons. In fact, she is frequently less encouraging.

The H-father has a specifically negative attitude toward his homosexual son as contrasted with his attitude toward his other children. The homosexual son is rarely the father's preferred child; rather, he is usually least preferred by his father. The H-father has the *capacity* to be affectionate and even preferential to sons but not to his homosexual son. In families where there are male children only, H-fathers prefer sons as frequently as do C-fathers; but, whereas the C-father more often prefers his patient-son to nonpatient sons, the H-father prefers a heterosexual son to his homosexual son nine times more frequently. In families with sons and daughters, the H-father prefers daughters to sons at statistically significant levels. His child preferences, as those of the H-mother, divide along sexual lines, though less sharply. The C-fathers do not show a gender preference pattern. This suggests that sexual factors play determining roles in the relationship of the H-father with his children, most particularly, factors of sexual rivalry with his homosexual son.

Negative attitudes toward brothers and positive attitudes toward sisters appear with greater frequency among homosexual than among comparison patients. The homosexual hates/fears his brothers more often than he hates/fears his sisters, while sibling hatred/fear among comparison patients does not indicate gender preference. The homosexual more often admires his sisters than he does his brothers while the comparison patient more often admires his brothers than he does his sisters. More homosexuals are hostile to brothers than are comparison patients, and more homosexual than comparison patients indicate positive feelings toward their sisters.

These data point to some of the origins of the homosexual's hostile attitudes toward males and covertly positive attitudes toward females. The homosexual is competitive with his brothers for the mother, but he is much less competitive with his sisters for the mother. The comparison group manifests no such differences in attitude toward brothers and sisters. However, the homosexual will compete with his sisters for the *father* and he will be hostile to sisters preferred by the father. This finding further attests to the seeking and striving for paternal-like affection noted among many homosexuals.

Despite the greater frequency of hostility and fear of brothers, the homosexual nevertheless wishes to identify with a brother more frequently than does the comparison patient. The tendency toward fraternal identification reflects the homosexual's greater need for male models with whom to identify, other than the father. Supporting this assumption, we found a greater trend toward admiring siblings who are preferred by the father than by the mother. Several homosexual patients wished to be like their admired sisters.

Homosexual patients who identified their partners with siblings can be divided into three categories:

Those who identified partner with an admired brother. We assume that the wish for a positive identification with an admired male who offers acceptance is a dominant psychodynamic characteristic of this group.

Those who identified the partner with a brother with whom the sibling interaction was predominantly hostile. Patients in this group "use" the partner to act-out hostile, destructive, and competitive attitudes toward males.

Patients who identified the partner with an admired sister. The cardinal dynamic among these cases is the covert expression of the love relationship with a sister.

Although the majority of homosexual patients studied did not have homosexual siblings, there were significantly more homosexual male siblings in the families of homosexual patients than occurred among the comparison group.

VI

The Triangular System

OUR ATTENTION thus far has been focused on the relationship of our patients with members of the *nuclear* family—their parents and siblings. A family may also be thought of as an extended system of relationships—grandparents, aunts, uncles, cousins—who maintain interchange of various kinds with each related nuclear family. Kinship influences and group membership are not, however, immediately pertinent to our present analysis. Our interest here is to consider the patient within the context of a three-member system—mother, father, and child.

As Parsons and Bales have emphasized, the nuclear family is not an independent unit but a small and highly differentiated social system interpenetrating with other structures and systems in the broader society. However, "that it [nuclear family] is itself a sub-system of a larger system is of course a sociological commonplace. But to break it, in turn, down into sub-systems is a less familiar way of looking at it. . . . In certain crucially important respects, the very young child does not participate in, is not fully a 'member' of his whole family, but only a sub-system of it, the mother-child sub-system. The marriage pair constitute another sub-system as may, for certain purposes, also the child with all his siblings, all the males in the family, all the females, etc. In fact, any combination of two or more members as differentiated from one or more other members may be treated as a *social* system which is a sub-system of the family as a whole."

We have selected the patient-mother-father unit for analysis as a sub-system since this unit system embraces basic interpersonal, interactive processes that lay the foundations of personality development. We believe that personality for the most part is forged within the triangular system of the nuclear family. It follows then that personality maladaptation must also be primarily rooted here.

Families with more than one child have more than one triangular system, each interpenetrating with other sub-systems of the nuclear family. If a child is the firstborn, his parent-child triad will differ environmentally from the second-, third-, or fourth-born; in fact, each such unit differs from others. The "only" child is destined to grow up in a "closed" triangular system as compared with the child who grows up in a nest of intermeshing "open" triads where other siblings are constantly influencing the interactive responses of the people around him. Parental roles may vary subtly or grossly from one triad to another. Certainly, as our data have shown, the psychological environment of the homosexual son differs critically from that of his siblings (Chapter V). The quality and style of parental attitudes and discipline, the personality and behavior of individual members, the resonating, reverberating communications, signals, and cues—verbal and nonverbal, conscious and unconscious—the vast, complex tapestry of all mutually interacting patterns operant in the family, all influence the dynamics of the triangular system.

In Chapters III and IV we classified the parents into descriptive categories on the basis of parent-child relations as reflected by item responses and the ways in which the responses "clustered." By selecting a specific mother category, such as CBI, we were able to arrive at some "hunches" about the triangular system. For example, if a CBI mother preferred her homosexual son to her other children, allied with him, consistently sided with him against her husband, protected him against his father, and had a reciprocal confidant relationship with him, a picture of a dyadic coalition between mother and son emerges in which the father appears as a kind of "isolate" within the triangular system. Although most fathers were detached from their H-sons, 13 H-fathers were not-detached. While the CBI mother-son and detached father-son triad suggests a dynamic structure of a pair and a singleton with mother and son closely allied, the CBI mother-son and not detached father-son triad suggests a high rate of parent-child interaction within the triangular system. Thus, the mother and father classifications which were originally constructed on the basis of responses to items probing parent-child relationships, are in themselves indicators of important elements which make up the triangular system.

Now let us recall that in the analysis of the mother-son relationship some of the main variables were close-binding intimacy, controlling dominance, detachment, and so forth; in the father-son relationship some of the major variables were detachment-hostility, indifference, ambivalence, and so forth. On the basis of these classifications of parents (Chapters III and IV) we were able to delineate 51 types of mother-son and father-son configurations. There were 8 mother-son classifications and 9 father-son classifications, permitting a possibility of 72 combinations—but as Table VI-1 shows, 51 such combinations actually emerged. (Note that there were 10 H-sons who had CBI mothers and detached-ambivalent fathers; 30 H-sons had CBI mothers and detached-hostile fathers; 3 C-sons had not-detached, hostile mothers and not-detached, hostile fathers, and so forth.)

TABLE VI-1 *Triangular Combinations*

	Mothers	Fathers	Sons	
			H	C
1.	Close-Binding Intimate	Detached-Ambivalent	10	6
2.	Close-Binding Intimate	Detached-Hostile	30	11
3.	Close-Binding Intimate	Detached-Indifferent	13	3
4.	Close-Binding Intimate	Detached-Dominating-Exploitative	1	0
5.	Close-Binding Intimate	Not-Detached-Warmly related	0	1
6.	Close-Binding Intimate	Not-Detached-Ambivalent	5	5
7.	Close-Binding Intimate	Not-Detached-Hostile	3	2
8.	Close-Binding Intimate	Not-Detached-Overprotective	1	4
9.	Close-Binding Intimate	Absent	8	0
10.	Close-Binding Intimate	Unclassified	2	0
11.	Controlling-Dominating	Detached-Ambivalent	1	9
12.	Controlling-Dominating	Detached-Hostile	4	7
13.	Controlling-Dominating	Detached-Indifferent	1	2
14.	Controlling-Dominating	Detached-Dominating-Exploitative	1	0
15.	Controlling-Dominating	Not-Detached-Warmly related	0	3
16.	Controlling-Dominating	Not-Detached-Ambivalent	0	3
17.	Controlling-Dominating	Not-Detached-Hostile	0	2
18.	Controlling-Dominating	Not-Detached-Overprotective	1	1
19.	Controlling-Dominating	Absent	1	0
20.	Not-Detached-Hostile	Detached-Ambivalent	1	1
21.	Not-Detached-Hostile	Detached-Hostile	5	1
22.	Not-Detached-Hostile	Detached-Indifferent	0	1
23.	Not-Detached-Hostile	Not-Detached-Hostile	0	3
24.	Not-Detached-Hostile	Not-Detached-Overprotective	1	0

TABLE VI-1 *Triangular Combinations* (Cont'd.)

	Mothers	Fathers	Sons H	Sons C
25.	Not-Detached-Hostile	Not-Detached-Absent	1	0
26.	Detached-Hostile	Detached-Ambivalent	1	0
27.	Detached-Hostile	Detached-Hostile	1	0
28.	Detached-Hostile	Detached-Indifferent	1	1
29.	Detached-Hostile	Not-Detached-Ambivalent	1	0
30.	Detached-Hostile	Not-Detached-Hostile	0	1
31.	Detached-Hostile	Absent	0	1
32.	Detached-Indifferent	Detached-Ambivalent	1	3
33.	Detached-Indifferent	Detached-Hostile	1	0
34.	Detached-Indifferent	Detached-Indifferent	1	1
35.	Detached-Indifferent	Detached-Dominating-Exploitative	1	0
36.	Detached-Indifferent	Not-Detached-Ambivalent	0	1
37.	Detached-Indifferent	Not-Detached-Hostile	1	0
38.	Detached-Indifferent	Absent	2	1
39.	Mother Surrogate	Detached-Hostile	1	1
40.	Mother Surrogate	Detached-Indifferent	1	0
41.	Unclassified	Detached-Hostile	2	1
42.	Unclassified	Detached-Indifferent	1	1
43.	Unclassified	Not-Detached-Hostile	0	2
44.	Unclassified	Absent	0	1
45.	Unclassified	Unclassified	0	1
46.	Not remarkable	Detached-Ambivalent	0	1
47.	Not remarkable	Detached-Hostile	0	4
48.	Not remarkable	Not-Detached-Warmly related	0	4
49.	Not remarkable	Not-Detached-Ambivalent	0	8
50.	Not remarkable	Not-Detached-Hostile	0	1
51.	Not remarkable	Absent	0	1
	TOTALS		106	100

As shown in Table VI-1, the most common grouping among the parental categories was the CBI mother paired with the detached-hostile father. Of 206 patients in our total sample, 41 had this type of parental combination—30 homosexuals and 11 comparisons. Of the 11 C-patients in this group, information about homosexual problems was available on 9 patients. Of these 9 C-patients, 6 had severe homosexual problems and one had moderately severe homosexual problems. Thus, 67 per cent of the C-patients with the combination of a CBI mother and detached-hostile father had severe homosexual problems as compared with 22 per cent of the C-patients who had severe homosexual problems distributed in the remainder of the parent categories in the C-sample. We are led to believe that the triad characterized by maternal close-binding intimacy and paternal detachment-hostility is the "classic" pattern most conducive to promoting homosexuality or severe homosexual problems in the son. To be sure, 76 sons became homosexual without this parental combination and 11 C-patients who had such parents did not become homosexual. The themes, nuances, combinations, coalitions, attitudes, feelings, beliefs, and the whole interplay of human interaction and responsivity within triangular systems are as numerous and varied as there are families with children. Nevertheless, in our construction certain parent-child combinations were *not* represented in the homosexual sample: Not remarkable mothers paired with any type of father, or Warmly related fathers paired with any type of mother were absent in the nuclear triads of homosexuals.

The next most common combinations were: CBI mother and detached-indifferent father (13 H-sons and 3 C-sons); CBI mother and detached-ambivalent father (10 H-sons and 6 C-sons); CBI mother and absent father (8 H-sons and 0 C-sons). These four groups account for 58 per cent of the total H-sample. The remainder (42 per cent) are distributed in 30 other combinations.

Relationship between the Parents

Another way of approaching the triangular system is through the study of the interparental relationship. Every nuclear family has behind it the life history of the parental pair including the manifold and multitudinous influences in the life experience of each that motivated a coupling in marriage. What about the parents in our study? Did their choices at the outset appear to represent to them a complementarity of personality and reciprocity of love and sexuality? Did neurotic maneuvers of one kind or another play a part in or wholly determine marital choice? Were their marriages happy at first only to become unsatisfactory later? Or did they maintain happy marriages though their offspring developed psychiatric problems? We can only infer what brought these marital pairs together, but we have reliable information of their ongoing relationships from the reports of sons to their psychoanalysts. Answers to questions probing the interparental relationship appear in Table VI-2.

Item 1: "Can the relationship between the parents be described as 'good,' 'fair,' or 'poor'?" Answers to Item 1 did not differentiate the

H- and C-parents. Few sons regarded the parental relationship as "good," although this designation appeared more frequently for C-parents. Patients regarded parental relationships as "poor" in more than half the cases in both groups and as "fair" among the rest. Of the total sample only 20 per cent recalled witnessing affectionate interchange between parents while 65 per cent recalled frequent arguments. Based on the marital data we have gathered, we assume that the need for psychoanalytic treatment among our patient sample indicates an association between poor parental marital relationships and maladaptive processes in the sons.

H-parents were significantly differentiated from C-parents on two

TABLE VI-2 *Questions Probing Interparental Relationships*

	H	C
N =	106	100
1. Can relations between parents be described as:		
Good	5	14
Fair	41	34
Poor	60	52
2 Were there open demonstrations of affection between parents?		
Yes	22	19
3. Were there frequent arguments between parents?		
Yes	68	65
4. How much time did mother spend with father?**		
Great deal	1	13
Average	44	49
Little	37	24
Very little	22	13
No answer	2	1
5. Did they share similar interests?**		
Yes	21	37
No	82	61
No answer	3	2
6. Did they usually eat together?		
Yes	73	73
No	29	27
No answer	4	

* .05 level of significance
** .01 level of significance
† .001 level of significance

items: as a group, C-parents spent more time with each other than did H-parents; they also more frequently shared each other's interests. Mutuality of interest and time spent together were judged as indicators of closeness which more frequently occurred among C-parents than among H-parents, significant at the .01 level. Based on our clinical observations, we have found that sharing of interests need not be based on the objective attractiveness of an "interest" to either marital partner; it rather reflects a satisfying, interpersonal attachment, e.g., a man may be a physicist and his wife an artist. She may indeed lack the technical background to understand the details of her husband's work and, conversely, he of hers. But a mutuality of sympathy, acceptance, concern, and respect will lead each to participate, even if tangentially, in the affairs of the other. Each will be interested in the partner's progress, activities, and so forth, without necessarily being knowledgeable or "attracted" to the work or interests as such.

TABLE VI-3 *Parental Dominance, Contempt, and Attitudes that the Spouse Is Inferior*

	H	C
N=	106	100
1. Which parent was dominant in family decisions?		
Mother	61	55
Father	42	39
Neither	1	5
No answer	2	1
2. Was contempt by one parent for the other a prominent part of the parental relationship?		
Yes	62	51
No	41	48
No answer	3	1
Which parent showed contempt?		
Mother	46	28*
Father	11	18
Reciprocal	5	5
3. Was one parent regarded as inferior by the other?		
Yes	66	55
No	37	44
No answer	3	1
Which one was judged as inferior?		
Mother	18	21
Father	46	29*
Reciprocal	2	5

We judged interparental *detachment* on the basis of time spent together. If an average or great deal of time was spent together, we judged them to be *not-detached;* if less than average, they were judged as *detached.* There were 18 H-parents who were not-detached and shared similar interests as compared with 35 C-parents, and 59 H-parents who were detached without sharing interests as compared to 36 C-parents.

In 103 H-families and 94 C-families one parent was dominant. In Westwood's study of homosexuals one parent was dominant in 109 of 127 families; 57 per cent were dominant mothers; 29 per cent were dominant fathers. In our study of 106 H-families 61 mothers were dominant (58 per cent) and 42 fathers (40 per cent), as compared with 55 of 100 C-mothers and 39 C-fathers.

Table VI-3 lists 3 items tapping parental dominance, attitudes of contempt toward the partner, and attitudes that the partner is inferior. The H-mother was contemptuous of her husband with significantly greater frequency than was the C-mother; the H-mother also regarded her spouse as her inferior more frequently.

Tables VI-4 and VI-5 are contingency tables showing the association between marital dominance and contempt for the partner. Among H-mothers dominance and contempt for husbands appeared with greater frequency than among C-mothers (46:28, significant at the .01 level).

Tables VI-6 and VI-7 show the association between marital dominance and the inferior position in which the spouse is regarded. One parent in the majority of H- and C-families regarded the spouse as inferior—66 H-parents and 55 C-parents (see Table VI-3). Mothers,

TABLE VI-4 *Mothers Who Were Dominant and Showed Contempt for Fathers*

	H		C	
	Mothers dominant	Not dominant	Mothers dominant	Not dominant
Mothers showed contempt for fathers	46	5	28	5
Did not	15	37	27	40

Significance: H .01; C .01

TABLE VI-5 *Fathers Who Were Dominant and Showed Contempt for Mothers*

	H		C	
	Fathers dominant	Not dominant	Fathers dominant	Not dominant
Fathers showed contempt for mothers	12	4	19	4
Did not	30	57	20	56

Significance: H .01; C .01

TABLE VI-6 *Mother Regarded Father as Inferior Associated with Maternal Dominance*

	H		C	
	Mother dominant	Not dominant	Mother dominant	Not dominant
Mother regarded father as inferior	43	5	30	4
Did not	18	37	25	41

Significance: H .001; C .001

TABLE VI-7 *Father Regarded Mother as Inferior Associated with Paternal Dominance*

	H		C	
	Father dominant	Not dominant	Father dominant	Not dominant
Father regarded mother as inferior	18	2	19	7
Did not	23	60	20	53

Significance: H .001; C .001

however, regarded fathers as inferior more frequently than was the case in the reverse direction.

There is a high positive correlation between the mother's contempt for her husband and maternal dominance in the family. Contempt for the husband was almost always accompanied by wifely dominance in both samples though wifely dominance was not necessarily accompanied by contempt for the husband. In one-half of the C-families the dominant mother was not contemptuous of her husband though in only one-quarter of the cases were the dominant H-mothers not contemptuous of marital partners.

As for the fathers, the data reveal that contempt for the wife was usually accompanied by dominance, a dynamic resembling that of wives who showed contempt for the husbands. Generalizing from our data, either partner of a marriage who has contempt for the spouse has an 86 per cent chance of being dominant, though the converse does not hold (Table VI-4). In our sample of dominant H-fathers, 72 per cent did not have contempt for their wives, while among dominant C-fathers 50 per cent did not have contempt for their wives. In comparing the fathers with the mothers we found that whereas the dominant H-father did not view his wife with contempt in 72 per cent of the cases, the dominant H-mother was not contemptuous of her husband in only 25 per cent of the cases. Thus, the H-father is more likely to be dominant without feeling contempt for the spouse than is the H-mother. The trend shifts for C-mothers and C-fathers—half of each group showed dominance without contempt for the marital partner.

Table VI-8 shows that in families where there is a pairing of CBI mothers with detached fathers, a significant positive association obtains between the wife's contempt for her husband and close-binding intimacy with the son.

TABLE VI-8 *Mother's Contempt for Father in CBI Mother—Detached Father Pairs as Against All Other Types of Parents*

	H		C	
	Mother had contempt	Did not	Mother had contempt	Did not
CBI mother-detached father pair	31	19	11	9
All others	20	33	22	57

Significance: H .05; C .05

Thus far in our analysis, feelings and expressions of contempt and attitudes that the spouse is inferior have been handled as two discrete variables. In the interest of conceptual economy they may be logically merged without loss of refinement into the unitary variable "minimizing." Henceforth we will refer to "dominant-minimizing" and "dominant-not minimizing" as a sequence of paired variables. Dominance represents the *power* position of one parent over the other while minimizing attitudes both express and evoke hostile affects. Minimization, as we have defined it, is a behavioral mode which may be motivated by a variety of defensive needs, e.g., it may be psychologically useful as justification for hostility and perhaps as a disguise for guilt. It may be a maneuver of denial for feelings of rejection, lack of acceptance by the spouse, and so forth. As behaviorally expressed, however, the recipient perceives minimization as a hostile attitude.

The nuclear family and its sub-systems contain power elements and its leaders exercise power prerogatives. In the democratic family, parental power and authority are shared and, relative to the situation, leadership by offspring is encouraged. The children of democratic families, therefore, may perceive power as an element of *parental* and individual responsibility rather than as a feminine or masculine attribute; and they learn that at appropriate times they too may exercise family leadership. In all but 9 families of the total patient sample, clear-cut dominance of one parent over the other was noted. In the H-group only one case was reported where neither parent was dominant. With few exceptions, patients were exposed to a sex-linked power image.

Since we conceive of the power structure as a central element in family life and its triangular sub-systems, we constructed four types of interparental classes based upon a "power-affect" parameter of marital dominance-minimization: dominant-minimizing father; dominant-not-minimizing father; dominant-minimizing mother; dominant-not-minimizing mother.

A fifth group contains 11 H-marital pairs and 5 C-marital pairs where no clear-cut dominance pattern emerged.

Table VI-9 presents the distribution of the total patient population in the four interparental classes. Note that the largest single aggregate

TABLE VI-9 *Distribution of Interparental Dominance-Minimizing Systems*

	H	C
1. Father Dominant-Minimizing	18	25
2. Father Dominant, Not-Minimizing	19	16
3. Mother Dominant-Minimizing	46	32
4. Mother Dominant, Not-Minimizing	12	22
5. Mixed Groups	11	5
	106	100

of cases in both the H- and C-samples appears in Class 3 where the mother was dominant and minimizing toward her husband. It includes 43 per cent of the H-sample and 32 per cent of the C-sample.

As shown in Table VI-10, 22 questionnaire items were selected to ascertain how affirmative answers were distributed in the four interparental classes. It was anticipated that such a breakdown would furnish clues to characteristics of each parental class.

A useful, rapid method for outlining salient characteristics of the

TABLE VI-10 *Interparental Dominance-Minimizing Systems (in per cent)*

	H				C			
Class	1	2	3	4	1	2	3	4
N =	18	19	46	12	25	16	32	22
1. Son hates father	83	58	63	50	44	38	41	36
2. Son fears father	94	79	59	67	88	69	31	41
3. Son hates mother	16	16	39	33	28	25	38	32
4. Son fears mother	22	21	59	50	28	18	66	50
5. Son respects father	28	21	22	67	44	75	28	50
6. Son respects mother	67	63	46	83	40	75	63	68
7. Son admires father	28	5	9	17	48	63	28	36
8. Son admires mother	33	63	48	56	44	56	41	50
9. Patient coped more easily with mother	83	68	46	67	56	50	34	41
10. Patient sided with mother	78	74	59	67	56	44	63	55
11. Feared physical injury from father	83	79	48	33	60	50	41	36
12. Feared genital injury	83	53	59	50	48	44	50	45
13. Aversion female genitals	89	74	65	83	24	38	44	27
14. Feared angering father	83	84	59	75	64	50	47	55
15. Mother allies with son	72	42	76	42	44	18	72	27
16. Mother openly prefers son to husband	72	42	74	33	44	18	75	32
17. Confidant/confidante relationship with mother	61	37	67	58	28	18	63	23
18. Mother overprotective	44	58	67	67	40	44	41	45
19. Patient is mother's favorite[a]	67	65	71	58	53	75	43	30
20. Mother is seductive	67	42	63	56	32	38	44	32
21. Mother spends great deal of time with son	67	42	52	58	20	25	47	18
22. Mother protected son from father	56	47	37	33	36	31	34	55

[a] Based on number of families where patient had siblings.

parent-child triad also becomes available by referring to Table VI-11. It presents the distribution of patients in the "cross-fire" of two sub-systems: parent-child combinations have been cross-tabulated with interparental power combinations. The triangular sub-systems may be viewed from these two perspectives: the parents' relatedness to the son and to each other. The table may at first glance appear complex but is not difficult to follow and can be readily understood by the reader. A code for the parental designations is included in Table VI-11A. The reader may refer to Chapters III and IV respectively for a review of all descriptive categories of mothers and fathers who were not included in the table because of a scattered distribution (55 sets of parents were distributed in 36 parent-son combinations).

TABLE VI-11 *Distribution of Cases in Interparental Systems*

			Class 1		Class 2		Class 3		Class 4		Group 5 (mixed)	
			H	C	H	C	H	C	H	C	H	C
1.	CBI/DA	(16)	1	1	2	0	7	3	0	2	0	0
2.	CBI/DH	(41)	7	2	8	2	11	5	3	1	1	1
3.	CBI/DI	(16)	0	0	0	0	9	3	2	0	2	0
4.	CBI/NDA	(10)	4	0	0	1	1	3	0	1	0	0
5.	CBI/NDH	(5)	1	1	0	0	0	0	1	1	1	0
6.	CBI/NDO	(4)	0	2	0	0	1	0	0	1	0	0
7.	CBI/Abs	(8)	0	0	0	0	2	0	2	0	4	0
8.	CD/DA	(10)	0	2	1	0	0	3	0	3	0	1
9.	CD/DH	(11)	0	4	1	1	1	1	2	1	0	0
10.	NDH/DH	(6)	1	1	2	0	2	0	0	0	0	0
11.	DI/DA	(4)	0	1	0	0	1	1	0	0	0	1
12.	Unc/DH	(4)	0	1	2	0	0	1	0	0	0	0
13.	NR/DH	(4)	0	1	0	0	0	0	0	2	0	1
14.	NR/WR	(5)	0	0	0	2	0	0	0	3	0	0
15.	NR/NDA	(7)	0	2	0	5	0	0	0	0	0	0
		151	14	18	16	11	35	20	10	15	8	4
36 Other systems		55	4	7	3	5	11	12	2	7	3	1
		206	18	25	19	16	46	32	12	22	11	5

Table VI-12 analyzes the association between marital dominance and dominating behavior toward the son. This table shows the distribution of dominating parent-son behavior in relation to interparental dominance-minimizing classes. Note that the dominant husband is also a dominating father and that the dominant wife is a dominating mother.

TABLE VI-11A *Code to Table VI-11*

		Mother	Father
1.	CBI/DA	Close-Binding Intimate	Detached-Ambivalent
2.	CBI/DH	Close-Binding Intimate	Detached-Hostile
3.	CBI/DI	Close-Binding Intimate	Detached-Indifferent
4.	CBI/NDA	Close-Binding Intimate	Not-Detached-Ambivalent
5.	CBI/NDH	Close-Binding Intimate	Not-Detached-Hostile
6.	CBI/NDO	Close-Binding Intimate	Not-Detached-Overprotective
7.	CBI/Abs	Close-Binding Intimate	Absent
8.	CD/DA	Controlling-Dominant	Detached-Ambivalent
9.	CD/DH	Controlling-Dominant	Detached-Hostile
10.	NDH/DH	Not-Detached-Hostile	Detached-Hostile
11.	DI/DA	Detached-Indifferent	Detached-Ambivalent
12.	Unc/DH	Unclassified	Detached-Hostile
13.	NR/DH	Not Remarkable	Detached-Hostile
14.	NR/WR	Not Remarkable	Warmly Related
15.	NR/NDA	Not Remarkable	Not-Detached-Ambivalent

TABLE VI-12 *Dominating Parent and Dominant Spouse*

		Total N in each class	Mother dominates son	Father dominates son
Class 1	H	18	8	17
	C	25	10	20
Class 2	H	19	13	15
	C	16	6	11
Class 3	H	46	43	4
	C	32	30	7
Class 4	H	12	11	3
	C	22	16	3
Group 5	H	11	11	3
	C	5	3	1

Table VI-13 shows the distribution of detached and not-detached marital pairs according to the four interparental *power-affect* classes.

Class I:
Father dominates and minimizes mother

Of 18 H-fathers and 9 C-fathers who were classified as *indifferent* to their sons, none appeared in Class 1. The H-fathers who were dominant and minimized their wives were either hostile or ambivalent

TABLE VI-13 *Interparental Detachment and Interparental Power Classes*

		Not-detached with similar interests	Not-detached without similar interests	Detached with similar interests	Detached without similar interests	Totals
Class 1	H	2	7	0	9	18
	C	6	4	0	15	25
Class 2	H	7	5	0	7	19
	C	10	6	0	0	16
Class 3	H	7	8	2	29	46
	C	7	9	1	15	32
Class 4	H	1	5	0	6	12
	C	10	6	0	6	22
Group 5	H	1	0	0	8	9 (2 No answers)
	C	2	1	1	1	5

to the sons whom they dominated. (Of 18 H-fathers, 17 dominated their sons; of 25 C-fathers, 20 dominated their sons. See Table VI-12.) Among the dominant husbands, including those who were not minimizing, there was only 1 indifferent father in 37 H-cases and none in 41 C-cases, significant at the .05 level. This datum is quite striking and strongly suggests that a dominant husband actively participated in the family and in the patient's triangular unit. Further supporting this premise is the finding that in the entire H-sample only 13 fathers were classified as not detached from their sons. Yet, of these 13 fathers, 6 appeared in Class 1. The over-representation of not detached fathers in Class 1 is significant beyond the .01 level. Of the 6 dominant-minimizing H-husbands who were not detached fathers, 4 were also not detached from their wives; 5 were married to women who had a close-binding intimate relationship with the homosexual son. In only 2 of these 18 H-cases, the husbands were both not detached from their wives and shared similar interests; in each instance the patient became heterosexual.

The various mother categories in Class 1 were distributed proportionately. For example, CBI mothers represent 69 per cent of the total number of H-mothers (73). Of the 18 H-mothers in Class 1, 72 per cent were CBI. Since there were more CBI H-mothers than CBI

C-mothers in the total sample, fewer CBI C-mothers appear here. The lowest percentage of H-mothers who dominated their sons, 8 of 18 (44 per cent) occur in Class 1; 10 of the 25 C-mothers (40 per cent) dominated their sons (see Table VI-12). Thus, when the father was dominant and minimized his wife, the mother tended to dominate the son less frequently than did mothers who were dominant-minimizing wives, significant at the .001 level. Relationships between marital pairs were significantly poorer in the C-group here than in any other class; their sons regarded the parental relationship as "poor" in 80 per cent of the cases. A comparable statistic emerged for the H-marital pairs; 67 per cent of the relationships were regarded as "poor," though Class 3 H-marriages were somewhat worse—72 per cent. It is self-evident that minimizing behavior on the part of one marital partner toward the other goes along with a poor relationship. However, when the item responses tapping "good," fair," or "poor" interparental relationships were tabulated in the *power-affect* classes, this permitted us to locate the class of marital pairing that had the best or poorest relationships; e.g., where the husband was dominant but not minimizing, the relationships were more frequently "fair" or "good" than when the mother was dominant but not minimizing.

In both H- and C-samples there was a higher percentage of patients who hated their fathers, feared them, and feared physical injury from them than in the other three classes. While no significant differences were revealed between Class 1 and Class 3 for H-patients on the item "feared father," fewer C-patients in Class 3 feared their fathers than in Class 1, which was significant at the .01 level. The highest percentage of H-patients who feared genital injury also occurred in Class 1. This is in accord with the association found between fear of genital injury and fear of physical injury from the father (Chapter IV). Further strengthening this association is the fact that fear of genital injury occurred frequently in a system where H-fathers were dominant and minimized their wives. Clearly, such H-fathers represented openly aggressive, threatening figures.

In Table VI-14 patients in Class 1 and Class 3 are compared in relation to the fear of genital injury. H-patients whose fathers were dominant-minimizing as husbands were more frequently fearful of genital injury than those in Class 3, which is significant at the .05 level.

In Table VI-15, the comparison of H-patients in Class 1 and Class 3 is restricted to those with CBI mothers. We note that H-

TABLE VI-14 *Comparison of Class 1 and Class 3 H-Patients in Regard to Fear of Genital Injury*

	Class 1	Class 3
Fears genital injury	14	22
Does not	4	24

Significance: .05

patients with fathers who were dominant-minimizing husbands and CBI mothers were significantly more often fearful of genital injury than were H-patients whose CBI mothers were the dominant-minimizing marital partner, significant at the .01 level.

TABLE VI-15 *Comparison of Class 1 and Class 3 H-Patients with CBI Mothers in Regard to Fear of Genital Injury*

	Class 1	Class 3
Fears genital injury	12	15
Does not	1	18

Significance: .01

A related finding is the significant association between Class 1 H-fathers and interference with the son's heterosexuality in adolescence, as shown by Table VI-16. Though Class I contains 12 detached

TABLE VI-16 *Dominant-Minimizing Husbands Associated with Interference with H-Patients' Heterosexuality*

	Husbands dominant-minimizing	Not dominant-minimizing
Fathers interfered with sons' heterosexuality	8	14
Did not	10	63

Significance: .05

H-fathers and 13 detached C-fathers, paternal emotional distance does not appear to deter these dominant-minimizing husbands from actively behaving within the triangular system as interferers and controllers, at least in situations which arouse or threaten them.

The H-patient's reaction to the parental power position in the

Class 1 marriage is of special interest. The association between parental dominance-minimization and the parent whom the son admires offers a degree of insight into his aspirations and identifications (see Table VI-10, items 7 and 8). The highest percentage of H-sons who admired their fathers and the lowest percentage of H-sons who admired their mothers of all marital class groupings occur here. There was a tendency for H-sons more frequently to *respect* fathers who were dominant-minimizing husbands than those who were dominant-not-minimizing husbands, while a significant preponderance of C-sons respected fathers who were dominant but *not* minimizing to the mothers. We found that significantly more homosexuals identified their partners with the father when he was a dominant-minimizing husband (Table VI-17). All patients who had a CBI mother and a detached-hostile father who was a dominant-minimizing husband, identified the homosexual partner with the father. Each hated and feared his father, which suggests that the choice of homosexual partners is in part determined by defensive and reparative mechanisms.

TABLE VI-17 *Dominant-Minimizing Husbands Associated with Patients' Identification of H-Partner*

	Husband dominant-minimizing	Not dominant-minimizing
Identified H-partner with father	14	32
Did not	4	45

Significance: .01

Significantly more H-sons found the mother easier to cope with when the father was a dominant-minimizing husband than did C-sons in this situation (Table VI-10, item 9). C-fathers in this triangular atmosphere were less hostile to their sons than were H-fathers. The highest percentage of patients in all classes who felt their mothers protected them from their fathers occurred among H-patients in this class (Table VI-10, item 22). But however much the father minimized his wife, she appeared to be a very important figure to these H-sons. In two-thirds or more of these cases, they respected the mother, spent a great deal of time with her, and were favorites.

Of the 18 H-patients in Class 1, 6 were able to make a shift in sexual adaptation and became heterosexual.

Class 2:
Father dominates but does not minimize mother

Class 2 marital pairs had the best interparental relationships of all classes in both the H- and C-samples. Only 21 per cent of the H-relationships were reported as "poor," compared to 67 per cent in Class 1 and 72 per cent in Class 3; the difference is significant at the .01 level. For the C-group 19 per cent were reported as "poor" compared to 80 per cent for Class 1 and 69 per cent for Class 3, significant at the .001 level. The majority of "good" relationships for both H- and C-samples were located in this class. For the H-parents, significantly more interparental relationships were not-detached in Class 2 than in Class 3, the difference reaching the .05 level; there were also more not-detached couples who shared similar interests than occurred in Class 3, significant at the .05 level (Table VI-13, items 3 and 4). For the C-group significantly more marital pairs were not-detched than occurred in Class 1, significant at the .05 level, and there were more not-detached relationships where the parents shared similar interests than in Class 3, significant at the .05 level. Despite the frequency of "fair" or "good" interparental relationships in this class, there was, however, a disproportionately large number of detached-hostile fathers in the H-sample, significant at the .01 level (Table VI-11). The C-group, on the other hand, had a disproportionately large number of not-detached, ambivalent C-fathers, which is in accord with the relationship between the parents.

Notable contrasts and similarities occurred between H- and C-samples in Class 2. Whereas the dominant, not minimizing husband was least admired by his H-son in all classes, he was most admired by his C-son here (Table VI-10, item 7). Among the H-patients only 21 per cent respected dominant, not-minimizing husbands, in contrast to 75 per cent of C-patients who respected dominant fathers who did *not* minimize their wives, significant at the .05 level. On the other hand, Class 2 patients achieved higher percentages on the item probing admiration for the mother than did sons in the other classes. Thus, despite similar interparental power structures in H- and C-triangular systems, interactive processes within triads varied markedly since types of mother-son and especially father-son sub-systems varied. The point to be emphasized is that though the marital relationship of both H- and C-parents could be grouped into four interparental power-affect classes, the parental roles were enacted in different types of triangular systems. Among Class 2 H-patients, the fathers appeared to be threatening figures and were feared as frequently as they were in Class 1, but among C-patients in Class 2 there was a trend toward a more positive father-son interaction. Here the dominant C-father was less frequently hated and feared than was the dominant C-father who minimized his wife. C-patients hated and feared their Class 2 dominant fathers less frequently despite the fact that these fathers dominated their sons almost as frequently (69 per cent) as did the comparable class of H-fathers (79 per cent).

On the item probing the son's siding with his mother in parental arguments, Class 1 and 2 H-patients do not differ though C-patients in Class 2 sided with the mother less frequently than they did in any other triad arrangement.

Fewer H- and C-mothers who were not minimized by their husbands preferred their sons to their husbands, allied with them, or had reciprocal confidant relationships with them, as compared to the mothers who were minimized. C-wives were significantly more often CBI mothers when they were dominant-minimizing to their husbands than when they were married to husbands who, though dominant, were not minimizing (Class 2). For the H-sample, where the father was dominant but did not minimize his wife, the mother dominated her son in 13 of 19 cases, which is more frequent, though not significantly so, than when the husband was dominant and minimizing. For the C-sample, fewer mothers in Class 2 dominated their sons than did H-mothers.

These H- and C-mothers were infrequently hated and feared by their sons and in both samples the fathers were significantly more often feared than were the mothers. For the H-patient the father was more often hated than was the mother. Even though the H-triad in Class 2 contains a dominant but not minimizing husband, he still frequently remained a hated and feared paternal figure. The H-patient feared him (79 per cent), feared angering him (84 per cent), seldom respected him (21 per cent), and hardly ever admired him (5 per cent).

Class 3:
Mother dominates and minimizes father

Here the mother is undisputedly the power figure. The highest percentage of "poor" interparental relationships in the H-group occurs here (72 per cent). For the C-group it is almost as high (69 per cent), though not as high as was reached by the Class 1 C-parents. Despite the poor quality of the marital relationships, one-third of the H-couples were not detached from each other, and in 7 of the 46 H-cases interests were shared (Table VI-13). In the C-group, one-half were not detached and 7 of 32 couples shared similar interests.

In both H- and C-samples the father was feared *less* frequently than in any other system whereas the mother was hated and feared *more* frequently. In 43 of 46 H-cases, and in 30 of 32 C-cases, the mothers dominated the patient (Table VI-12). Yet, for the H-patients, hatred of the mother (39 per cent) never reached the proportions of hatred for the father (63 per cent) while among C-patients the mother was hated as frequently as the father (Table VI-10). On the item probing fear, Class 3 H-sons feared the mother as frequently as they feared the father but the C-sons feared the mother twice as often as the father. Even where the H-mother was the unchallenged power figure, it was the *H-father* who emerged as the more hated figure. In this class we find the fathers who defaulted in their parental role and resigned the "field" to their wives. We assume that one important determinant of filial hatred and lack of respect for these fathers was paternal failure to assume a protective role against the "castrating matriarchs" of this group. As Table VI-18 shows, Class 3 H-sons respected their fathers far less frequently when the mothers were CBI than when they were not CBI.

TABLE VI-18 *Respect of Father Associated with CBI and Non-CBI Class 3 H-Mothers*

	Patient respects father	Does not
H-mother CBI and Class 3	4	29
H-mother non-CBI and Class 3	6	7

Significance: .05

The lack of respect for fathers in Class 3 occurred particularly when the CBI mother was married to a detached-hostile father. Among the 11 cases where the triangular system was characterized by a CBI mother and detached-hostile father, *no son* respected his father.

In both the H- and C-samples of Class 3, the highest percentages were achieved on three items which most clearly reflect an over-intimate mother-son relationship: Mothers allied with sons against the father; mothers openly preferred sons to husbands; mothers and sons had reciprocal confidant relationships. The high percentages may be explained on the bases that in the C-sample CBI mothers were significantly over-represented in Class 3.

If we juxtapose the H-son with his parental pair the frequency of filial hatred of the mother occurred as follows:

(a) CBI-detached-hostile. Of 11 H-sons, 1 hated his mother (9 per cent).

(b) CBI-all types of fathers (DH excepted). Of 22 H-sons, 9 hated the mother (41 per cent).

(c) Non-CBI-all types of fathers. Of 13 H-sons, 8 hated the mother (62 per cent).

On the item, "Hatred of the mother," patients in category (a) differ from patients in category (c) at the .05 level. Patients in category (a) differ from patients in category (b), though not significantly. Of the CBI/DH pairs, the mother achieved the highest percentages on having favored the H-son (11 of 11), in having been seductive with him (10 of 11), in having allied with him against the husband, and in having openly preferred the son to the husband (10 of 11). She made a confidant of her son (10 of 11) and was overprotective (9 of 11). She did not differ substantially from other CBI mothers on these items, yet where the father reacted to his H-son with detachment and hostility, the son rarely hated his mother. The psychodynamics suggested are that the same sons who hated their fathers (10 of 11) and feared them (10 of 11) dared not allow hatred of the mother in the presence of a hostile, threatening father to enter conscious awareness. These sons could not psychologically "afford" to hate both parents since the mother was needed as protection against the destructive father. In support of this psychodynamic assumption, let us turn again to the item, "Feared mother." Among H-sons in Class 3 we find the highest percentage of all four classes who feared her (59 per cent). If we break "fear" down into the same groupings as we did previously in the analysis of Class 3 H-sons who *hated* their mothers, we find:

(a) CBI-detached-hostile. Of 11, 7 feared mother (64 per cent).

(b) CBI-other types of fathers (DH excepted). Of 22 H-sons, 12 (55 per cent) feared mother.

(c) Non-CBI-other types of fathers. Of 13 H-sons, 8 feared mother (61 per cent).

While Class 3 H-patients with parents who were CBI/DH are

significantly underrepresented for hating mothers, they are about equally represented for *fearing* mothers.

These statistics vary for the C-sample. Most sons who had *CBI-detached-hostile* sets of parents in Class 3 both hated and feared their mothers. The psychodynamics suggested for these C-patients are that they were more frequently sufficiently free of anxiety to have permitted conscious awareness of hatred of their mothers. As has been discussed throughout this report, even those C-patients who fall into the same categories as the H-patients tend consistently to show "healthier" trends, indicating that in the C-families the interactions within triangular systems promote less serious psychopathology than occur within matched H-triangular categories.

The not-detached, overprotective H-fathers totaled only 3 in the entire patient sample. Each appeared in Class 3, and of the 5 overprotective C-fathers 2 appeared here. It is possible that these fathers developed reaction formations to their own fears of threatening females projecting their own anxieties onto their sons, expressed in overprotective attitudes and behavior. Overprotection cast these fathers into roles usually associated with mothers. Other not-detached C-fathers appear here less frequently than expected, though the difference in expected frequency does not quite achieve the .05 level.

It is noteworthy that *none* of the 19 C-mothers who were classified as not remarkable fall within the mother dominant-minimizing marital class. The absence of these mothers is significant at the .05 level.

Of the 46 H-patients in Class 3, 11 became heterosexual. In this class there were 11 cases who had CBI mothers and detached-hostile fathers. Only 1 of the 11 patients became heterosexual. This represents one of the lowest rates of shift in sexual adaptation in our study.

Class 4:
Mother dominates but does not minimize father

There were 12 H-cases and 22 C-cases in this class. Although the mothers of both homosexuals and comparison patients were dominant in the interparental relationship, the triangular systems of each sample differed markedly. The marital relationships were regarded as "poor" for 41 per cent of the H-sample and 32 per cent for the C-sample. Only 1 set of H-parents was reported as sharing interests while 10 sets of C-parents were so reported.

Patients here had the following characteristics in common: The majority of mothers were respected and about one-half were admired (Table VI-10). As in Class 3, these dominant wives also dominated their sons more frequently than when the father was dominant—in the H-sample 11 of 12; in the C-sample 16 of 22 (Table VI-12). These mothers were more frequently hated and feared than when the father was the dominant spouse. The Class 4 fathers, on the other hand, were hated and feared less frequently than when they were dominant and minimized their wives. The lowest percentage of patients who feared physical injury from the father was noted for this class. Items reflecting maternal close-binding intimacy achieved lower percentages than in Class 3; for the C-sample the difference between frequency of CBI mothers in Classes 3 and 4 is significant at the .05 level. Yet, two-thirds of the H-mothers and about one-half of the C-mothers here were overprotective. Of all classes, these C-mothers achieved the highest percentage on the item, "Protected son from father."

Although the interparental power parameter for patients in both H- and C-samples are similar, again, the types of triangular systems differ. In the H-triads *most* of the fathers were hostile and several were indifferent; most of the mothers were CBI. Among the C-triads, only 7 patients had fathers who were hostile and only 1 patient had an indifferent father—others were either ambivalent or warmly related to their patient-sons. Among the mothers there were 6 CBI, 6 controlling-dominating, 6 not remarkable, 2 detached-poorly related and 2 not detached-hostile. The Class 4 C-sample contains a greater heterogeneity of triangular systems than does the H-sample, particularly in the distribution of types of mothers. The C-wife who was dominant and had not minimized her husband had a wider range of maternal relatedness to her patient-son—she was CBI in some instances and not remarkable in others. The dominant but not minimizing H-wife was most likely to be a CBI mother (75 per cent). Among the H-husbands here none showed affection to the patient-son while the C-husbands of the same class showed the patient-son affection in 13 of 22 cases.

The fact that the mother was the dominant spouse appears to have tempered the H-son's perception of his hostile father. Fewer H-sons consciously hated him than did H-sons in other classes, and we found the lowest percentage here of all patients in the four classes who feared physical injury from him. This apparent advantage may occur at the price of a more frequent and greater dependency upon the mother; 80 per cent of these H-patients were reported as excessively dependent upon their mothers and 50 per cent were reported as having been clinging children. Only 2 of the 12 H-sons identified the homosexual partner with the father as compared with the 14 of 18 H-sons who made such an identification when the father was the dominant-minimizing spouse, significant at the .05 level. In 2 of the 12 H-cases, the homosexual partner was identified with the mother. Despite frequent maternal protection of the patient from these fathers, most H-sons in this class were fearful of angering them by any show of self-assertiveness.

SOME COMPARISONS AMONG THE INTERPARENTAL CLASSES

Dominance. Fathers (Classes 1 and 2) as compared with mothers (Classes 3 and 4)

(a) *Fear of Physical Injury.* Where husbands were dominant, the patient-sons significantly more often feared physical injury from fathers than when the mother was the dominant spouse. For the H-sample the difference is significant at the .001 level; Table VI-19 presents these statistics. Table VI-20 and VI-21 show a further analysis of these findings. The H-sample is divided into those who had CBI mothers and those who had not. When H-patients had mothers who were CBI and the fathers were dominant husbands, the association between having such fathers and fearing physical injury from them is significant at the .01 level. When H-sons of such fathers had mothers who were *not* CBI, the association between fearing such fathers and fearing physical injury from them is not significant.

TABLE VI-19 *Parental Dominance Associated with Fear of Physical Injury from Father*

	H		C	
	Fathers dominant Classes 1, 2	Mothers dominant Classes 3, 4	Fathers dominant Classes 1, 2	Mothers dominant Classes 3, 4
Feared physical injury from father	30	26	25	20
Did not	6	33	16	34

Significance: H .001; C not significant

TABLE VI-20 *Parental Dominance in H-Sample Where Mothers are CBI Associated with Fear of Physical Injury from Father*

	Fathers dominant Classes 1, 2	Mothers dominant Classes 3, 4
Feared physical injury from father	21	18
Did not	4	24

Significance: .01

TABLE VI-21 *Parental Dominance in H-Sample Where Mothers Are Not CBI Associated with Fear of Physical Injury from Father*

	Fathers dominant Classes 1, 2	Mothers dominant Classes 3, 4
Feared physical injury from father	9	8
Did not	2	9

Not significant

(b) *Hatred and Fear.* When the father was a dominant husband he was consciously hated somewhat more frequently in the H-sample than when the wife was dominant, but not significantly so. He was, however, significantly more often feared when he was the dominant spouse in the H-sample, significant at the .05 level, but for the C-sample the difference is significant at the .001 level (Table VI-22).

When mothers were dominant wives they were feared significantly more often by patient-sons than when fathers were the dominant spouse (Table VI-23). For the H-sample, mothers who were dominant wives were hated significantly more often than when they were not

TABLE VI-22 *Fear of Father When He Is Dominant Compared with Fear of Father When Mother Is Dominant*

	H		C	
	Fathers dominant Classes 1, 2	Mothers dominant Classes 3, 4	Fathers dominant Classes 1, 2	Mothers dominant Classes 3, 4
Feared father	32	35	33	19
Did not	5	23	8	35

Significance: H .05; C .001

TABLE VI-23 *Fear of Mother When She Is Dominant Compared with Fear of Mother When Father Is Dominant*

	H		C	
	Mothers dominant Classes 3, 4	Fathers dominant Classes 1, 2	Mothers dominant Classes 3, 4	Fathers dominant Classes 1, 2
Feared mother	33	8	32	10
Did not	25	29	23	30

Significance: H .001; C. 01

dominant wives. This does not obtain for the C-sample. The difference (Table VI-10) is accounted for by the fact that fewer H-sons than C-sons hated their mothers when the fathers were dominant for reasons which were discussed on page 160.

The difference between H- and C-patients in reactions of hatred and fear of the parents are highlighted by the following ratios:

Ratio between hating father and hating mother.
Father Dominant: H-patients = 4:1; C-patients = 1.5:1
Mother Dominant: H-patients = 3:1; C-patients = 1:1

Ratio between fearing father and fearing mother.
Father Dominant: H-patient = 4:1; C-patient = 3.4:1
Mother Dominant: H-patient = 1.2:1; C-patient = 1:1.6

Thus, the H- father emerges as the predominantly hated and feared parent.

Interparental Minimization. Class 1 and Class 3 as compared with Class 2 and Class 4

Mothers allied with son and openly preferred him to the husband. When either parent minimized the other, the minimized or minimizing *mothers* (Class 1 and 3) more frequently allied with their sons against their husbands than occurred in Classes 2 and 4, significant for H-mothers at the .05 level; significant for C-mothers at the .01 level; and significantly more mothers openly preferred their patient-sons to their husbands, significant for H-mothers at the .05 level and significant for C-mothers at the .01 level (Table VI-10).

From the point of view of the family systematics we have presented, namely the triangular system, the case which follows is illustrative. Several articulating sub-systems will be discernible, and the inherent psychologic themes which brought the patient to a sexual adaptation oscillating between homosexuality and heterosexuality, before psychoanalytic intervention and a sexually adaptive resolution, will be outlined. Aspects of treatment and psychodynamics are only occasionally alluded to. The importance of the parent-child interaction in sexual outcome is, however, highlighted.

CASE NO. 89

The patient was born and reared in a small northern city. His mother had been the youngest and only girl of a family of many sons and she was petted and spoiled by her well-to-do father who pridefully traced his ancestry to the early American colonists. He had hoped his beautiful daughter would marry a man of greater social distinction than the owner of a men's haberdashery. The grandfather died shortly before the patient was born and his widow came to live with her daughter and son-in-law. An Irish housekeeper who had been with the family since her immigration was brought along and she, too, joined the household.

The patient was a healthy, strapping child. His grandmother and the housekeeper would often tell him how much he resembled his maternal grandfather—dark-eyed, ruddy complexion, and wiry. The patient had no other siblings and he was doted upon by these two women. In contrast, his mother was harsh, often brutal, and would fly into rages which appeared quite irrational. Should the patient's behavior suggest even the slightest infraction she would beat him unmercifully. Then the two older women would swoop down "like protective angels" to extricate the boy from these hysterical, sadistic situations. He would be confused as to why his mother treated him as she did since he usually could find no reason for it. He did recall the reason for being very badly beaten by her when he was about six years old. He was caught playing sexual games with a little girl his own age who lived near-by. After this incident, he stopped playing with girls. The patient's father was never corporally punitive. He was an extremely stingy and insensitive man and the patient would become intensely resentful at having reasonable requests turned down by both parents since he knew they could afford the small luxuries he would ask for occasionally. He would have to wheedle money out of them.

The mother was self-centered, vain, suspicious. She had no friends outside her own large, sprawling family; there was hardly any contact with her husband's people who lived in a near-by city. She had always felt herself to be superior to him and lost few opportunities to emphasize their difference in social status. The mother and grandmother were talkative women and they spent much of their time in conversations centering about family affairs, ancestry, marriages, deaths, inheritances, feuds. The patient would lend a sharp ear and became quite as interested as they. The patient's social contacts, too, remained largely within the maternal family. His friends consisted mostly of his many cousins. In his preadolescence he made a deep identification with military heroes of the Revolutionary War and he built a rich fantasy life around major figures in early American history. He read prodigiously on this subject and spent most of his spare time occupied with his books. Neither parent interfered with this pursuit. They made it quite clear that they expected him to enter a profession some day and reading was viewed as a preparation for it.

The father enjoyed hunting and fishing. Occasionally, he would make a feeble attempt to have the patient come along but somehow both the mother and grandmother found some excuse to prevent such outings. The patient did not recall fearing guns or having squeamish feelings about killing animals or birds, but neither did he recall eagerness to accompany his father as did other boys. As an adolescent, and later, the patient never went to his father's shop to help out. He was never asked to nor did it ever occur to him to do so since he considered it below his dignity as the young gentleman and scholar he fancied himself to be. Yet, the father enjoyed running the shop. He was a rather garrulous man, had a surface affability, and liked to swap stories and chat with his customers, savoring the tid-bits of news and gossip he picked up. The mother never set foot into the store. It was a thing apart from her life. Reflecting the mother's attitude, the patient harbored a feeling of shame about his father's occupation and when he went to college he concealed from his wealthy fraternity brothers that his father ran a men's furnishings store.

The grandmother and father get along quite well. There seemed to be an unspoken pact between them and she tended to defend him when her daughter's carping and criticisms got out of bounds. She was hardly reticent in her affection for her grandson, however.

The grandmother-housekeeper combination were remembered by the patient with uncomplicated feelings of love.

The patient had his first homosexual experience when he was about twelve years old with a boy of his own age whom he had admired a good deal as the brightest boy in the school. They were in the toilet together and became involved in mutual masturbation. He then began to drift from boy to boy in the social inner circle, having sporadic masturbatory experiences with them. His homosexual activities continued at high school with boys who were either outstandingly gifted students or came from the leading families of the local citizenry. His sexual preferences began to form around performing fellatio.

When the patient was away at college, the housekeeper died and shortly after he graduated his grandmother passed away. He felt a deep sense of loss, especially when his grandmother died, since he was left with parents who were ambivalent, demanding, and rigid. He had a profound admiration for his mother's beauty which for him compensated somewhat for her maternal shortcomings.

The patient went on having sporadic homosexual affairs at college but he also began to date girls. As he was a very attractive young man, interesting and kind, the girls pursued him. After graduation, the patient entered postgraduate training; he took his doctorate and became a history professor at a western college. During his studies, the patient became ill with serious infectious hepatitis. Although his parents were informed of the serious nature of his illness and that he might possibly not survive, they did not go West to see him. His mother "did not feel up to it," and the father did not care to leave her behind. The patient was bitter and resentful. Some months after his recovery he had his first heterosexual intercourse. He recalled little conscious anxiety with this experience. His homosexual interests declined and he began to go out with women on a more serious basis. He met a pretty young woman from a wealthy, socially prominent family and soon found himself very much attached to her and in love. They began to live together and planned to marry. As the date drew nearer, the patient began to develop marked anxiety, began to question his capacity to remain heterosexual, and finally broke the engagement. He resigned his post and came to New York depressed, agitated, and drinking heavily.

With the inheritance his grandmother had left him he decided after some aimless months to take a trip around the world. During his sojourn in the Orient, he became intensely interested in Eastern art and history. His fascination for the subject prompted him to pursue Oriental studies at one of the New York universities. Back in New York, he became active socially once more and soon met another woman—again, wealthy and socially prominent. She was bright, witty and beautiful. In due course, he began to think of marriage but found out shortly after she accepted his proposal that she was having a concurrent affair with another man. The engagement was broken and this was the last of his heterosexuality for several years to come. He immediately became involved in a homosexual affair with a college professor and began to live with him.

A serious depression brought him into analysis. He felt hopeless about his homosexuality, had lost interest in his work, and found himself thinking about suicide. After about five years of intensive psychoanalytic treatment, he began to venture toward women again. After a courtship filled with anxiety and inner torment, which he attempted to alleviate by the use of alcohol, he married a Canadian woman. She was much like his grandmother physically, and the patient was quite aware of the similarity between them. This girl, however, was neither wealthy nor socially prominent. She came from a family background of intellectuality, though she herself was not given to such interests. She was intelligent, straightforward, and devoted to him. At first, his sexual performance in marriage was satisfactory but after some months he began to have potency difficulties and would resort to alcohol from time to time. In the second year, the marriage became more stable. No homosexual experiences intervened between the time he met his wife and his termination of psychoanalysis.

SUMMARY: We may infer that the mother's relationship with her own mother was seriously disturbed, in that the grandmother seemed to have preferred her sons to her only daughter, who was favored by the grandfather. The grandmother, buttressed by the housekeeper, competed with her daughter for the grandson; the daughter, in turn, competed with her own son for the grandmother. On a deeper level, the mother probably identified her son with her own father whom the child was stated to have resembled. As discussed on page 68 of Chapter III, women who have incestuous guilt feelings sometimes attempt to expiate their guilt by rejecting the son identified with the incestuous object. This mother seemed to beat such feelings down in herself by literally beating down her son, the living evidence of forbidden impulses. As a mother she was not CBI but controlling-dominating. As a wife, she was the dominant partner who minimized her husband. Evidence of her dominance may be seen in her ascendancy in decisions as to the patient's relationship with his father, i.e., hunting trips, and helping at the store. When the patient was desperately ill, it was she who decided against visiting him. Her belittling of her husband formed the social content on which the patient's snobbery developed. Social snobbery is not infrequent among homosexuals and usually evolves out of a situation where either parent is minimized. In order to preclude a similar humiliation the *reference group* of homosexuals who have had a minimized parent may become the perceived socially superior class. Elegance, perfection, and "the best" are side-products of denial of unacceptability.

The father, too, was upwardly striving for he married a woman from a class he considered to be above his own. As a way of maintaining the social distance between them, the mother participated in none of her husband's interests. Their common enjoyment—the affairs of others—were experienced in different settings. The father was able to win acceptance from his mother-in-law but on the basis of her preference for males. (He was classified as a detached-indifferent father.) Apart from his interest in his son's economic future, there was little involvement between father and son.

The patient grew up in an atmosphere of ancestral pride stemming from the maternal family. The grandfather rather than the father was put forward as a model for the boy but, at least, he had a strong *imagined* figure for identification in the presence of a father who neither protected the patient from the mother nor won his respect. This triad exemplifies an interactional communion of meager content. The mother, father, and son were, for the most part, weakly joined, though a much higher rate of interaction occurred between the patient and his mother, much of it hostile. The patient's homosexual partners in boyhood and later when he was an adult were clearly males who would be acceptable to the mother, a reparative maneuver in the direction of maternal acceptance. Her sexual restrictiveness is well illustrated by the way she interdicted her son's early heterosexual experimentation.

Were it not for the relationship with the grandmother and the housekeeper, we venture to speculate that the patient would have been exclusively homosexual. The unambiguous love and support from these women seemed to have given him enough confidence with women to permit him to enter into heterosexual relationships.

The grandmother-housekeeper-patient triad provided the model for a good parent-child relationship, except that this parental unity, in a sense, was "homosexual," since it was an ipsosexual pair who provided a "good" parental image. Yet, the patient also had independent dyadic relationships with each.

Summary

In ordering our data within the framework of family sub-systems, the sexual adaptation of patients in psychoanalysis may be understood from a point of view which departs from the more familiar analysis of individual behavior and motivation. By constructing classifications of mother-son, father-son, and interparental power-affect parameters, we have designed a systematic way of studying the patient in a triangular interaction with his parents. The "classical" homosexual triangular pattern is one where the mother is CBI and is dominant and minimizing toward a husband who is a detached father, particularly a hostile-detached one. From our statistical analysis, the chances appear to be high that any son exposed to this parental combination will become homosexual or develop severe homosexual problems.

VII

Developmental Aspects of the Prehomosexual Child

CONSTITUTIONAL FACTORS are still often relied upon to "explain" the characteristics of the developing prehomosexual child. Freud's theories place emphasis on both experiential and constitutional determinants. The latter includes the exaggerated influence of pregenital erotogenic zones as well as inherent drives toward passivity. Passivity in females is assumed to be essential for the patterning of the feminine role; while in some males the imbalance between instinctual passivity and aggression is deemed to be operant in certain forms of homosexuality (passive) or "latent" homosexuality. It is a biologic commonplace that there are constitutional differences and variations. But the reliance upon constitutional factors to account for social deviance and for the psychopathology involved in homosexuality appears to us, as indeed it does to other researchers, to be unwarranted; in other words, the constitutional tendency idea invoked as a basis for homosexuality is, after all, but another way of saying "he was born that way." Psychiatric theories of homosexuality which depend upon formulations having to do with inherent constitutional traits have been based upon unsupported assumptions which, however ingenious and convenient, appear to us to be discordant with the data. Our findings point to the homosexual adaptation as an outcome of exposure to highly pathologic parent-child relationships and early life situations.

We were oriented to seeking out those aspects of child behavior which differentiated the homosexual patients from the comparison cases and to locating the derivatives of these differences within the nuclear family. Six items in our questionnaire probed developmental characteristics related to fears, sociability, and play activities, and these items clearly differentiated the homosexual from the comparison sample at levels of statistical significance all at .001, and beyond. These items were used in constructing a Developmental Cumulative Score (see Appendix B) as a basis for rating each patient. The ratings ranged from zero for those responses which indicated a relative absence of developmental disorder, to 6 for responses judged as revealing the greatest degree of disorder. Only 10 per cent of the H-patients scored 2 or less while 62 per cent of C-patients scored 2 or less. The six items are presented in Table VII-1, (items 1 through 6) as are 2 other related items (7 and 8) which also significantly differentiated the H- from the C-patient (at .01 level). Seventy-five per cent of the H-patients were excessively fearful of physical injury in childhood and almost 90 per cent avoided the fights engaged in by most boys. Among the C-patients 46 per cent were unusually fearful of injury and 55 per cent avoided fights. Of the prehomosexual children 83 per cent did not participate in competitive games and sports, as compared with 37 per cent of the comparison sample who did not. Only 17 H-patients were reported ever to have played baseball while 62 C-patients had played baseball in childhood. In 60 per cent of the cases the H-patient had been an isolate in his peer relations and in 33 per cent of the H-cases he had played predominantly with girls. Inasmuch as the results of the "Six Score" indicated that there had been sharply divergent styles of childhood behavior between the H- and C-groups up to adolescence, our purpose was to compare these item responses with our data on family interaction and to test for associations between patterns of childhood behavior and psychopathology in parent-child relationships.

Excessive fear of injury in childhood

Our data indicate that excessive fear of injury in childhood is associated with various parental attitudes and behavior. In Table VII-2 we note a positive association between excessive fear of physical injury in childhood and (1) mother was unduly concerned about protecting son from physical injury; (2) mother was unduly restrictive of play and social activities; (3) father was minimizing of son; (4) son both

TABLE VII-1 *Some Characteristics in Childhood (in per cent)*

	H	C
N =	106	100
1. Patient was excessively fearful of physical injury in childhood	75	46†
2. Patient avoided physical fights	89	55†
3. Play activity before puberty was predominantly with girls	33	10†
4. Patient was a "lone wolf" in childhood	60	27†
5. Patient participated in competitive group games	17	63†
6. Patient played baseball	16	62†
7. Patient was a clinging child[a]	50	25**
8. Patient was reluctant to start school[a]	43	23**

[a] Based on 96 cases
* .05 level of significance
** .01 level of significance
† .001 level of significance

TABLE VII-2 *Excessive Fear of Physical Injury in Childhood Associated with Five Other Items*

Item	Affirmative responses to each item: H (96)	C (96)	Excessive fear of physical injury in childhood H (73) C (44)	Number who also gave affirmative response to listed items: H	C
1	56	37	Mother unduly concerned about protecting son from physical injury	44	22*
2	47	25	Mother unduly restrictive of physical and social activities	38	19**
	H (103)	C (100)		H (80)	C (46)
3	68	42	Father minimizing of son	55	29†
4	60	31	Son both hated/feared father	49	20*
5	48	36	Father classified as hostile	40	23*

Each number in the last two columns is the frequency of cases in the positive-positive cell of a contingency table involving Excessive fear of injury with the specified questionnaire item. The indication of level of significance applies to that whole contingency table.

hated and feared father; (5) father was classified as *hostile* to patient-son. The association between each item and excessive fear of injury in childhood is significant for the C-sample but does not reach the .05 level in any instance for the H-sample. This occurred despite the fact that 44 of the 56 H-patients whose mothers were unduly protective against physical injury also were excessively fearful of injury; 38 of the 47 having mothers who were over-restrictive, excessively feared injury, as well as 55 of the 68 H-patients whose fathers were minimizing; and so on down the table. Why did not these individual items reach statistical significance in the H-sample? We postulated that for the H-patients there were so many factors creating excessive fear of injury that the association of any single variable with excessive fear of injury in childhood was masked. With this assumption in mind, we adopted two procedures. First, we assembled 4 mother-related items reflecting three parameters of maternal behavior: maternal over-concern regarding health, and injury; maternal restrictiveness; maternal infantilizing behavior. We then tested for a positive association between the affirmatively answered cluster of 4 mother-related items and an affirmative response to the item tapping excessive fear of injury during childhood (Table VII-3). There is a marked association among the H-sample (beyond .01 level) between the 4 mother-related items, and the son's excessive fear of injury in childhood, but not a significant association among the C-sample. Note that there are 37 H- and only 13 C-patients who had excessive fears in childhood and for whom there were affirmative answers to all 4 mother-related items. The hypothesis that the H and the C distributions were drawn from the same sample was tested and rejected at the .001 level of confidence.

Secondly, we assembled 9 items—6 mother-related and 3 father-related—and constructed a Cumulative Score assigning equal weight to each item. These 6 mother-related items included the 4 items in Table VII-3 as well as 2 additional items tapping maternal interference with the son's assertiveness. The 3 father-related items were: patient consciously hated father; patient consciously feared father; father was contemptuous of his son and/or humiliated him.

Table VII-4 presents the distribution of the cumulative scores for both H- and C-samples. Table VII-5 shows the separation of those cases with affirmative answers to 4 or fewer items from those with 5 or more items. It also shows the association between the number of cases with scores of 4 or less, and those with scores of 5 or more, to the item: "Excessive fear of injury during childhood." When the data are handled in this manner, the significant association between excessive fear of injury in childhood and parental attitudes and behavior is established for the H-sample as shown in Tables VII-3, VII-4, and VII-5.

TABLE VII-3 *Cluster of Mother-Related Items*[a] *Associated with Excessive Fear of Physical Injury*

	H		C	
	Affirmative responses to all 4 items	No affirmative responses	Affirmative responses to all 4 items	No affirmative responses
Excessive fear of physical injury in childhood	37	36	13	30
No excessive fear	3	20	7	46

[a] Item 1. Mother was unduly concerned about patient's health in childhood.

Item 2. Mother was unduly concerned about protecting patient from physical injury in childhood.

Item 3. Mother's concern about health or injury caused her to interfere with or restrict patient's play, social or other activities.

Item 4. Mother babied patient.

Significance: H .01; C not significant

TABLE VII-4 *Distribution of Cumulative Scores for Parent-Related Items*

	H				C			
Cumulative scores	Excessive fear		No excessive fear		Excessive fear		No excessive fear	
N =	69		23		43		53	
0	0	0%	3	13%	1	2%	5	9%
1	2	3%	1	4%	2	5%	16	30%
2	5	7%	1	4%	6	14%	4	8%
3	7	10%	3	13%	5	12%	9	17%
4	10	14%	6	26%	8	19%	6	11%
5	8	12%	3	13%	7	16%	5	9%
6	10	14%	4	17%	3	7%	3	6%
7	10	14%	0	0%	4	9%	2	4%
8	12	17%	1	4%	6	14%	2	4%
9	5	7%	1	4%	1	2%	1	2%
Average for each group	5.56		4		4.63		3	

The difference between the means of groups 1 and 3 significant at .05 level; the difference between means of groups 1 and 2, and between 3 and 4, is beyond the .01 level.

TABLE VII-5 *Excessive Fear of Physical Injury Associated with Distribution of Cumulative Score*

	H		C	
	Score of 4 or less	Score of 5 or more	Score of 4 or less	Score of 5 or more
Excessive fear of physical injury	24	45	22	21
No excessive fear	14	9	40	13

Based on samples of 96 (see Chapter II); 3 fathers absent; 5 items not answered in 1 case.

Significance: H .05; C .05

In Table VII-3 we note a significant association between the cluster of 4 mother-related items (3 items are included in Table VII-2) and excessive fear of physical injury in childhood for the H-group at a .01 level; the association for the C-group is not significant. Yet for the C-group these same items were significant when tested individually, and attained higher levels of significance, while in the H-sample the individual items did not reach significance but the *cluster* did. This supports our assumption that in the H-group there is a *broader spectrum* of deleterious maternal influences in addition to the fact that more H-mothers than C-mothers exercised unfavorable influences, as described in Chapter III.

In Table VII-4 we note that in the H-sample 38 per cent of the cases with excessive fear of physical injury in childhood scored 7 or more as compared to only 8 per cent of the H-cases without excessive fear. In the C-sample, the comparable statistics are: 25 per cent of patients with excessive fear of injury scored 7 or more, while of those who were not excessively fearful, 10 per cent scored 7 or over; 64 per cent of the C-group without excessive fear scored 3 or less as compared to 33 per cent who were fearful and scored so low. In the H-sample, this difference does not appear in the low score range since most H-patients (80 per cent) scored 3 or more—further evidence of the pervasiveness of pathologic parent-child relatedness. The average score for the excessively fearful H-group was 5.56; for the H-group who were not excessively fearful the average score was 4. In the C-group, the average score for the excessively fearful was 4.63 and for those not excessively fearful the average score was 3.

In Table VII-5 we note a significant association (.05 level) between the number of H- and C-cases who scored 4 or less and cases who scored 5 or more and the item, "Excessive fear of injury in childhood." However, there are 45 H- and 21 C-patients who were both excessively fearful in childhood and scored 5 or more; and 14 H- and 40 C-patients who were not excessively fearful, and scored 4 or less on the mother-related items. The hypothesis that the H- and C-samples in the table might be drawn from the same population is rejected at the .001 level of confidence.

Excessive fear of injury in the childhood of the patient sample is related, on the one hand, to paternal hostility, and on the other, to a pattern of maternal overindulgence and overprotectiveness in concert with social and sexual restrictiveness. Few mothers in the total patient sample were classified as "hostile." Of 206 patients, 22 had mothers who were so classified; of the 12 with hostile H-mothers, 9 were excessively fearful of injury while of those 10 with hostile C-mothers, 5 were excessively fearful. No statistical association was established between maternal hostility and excessive fear of injury in the sons. *Paternal* hostility and engulfing maternalism emerge throughout our findings as having had the most telling destructive impact. One might argue that if the roles of the parents were reversed, that is, if a sample of mothers were more frequently hostile and the majority of the fathers were CBI, the effects on the son would compare to our findings. Judging from our data, however, we are led to the conclusion that the *father's* hostility produces a qualitatively different effect from that of a mother in that paternal hostility seems to be perceived as far more threatening to a son than does hostility by the mother. For example, the association in the C-group between paternal hostility and excessive fear of injury was at the .01 level of significance whereas *no association* was found for maternal hostility and excessive fear of physical injury.

EXCESSIVE FEAR OF INJURY AND SYMPTOMS OF SEXUAL DISTURBANCES

The question arises as to why symptoms of sexual disturbances manifested in masturbatory guilt, aversion to female genitalia, and the wish for a larger penis are associated with excessive fear of physical injury in childhood (Table VII-6). Our discussion will include in-

TABLE VII-6 *Excessive Fear of Physical Injury Associated with Symptoms of Sexual Disturbances*

Item	Affirmative responses to items 1-3 H (106)	Affirmative responses to items 1-3 C (100)	Excessive fear of physical injury in childhood H (80) C (46)	Number who also gave affirmative response to listed items H	Number who also gave affirmative response to listed items C
1	56	48	Much guilt about masturbation	50**	22
2	74	34	Aversion to female genitalia	61*	21*
3	46	35	Genitals are smaller than desired	39	22*

Each number in the last two columns is the frequency of cases in the positive-positive cell of a contingency table involving Excessive fear of injury with the specified questionnaire item. The indication of level of significance applies to that whole contingency table.

ferences based upon our data and inferences derived from clinical observations.

The data of this study and the vast amount of clinical evidence in the psychoanalytic literature indicate that sexual symptomatology in later life has its roots in childhood. We assume that a reciprocal interaction was operant between the patients' excessive fear of injury and the psychodynamics underlying their sexual symptoms. Firstly, unrealistic and harsh parental sexual prohibitions were particularly noted in the backgrounds of the homosexuals. The H-mothers in our study have been more frequently and more pervasively injurious to the sexual development of the patients than have the C-mothers. The H-mothers discouraged and interfered with heterosexuality significantly more often. One-third of the fathers in both H- and C-samples were puritanical and, we assume, acted in concert with the mothers in sexually restricting their patient-sons, particularly the prehomosexual sons. *Much guilt* about masturbation in childhood was reported for 56 H-patients and 48 C-patients while *no masturbatory guilt* was reported for only 8 H-patients and 5 C-patients, clearly pointing to the presence of varying degrees of guilt among almost all the patients. However, masturbatory guilt and excessive fear of injury in childhood were significantly associated for the H-sample only (.01 level).

Children who have been intimidated by parents and consequently have become pathologically submissive are unusually sensitive and responsive to parental prohibitions, sexual and other. The vulnerability to parental prohibitions extends sexual impairment in that the continuing submissiveness of the child serves to further inhibit him in forbidden zones of behavior. Any impairment of function which has been parentally induced increases the fear of parents (or transferential surrogates) and intensifies the anticipation of injury from external agents.

Secondly, fear and guilt about incestuous impulses, usually unconscious (Oedipus Complex), have been demonstrated by many psychoanalysts in the course of treating adults and children. The overcloseness and seductiveness of the majority of H-mothers (CBI) tended to reinforce and strengthen incestuous impulses. Antisexual maternal attitudes articulating with paternal hostility and rejection fostered fearful attitudes about such wishes. The child who is beset by an expectation of injury for sexual feelings toward a tabooed object comes to fear not only the expression of sexual behavior but the discovery of the impulses themselves. His uncertainty about self-controlling mechanisms leaves him in a state of chronic apprehension and guardedness since he fears retaliative attack. His fears are then projected to external sources, sexual and nonsexual, creating a generalized fear of attack. Phobias (fears of mice and insects, etc.) are a common manifestation of such displaced fears. Thus sexual fears interdigitate with all other fears. The excessively fearful child overestimates the dangers of any situation, including play situations, in which potential injury is perceived.

We interpret *aversion to female genitalia* as a defensive reaction formation to a fear of heterosexual activity and a manifestation of severe sexual impairment. The association between this aversion and excessive fear of injury in childhood is significant at the .05 level in the H- and C-samples.

The *wish to have a larger penis,* in general, reflects a feeling of unacceptability and inadequacy, in particular a feeling of sexual inadequacy: a belief, usually unconsciously held, that sexual functioning has been injured and is vulnerable to further injury; a wish to supersede other males who are feared and regarded as superior. The wish for a larger penis and excessive fearfulness is significantly associated for C-sample at the .05 level.

In summary, excessive fearfulness of injury in childhood tends to reinforce those factors which have already disturbed sexual development and, conversely, sexual apprehensiveness tends to reinforce apprehensiveness about most other activities.

Dependency

Table VII-7 presents items probing excessive dependency[1] upon the parents. The entire subject of dependency has been widely discussed in the psychoanalytic literature. I. Bieber has pointed out that dependency is not "instinctual" although terms such as "passive longings," "passive oral strivings," "infantile longings," "dependency drives," and so forth, suggest at least an affinity to instincts. Actually, the physiobiologic dependence of children is often confused with pathologic dependency arising from psychologic disabilities. "Pathologic dependency is never primary; it is always secondary to the neurotic inhibition of function."

TABLE VII-7 *Pathologic Dependency*

	H	C
1. Patient was excessively dependent on mother in childhood	61	40**
2. Patient was excessively dependent on father in childhood	7	18*
3. Patient frequently turned for protection to:		
mother	52	29†
father	2	2
4. Patient was clinging child	50	25†
5. Patient was reluctant to start school	43	23**

Based on samples of 96 (see Chapter II)

Item 1, "Was the patient excessively dependent upon the mother in childhood?" was answered for 93 H-cases of whom 61 (66 per cent) were reported to have been excessively dependent upon her but only 8 had this relationship with the father. Of 96 responses for the C-sample, 42 per cent were excessively dependent upon the mother and 19 per cent upon the father; only 2 patients in each sample usually turned to the father for protection. These statistics conformed with expectations in view of the frequency of distance and hostility between the H-father and son and the frequency of close-binding intimacy between the H-mother and son.

[1] Our reference to "excessive dependency" should not be taken as a quantifying concept. In our usage, it is synonymous with "pathologic dependency."

Table VII-8 reveals a significant association between sons "babied" by mother and a history of having been a clinging child. The relationship between maternal infantilization of the prehomosexual child and his pathologic dependency is thus underscored. Maternal interference with heterosexuality and filial "clinging" is significant, at the .01 level, for the H-sample only (Table VII-9). An association between having been a "clinging" child and aversion to female genitalia was found to be significant at the .01 level for the H-sample (Table VII-10). These associations point to the relationship between severity of sexual impairment and an early history of pathologic dependency. In our view, the excessive dependency noted in the prehomosexual child follows upon inhibition of resourceful behavior. Such inhibitions were linked by our data to the restrictions and intrusiveness consequent to "babying," overprotection, demasculinizing attitudes, and interference with heterosexual and social activities.

TABLE VII-8 *Clinging Child Associated with Mother Babied Son*

	H		C	
	Clinging child	Not clinging	Clinging child	Not clinging
Mother babied son	36	23	16	23
Did not	12	25	10	48

Significance: H .05; C .01

TABLE VII-9 *Clinging Child Associated with Mother Interfered with Heterosexual Activities (H-Sample Only)*

	Mother interfered	Did not
Clinging child	38	10
Not clinging	21	21

Significance: .01

TABLE VII-10 *Clinging Child Associated with Aversion to Female Genitalia*

	H		C	
	Clinging child	Not clinging	Clinging child	Not clinging
Aversion	41	21	7	26
No aversion	7	20	18	42

Significance: H .01; C not significant

Peer relations

Pathologic dependency upon the mother generally goes along with physical timidity, lack of assertiveness, and a sense of inadequate mastery in coping with peer groups and their activities. A "lone wolf" pattern of childhood behavior was noted in 27 per cent of the C-patients and in 60 per cent of the homosexuals. Fears about the usual "risks" in the rough and tumble of boyhood games are quickly sensed by peers who mistreat and humiliate or reject the playmate who is not "regular" since he does not conform to group standards. The peer group is also alert to over-close attachment to the mother by a playmate who may be called "sissy" or told "go suck your mother's titty." The frequent "lone wolf" pattern noted among prehomosexual boys need not, however, be based upon group expulsion. Boys may isolate themselves from their playmates because of felt inadequacy and a sense of deep shame about their over-closeness to the mother which includes unconscious guilt about incestuous feelings. The fear of anticipated humiliation drives many such boys from contact with peers.

As Table VII-1 indicated, one-third of the prehomosexuals played predominantly with girls. A significant association between excessive fear of physical injury and playing predominantly with girls points to the choice of female playmates as a partial solution to the fear of participating in the activities of other boys who may be physically injurious as well as humiliating (Table VII-11).

Table VII-12 shows a significant association, at the .01 level, between playing predominantly with girls and a "lone wolf" pattern, suggesting that the choice of girls over boys was essentially part of a superficial social relatedness and that fear and inability to play with

TABLE VII-11 *Association Between: "Excessive Fear of Physical Injury" and "Played Mostly with Girls"*

	H		C	
	Played mostly with girls	Did not	Played mostly with girls	Did not
Excessive fear of physical injury	32	48	8	38
No excessive fear	4	22	2	52

Significance: H .05; C .05

TABLE VII-12 *Association Between "Played Mostly with Girls" and "Was Lone Wolf in Childhood" (H-Sample Only)*

	Was lone wolf in childhood	Was not
Played mostly with girls	28	7
Did not	36	35

Significance: .01

boys left little alternative. The possibility that playing with girls served to gratify heterosexual interests may well have played a part in the choice of girl playmates but such interests were not apt to have been expressed in overt behavior. No association was found between playing predominantly with girls and punishment for sexual play with girls. Since most mothers of prehomosexuals were sexually over-restrictive and over-controlling, it is unlikely that overt indications of sexual interest in girl companions would have gone unnoticed or unimpeded. If such were the case, we would have expected more prehomosexuals to have been punished for sex play with girls. It is likely that these H-mothers recognized playing predominantly with girls as atypical of boyhood behavior.

SOME PHYSICAL CHARACTERISTICS OF H-PATIENTS DURING CHILDHOOD

The members of the Research Committee have clinically observed many patients, particularly homosexuals, who reported "inherent" physical disabilities in childhood: (a) frailty; (b) clumsiness; (c) effeminacy. Table VII-13 presents the responses to the items: (1) "Describe the patient's physical make-up in childhood (e.g., frail, clumsy, athletic, well-coōrdinated, overweight, other)." (2) "Were there any effeminate affectations of voice, gesture, etc? Describe same currently."

Frailty

Webster defined "frail" as "weak, brittle, fragile, feeble, delicate." In common usage it seems to have the connotation of uncertain health and vulnerability to disease. Although 47 H-patients described themselves as frail in childhood, only 2 of this group had suffered a severe

TABLE VII-13 *Physical Make-up in Childhood and Maturity*

	H	C
Physical make-up in childhood:		
Athletic	12	39†
Well-coördinated	12	49†
Overweight	15	9
Clumsy	22	10*
Frail	47	20†
Effeminate	26	2†
Physical make-up in maturity:		
Athletic	17	37**
Well-coördinated	12	37†
Frail	17	9
Effeminate	26	4†

Based on samples of 96

illness in early life; 1 H-patient who had not described himself as "frail" had had a severe illness in childhood. Among 20 C-patients who were presumably frail in childhood, 4 had had a serious illness while 6 had suffered serious illness in childhood but did not consider themselves to have been frail. Thus, illness itself does not account for the preponderance of H-patients over C-patients who thought of themselves as frail during childhood. In fact, the histories of both samples reveal an over-all excellent state of physical health with a somewhat better health record noted among the H-patients. This concept of *frailty,* then, is rarely based on reality. A self-concept of frailty may be developed through over-anxious parents, usually the mother, who communicate to the child their own preoccupations with health and safety; or a need for a fragile façade to conceal effectiveness, consciously or unconsciously associated with masculinity, inasmuch as an open presentation of masculine behavior provokes intense anxiety when the parents have been demasculinizing; or a displacement to the body image of a sense of impotence and vulnerability consequent to the disabilities associated with maladaptive personality development.

Table VII-14 shows the association between childhood frailty and maternal over-concern with health and injury among the H-sample, significant at the .001 level. The history of good health among the H-sample indicates that this association is not based on realistic maternal reactions to sick children. In general, the data of this study point to a connection between maternal neuroticism and the promotion of a concept of frailty in the patient. Of all the H-patients who were frail as children, 73 per cent had mothers who interfered with their sons' heterosexual activities in adolescence. Interestingly, while 47 H-patients thought of themselves as frail in childhood, only 17 had this belief in adulthood. We assume that the development of a feeling of well-being, particularly observed among *body-builders,* is a reparative technique for feelings of inadequacy and castrated masculinity. Frailty becomes inconsistent with these defensive needs.

TABLE VII-14 *Frailty in Childhood Associated with Mother Unduly Concerned about Health and Physical Injury (H-Sample Only)*

	Mother unduly concerned	Not unduly concerned
Frail in childhood	32	15
Not frail	15	32

Significance: .001

Clumsiness

Very few H-patients viewed themselves as having been well-coördinated or athletic, and outright clumsiness in childhood was reported by 22 H-patients. Apart from the rare occurrence of congenital dyskinesia, the human organism is potentially well-coördinated. Though varying rates and patterns of maturation are observable, the neurologically normal child attains at least competent levels of motor coördination long before early adolescence. As a rule, difficulties in coördination, or clumsiness, are the consequences of *anxiety* about effective motor performance. For example, we have been particularly struck by the H-patients' attitude toward baseball. Two major themes have been delineated in their dreams: the fear of the "fast" ball, apprehensively anticipated as injuring their genitals (castration anxiety); the inability to bat; the bat splinters, collapses, or the ball is weakly hit (fear of lack of mastery, fear of humiliation, impotence). Athletic ability usually implies participation with others in competitive sports. Inasmuch as most H-patients avoided competitive sports, they tended to dissociate themselves from athletics. The frequency of body-building, noted post-childhood, was apparently not perceived as athletic, despite the physiologic demands of weight-lifting, exercises, and so forth.

Effeminacy

In popular thinking there is a connection between male homosexuality and effeminacy and between effeminacy in males and the biosocial characteristics of females. The effeminate male is thought to be "like" a female in certain ways: voice, intonation, gesture, posture, and other behaviors. The patterns of behavior associated with effeminacy in males, however, are not typical of women. Exaggerated shrugging, "wrist-breaking," lisping, hand-to-hip posturing, effusiveness, and so forth, when observed in women appear to be bizarre rather than feminine. When these gesture-voice affectations are taken on by effeminate males the motoric pattern does not suggest freedom of movement but gives the appearance of constriction and inhibition since the movements are confined to small arcs in space; they are directed inwardly toward the midline of the body rather than away from it. We have noted also that, in some cases, a shoulder tic has been organized and incorporated into a gesture of effeminacy. The effeminate behavior noted among some homosexuals appears to us as neither "masculine" nor "feminine"—it is *sui generis,* i.e., it expresses some caricaturing of female mannerisms but is set within a behavioral framework of motoric constriction and inhibition.

In the *Three Contributions to the Theory of Sexuality* Freud stated: "In men, the most perfect psychic manliness may be united with the inversion (homosexuality)." In our H-sample, no manifestations of effeminacy were apparent in 65 per cent of the cases. The responding psychoanalysts reported evidences of effeminate behavior in voice and gesture in 33 cases of a 96 H-patient sample (34 per cent) some time in their lives; 26 in childhood, 26 as adults. In 19 cases, effeminacy was reported as unchanged from childhood to adulthood while in 7 cases the patients had been effeminate as children but showed no evidence of such traits as adults. On the other hand, 7 patients were presumably not effeminate as children but showed effeminacy as adults. The responding psychoanalysts included descriptive notations which revealed that, in the main, effeminacy in patients was mild, and in only 2 cases was the effeminacy of a pronounced type. In the group interviewed by Westwood in England, 10 per cent were reported to have pronounced effeminate mannerisms and 9 per cent slight effeminate mannerisms. In the H-sample we studied, 2 per cent were markedly effeminate while 25 per cent (26 of 96) were described as having mild effeminate traits currently. The ratio of 19 per cent to 27 per cent falls within a comparable range of sampling differences.

A search was made to locate significant associations between the item tapping effeminacy and other items, e.g., "fear of injury in childhood," "avoidance of competitive games," "mother's most favored or least favored child," "mother feminizing or seductive or overprotective," "mother's confidant," "father's least favored child," "fear of father," "respect for father," "time spent with father," "fear or aversion toward female genitalia," or "fear of injury to own genitals." No significant associations were found. Nor did we find any association between effeminacy and a desire to be a woman. Of 96 H-patients investigated for this item, 38 wanted to be women, and of these, 15 were effeminate. The absence of an association between effeminacy and a desire to be a woman supports our assumption that effeminacy is an unconscious masking of masculinity rather than an emulation of femininity. The absence of a significant association, however, does not preclude the possibility that where effeminacy and wanting to be a woman co-exist, as it did in 15 patients, a psychodynamic relationship may obtain.

On the whole, scant evidence of effeminacy occurred among the C-patients. Of 96 patients, 4 were effeminate in adulthood; 2 had been effeminate in childhood. The wish to be a woman was reported for 8 C-patients.

Earliest sexual experiences

The preadolescent sexual history of the homosexual varies distinctly from that of the heterosexual, even excluding choice of sexual object. Significantly more homosexuals start sexual activity before adolescence than do heterosexuals and more homosexuals are *more frequently* sexually active during preadolescence, early adolescence, and adulthood than are heterosexuals, significant at the .01 level. Table VII-15 lists the age at which patients recalled their first experience of sexual arousal by looking, dreaming, and fantasying about a male or female.

About half the H-sample were reported to have been aroused by the thought or sight of a female at some time in their lives; the total number of C-patients so reported is significantly greater. The striking fact noted is that more than 65 per cent of the C-group recalled heterosexual arousal before 10 years of age and none was reported as having had first sexual arousal after 14 years of age. Among the H-patients, there is an extremely wide age range during which arousal was recalled; thus, 35 per cent recalled first heterosexual arousal after 15, even as late as 40 years of age. One would expect concentrations of sexual arousal at puberty and early adolescence. The delays among the H-patients are outstanding. It raises the question as to whether repression of earlier memories had occurred; our strong impression is that it had.

Sexual arousal as a consequence of dreaming, fantasying, or looking at males was recalled by 75 per cent of the H-patients but only by 17 per cent of the C-patients. The bulk of these memories were placed in the earlier years before 14.

TABLE VII-15 *Age of Remembrance of First Arousal at Thought or Sight of Male and Female Figure*

	Thought or sight of female		Thought or sight of male	
Age	H	C	H	C
10 or less	22	43	31	7
11-12	5	13	14	2
13-14	6	9	20	3
15-16	6		5	2
17-20	4		3	
21-29	5		2	
30-39	3			3
40-	1			
TOTALS	52	65	75	17

Responses to the item tapping first heterosexual genital contact were obtained for 68 H-patients (median age, 20-22) and for 84 C-patients (median age 19-20; Table VII-16). By genital contact we refer to sexual activity where the genitals of the patient, partner, or both are involved in sexual activity. It does not necessarily involve sexual intercourse but may include petting and masturbation of one participant by the other. Heterosexual experiences of this order before the age of 10 were reported in 2 cases in each sample. Of the 84 C-patients, 85 per cent had had their first heterosexual genital contact between the ages of 15 and 24. Of 68 H-patients, 25 per cent made a first heterosexual attempt after the age of 25, in contrast to 7 per cent of 84 C-patients who delayed so long.

A quite different pattern emerges regarding the ages at which the first homosexual genital contact occurred. Of the 96 homosexuals and

22 comparisons who were reported to have had such contact, 29 H-patients and 11 C-patients had homosexual genital experiences by the age of 10 in which their own or a partner's genitals were involved. Before 15 years of age 58 of 96 H-patients (60 per cent) had had homosexual relationships while only 7 C-patients had had a heterosexual contact before that age. Hence, while homosexual experiences often occur during the prepubertal period and may be well established by adolescence, heterosexual experiences tend to be initiated in later adolescence and early adulthood. In Westwood's study of 127 British male homosexuals who volunteered to be interviewed, data were obtained on early homosexual experiences. Homosexual contacts before age 15 were reported in 31 per cent of the group, and before age 16 in 81 per cent.

In view of a common belief that seduction by an older, experienced homosexual may induce homosexuality in a child, some of the features reported about the first homosexual contact are of interest. In these childhood encounters (72 patients had had their first homosexual contact by the age of 16), the partner was described as approximately of the same age in nearly 60 per cent of the cases. The partner was more than two years older than the patient in about 35 per cent of the cases including 13 homosexuals who reported their first partner to be at least 10 years older.

TABLE VII-16 *Age of First Sexual Contacts*

	First genital contact				First homosexual contact involving orifice	Attempt first intercourse[a]	
	Heterosexual N = 96		Homosexual N = 96				
Age	H	C	H	C	H	H	C
10 or less	2	2	29	11	7		
11-14	2	5	29	8	13	1	1
15-16	3	10	14		12	3	9
17-18	7	18	10		14	6	19
19-20	19	17	2	2	9	19	22
21-24	18	26	9		17	19	32
25-29	5	4	2	1	7	8	7
30-39	10	2	1		2	8	3
40-	2					3	
Total reporting	68	84	96	22	81	67	93

[a] 37 H-patients reported success at first intercourse; 28 never tried.

Of the 58 homosexuals and 19 heterosexuals who had had their first homosexual contact by 14 years of age, 25 H-patients and 8 C-patients claimed seduction. Now, whether an actual seduction took place is open to question since the burden of guilt and responsibility may have been projected to the partner. Several responding psychoanalysts wrote impressionistic comments, including quotations from patients, i.e., "I was seeking it," "I was cruising." Three psychoanalysts questioned the patient's claim of seduction and noted that the activity was mutual masturbation. Further, a sexually preoccupied child might actively "drift" into a situation where an adult homosexual could promote some type of sex play which the child might rationalize as seduction. But assuming that the claimed seductions did, in fact, occur, it would account only for 25 H-patients and leave unexplained the heterosexual adaptation of the 8 C-patients who also were "seduced" before the age of 14. It was Westwood's opinion that seduction had no appreciable effect among his "contacts" in the establishment of a homosexual pattern. He also pointed out that the so-called "victim" was often the tempting seducer who encouraged or actively sought the sexual act with the older male. He found no correlation between the sexual technique employed in the first homosexual experience and the later preferred practices.

The fifth column of Table VII-16 presents the age at which H-patients reported their first homosexual experiences utilizing some bodily orifice as "insertees" or "insertors." Intromission occurred somewhat later than did other homosexual acts; 32 per cent reported this initial experience after 21 years of age.

Columns 6 and 7 of Table VII-16 list the age of the first attempt at heterosexual intercourse, whether or not successful. A total of 28 homosexuals were reported *never* to have attempted intercourse with a female. Attempts were reported in 67 H-cases and in 93 C-cases (on the basis of 96 cases in each sample). In one H-case and one C-case heterosexual intercourse was attempted between the ages of 13 and 14; the median age for C-patients was 20 and for H-patients 21-22. Only 3 C-patients first attempted intercourse beyond the age of 30 while 17 per cent of the H-patients who made a heterosexual attempt did so after 30 years of age. Success on the first attempt was reported by 55 per cent of the H-patients who ventured to have heterosexual intercourse and by 70 per cent of the C-patients who tried, a significant difference.

The data in Tables VII-15 and VII-16 show a striking similarity to some of the material published in *The Ladder* questionnaire study referred to in Chapter II. In the present study 68 per cent of the H-cases reported arousal by the sight or fantasy of a male figure before the age of 15; 58 per cent of *The Ladder* sample noted the awareness of sexual arousal at the thought or sight of a male figure before age 15. In the group we studied 60 per cent reported first homosexual experience before age 15, *The Ladder* reported 52 per cent. Among our patient sample 30 per cent were bisexual, and among *The Ladder* group 38 per cent were so reported. These statistics are all well within the limits of samples from the same population, and therefore support the position that the findings of each study may have significance beyond the individuals represented in either investigation.

We found that the homosexuals were more often excessively preoccupied with sexuality in childhood; that a greater proportion of H- than of C-patients had childhood sexual fantasies about males and that fewer H-patients had such fantasies about females; that most of the H-patients had participated in homosexual activity in preadolescence or early adolescence in contrast to the C-patients who began sexual activities later.

Identification

The term "identification" is difficult to define precisely and concepts of identification are as broad as they are sometimes vague. In the plethora of references to identification, formulations vary from conscious imitation to unconscious patterning or modeling, including many intervening forms of personality and behavioral "matching." Since there is a large area of subjective interpretation of its meaning among psychoanalysts, we avoided questions that might tap heterogeneous evaluations of identification processes and we stayed close to the line of conscious and objective parameters. Therefore, we limited ourselves to the items: "Did the patient ever want to be a woman?" and "Whom did the patients want to be like in childhood?"

"Did the patient want to be a woman?"

This question was answered affirmatively for 41 homosexual patients and 8 comparison patients. Since the number of answers for the C-sample is small, Table VII-17 presents significant items which are related to the wish to be a woman for H-patients only.

TABLE VII-17 *Did Patient Ever Want to Be a Woman?*

	Wanted to be a woman	
	Yes 41	No 61
Patient wanted to be like mother (18)	1**	3
Patient wanted to be like a sister (6)	6**	0
An older sister was father's favorite (20)	13*	7
An older sister was admired (21)	16**	5
Son accepted father (24)	4**	20

Of 18 H-patients who wanted to be like their mother 14 wanted to be a woman, significant at the .01 level. Of 6 H-patients who wanted to be like a sister, all had expressed a desire to be like a woman at some time in her life. In 21 H-cases, the patient admired a sister, and of these cases 16 H-patients had wanted to be a woman, significant at .01. The data suggest that the wish in a male to be a woman is related to a wish for paternal acceptance and admiration which is perceived as being given to a female. In the sample studied this perception was generally accurate. Where the son accepted his father, only 4 of 24 wanted to be a woman. A good relationship with the father is negatively correlated with a desire to be a woman. Table VII-18 presents the responses to the question "Whom did the patient want to be like?"

TABLE VII-18 *Some Trends in Patient Identification*

	H	C
1. Whom did the patient want to be like?		
Mother	18	1†
Sister or other female	7	1
TOTAL	25	2†
Father	12	20
Brother	12	5
Other male	12	17
TOTAL	36	42

"Whom did the patient want to be like in childhood?"

(Of 106 H-patients, responses were given for 70 cases, and of 100 C-patients, responses were given for 58 cases.)

Father: Of 12 H-patients who had wanted to be like the father, 6 had Class 1 parents (see Chapter VI), 4 had Class 4 parents and 2 had Class 3 parents (these mothers in Class 3 were reported to have gross psychiatric disorders). None of these 12 H-patients had a detached-indifferent father; the distribution of other paternal types was proportionately represented. A trend toward paternal acceptance and affection was noted and, in turn, the sons predominantly accepted and respected the father. The patient admired a female sibling in 6 cases and in 8 the patients hated a sibling—7 of them brothers. Of the 12 patients, 4 were diagnosed as schizophrenic and 3 of the 4 were "effeminate." The responding psychoanalysts reported 5 patients who identified the homosexual partner with the father and of these 5 fathers, 4 had been dominant in interparental relations. Three other patients sought a partner who the psychoanalyst believed was identified with a family member. In one instance, the identification was with a hated brother and in the other two cases with the mother.

Most of the 20 C-patients who had identified with the father respected and admired him; all but 2 fathers were dominant in interparental relationships; 14 were in Class 2 and 4 were in Class 1; 2 others were in Class 3. Detached-indifferent and hostile fathers were absent among the group of C-patients who had wanted to be like the father. CBI mothers were underrepresented.

Brother. In 12 homosexual cases, the patient had wished to be like a brother. The interparental relationships in most of these cases were Class 3. No patient in this group either respected or admired his father, 9 of whom were detached-hostile. In no case was the son the father's favorite while 6 patients were favored by the mother who preferred her H-son to the patient's brother. In 4 of these 6 cases, the father preferred this brother to the patient. In all instances, the patient wanted to be like the paternally preferred brother. In 8 cases, the homosexual partner was identified with a brother (see Chapter V).

In 12 homosexual cases, the patients wished to be like a male who was not a member of the nuclear family. In 10 cases one or the other parent was dominant-minimizing while in the other 2 cases the parents had reciprocal contempt for each other. The father was hated and feared in 11 cases (in one case the father had died during the patient's childhood). In 5 cases, the H-patient followed his mother's expressed wish to emulate her choice of an "ideal." In 2 cases, these "ideals" were maternal uncles and 3 were other males whom the mother greatly admired and whom she pictured as more powerful than, and generally superior to, the patient's father. One mother had wanted her H-son to be like the deceased father. In 7 other cases, the patients chose "athletes," "geniuses," and other figures of heroic stature as the males they wished to be.

Only 5 comparison patients had wanted to be like a brother while 17 had wanted to be like some other male. The C-patients who had wanted to be like a male other than their father presented a more disturbed psychiatric picture than had C-patients who as children had wanted to be like their father. Among this group 7 were schizophrenic (4 was the statistically expected number); 4 had wanted to be a woman at some time in their lives. In terms of parent-son interaction 10 had CBI mothers but only 2 had hostile fathers; the others were ambivalent or indifferent. The mother was the dominant spouse in 14 C-families and of this group 10 were in Class 3. The patient was his mother's favorite in 7 cases. Eight mothers had wanted the C-son to be like a person of their own choice, and in all these cases the sons also wanted to be like the males the mothers admired.

In sum, of these C-patients 5 had wanted to be like a brother and 5 like a maternal uncle or grandfather. Others had wanted to be like a "strong man," "a benevolent despot," "an army general," "a heroic football player," "a western cowboy," and "Daniel Boone."

Mother. A group of 18 homosexuals had wanted to be like their mother. Among them 8 were schizophrenic and 6 of these had wanted to be a woman at some time in life. Of 5 who were "effeminate," 4 had wanted to be a woman and 2 were schizophrenic. Of the 18 cases 15 had wanted to be a woman thus differing from the remaining H-sample beyond the .05 level of significance. Eight parental pairs were classified as Class 3, and 2 as Class 4; 14 mothers were CBI; patterns of family atmosphere and parent-son categories were, however, about equally represented. The H-son was the mother's favorite in 14 cases, and 11 of these mothers also accepted and admired her H-son. In the total H-sample, in 6 cases the mother had wanted her son to be like her; 5 of these mothers are represented within this group.

The fathers preferred a brother or a sister in 16 of 17 cases where the patients had a sibling. In 10 cases the H-son was least favored, yet in 9 cases the father had wanted the patient to be like him, but the son was least favored by 7 of these fathers and of these 6 patients wanted to be a woman. In 4 cases the mother opposed the father's wish; she wanted her H-son to be like herself, instead. Only 1 H-son here accepted and respected his father; however, 5 patients admired a brother, 4 of whom were the father's favorite. Of 4 sisters whom patients admired, 3 were the father's favorite. In the fourth case, the father preferred an older brother and the mother preferred a younger brother.

Though these patients had wished to be like the mother, the characteristics sought in the homosexual partner in 7 cases were like those of the father; these patients were also least favored by the father. In 8 cases, the characteristics sought in the partner were those of a brother or sister who had been the father's preferred child. In 2 instances the father preferred a brother but the patient sought a partner like the father. It is of interest that of 18 homosexuals who said they had wanted to be like their mothers, only 2 had chosen a partner whose characteristics were identified with her.

Only one comparison patient had wanted to be like his mother; he was diagnosed as schizophrenic.

Sister. Six homosexuals had wanted to be like a sister; 2 had male siblings. All had wanted to be a woman; 3 were effeminate and 2 were schizophrenic. The parents were in Class 1 or 3. Five mothers were CBI and 4 were paired with fathers who were *hostile*. In 3 cases the patient was favored by his mother. Each of the 6 mothers discouraged masculine behavior and attitudes or encouraged feminine ones; 5 of these sons either hated or feared the mother, an overrepresentation of hostility to the mother as compared with the rest of the H-sample. One patient hated and feared the sister whom he had wanted to be like while 5 admired the sister they wished to be like. Of the 6 H-patients 4 identified the partner with a member of the nuclear family; in only one case was the identification made with the sister, and in the 3 other cases the identification was with the father. Five patients sought masculine qualities in the partner. Only 1 comparison case had wanted to be like his sister.

In cases where the patient had wanted to be like his father, the father was usually the dominant spouse; or if he was not, his wife did not minimize him. In these cases the father-son relationship showed a group trend toward mutual acceptance and respect. Among the C-sons who wished to be like the father, clearly positive aspects in the relationship were noted. Where H-patients wished to be like a brother, a poor relationship existed with the father in all instances. This was also evident when the H-patient wished to be like some male outside the nuclear family. Heterosexual patients who wished to be like a male other than the father were among the more disturbed cases in the C-sample. When an H-patient wanted to be like his mother she was usually a Class 3 wife who was dominant in the family and minimized her husband. In addition, she was most often CBI and demasculinizing; in about one-third of the cases she wanted her H-son to be like herself. Only 2 of these patients sought maternal characteristics in their homosexual partners; the majority sought masculine qualities. In the 6 H-cases where the patient wished to be like a sister, all had wanted to be like a woman at some time. All had demasculinizing mothers; all had fathers who had rejected them.

Three case histories follow which focus on some of the early disturbing influences interfering with heterosexual development in the life of one bisexual and two homosexual patients.

CASE NO. 1

The patient's mother was more close-binding intimate and overprotective than warmly affectionate. His father, pleasant but detached and ineffectual, was dominated by his wife. The patient shared a bedroom with his sister, a strong-minded, independent girl, five years his junior, whom he secretly envied. During the first few years of his life the patient was a focal point of attention since he was the first son and the first grandson on both sides of the family. He was said to be a "lovely" boy. Always trying to please, he never took a stand in an argument. In his pre-school days he was indulged by his mother and doted upon by his aunts but he had few peermates. In his early school years, his isolation from male peers persisted. He played with girls and often played alone with dolls. He was called a "sissy." Once his teacher asked him and a little girl who lived near-by to stay after school to clean up. His arrival home late and in the company of a girl greatly upset his mother who thought surely something sexual must have occurred. The only time he recalled a beating from his father, who also threatened to take him to the police, was when the patient and a girl were discovered inspecting each other's genitals. It had been the mother who had urged the father on, but during the whipping she implored him to stop.

The patient had asthma between the ages of six and twelve but he was neither weak nor unskilled in athletics. He did not enjoy playing baseball—it was the batting, he said, that bothered him, with everyone watching him and demanding some spectacular hit.

He felt he could not bear the humiliation of a failure. His mother could see the ball games through the window. She encouraged him to play but when games were started he would hide out.

In preadolescence and adolescence he was much favored and even "courted" by adult female relatives. He would be dated for shows, dinners, and evenings out, and he learned to hint for things he wanted. His mother was jealous and possessive. He liked her to be possessive of him yet feared to hurt her. He developed tact and finesse so that he would say just the thing to please her. The patient reported, "I was obliging and agreeable like my father," but unlike his father, he learned to lie to his mother, to charm and flatter her. She believed she knew her son's every thought yet she often turned to him for advice.

At the age of thirteen he met a slightly older boy who became the first person outside the family with whom he had a continuing relationship albeit a homosexual one. He was compulsive about engaging in this secret act and tried to meet his partner at every available opportunity. He feared his mother might in some way see through him, find out, and pounce upon him. There was a great turmoil when, some six years later, he made it obvious to his parents that he was having a homosexual affair. They were very distressed and worried about what the neighbors would think. He stood his ground and quietly moved out. "I thought my mother would collapse when she found out I moved." She could not believe her son would dare flout her control, nor could she believe he had the strength to assert himself against her. She predicted that he would come "crawling back" in less than a week. Vindictively, she froze the funds of their joint bank account.

He had entered into a fairly permanent relationship with an insecure, frightened young man. The patient did the cooking, sewing, and managing of their apartment while the partner, a compulsive cleaner, kept things in perfect order. When the two went shopping together, the patient would insist on walking ahead and his partner would trot along behind just as the patient used to follow his mother on her occasional shopping sprees which seemed to him like holiday celebrations.

The patient was sturdy and tall but had effeminate gestures and speech. Asked if he had ever wanted to be a woman he felt certain he had not. During sessions when he talked of his father he summed up his opinion of him with the comment, "He was a nothing." The patient "loathed" being touched by him. Early in treatment the patient had the following dreams:

Dream 1: "I was at a group therapy meeting with women and men. We all had a textbook called *The Stone Age,* because people today all have stone faces. One class was observing children and they all looked female. I said 'she' to one child and it was a 'he.' Then one of the children's fathers came and got the child and he yelled at the therapist because boys and girls were playing together in the same area."

Dream 2: "There was a very handsome woman, well dressed in a purple wool suit, and purple shoes, and a wide-brimmed hat. She was very buxom, like Mae West. She was very seductive and sexy like; that was all she wanted. I kept putting her off with flattery and praise but all she wanted was to go to bed with me. It was very uncomfortable. Suddenly I was getting a haircut (mother was *never* pleased with any haircut) and this one came out wild, like that purple hat she was wearing. I didn't know what to do but finally my friend told me, 'Go home! Show your mother your haircut.' "

CASE NO. 2

This was an only son who had two older sisters. He was bisexual when he entered psychoanalysis. He had been waiting for the Big Break when he would be discovered as a genius in any of several artistic and dramatic fields in each of which he felt he had outstanding talent.

His puritanical mother was affectionate to him only when he was a small boy. As he matured, she would alternate between being sweet to him and sharply critical, always comparing him unfavorably with some other neighboring young man. His father was unpredictable. On the whole he was an inhibited man, preoccupied with his own problems. He was, for the most part, indifferent to his son. Yet he had a flair and a style that was attractive and which the son picked up.

The patient was a handsome child and his mother dressed him carefully never allowing him to get his clothes rumpled or dirty. He was watched over by his mother, aunts, and grandmother. One of them always seemed to be admonishing him not to play too rough, not to get hurt and warning the other boys not to attack him. His mother accompanied him to and from school, about five blocks away, until he was eight years old. He was afraid to play baseball though his coördination was good. He feared catching a fast ball and could not bat well.

The strains between the parents were dramatized around the

wife's assertion that the father's side of the family was not much good; only her side was worth while. The son found himself increasingly alienated from his father and on the side of his mother and her relatives. The mother would cuddle a niece but never demonstrated any affection for him. She whipped him on occasion and sometimes instigated the father to do so. He would beat the boy with fury.

His mother bathed the patient until he was eleven or twelve and in recalling this during psychoanalysis he wondered why he would try to lean forward in the tub to conceal his genitals from her. A frequent childhood fantasy which he associated with his physical attractiveness was that he might be kidnaped and held for high ransom. As the fantasy would unfold he would become frightened and scamper to his parents' bed, seeking reassurance. Usually he would get between them turning his back to his father but was very aware of him. He would fondle or hold his mother, a rare opportunity for warm closeness, delighting in her smooth skin.

His earliest sexual memories involved explorations with a girl in the apartment house in which they lived. This activity was suspected by some teen-age boys who teased and derided him. His older sister and her girl friend also teased him and threatened to "cut off his pipe stem" if he were not good.

A maternal uncle, very much admired by the boy, belonged to a bachelors' club that had a room decorated with animal skins, guns, swords, and trophies. The romance of this room was used by the uncle to introduce the patient into homosexuality. Their homosexual activities continued for several years during the patient's preadolescence.

In his early teens the patient slept across a hall from his parents whose room had no door. He could see and hear their sexual activity and strained to know more. He could not believe his mother had sexual intercourse by her own desire. Indeed, he denied to himself her participation and developed great hatred for the "bestiality" of his father. Once the boy found and destroyed his father's contraceptives.

During the patient's adolescence he had a variety of brief homosexual contacts with neighboring boys. When later on he moved from home he would have occasional pick-ups but also settled into an odd relationship with a divorcée, older than he, with a small child. The patient maintained his own room which helped keep the relationship remote yet he was very dependent upon her in many ways. He behaved tyrannically after the manner of a spoiled child. When she finally broke with him to join with a man more likely to marry her, the patient was quite upset to be faced with desertion; he felt he wanted her back desperately. On the other hand, her love for him did seem impossibly shallow if she could leave him so easily. He then sought girls who were innocent-looking, wore no make-up, were round in face and figure, and were sexually provocative, an image combining his mother and previous love. His ensuing heterosexual relationships were always melodramatic entanglements but he persisted in them, assuring himself each time that if they loved each other all problems would disappear. At the same time he might compulsively seek a homosexual pick-up at a corner or a bar. These contacts would be uncomplicated and direct.

The fantasy of being a smashing success lingered on: as soon as a famous stage director, movie magnate, or art critic saw his work which he would modestly present, his talent would be immediately recognized and he would be employed at a fabulous salary. Or he would dream of being chosen by some world-famous man as a protégé to be subsidized until he achieved solid success.

Dream 1: "I am visiting a couple I admire. The man is a successful artist. The wife is big-breasted, virginal looking. They have two nice children. At first I talk admiringly to the husband about his work. Then he and one child are occupied in a corner of the room while I stay with the wife and the other child. They are on a bed and the child is put to one side. I make advances to her and she does not resist."

Dream 2: He is a member of a boys' club where the convention is that they casually kill each other under the appropriate circumstances. "I am sitting in the club room (patient associated the room to his uncle's club). Then I am in the shower and a club member who is sitting on the toilet says to me, 'I want to kill you.' I sort of put him off for a while and then I say, 'All right, I'll serve you.' He jumps on my back and begins to bite my neck. Then I woke up."

CASE NO. 3

The patient is a short, energetic, smiling young man who entered psychoanalysis because he felt insecure, afraid, even stupid, and at times blocked completely. His shifts from boldness to stark fear discouraged him from becoming an actor.

In his early years his mother was close-binding and over-intimate. Later on she became preoccupied with her own problems and was detached and critical of him. His father, much his mother's senior, was detached from both. The parents were immigrants who had married for reasons related to family customs. Neither cared for the other—neither had much self-esteem. In the early years of their marriage, the father appeared more devoted to his own mother and brother than to his wife and son; he usually visited his mother before coming home evenings. The wife absorbed herself with the son. The patient recalled that whenever the father tried to dress or bathe him he would scream hysterically for his mother. On occasion he would dress up in her clothes and parade and show off before his amused father.

When the patient was about seven years old his father died. The mother had to go out to work, and during the day the patient was left with his maternal grandmother and an aunt in a household with several other grandchildren, all more favored than he. He felt unwanted and a nuisance. His mother would not let him go to school alone; "It was my funny, old, foreign-speaking grandfather who took me." He was ridiculed by the other boys.

Once he was caught in reciprocal explorations with a girl where each was trying to stick a lollypop handle into the other's anus. He was severely beaten. The following summer the girl was killed in an accident.

The collection of families lived in the country for a while and they had outdoor toilets. He would peek into the toilet to watch his aunts there and found the act of wiping the genitals to be exceedingly disgusting. At one time his mother told him that at birth he had a very large head and that it had been very difficult to get it through. He felt women's sexual areas to be very messy in contrast to the neat and clean male genital.

In his early teens he slept in the same room with his mother and hated it. When she started to work he did the shopping, cleaning, and cooking. During this period he enjoyed the company of his aunts and was often invited to talk with them in the afternoons as they were dressing. Some sought his advice and showed that they admired him.

His mother fought with all his uncles and he, too, felt they were his enemies. They all bullied him. One uncle threatened to cut off his penis. Once this uncle suggested that the patient should be in an orphanage. He had many fights with his cousins, especially an envied older one who was overindulged. He also had fights with a group of neighboring boys who were brothers. In one scuffle his penis was injured and required medical attention. He later engaged in homosexual affairs with these boys and others. The males who bullied him or whom he envied were the ones about whom he had homosexual fantasies; in some cases he would have homosexual relations. His imagery would often consist of visualizing the partner spread-eagled on a bed for the patient to approach; or he himself would be bound and tied and the partner would be the sexual aggressor.

When he began to go out on his own at eighteen or so, he felt that though he was ugly he could somehow make it up with charm. He worked with compulsive persistence to get attention and to prove that he was attractive. He did not feel at ease with most men, only with "gay" ones. It was usually when he felt defeated, frustrated, or rejected that he would go "cruising." Mostly he would try to get two of three homosexuals at a bar to compete for him. It was a great pleasure to let them discover that small as he was in stature, he had a huge penis.

He had recurrent dreams that he was walking down a street and was shot and killed by a gang member or some unknown person. Once he had what he called a "horrible dream of intercourse with my mother."

Summary

Our questionnaire revealed patterns of prehomosexual childhood and preadolescent behavior that differed in fundamental and crucial ways from the characteristics noted during the early years of the comparison patients. Excessive fear of physical injury in childhood was noted among three-quarters of the H-patients, and most avoided fights. Less than one-fifth participated in the usual games of boys. Over half were isolates; one-third played predominantly with girls.

Excessive fear of physical injury in both the H- and C-samples was found to be significantly associated with psychopathologic parental behavior. Patients who were apprehensive about being hurt had mothers who were overconcerned about health and injury; they were socially restrictive and interfered with self-assertiveness and heterosexuality. The fathers were mostly hostile and rejecting. Much guilt about masturbation was significantly associated with excessive fear of injury among prehomosexual children while pathologic attitudes toward male and female genitals were significantly associated with fear of injury in both patient samples. The significant association between pathologic sexual attitudes and excessive fear of injury is assumed to connote a reciprocal interaction between fearfulness in childhood and the psychodynamics underlying disturbances in sexual development.

Evidences of early pathologic dependency were present in about one-half of the homosexuals. Excessive dependency was significantly associated with maternal infantilization, interference with heterosexual activity, excessive fear of injury, and aversion to female genitalia. Parental behavior which stimulated fear and anxiety in the child was seen as inhibiting self-assertiveness and fostering the development of pathologic dependency.

Defense-avoidance behavior with peer groups was characteristic of most homosexuals in our sample. In 61 per cent of these cases isolation from other children was noted though many played predominantly with girls. Significant associations were found between playing predominantly with girls and excessive fear of injury, a "lone wolf" pattern, and paternal hostility. We propose that fear of exposure to humiliative jibes of playmates and shame about felt inadequacy and overattachment to a CBI mother contributed to the withdrawal from male peer groups. Lack of paternal support and overtly contemptuous attitudes for the failure to be tough, reinforced a sense of shame and impotence.

Our questionnaire contained items probing childhood and current physical characteristics of our patient sample. Few homosexuals were purportedly athletic or well coördinated in childhood; almost one-half thought of themselves as frail and about one-quarter were effeminate. The patients' assessment of poor coördination is assumed to be the consequence of anxiety and muscle tension associated with fear about participating in games and competitive sports. Though 47 homosexuals regarded themselves as frail in childhood, only 17 of these continued to consider themselves to be frail. Since serious illness in childhood was rare and the over-all health record was excellent, the self-appraisal of frailty is clearly based upon considerations other than standards of health and vigor. Of 26 H-patients who were effeminate in childhood, 19 continued to be effeminate. In all, 33 homosexuals had been effeminate at some time in life. No significant associations were found between effeminacy and other variables including the wish to be a woman. We interpret effeminacy as a defense façade to conceal masculinity.

The childhood and adolescent sexual histories of homosexuals and comparison patients showed distinct contrasts. We found that prehomosexuals tend to begin genital sexual activities with a partner earlier and have them much more frequently than do heterosexuals. More than half the H-sample had had homosexual experiences by the age of 14 as compared with only one-fifth of the C-sample. Heterosexual intercourse was attempted by 70 per cent of the H-patients; but whereas one-quarter of the C-patients were initiated by age 18, less than 10 per cent of the homosexuals had made a heterosexual attempt by this age. Thus, heterosexuals began heterosexual activity *later* than homosexuals began homosexual activity though most H-patients made a delayed heterosexual attempt.

The process of identification was explored on the level of conscious wishes "to be like" someone. The expressed desire to be a woman occurred significantly more often among homosexuals who had wanted to be like their mother, or a sister, particularly one whom the patient or his father admired. Homosexuals who had had accepting attitudes toward their father wanted to be a woman infrequently. Only 2 C-patients had wanted to be like the mother or a sister, as contrasted to 24 H-patients. Among the 12 homosexuals who had wanted to be like their father the paternal-filial relationship was better than among other homosexuals. Where the father was the model, he was dominant in family decisions. All 12 homosexuals who had wanted to be like a brother, usually an admired brother, had a poor father-son relationship.

Twelve H-patients had wanted to be like some male outside the nuclear family. The relationship of these patients to members of the nuclear family was poor.

The best father-son relationships in the total sample were noted for the 20 comparison patients who had wanted to be like their father. The 17 C-patients who had wished to be like a male other than their father were among the most disturbed segment of the C-sample.

VIII

Homosexuality in Adolescence[1]

THE FORCES that determine a homosexual adaptation lend themselves more easily and at times more dramatically to observation in adolescence since sexual conflicts are so much closer to the surface in the adolescent period.

This report is based on a study of 30 male adolescent homosexuals. Of these patients, 23 were studied in the male adolescent ward at Bellevue Hospital, 6 at the University Hospital Adolescent Clinic, and 1 was seen in private practice. All patients selected were actively homosexual. Boys who had had isolated homosexual experiences but who appeared to be heterosexual were excluded. The patients were referred by the Children's Court of the City of New York, the Bureau of Child Guidance, various social agencies, and parents; some, particularly those seen at the Clinic, came of their own volition.

The presenting problems included a bizarre, disturbed, or destructive behavior in the home; truancy, vagrancy, or long absence from the home, with or without complaints that the boys were consorting with homosexuals or engaging in homosexual activity. One boy was charged with sexual and sadistic attacks on girls, another with arson. One boy was apprehended for voyeuristic activity while another made a homi-

[1] The authors express appreciation to Dr. Arthur Zitrin, Director of Bellevue Hospital, for permission to include the data obtained during a three-year study at the Adolescent Service of Bellevue Hospital. This study was carried out by the late Dr. Paul Zimmering, Senior Psychiatrist of the Male Adolescent Service and by Dr. Paul Dince, who was at that time Public Health Service Fellow in Psychiatry.

cidal attempt on his mother. Those who sought help independently complained of severe anxiety, depression, or school difficulties.

Although all cases were not studied with uniform intensity—a few were interviewed only a few times—most were seen for a dozen or more sessions. The behavior and social relationships of most of the boys were studied in the group setting of a hospital ward. Wherever possible, both parents were interviewed in order to obtain validating collateral information and to make a personality evaluation of the parents. Emphasis was directed toward the interparental relationship and the relationship of each parent to the patient.

Diagnosis

About one-half the patients were diagnosed as suffering from "schizophrenia." With two exceptions, the remainder of the patients were considered to be "schizoid" or "schizophrenic personalities." Many of the patients who were not diagnosed as overtly schizophrenic had schizophrenic Rorschach protocols, as had the boys in the total sample who had strongly identified themselves with girls.

Classification

It was extremely difficult to fit the patients of this study into meaningful categories. They could, however, be classified to some extent according to the degree to which they identified themselves with females. There were boys who apparently had renounced heterosexual strivings, and had played a feminine role in sexuality as well as in life style. They had markedly effeminate mannerisms, most of which were exaggerated imitations of behavior presumably used by women to attract men sexually. These boys tended to become homosexual "mistresses" who frequently sought a protective partner. Histories often revealed a marked feminine identification since early childhood. They tended not to masturbate, were usually averse to involving their penises in the sex act, and strove for spontaneous orgasm. Psychological testing revealed confusion, conflict, and indecision as to choice of sexual role. The histories, dreams, and fantasies of even the most effeminate boys, however, revealed heterosexual strivings manifested especially in early puberty.

Many such boys often openly questioned whether it was preferable to be a boy or a girl. One quite effeminate adolescent, a transvestite with a long history of homosexuality, stated in his initial interview that he always knew he was a homosexual. "I want to be a girl," he said, "I always wanted to be a girl." At a subsequent interview he vacillated between saying that he wanted to be a man and that he wanted to be a woman. The preference, he indicated, was to be a man, but that he had no choice. At a still later interview when he was quite comfortable with the psychiatrist whom he had begun to trust, he stated, "I would like to be a psychiatrist—a man like you. I want to be a father just like every other father. I would prefer not to be a homosexual but I can't help myself. I'm half boy and half girl." It was then he revealed, and with considerable anxiety, that at the age of twelve he had been sexually excited by an older sister. Most of the boys in the group revealed that they had had heterosexual fantasies during puberty, which were sometimes of very brief duration and were then apparently banished from awareness. Some patients had displayed sporadic heterosexual strivings despite overt effeminacy.

The contrasting group was composed of boys who were undergoing a crisis in defining themselves sexually. Although actively homosexual, their masculine strivings were prominent. Effeminate traits were much less observable and sometimes apparent only to the most discerning. Some were "insertors" (see Chapter IX) in the homosexual act with varying degrees of acceptance of this role while some preferred the "insertee" role exclusively. In general, they alternated the roles, and sought different types of partners accordingly. Sometimes these patients would shift roles during the course of the same sexual experience or adopt both roles simultaneously.

The group in an adaptive crisis was much larger and more diversified; its members generally showed more evidence of overt anxiety and a greater variety of disturbed behavior. It included most of the homosexual prostitutes, the voyeurist, the fire-setter, the boy who attacked girls sadistically, and so on. One boy was a compulsive masturbator who used his stepfather's condoms in the masturbatory act with the explanation that it made him "come quicker." Many were given to hypermasculine posturings, preoccupation with body building, and Don Juan affectations. Some of the homosexual prostitutes tried to conceal their psychological stake in homosexuality by protesting that they catered to homosexuals for financial gain only. After several interviews this pretense was generally abandoned. While there was considerable conflict about masculinity and a strong tendency to handle problems through homosexual maneuvers, masculine strivings were persistent and in evidence among the group still in flux. Destructive and expropriative behavior occurred mainly among these boys. One had robbed all his homosexual partners at the point of a knife. Another had reported approximately fifty homosexual assaults upon him by men, several of whom were arrested and sentenced before the authorities discovered his game. Another sought out virile-looking men, the type he wished to be like, for the purpose of performing fellatio upon them. This boy complained bitterly that his father never gave him the things he wanted. He was involved in seven instances of housebreaking, all solitary adventures, stealing male effects exclusively. He specifically sought out men's jewelry which he never used and usually threw away. On the occasion of his last housebreaking he could find nothing to steal and so set fire to the apartment. When asked why he had done this and how he felt when he set the fire, he said that he was angry and hurt because he was unable to find anything he wanted, and that "it was like when I don't get what I want from my father." Another older adolescent who sought virile-looking partners in order to perform fellatio, then pederasty, upon them, described his feelings during the act in this way: "It's as if there were only one penis and he had it; when I sucked it, it was mine." This same young man was one of those in the entire sample who had had sexual intercourse with a girl. "When I like a girl I feel as if I have no right, as if I didn't have permission. Then I feel as if I am no good in some way . . . have to be recognized by some man."

In one boy sexual fantasies occurring during prepuberty and puberty centered upon his mother almost exclusively. One type of homosexual activity in which he engaged involved the search for a masculine ideal (usually a compulsive activity following mounting anxiety). The second activity was more pleasurable and relaxed and involved another boy: "He was just like me." The partner was an effeminate homosexual. They shared many interests and intimacies; they embraced and kissed each other when they met. Apparently, they had a genuine liking for one another. Their sexual activities consisted of mutual fellatio, during which they coöperated in a mutual fantasy. Each one imagined that he was the other and that at the same time each was a mature woman performing fellatio on this image of himself.

Homosexuality as a defensive adaptation

The effeminate adolescents related comfortably to other effeminate homosexuals and to lesbians and women considered as asexual, but became very anxious in the presence of a female perceived as "sexual." Many patients suffered marked anxiety at the prospect of any heterosexual contact. Several older boys had girl friends and had engaged in limited petting with them, but had never experienced erection or sexual excitement. One such patient spent the night at the home of his girl friend when her parents were away. She came to his bed dressed only in pajamas and lay down next to him. He became "numb," "without feeling," "paralyzed." Within a few days he yielded to a compulsive urge to go to a Greenwich Village bar and pick up a homosexual. Another boy, after a long period of total sexual abstinence, was stimulated sexually by a girl whom he had escorted for the evening. He felt sexually excited when he bade her good night at her door. He began to experience extreme anxiety and upon leaving compulsively picked up a homosexual—this in the face of tormenting self-recriminations, for he had broken his resolve to give up homosexuality.

In several instances effeminate homosexuals in the ward became very anxious and disturbed whenever they felt compelled to act like boys. Once they could assume an effeminate guise, they appeared happy and relaxed, if other boys in the ward did not torment them too much. One such boy patient was cheerful, sociable, and outgoing; he described himself as the "ward queen," but engaged in no homosexual activity during his hospitalization since he had no sexual interest in boys of his own age. He appeared unafraid of his peers but defended himself in fighting much the way a girl would. On his second admission, several months later, the ward patients were unusually tough and aggressive. The boy was unable to act effeminately for he felt he had to put up an appearance of masculinity. He was extremely uncomfortable, unhappy, and fearful of the other boys. He solved his problem, however, by seducing the bully of the ward and under his protection was able once again to become effeminate. He became cheerful and spontaneous once more. The same boy stated that though he experienced nocturnal emissions he could not masturbate by manipulating his own penis. He enjoyed various types of homosexual activity in which he played a "feminine" role and would experience spontaneous orgasm. When his homosexual partner performed fellatio upon him, he experienced intense itching in his genital region and he was moved to uncontrollable laughter which put a stop to the act. On one occasion when he was coaxed into performing anal intercourse upon his partner he experienced a sharp pain in his penis and had to desist. His rectal area, he revealed, was neither ticklish nor sensitive. The tickling and pain reactions may be compared to psychogenic dyspareunia in the female—a somatic defense against anxiety.

Another adolescent homosexual persisted in testing the male authorities during the early period of his hospitalization. Without provocation, he approached a male attendant and cursed him obscenely. The attendant was somewhat surprised but ignored the boy. He repeated this behavior with the other male attendants and in each case met with a nonpunitive response. He grew quite bold, assumed a very aggressive façade, and talked about having a girl friend in the girls' ward who, it developed, was a lesbian. Later, when a new group of aggressive boys came to the ward, the equilibrium he had established was upset and he reverted to extreme effeminacy.

Another patient was a schizophrenic adolescent who had received intensive shock therapy at another institution during the course of which he suddenly developed a high-pitched voice. The psychiatrist was uncertain whether he was trying to mimic a girl or a child. When the patient was told that it seemed as if he wanted to be a child, he replied, "I don't want to be any older. I want to play children's games." When asked if he saw no fun in being older, he answered, "Yes, but that has to do with sex. Sex is ugly. Sex has a lot to do with growing up. I don't want to commit myself to sex. The real trouble started when I dyed my hair when my mother wasn't there. I began putting on women's clothes . . ." and so on.

These boys, in general, viewed heterosexuality as dangerous. The effeminate homosexuals were often fully prepared to discuss homosexual activity, frequently in great detail. But they required a great deal of reassurance to admit to heterosexual fantasies and minor heterosexual experiences. Only 3 boys out of 30 admitted to any genital contact with girls. One boy, the housebreaker previously discussed, had attempted intercourse at a girl's insistence but he had a weak erection and withdrew. Another boy, a would-be Don Juan, exaggerated his heterosexual experiences but admitted that he always ejaculated prematurely. A third boy, after much difficulty, established a sexual relationship of some duration with a girl, but withdrew from the relationship when a rival appeared. The patient perceived his withdrawal as a rejection by the girl and thereafter was exclusively homosexual.

Family relationships

The histories of the patients revealed the following features in almost every instance: In childhood there was an avoidance of the usual ball games and other competitive activities with boys; they played only with girls or with boys much younger than themselves; they were restricted and overprotected by their mothers, particularly in aggressive games. Some mothers kept the child from all socialization with other children; in one case until the age of twelve. One mother surrogate who was the patient's aunt (and legal guardian), tied the boy to a tether in the yard whenever she left the house; she permitted him no companions. In three cases, the mother had wanted a girl (more specifically, a "nonmasculine" child), and repeatedly expressed to the patient the wish that he were a girl. Each boy had been treated like a girl for a time.

Not a single family situation was reasonably normal and healthy. In 10 cases, the fathers were described as brutal. Some of these were alcoholic and prone to violent rages when drunk. The father would frequently beat the boy and sometimes the mother as well. One boy chose vagrancy in preference to living with a father of whom he was terrified. Another boy ran away from home several times because he feared his father's beatings. Both these boys expressed the fear that their fathers would kill them. Unlike many other boys in the group, they did not feel their mothers could protect them from the destructive fathers.

Twenty boys in the study group expressed open fear and hatred of the father in the first or second interview. These feelings were easily elicited. Only one boy in the series stated that he liked his father (a father surrogate). In 10 instances, fear and hatred could be understood on the basis of the father's brutal behavior. Some of the hated fathers, however, were nonthreatening and timid men. In general, open expression of hatred of a father, even a punitive one, is uncommon in adolescent patients. Some patients in the study remarked with some perplexity that they did not understand such feelings since their siblings seemed to get along with the father. In fact, their sisters were often very fond of the father. Mothers sometimes commented that of all the children the patient was singular in fearing and disliking the father. In one family a meek and timid father was very dependent upon and submissive to his wife. She stated she had never loved her husband and that sexual relations with him had been infrequent and unsatisfactory. When her husband entered military service, she established a sexual relationship with another man. When the husband returned home the lover appeared and announced to him that he wished to marry his wife. The husband left his home without any protest. The mother reported that as her husband was leaving, the patient stuck his tongue out at his father in a final gesture of hostility, derision, and, probably, victory. Another patient, an only child adopted in infancy, had once visited his ill mother at a hospital. When the father approached the sickbed, the mother leveled an extremely vituperative, insulting verbal assault at him, telling him to get away, but at the same time beckoning the boy to her. The patient stated that he was moved at this point to uncontrollable laughter. He appeared to relish the experience once again in relating it.

The alienation of these sons from the father generally began at a very young age. One boy stated: "When I was three I used to see my father but I didn't know who he was until my mother told me. My father was giving my brother a bath. I was looking at him and wondered, 'Who is he?' My mother told me he was my father. I didn't know what a father was. The last thing I learned to say was 'Dada.' I was always afraid of my father when he looked at me. I was afraid of no one else."

Three boys in the group expressed strong fear of the mother. One of these mothers was as cruel to her son as was the father. She deliberately burned the boy's hand on a stove the only time he raised his hand to her in anger. Most mothers were domineering and restricting as well as overprotective, although the domination often took on a superficially benign aspect. Two mothers stated that they could deny their sons nothing, but at the same time they would not permit their sons out of sight; these mothers constantly supervised their son's activities and did not permit ordinary socialization. Some boys showed strong undercurrents of hostility toward their mothers, which were expressed with great difficulty, and several were not consciously aware of these feelings. They showed unusual fear of incurring the mother's displeasure; when they did so, they reacted with anxiety and guilt, and felt impelled to make restitution. With few exceptions, the sons were very close to the mother and expressed great love and adoration for her.

They were the mother's favorites and yet they were always submissive. Most saw the mother as a protection against the feared father. They saw themselves, or preferred to see themselves, in league with the mother against the father. In these instances, the father was derogated and assigned a minor role in the family. The derogation was usually rationalized on the grounds that the father was crude and that he was unimportant.

Two of the boys had slept with the mother up to the time of admission to the hospital while the father slept in another room. One boy described being cuddled in the mother's arms like a baby at the age of fifteen. These relationships were scrupulously asexual on the surface but the situation was apparently sexually stimulating.

While heterosexual fantasies were difficult to elicit, those obtained were frank or thinly disguised incestuous fantasies. One boy who had an inordinate interest in the sexual activity of his mother and new stepfather and who masturbated into his stepfather's condoms always fantasied a red-haired girl whom he had seen on his street. His mother had striking red hair. Another boy discussed freely his preoccupation with his mother's body and her breasts, although during masturbation he always fantasied his mother in a sexual relationship with another man. The only patient in the group who developed a sexual relationship with a girl over a period of time was obviously embarrassed when he announced that his girl friend bore the same given name as his mother.

One very effeminate homosexual boy had been adopted in infancy by his grandparents. His grandmother was an extremely tyrannical, punitive person who dominated a family consisting of her husband, the patient, and eight nieces and cousins. He was not permitted to play on the street nor to have any friends. The grandmother and other female relatives dressed him as a girl and were delighted by this game. He had no memory of sex until the age of thirteen when he was stimulated by the sight of the bare legs of a female cousin. He had an erection and retired to the bathroom because of embarrassment. His thought was that he had some disease which caused swelling of his penis. He manipulated his penis while he fantasied intercourse with his cousin. He then forced himself to put an end to these thoughts; the erection subsided and he rejoined the family. The next morning he awoke with an erection and once again fantasied sexual relations with his cousin. On one occasion he walked in on his grandmother while she was in her bath, whereupon she shouted at him. That day he began to masturbate with sexual fantasies about his grandmother; he became frightened and shut out the fantasies. Shortly after this incident, he saw a woman whose skirt had been raised by the wind and he subsequently made use of this image in his masturbatory fantasies. The persistence of this fantasy remained a mystery to him until he associated it with his grandmother's epilepsy. During her seizure she always pulled her skirt up above her waist.

It had been explained to one of the boys in the ward who was struggling with the problem of his homosexuality that much of his difficulty related to his fear of sex with women. He was obviously unimpressed and in relating this episode to the ward secretary dismissed the idea as "absurd" since he had sexual feelings only for his foster mother with whom he lived from the age of seven to fourteen.

Although the relatedness of these mothers to their sons was very close and frequently seductive, they discouraged masculine activities and attitudes in the boys and, conversely, encouraged feminine interests and behavior. The mothers showed a remarkable lack of concern about the effeminate behavior of their sons and of their homosexuality until a point was reached where unfavorable comment came from neighbors, or their sons became involved with the Children's Court.

These mothers placed great value on what they considered the "esthetic" activities of the son and contrasted these activities with the "vulgar" ones of the father. One mother became quite upset when a female psychiatrist inquired into the patient's masturbation. The mother was "disgusted," stating emphatically that her son did not masturbate; that she examined his clothes regularly and found no evidence of such activity. Another mother, thinking that the psychiatrist was being critical, exclaimed with some heat, "If being a boy is to go out and steal and play with yourself, I'm glad L. is the way he is." Many mothers did not seem to know that there was anything unusual about their sons. On the whole, the mothers seemed unperturbed about the sons' homosexuality and expressed no desire for change.

When there were siblings in the family the rivalry of the patients was open, extreme, and at times dangerous. There were instances in which the parents were unable to leave the siblings alone together. In one family a half-sibling had to be removed from the home for his protection.

In considering the interparental relationships, no instance of mutual love and respect could be found. The fathers sometimes dominated the household by tyranny and terror, bolstered by alcohol. The mothers, however, usually controlled family affairs down to the last detail. With the exception of mothers who were newly remarried, sexual relations between the parents were minimal, occurring in some instances only when the father was drunk and forced himself upon the mother. Invariably, open displays of affection between the parents were nonexistent. In two families, extreme religious asceticism forbade all pleasure; one father boasted that nothing had ever occurred in his family of which he could be ashamed. In fact, his children had never even seen him kiss his wife.

The mother of an adolescent transvestite was studied individually in a psychoanalytic treatment situation. She was in her middle thirties; her presenting symptom was cancerophobia. She was married to a professional man and had three children, all boys. The oldest boy, then thirteen years of age, was a transvestite. The mother had been a tomboy in her adolescence and had been overattached to her own mother. She found her father physically repulsive although she remarked that he was generally considered to be a handsome man. She was frigid in sexual relations. Her husband, a nonassertive individual, submitted to most of her unreasonable demands without complaint.

She had wanted her first child to be a girl and was deeply disappointed when she had a boy. For about two years she raised him as a girl, taking great pleasure in dressing him prettily. Between the ages of two and five he slept with his mother during the time the father was in the armed forces. She stated that it gave her a special kind of pleasure to sleep with the boy. With her second pregnancy she was once again disappointed by the birth of another son. She rejected him, felt he was ugly, particularly his penis which, she declared with a shudder, was "large and ugly." When her third boy was born, she was resigned and has even liked him in a somewhat detached way. She was tyrannical and exacting in her maternal role. The two older children did much of the housework and they catered to her every whim and demand. She was very involved emotionally with the oldest son with whom she had frequent talks about sex, ostensibly for the purpose of teaching him "the facts of life." She would not permit him to go to bed without her kissing him good night, but she was able to forego this practice with her other sons. When her husband was away she slept with this son because "I don't like to sleep alone." She stated that he meant more to her than anyone else, but admitted that she was most severe with him. She constantly criticized and corrected him. The two youngest boys ran about playing cops and robbers, dressed in dungarees, getting themselves dirty, but she was unable to tolerate such behavior in the oldest boy. She sewed up the pockets of his trousers so that he would not be able to reach his penis. She constantly berated the father for showing no interest in this boy and she suspected that the father was jealous of him. She recalled that prior to and following the birth of their firstborn the father repeatedly expressed concern that the child would take his, the husband's, place in the mother's affections. His favorite was the youngest boy. According to the mother, the father's eyes "lit up" whenever this youngster entered the room. She described him as a "regular boy" who was not afraid of her, who usually got his way with both parents, and who was happy-go-lucky. The middle child was very submissive, felt rejected, and spent his time dusting the furniture. At the same time, he had many companions, had a good relationship with the youngest boy, and as an adolescent became involved in a sexual experience with a somewhat older girl. The oldest boy was quite successful at school, had few companions, did not play in ball games or engage in other competitive games with boys, was very jealous of his brothers, and was not liked by them. He was alienated from his father.

The following case illustrates the mother's transference to her son from a relationship with a loved brother. This is an older adolescent in our series whose mother had a close, adoring relationship with her younger brother who had died when the patient was seven. From his earliest memory he had been told by his mother that he looked like his uncle, that he had the same "sensitive and artistic nature," and that she wanted him to grow up to be just like her brother. The mother's need to identify her son with her brother reached such proportions that the patient was not allowed to leave the house on the anniversary of his uncle's death, because she was convinced something catastrophic would happen to him. The patient saw nothing inappropriate in this for he had long since accepted the role assigned to him by his mother.

Summary

A study of 30 male adolescent homosexuals, 23 of whom were hospitalized in the Adolescent Ward of Bellevue Psychiatric Hospital, has been presented. The study included interviews with many of the parents. About half the patients were diagnosed as "schizophrenic" and the other half as "schizoid" or "schizophrenic personalities." The adolescents could be subdivided into two groups based upon the criterion of effeminacy. One group was composed of markedly effeminite boys who had apparently accepted both their effeminacy and homosexuality. They manifested no obvious evidences of homosexual conflict. The majority of these patients openly proclaimed their wish to be a female. When trust in the psychiatrist was established, however, they revealed heterosexual fantasies and incidents of heterosexual excitation as well as wishes to be a male. When the ward group did not grossly interfere with the effeminite behavior of the homosexuals, they were not manifestly anxious. At those times when these patients were compelled to drop their effeminate façade, they responded with anxiety.

In the second group, many were given to hypermasculine affectations. These boys were more overtly anxious and their behavior was more disordered. In both groups heterosexual fantasies and activities were accompanied by severe anxiety and inhibition.

The parents of these adolescents, particularly the mothers, were similar in behavior and attitudes to those described in Chapters III and IV. The fathers were more frequently brutal (10 of 30) than in our adult sample (20 of 103 were physically cruel). One gains the impression that the ineffectual fathers of the adolescent homosexuals were more ineffectual than were the fathers of our adult homosexual sample. As was the case among our H-sample, the interparental relationships among the parents of the hospitalized adolescents were most frequently poor and no parent-child relationship could be regarded as reasonably normal.

IX

The Sexual Adaptation of the Male Homosexual

We consider homosexuality to be a pathologic bio-social, psychosexual adaptation consequent to pervasive fears surrounding the expression of heterosexual impulses. In our view, every homosexual is, in reality, a "latent" heterosexual; hence we expected to find evidences of heterosexual strivings among the H-patients of our study.

Heterosexual manifestations in the homosexual patients

Aside from the finding that 67 per cent of H-patients chose to maintain social contacts with women, the most obvious evidence of heterosexual interest was the fact that many homosexuals reported the presence of, or the conscious suppression of, heterosexual desires at one time or another. In our sample, 30 (28 per cent) of the H-patients were "bisexual," some of whom had had sustained heterosexual relationships (in some instances, marriage and children) while at the same time engaging in clandestine homosexual relationships.[1]

Although many homosexuals seem unperturbed by public knowledge of their sexual deviation, 90 per cent of the H-patients in this study were concerned about exposure of their homosexuality. Of 106 H-patients, 64 (60 per cent) had come into psychoanalysis in order

[1] Westwood found only 18 per cent of his British sample to be "bisexual."

to overcome homosexuality. It is to be expected that many in this group would wish to avoid revealing their homosexuality, except to their homosexual contacts. The homosexual activities of most of our patients had been largely clandestine—sometimes brief encounters with pick-ups while "cruising," and at other times sustained relationships which were kept secret from most acquaintances.

Among 76 H-patients who did not show a distinctly bisexual pattern of behavior, there were nevertheless evidences of heterosexual tendencies. Of these there were 41 (39 per cent of the total sample and 54 per cent of the nonbisexual group) who had had at least one experience in heterosexual intercourse—in 26 cases prior to the age of 25 years (of which 22 had been successful attempts), and 15 others after the age of 25 years (of which 11 had been successful). Potency difficulties in heterosexual relations were reported in 47 H-cases (44 per cent, which includes 16 bisexuals) and in 34 comparison patients, a difference which is not significant; however, with the exclusion of 28 H-patients (26 per cent) who had never attempted heterosexual intercourse and 4 nonbisexuals (4 per cent) for whom there was no answer on this question, the percentage of homosexuals with impaired heterosexual potency rose to 63 per cent (47/74). In homosexual relations, potency difficulties were reported for 18 per cent of the H-sample (19 patients, of whom only 3 were bisexuals. See Tables IX-1A and IX-1B).

Little difference appeared in the incidence of fantasies during

TABLE IX-1A *Heterosexual Manifestations (A)*

	Exclusive homosexuals[a]		Bisexuals[b]	Comparisons[c]
	Total	Successful first experience		
1. First heterosexual experience:				
(a) before 25	26	22	17	84
(b) after 25	15	11	5	10
(c) age not stated	0	0	8	2
2. Never attempted heterosexual intercourse	28	0	0	0

[a] N = 76
[b] N = 30
[c] N = 100

TABLE IX-1B *Heterosexual Manifestations (B) (in per cent)*

	H	C
N=	106	100
1. Potency difficulties:		
(a) heterosexual intercourse	44	34
(b) homosexual intercourse	18	
2. Fantasies:		
(a) during heterosexual intercourse	20	31
(b) during homosexual intercourse	24	
3. Manifest dream content:		
(a) erotic heterosexual activity	47	87
(b) erotic homosexual activity	87	25
(c) incestuous activity	33	38

intercourse when homosexuals and heterosexuals were compared; however, the manifest dream-content of the two groups revealed interesting data. About one-third of each group had dreams with incestuous content. Erotic heterosexual dreams occurred in 87 per cent of the comparisons, while the same percentage of homosexuals had erotic homosexual dreams; but almost one-half of the homosexuals also reported erotic *heterosexual* dreams, in contrast to 25 per cent of comparisons with *homosexual* dream-content. Clearly, the sexual content of dreams varies in both groups, yet the homosexuals as a group showed no exclusive interest in males in their dream-life. It is also noteworthy that there were twice as many homosexuals who had heterosexual dreams as heterosexuals who had homosexual dreams. Even among the 28 homosexuals who had never attempted heterosexual intercourse, 8 were reported who had manifestly heterosexual dreams. In an analysis of the 76 homosexuals who were not bisexual, it was found that 56 (74 per cent) had an aversion for female genitalia, but this strong phobic attitude did not exclude manifest heterosexual dream-content; almost half of these 56 cases brought such dreams to their psychoanalysts. The tendency toward heterosexual dreams was even more sharply illustrated by 23 of these 56 H-patients with aversion for female genitalia who had a history of never having had a successful heterosexual experience: 9 of the 23 reported dreams with manifest heterosexual activity. On the other hand, of the 44 homosexuals with impaired potency in heterosexual relations, 24 did *not* report manifestly heterosexual dreams.

An outstanding finding in the responses on dream content was the occurrence of erotic heterosexual activity in the manifest dream content of almost one-half of the H-patients. If it were possible to assess the *disguised* heterosexual elements represented in the latent content of the dreams, a substantial increase in the number of homosexuals with heterosexual dreams seems likely.

Following are some examples of dreams of homosexuals:

THEME OF INCEST WITH MOTHER (from an exclusively homosexual patient):

"I am in a public toilet. I am about to do mutual masturbation with a man, a homosexual. A group of women come in, and one of them squats over the shower-basin to urinate; she is jovial and talks with the other women. I am annoyed—it's preventing me from masturbating with the man. Then a group of foolish brown-skinned girls come in. *Then* I had a vague dream of women teachers hitting with rulers. *Then* a vague dream of being in bed with my mother, and deciding to test myself out in intercourse with her." A dream of another night was told immediately following the foregoing: "I am arguing with my father. I tell him to sit down, and I push him down into a seat. He doesn't fight back."

THEME OF INCEST WITH A SISTER (from an exclusively homosexual patient who prefers to be the "insertee" in anal intercourse):

"I dream that I see my sister naked, and it makes me angry. I'm afraid I'll get sexually aroused and I wouldn't want her or anyone to see it."

"I get depressed when I see evidences of heterosexuality in myself."

HETEROSEXUAL THEME (from the same "insertee"):

"I'm standing with a girl, kissing her. I feel sexually aroused, maybe with an erection. Then the scene changes. I'm searching for a man to have sex with."

HETEROSEXUAL THEME (from an exclusively homosexual patient):

"I am back at college taking courses, after 10 years. I'm on a hilltop. I go to a rooming house for a room. I can't get one, but a fat Negro maid shows me the room I used to have—it's now occupied by someone else. Then I go looking for a restaurant, because I'm hungry. A girl drives along in a car and offers to help me find a restaurant. We ride off in her car and she's very friendly with me. We embrace and pet, and she puts her hands down my back, down to the buttocks, and she pushes up my scrotum from behind. She asks if I have a 'rubber' and I visualized it as being attached to a pull-ring from the string of a window-shade. Then I'm in her room. She's lying on the bed and I'm sitting on the edge of the bed with my shirt off. I'm concerned about being seen through the window, so I pull down the shade. I woke up scared."

HETEROSEXUAL THEME (from an exclusively homosexual patient who had never attempted heterosexual intercourse because of intense anxiety):

"A woman's hand grabs my penis while she's having intercourse with another man."

HETEROSEXUAL THEME (from an exclusively homosexual patient who prefers to insert his penis into his partner's mouth or anus, but frequently engages in various other homosexual acts):

"I was married. I married a cute and lovely girl. I had sex relations with her. A day passed, and she evolved into an elderly woman."

THEME OF INCEST WITH MOTHER (from a bisexual patient):

"Mother is on the bed—soft, plump, with no make-up, smooth skin. I am looking at her, talking; but it is understood that we are about to go to bed together." Another dream the same night: "Father is sitting on a couch, dejected. I am standing, aware of his depressed feelings and his needs. Condescendingly and consolingly, I put my penis into his mouth. Father remains inactive, and I move to ejaculation."

HETEROSEXUAL THEME (from an exclusively homosexual patient with a strong aversion for female breasts as well as for female genitalia):

"I'm in a Turkish bath, but I am dressed and I'm painting a picture. I'm being shown how to paint by a woman with big breasts. She embraces me and I enjoy the warm pleasant feeling. Then we go down a fire escape. I lead the way." Another dream the same night: "I go from one house to another, kissing many girls, who welcome it, except for lesbians. The lesbians submit to being kissed by me after I tell them I have to kiss as many girls as possible—for a contest. I enjoyed all the kissing. Then I'm dressed up as a 'cavalier,' with a heart-shaped shield and a spear —'St. Valentine'—maybe as the winner of the contest."

HETEROSEXUAL THEME (from an exclusively homosexual patient who limits himself to the role of "insertee" in anal intercourse):

"A woman with a baby-carriage complains that the baby was attacked by a German shepherd dog and a bear. I see a man leading the two animals away on a leash. I hope no drastic punishment would be given them. Then I had a heterosexual dream: I am in love with a girl, and I want to marry her. I have the desire to fondle her but only up to a point. I'm concerned with whether I will be able to satisfy her sexually. It's unusual for me to have such an obviously heterosexual dream."

Although the 30 bisexuals in this study were not differentiated as a group distinct from the rest of the H-sample, certain trends appeared which are summarized in Table IX-2.

TABLE IX-2 *The Bisexual Homosexual*

	Bisexuals	Others
N=	30	76
1. Effeminate in childhood	3 (10%)	23 (30%)*
2. "Lone wolf" in childhood	12 (40%)	52 (69%)
3. "Lone wolf" in childhood and first homosexual behavior before 14	3/12 (25%)	25/52 (49%)
4. Score 5 or 6 (Developmental)	10 (33%)	40 (52%)
5. Competitive:		
overtly	11 (37%)	19 (25%)
covertly	17 (57%)	61 (80%)*
6. Impaired potency:		
heterosexual	16 (53%)	31/41 (76%)
homosexual	3 (10%)	16 (21%)
7. Homosexual partner regarded as warm and sensitive	16 (53%)	20 (26%)
8. Mother close-binding	17 (57%)	56 (74%)
9. Mother hostile-detached and not-detached and/or controlling-dominating	12 (40%)	9 (12%)

* .05 level of significance
** .01 level of significance
† .001 level of significance

In those items of Table IX-2 which deal with childhood, the bisexuals show a lower frequency of behavior patterns which connote inhibition of assertive behavior.

A general indicator of this inhibitory pattern is the set of six developmental questions designated as "Six Score" (see Chapter VII). The higher the score (6 would be the highest attainable score), the more restricted was the individual's behavior during childhood. Bisexuals with a score of either 5 or 6 totaled 10 (33 per cent), while among the other 76 homosexuals there were 40 (52 per cent) with such scores.

One of the items included in the "Six Score" probes the patient's tendency to keep to himself in childhood ("lone wolf"). It was found that there is a lower frequency of a "lone wolf" pattern among bisexuals —40 per cent as compared to 69 per cent among the rest of the H-patients.

Of the 12 bisexuals who had been "lone wolves," only 3 (25 per cent) had begun their homosexual activities prior to the age of 14 years, whereas 25 (49 per cent) of the "lone wolves" among the rest of the homosexuals had started homoerotic behavior at so early an age.

Effeminacy in childhood is reported by only 3 bisexuals, of a total of 26 cases of childhood effeminacy in the entire H-sample. Considering the bisexuals separately, the incidence of childhood effeminacy is 10 per cent, compared to 30 per cent in the rest of the homosexual group—which approximates the .05 level of statistical significance.

The foregoing data suggest that the bisexual shows evidence of less serious psychopathology than the homosexual who has avoided heterosexual activity completely or has indulged in it only sporadically. The contrast may be illustrated by (a) a bisexual patient who was not effeminate in childhood, preferred to be in the company of male peers in his childhood activities, was sufficiently assertive at times to seek a leadership role despite anxieties about it, and who did not begin homoerotic activity (largely, performing fellatio) until late adolescence, and (b) a homosexual patient with a history of effeminacy in childhood, including playing with dolls, who preferred to play at home by himself much of the time, often with a female dog to which he was closely attached, who envied and idolized other boys but had little contact with them, and who began homosexual activities (performing fellatio on other boys, his preferred practice) when he was 11 years old. While the first bisexual patient had been heterosexually aroused with a desire for heterosexual intercourse since his early teens, and had had sexual relations with girls several times before he reached the age of 25, the second homosexual patient had no conscious desire for genital contact with a female, but he had made an unsuccessful attempt at intercourse with a much older woman whom he had picked up ("I was determined to lose my virginity").

Data on the mother-son relationship reveal a much higher incidence among bisexuals of mothers who are hostile-rejecting and/or dominating—12 of 30 bisexuals (40 per cent), compared to 9 cases (12 per cent) among the rest of the homosexuals, significant at the .05 level. However, the less frequent occurrence of the CBI mother among the bisexuals (57 per cent compared to 74 per cent for the other homosexuals) does not reach statistical significance. It appears that a mother whose relationship with her son was predominantly hostile or dominating was less likely to inhibit heterosexual strivings than was the CBI mother.

With respect to sexual potency, it is to be expected that the bisexual had potency difficulties less frequently than the homosexual who had only occasionally (if at all) attempted intercourse with a woman. Of the 30 bisexuals 16 (53 per cent) have reported impaired potency with women, while 31 of the 41 remaining homosexuals (76 per cent) who had attempted sex relations with women experienced potency difficulties. The bisexuals also showed less frequent occurrence of impaired potency in their relations with homosexual partners: 3 (10 per cent) compared to 16 (21 per cent) among the other homosexuals.

In 16 of the 30 cases (53 per cent) the bisexual regarded his homosexual partner as a warm and sensitive person, while only 20 of the other 76 homosexuals (26 per cent) had this feeling about their partners. The apparently lesser dependency of the bisexuals upon homosexuals for erotic gratification may influence their greater selectivity in the personal qualities of their partners. In addition, bisexuals appear to be less seriously damaged psychologically than are exclusively homosexual patients and seem able to enter into interpersonal relationships which are, in general, less frequently fraught with anxiety and conflict.

Despite heterosexual activity, there are proportionately about as many bisexuals as other homosexuals in our study who were reported to prefer accepting the partner's penis into a bodily orifice; nor is there a disproportionate number of bisexuals with a predilection for inserting the penis into the partner's orifices. Similarly, data regarding attitudes towards women, aversion for female genitalia, fear of injury to one's own genitalia, and masturbatory guilt, reveal approximately the same proportions for the bisexuals as for the homosexual group as a whole. Although positive correlations might have been expected on items tapping the so-called "masculine" role in homosexual practices—all of which have some bearing on the bisexual's capacity for sexual contact with the opposite sex—no such correlations emerged.

In adulthood, more bisexuals manifested *overt* competitiveness than did other homosexuals, though the difference is not statistically significant; however, *covert* competitiveness was reported in significantly fewer instances among the bisexuals: 17 bisexuals (57 per cent) compared to 61 (80 per cent) among the rest of the homosexuals. It can be assumed that competitiveness becomes covert through fear of openly expressing it. Here again the bisexuals appear more capable of assertive behavior.

The foregoing data indicate that male homosexuals give evidence of a basic heterosexual potential—most clearly discernible in the bisexual but also evident in exclusively homosexual patients—specifically in the forms of (a) the inclusion of women in their social lives, (b) sufficient interest in women to attempt heterosexual intercourse, despite fears, and (c) the occurrence of frankly heterosexual dreams.

Homosexual practices: attitudes toward male genitals

Dissatisfaction with the size of genitals (Table IX-3) was reported for 46 homosexuals. Although such dissatisfaction was usually associated with the feeling that the genitals were smaller than normal, there were several homosexuals who did not consider their genitals smaller than normal but who nevertheless would have wanted them to be larger. Of the H-patients who felt their genitals to be too small 32 (70 per cent) expressed a desire for a partner with a large penis (see Table IX-4A). However, among the 60 homosexuals who appeared content with the size of their genitals, only 28 (47 per cent) desired a partner with a large penis, so that within this group there was an almost equal distribution of those who sought a partner with a large penis and those who did not.

Among the 74 homosexuals who had reported fear or aversion towards female genitalia, the desire for a partner with a large penis was more prevalent, though not statistically significant: 63 per cent of this group showed this predilection, compared to 41 per cent of those talia and fear of genital injury for the H group, but not for the C group (Table IX-4B).

Although more than half of the homosexuals sought a partner with a large penis, this did not necessarily mean that the partner must also possess other predominantly "masculine" qualities, nor did this preference show any correlation with either the "insertor" or the "insertee" role in the sexual act.

Table IX-5A deals with the presence or absence of fear of genital injury or genital disease among those homosexuals who considered their own genitals too small and also sought a partner with a large penis. Of the 32 homosexuals in this category 23 (72 per cent) had expressed a fear of genital injury, and 9 did not. In contrast, among the 28 homo-

TABLE IX-3 *Homosexuals' Feelings about Genitalia*

N =	H 106		C 100
1. Patient feels his genitals smaller than normal	38%	(40)[a]	28%
2. Patient feels his genitals smaller than he desires	43%	(46)[b]	35%
3. Patient has fear/aversion towards female genitalia	70%	(74)	34%**
4. Fear of disease/injury to own genitals	54%	(57)	43%
5. Fear of disease/injury to own genitals and fear/aversion to female genitalia	42%	(45)	8%**
6. Patient seeks partner with large penis:	56%	(60)	
(a) Patients with fear/aversion to female genitalia	63%	(47/74)	
(b) Patients with no fear/aversion to female genitalia	41%	(13/32)	
7. Patient has special interest in partner's buttocks	34%	(36)	

TABLE IX-4A *Homosexuals' Desire for Partner with Large Penis*

	Desires partner with large penis	Does not desire partner with large penis
Genitals too small (46)	32	14
Genitals not too small (60)	28	32

[a] Includes 2 homosexuals who had no desire for larger genitals and no interest in a partner with a large penis.

[b] Includes 9 homosexuals not regarding genitals as smaller than normal.

TABLE IX-4B *Association Between Fear of Genital Injury and Aversion to Female Genitalia*

	H		C	
	Fears genital injury	Does not	Fears genital injury	Does not
Aversion	47	27	23	11
No aversion	10	22	20	46

Significance: H .01; C .001

sexuals who did *not* feel their genitals to be too small and who did *not* desire a partner with a large penis, only 6 individuals (21 per cent) expressed a fear of genital injury and 22 did not.

There were 9 homosexuals who were reported as feeling that their genitals were smaller than they wished but who had not indicated that they regarded their genitals as smaller than normal. In this group 7 H-patients were attracted to a partner with a large penis and in addition were fearful of injury to their own genitals.

In the homosexuals, morbid fear of injury to one's own genitals is predominantly associated with fear/aversion to female genitalia: Of 57 H-cases with fear of injury to the genitals, 45 patients (79 per cent) also had fear/aversion toward female genitalia. On the other hand, of the 43 C-patients who feared injury to their own genitals, only 8 (19 per cent) had concomitant fear/aversion toward female genitalia (see Table IX-3). Of the 45 H-patients with fear of injury to their own genitals as well as fear/aversion toward female genitalia, 34 (76 per cent) desired a partner with a large penis, and 11 (24 per cent) did not (see Table IX-5B). H-patients who had fear/aversion toward female genitalia *without* associated fear of genital injury were approximately evenly divided between those who desired a partner with a large penis and those who did not (14:13); of the 11 homosexuals who feared genital injury but did *not* have fear/aversion to the female genitalia, only 2 sought a partner with a large penis. The desire for a partner with a large penis is therefore significantly correlated with the following factors: One's own genitals considered too small; fear of injury to one's own genitals; and fear/aversion toward female genitalia. However, it must be noted that a substantial minority of H-patients who sought partners with a large penis did not have all of the foregoing attitudes, and many others were reported as not particularly concerned with the size of the partner's penis. In those homosexuals who do have this constellation of findings, it appears that fear of genital injury is in some way associated with a phobic attitude toward female genitalia, and a partner with a large penis seems to keep these anxieties at a minimum.

The significant association between the H-patients' belief that their own penis is too small and the search for a homosexual partner with a large penis suggests among many complex determinants that this quest is (a) partly reparative in that sexual acceptance from another male with a large penis will compensate for feelings of inadequacy as a "castrate"; (b) partly acquisitive as a way of attaching to themselves the partner's penis and symbolically incorporating the partner's sexual power; and (c) partly a magical belief that the larger the penis, the greater the sexual pleasure.

This theme is illustrated in the following dream of a bisexual patient:

> "I am 'shooting' a movie set on the beach, at dusk—I'm about finished. A big man comes up, asks to borrow the lights and stands. I am hesitant but my assistant says, 'Why not?' So the man takes them away. Then I get uneasy at having allowed this. I decide to go down to the beach to tell the man to be careful. Aggressively I approach to tell him, but suddenly I grasp his genitals. . . . There is a scene shift. Now I am explaining to a childhood friend or neighbor about this great penis I have in my hands. Playfully I hold the penis and balls over myself, in place, and the penis becomes erect! Amused, I think: Well, now, it would be possible with so long a penis to suck myself! I wonder about the semen: If it should be my own then it would not be worth very much, but if it were really that man's, then it should be quite potent!"

With respect to the 36 homosexuals in the sample (approximately one-third) who had a special interest in the buttocks of their partners, no significant positive correlations could be found with the nature of other sexual practices or with the type of partner, nor was there any significant correlation in those cases in which the patient was attracted to both a large penis and the buttocks.

Preferences for different types of homosexual relations are shown in Table IX-6. Mutual masturbation, often an initiating activity preliminary to an anal or oral contact, was practiced by 47 per cent of homosexuals. The practice of mutual fellatio was reported by 27 per cent of the homosexuals. Others preferred inserting the penis into the mouth or anus of the partner (36 per cent), or allowing the partner to insert into them (31 per cent). However, a substantial proportion of the H-sample (24 per cent) expressed no special preferences, reporting the practice of any or all of the foregoing activities. In spite of their expressed preferences, many homosexuals will sometimes assume a sexual role they do *not* prefer—depending upon the circumstances and the nature of the relationship with the partner of the moment. For example, a homosexual who prefers to insert his penis into his partner's mouth or anus may be attracted to a man who is not "warm" toward him; he may try to please such a partner in an attempt to elicit the "warmth" he desires, by allowing himself to be used in whatever manner the partner may wish: for example, allowing his own anus to be used by the partner for anal intercourse when such an act gives no pleasure to him as the "insertee," and may even be painful.

THE HOMOSEXUAL'S PARTNER

The personal attributes of the homosexual partner are of more importance in cases of more permanent relationships than in purely

TABLE IX-5A *Homosexuals with "Too Small" Genitals Associated with Desire for Partner with Large Penis, and Fear of Genital Injury*

	Genitals "too small" and seeks partner with large penis (32)	Genitals not "too small" and does not seek partner with large penis (28)
Fear of genital injury (29)	23	6
No fear (31)	9	22

Significance: .001

TABLE IX-5B *Fear of Genital Injury and Aversion to Female Genitalia Associated with Desire for Partner with Large Penis*

	Fear of genital injury and aversion to female genitalia	Fear of genital injury only	Aversion to female genitalia only	Neither
Seeks partner with large penis	34	2	14	9
Does not	11	9	13	12

TABLE IX-6 *Preferences in Homosexual Activity*

	N = 106	
1. Prefers to insert penis:		
(a) into partner's mouth	2%	(2)
(b) into partner's anus	8%	(8)
(c) no orifice preferences	26%	(28)
Total	36%	(38)
2. Prefers partner's penis inserted:		
(a) into mouth	17%	(18)
(b) into anus	14%	(15)
(c) no orifice preferences	0	
Total	31%	(33)
3. Practices insertion into partner as well as partner's insertion into patient, with *no preference for either*	24%	(25)
4. Practices mutual fellatio ("69")	27%	(28)
5. Practices mutual masturbation	47%	(50)

transient and temporary liaisons. Consequently, our findings regarding the homosexual's partner are more applicable to more durable homosexual pairings than to the transient contact; nevertheless, many homosexuals sought similar attributes in both the permanent and transient relationship. This tendency appears in the finding that the partner was believed to be a warm, sensitive person in 34 per cent of permanent relationships (36/106) and in 25 per cent of transient relationships (27/106), a divergence which is not statistically significant.

As Table IX-10 indicates, most homosexuals in this study were attracted to "masculine" qualities in another male, although a substantial minority (21 per cent) showed a preference for "feminine" qualities. Concepts of "masculinity" and "femininity" generally conform to cultural stereotypes though such concepts may be highly idiosyncratic and related to family members. The responding psychoanalysts reported that the partner in 61 per cent of the cases was identified, consciously or unconsciously, with some member of the nuclear family (see Tables IX-7 and IX-8). It was found that when the patient identified the homosexual partner with the father or brother, masculine characteristics would usually be sought in the partner; similarly, when a patient identified the partner with the mother or sister, he usually sought feminine traits in the partner.

A group of 19 H-patients could not be consistently rated, since fluctuating and combining identifications occurred. According to the responding psychoanalysts, some of this group identified the partner with a male member of the family yet sought feminine traits, while others identified the partner with a female member of the family yet sought masculine traits, or they identified the partner (at different times, or at one and the same time) with both mother or sister and father or brother while seeking masculine traits (see Table IX-8).

There is some evidence, as presented in Table IX-9, that certain types of parental relationships have an influence on the predilections of the homosexual in his choice of partner. The most prominent example of such influence is a mother who interferes with her son's heterosexual activities after adolescence, combined with a father who is minimizing in his attitude toward his son (42 cases). This constellation seems to have influenced the H-son toward a choice of partner who was identified with a male member of the nuclear family (23 cases, or 55 per cent) and away from the choice of a partner identified with a female member of the family (2 cases, or 5 per cent). Thus, the greater the destructive influence of both parents upon the homosexual son's heterosexuality, the further he moves from female sexual contact and from characteristics he may perceive as "feminine" in his homosexual partner.

Attitudes of the patient about certain personal qualities of the partner and the feelings between them are presented in Table IX-10. Although homosexuality provides a means of obtaining sexual gratification, the total homosexual relationship is a highly complex interpersonal constellation. It is quite clear that a significant number of homosexuals sought specific qualities in their partners in order to fulfill

TABLE IX-7 *Responding Psychoanalysts' Opinion: Homosexual Partner Identified with a Family Member*

Father	29%	(31)	Mother	6%	(6)
Brother	7%	(7)	Sister	1%	(1)
Father and brother	8%	(8)	Mother and sister	4%	(4)
	44%	(46)		11%	(11)

Identified with:		
Both mother and father	5%	(5)
Father, mother, and sister	1%	(1)
Father, brother, and mother	1%	(1)
Brother and sister	1%	(1)
	8%	(8)

a variety of subjective needs, both sexual and nonsexual. Seeking feminine qualities in a male partner, for instance, may be a part of a covert attempt to gratify heterosexual desires. On the other hand, the quest for male qualities in a partner often subserves a series of defensive and reparative needs, e.g., obtaining the affection of a "father" in instances where the patient had not experienced paternal affection; identification with and dependency upon a "masculine figure"; irrational destructive or predatory maneuvers; and others. Two interesting examples of the acting-out of irrational destructive impulses were observed by one member of our Committee during his military service: (1) A soldier repeatedly became involved in homosexual activity with officers; in each instance he exposed the officer; the officer would be court-martialed while the soldier would merely be transferred to another installation.

TABLE IX-8 *Responding Psychoanalysts' Opinion: Family Identification and Sex-Role Characteristics of Partner*

Partner identified with:		Masculine traits desired:	Feminine traits desired:
1. Father		25	5
2. Father: no answer re masculine or feminine traits	1		
3. Brother		5	0
4. Brother: masculine *and* feminine traits	1		
5. Brother: no concern with masculine/feminine	1		
6. Father and brother		7	1
7. Father and mother		4	1
8. Father, mother, and brother		1	0
9. Father, mother, and sister		1	0
10. Mother		2	4
11. Sister		0	1
12. Mother and sister		2	2
13. Brother and sister		1	0
14. The patient himself		1	0
15. No identification with family member		24	8
16. No identification reported; no reported concern with masculine/feminine traits:	8		
TOTALS		73	22

TABLE IX-9 *Identification of Partner, as Related to Heterosexually Interfering Mother and Minimizing Father*

	Mother interferes	
	Yes	No
Father minimizing:	42	19
Partner like father, brother	23	10
Partner like mother, sister	2	4
Father *not* minimizing:	18	10
Partner like father, brother	6	4
Partner like mother, sister	5	3

(2) A man suspected correctly that he had a gonorrheal infection; he attempted to infect as many men as he could in homosexual intercourse before finally undergoing treatment for venereal disease.

Of the many qualities sought by patients in the homosexual partner, the following were included in our questionnaire: Warmth, friendliness, permissiveness, and contact. The semantic difficulties involved in the precise differentiation of these four qualities require us to interpret the statistics with caution. It appears that physical *contact* is commonly sought by the homosexual in his relationship with a partner. This does not necessarily imply contact through the sexual act only. Many homosexual patients report great satisfaction from any type of physical closeness to a desired partner.

Items 4-7 of Table IX-10 present information as interpreted by the responding psychoanalysts. Nearly 80 per cent of the H-patients

TABLE IX-10 *Qualities Sought in Homosexual Partner*

	N = 106	
1. Predominantly masculine qualities desired	69%	(73)
2. Predominantly feminine qualities desired	21%	(22)
3. Partner sought for:		
warmth	42%	(45)
friendliness	44%	(47)
permissiveness	24%	(25)
contact	59%	(63)
4. Patient receives warmth from partner	51%	(54)
5. Patient gives warmth to partner	48%	(51)
6. Patient regards self as warm and sensitive	79%	(84)
7. Patient regards partner as warm and sensitive:		
in permanent relationships	34%	(36)
in transient relationships	25%	(27)

were said to regard themselves as "warm" persons, yet only 51 per cent were reported to give or receive warmth in the homosexual relationship and even fewer regarded the partner as warm and sensitive. That one's personal warmth is not matched by others may indicate unfulfilled longings for warmth that homosexuality does not gratify. However, the more precise psychodynamic implications would require a special study.

The following description of two young male homosexuals who had been living together for about a year *illustrates certain aspects of the homosexual-partner interrelationship:*

> One young man, A., is rather self-confident, effective in his vocation, and takes pride in it, enjoys being admired for proficiency in his work, and for his manner of dress; he presents a cheerful, outgoing appearance. In contrast, his partner, B., is withdrawn, fearful, and moody; he does not like to be "watched" by people; he is very envious of A.'s sociability and jealous of A.'s wide circle of friends; he wants constantly to be told that he is loved by A. On one occasion, when a beach outing had been planned with two other friends, B. pretended to be sick because of his apprehension about going out in public. When A. went on the outing without him, B. was furious on the ground that this "test of love" had failed. In housekeeping, A. was easy-going and rather careless, but liked to cook. On the other hand, B. was a meticulous, compulsive housecleaner, who fussed about household details. Their sexual practices varied from time to time. B. was passionate, with frequent desires for sexual excitement and sexual release; he was more insistent on being an anal insertor, while A. was more content with holding and closeness, and preferred oral or manual sexual practices.

A quotation from a homosexual patient illustrates his feelings about the choice of a homosexual partner:

> "I want to be a man, so I try to seduce males the way Mother does, and to possess them, absorb them. I try to *take* from the handsome males what I do not have. But when I flirt with girls it is usually before males whose admiration I want. I want to prove to them how masculine I am. I feel I can't be a real man, so I try to seduce and to top rival males who I think are also bluffing. I do want a father! I'd like to have my own father—I'd submit to him. I cannot get away from that *trap* of my mother . . . and whenever I get into an argument with her, or

she is angry with me, I find that in my frustration and agitation I seem to seek out some male to exploit sexually, and prove myself, and get even with him."

A patient who prefers transient homosexual contacts is exemplified by the following case:

This shy young man had had a "passionate" homosexual affair which lasted almost a year, but the pair were quite incompatible in ideas, attitudes, and general life interests. Since then, this patient would haunt the halls of libraries and colleges looking for someone new. Other homosexuals whom he saw on such occasions were not what he wanted. He would have liked to find some older male who would not reject him and who had something of intellectual interest to offer. But if no such "intellectual" turned up, an older Negro was a most likely prospect, since he was less apt to refuse, and less apt to hurt the young man's pride. This patient sought a partner with a large penis, and preferred to be an anal insertee.

A bisexual's feelings about object-choice:

The type of girl in whom he could be interested was identified with both mother and sister. She should be voluptuous, use no make-up, and be "virginal" in appearance. But she should also be the forward one. She should have intrigues and affairs with others, so that there are suspicions and agonies about her actual or supposed infidelity, and doubts about his own merit in contrast to the rival. In his relationships with homosexual partners, he was very selective. He sought someone whom he admired for those qualities he believed to be lacking in himself, e.g., social manners, appearance, strength, and so forth. He then attempted to out-do his partner in these same qualities. His homosexual affairs involved achieving some mastery over another male. He has on occasion tenderly "seduced" another homosexual who seemed timorous, an approach which he himself would have liked.

Distinguishing Insertors and Insertees

The psychological concepts of "activity" and "passivity" related to sexual roles and sexual activities are not clear-cut.[2] In the act of

[2] Westwood found that the homosexuals he studied could not be divided into "active" or "passive" by reference to sexual technique.

fellatio, for example, it is incorrect to judge one participant as "active" and the other "passive." Is the individual who is using his mouth as receptor in the act of sucking, passive? From a kinetic orientation he is not. It becomes clear that concepts of activity and passivity to describe role behavior are not operationally useful. For this reason we have adopted the terms "insertor" and "insertee." The insertor intromits his penis into an orifice. The insertee accepts the penis into his orifice. There can be no question in any particular act (other than in mutual fellatio—"69") who is the insertor and who the insertee. Furthermore, our study has found that many homosexuals fall readily into one or the other of these two categories. Of the 106 homosexuals, 38 (36 per cent) were predominantly insertors and 33 (31 per cent) were predominantly insertees (see Table IX-6). Among the insertees, approximately half (15) expressed a preference for the anus, while the rest (18) preferred the mouth. Although no major differences emerged between those insertees who preferred insertion into the mouth and those who had a predilection for anal insertion, a trend appeared in the data concerning excessive fear of injury during childhood. Of the 26 homosexuals who did *not* have such a fear, there were 17 insertees, of whom 12 preferred fellatio and only 5 preferred anal insertion, a finding which almost reaches the .05 level of significance. It is also noteworthy that of the 17 insertees in our sample who became heterosexual during their psychoanalytic treatment 13 had preferred the use of the mouth and only 4 had preferred anal insertion. The oral insertee therefore seems to show a greater potential than the anal insertee for becoming heterosexual. An interesting finding emerged when the sex of the psychoanalyst was correlated with the orifice preferred by the homosexual who assumes the role of insertee. (This includes some patients who are not predominantly insertees. See Table IX-11.) Only 2 patients who preferred insertion into the anus had chosen female analysts, in contrast to 27 H-patients who were treated by male psychoanalysts, whereas those with a preference for the role of oral insertee were about evenly distributed between male and female therapists. It is likely that the revelation to a woman therapist of intimate sexual matters concerned with the anus may generate intolerable anxiety in most homosexuals. Only 10 of the 38 insertors expressed preference regarding the partner's orifices; 2 preferred the use of the partner's mouth, and 8 preferred the partner's anus. Forty-two per cent of the insertors (16 cases) were unwilling

TABLE IX-11 *Insertee's Preference for an Orifice, in Relation to the Sex of His Psychoanalyst*

	Male psychoanalyst	Female psychoanalyst	Total
Prefers mouth	17	15	32
Prefers anus	27	2	29†
Others (incl. no answer)	43	2	45
			106

under any circumstances to allow their own orifices to be used by the partner.

As seen in Table IX-12, masculine qualities were desired in the partner by 25 insertors (66 per cent) and feminine qualities were sought by 10 (26 per cent), as compared to 28 insertees (85 per cent) who sought masculine qualities in the partner and 3 insertees (9 per cent) who sought feminine qualities. In the opinions of the responding psychoanalysts, partners wtih masculine qualities were identified with a father and/or a brother by 10 insertors, with a mother and/or a sister by 2 insertors, and with both mother and father by 3 insertors. In addition, one insertor identified his partner with a brother and desired both masculine and feminine qualities in him. For the insertees, partners wtih masculine qualities were identified with a father and/or a brother by 20, and with both father and mother by 1 such patient. Partners with feminine qualities were identified with a mother and/or a sister by 4 insertors, and with a father and/or a brother by 3 insertors. For the insertees, partners with feminine qualities were identified with the mother by 2 patients, and with the father by one patient. Whereas identification with a male member of the family was associated with a desire for masculine attributes in the partner, and identification with a female member of the family was associated with a desire for feminine attributes in a majority of both insertors and insertees, the number of instances of mixed masculine-feminine identifications was greater among the insertors: 9 insertors sought partners with "gender traits" opposite to the sex of the family member with whom the partner was identified; this was true for only 2 insertees, a contrast which approximates the .05 level of significance.

The data in Table IX-12 may be more dramatically formulated as follows: Whereas the ratio of those seeking masculine qualities to those seeking feminine qualities in the partner among the insertees was 9:1, the corresponding ratio among insertors was 2.5:1. A preponderance of partners with consistent masculine attributes and identifications would be expected among patients with an insertee orientation in homosexual practices. However, among the insertors, only 7 patients (19 per cent) clearly identified the partner with a female figure, associated with a desire for feminine attributes in him, while 20 insertors (53 per cent) clearly identified the partner with a masculine figure and had a desire for masculine attributes; 9 others were reported to have mixed masculine-feminine identifications (24 per cent).

A noteworthy finding was the proportion of insertees among bisexuals. One might conceive of the bisexual as "more masculine" than the exclusive homosexual, since sexual behavior, in part, is carried out with women. One might also be inclined to identify the insertor role with a masculine role and the insertee with a feminine role. In this context, one would expect few if any insertees to be bisexual since

TABLE IX-12 *Identification of Homosexual Partners*

	Insertors (38)		Insertees (33)	
1. Father or brother identification:				
masculine qualities desired	26%	(10)	61%	(20)**
feminine qualities desired	8%	(3)	3%	(1)
2. Masculine qualities desired: no identification with family member	26%	(10)	21%	(7)
3. Mother or sister identification:				
feminine qualities desired	10%	(4)	6%	(2)
masculine qualities desired	5%	(2)	0	
4. Feminine qualities desired: no identification with family member	8%	(3)	0	
5. Father and mother identification:				
masculine qualities desired	8%	(3)	3%	(1)
6. Brother identification:				
masculine and feminine qualities desired	3%	(1)	0	
7. None of the above	5%	(2)	5%	(2)
8. Father or brother identification and/or masculine qualities desired	53%	(20)	82%	(27)**
9. Mother or sister identification and/or feminine qualities desired	19%	(7)	6%	(2)
10. Mixed masculine-feminine identification	24%	(9)	6%	(2)

they are obviously insertors in the heterosexual act. Contrary to these expectations, our study found as many bisexuals among insertees (9 in 33) as among insertors (10 in 38).

The sexual behavior of the bisexual provides some insight into the psychologic meaning of ipso- and heterosexual relationships. If one looks upon bisexual behavior as representing complementary patterns, then heterosexuality fulfills primary sex goals and homosexuality fulfills defensive needs in regard to a male who is potentially threatening or rejecting as punishment for heterosexuality. In the role of insertee, the bisexual placates and submits to his partner as the symbolic representative of the feared father image. In the role of insertor he dominates and controls this image as a safety maneuver. In both roles he may be acting-out propitiating techniques out of a feeling of guilt.

Table IX-13 shows a comparison of insertors and insertees in regard to certain aspects of their relationships with parents. The insertee's relationship with his father is most frequently characterized by submission to a feared father who is angered (the son believes) by any assertive behavior, and from whom many of the mothers have protected the sons. Most insertees (67 per cent) were found to use submission as a technique for coping with their fathers, in contrast

TABLE IX-13 *Insertors and Insertees: Relations with Parents*

		Insertors (38)	Insertees (33)
1.	Father angered by son's assertiveness	50% (19)	85% (28)**
2.	Son submissive to father	37% (14)	67% (22)*
3.	Son afraid of father	55% (21)	76% (25)
4.	Mother protected son from father	29% (11)	55% (18)*
5.	Son felt he could cope with mother more easily than with father	37% (14)	76% (25)**
6.	Mother overprotective	53% (20)	85% (28)*
7.	Mother overprotective re injury	47% (18)	79% (26)*
8.	Mother overprotective re play	37% (14)	64% (21)*
9.	Son was mother's confidant	37% (14)	82% (27)**
10.	Son is mother's favorite[a]	59% (20/34)	84% (26/31)*
11.	Son is mother's least-favored[a]	29% (10/34)	6% (2/31)*
12.	Guilt about masturbation:		
	much	40% (15)	70% (23)*
	some	32% (12)	21% (7)
	little	10% (4)	9% (3)
	none	18% (7)	0% (0)*

[a] Only children excluded

to only 37 per cent of the insertors. Compared to the insertors, twice as many insertees felt they could cope with their mothers more easily than with their fathers. The insertee's mother, in addition to her frequent overprotectiveness, was more often close-binding, and more often spent a "great deal of time" with her son; he was more often her favorite and her confidant. This parental impact is reflected in more frequently reported guilt over masturbation among insertees compared to the insertors, further indicating that more insertees have been discouraged from self-assertiveness (which includes *sexual* self-assertion) by the restricting effects of the mother's behavior and the intimidating influence of a threatening father. It is noteworthy that of the insertors only 18 per cent were reported to be free of guilt about masturbation, but that *none* of the insertees were free of such guilt.

The following is an account of a homosexual who prefers to be an insertor:

> C. did not appear effeminate but had been so in his childhood. He was fearful of his father (as was his more timid and submissive younger brother). The father's violent temper would be vented on the mother, as well as on the patient and his brother. Quarrels between the parents were commonplace, as well as expressions of mutual contempt. C. and his brother would often receive beatings in the course of the father's outbursts. When he was not angry he was a fairly reasonable and helpful parent, but he was neither affectionate nor close to either sibling. The mother was also unaffectionate; she was predominantly critical, demanding, complaining, and easily angered. C. often quarreled with her, in futile attempts to cope with her. A constant complaint against her was her frequent seductive parading through the house in scant attire, which enraged the patient. No amount of pleading or yelling at her had ever succeeded in altering her behavior. At times, C. would beat up his brother in a fit of rage but he discontinued this behavior in mid-adolescence and told his psychoanalyst that he presently felt deep regret and guilt for so maltreating his brother. Around the age of ten or twelve C. began to seek out homosexual experiences with older boys. He engaged in mutual masturbation and would also perform fellatio. His real source of sexual pleasure had always been as an insertor, and he soon gave up other practices. From the time he was a teen-ager he has limited himself to oral insertion. Occasionally, however, he would engage in anal intercourse (as insertor). Although he

had had a liaison with an older boy which lasted many months during early adolescence, he never again had a permanent type of relationship with another homosexual. He preferred to pick up masculine-looking homosexuals of his own age or older; he would usually have the impulse to do so after he had been frustrated or angered. In the homosexual act he described feelings of power, contempt, triumph; he exulted in the idea that he was humiliating his partner whom he usually identified with his father.

C. had always been interested in girls but felt insecure about their interest in him since he considered himself not "masculine" enough. Despite anxiety he made contacts with women at parties and elsewhere. He occasionally had dates with girls and, at times, engaged in mild petting. A meaningful heterosexual relationship developed with the rather nonassertive, retiring daughter of his employer. This relationship developed into an intimate love affair with much necking and petting, and finally with frequent sexual intercourse. It was this relationship which propelled him into psychoanalytic treatment; he was disturbed by his continuing homosexual urges which he wanted to conceal from his fiancée though he had great guilt about not revealing his problems to her.

Some aspects of the life history of the homosexual who prefers the role of insertee are illustrated by the following case:

In childhood, D. had been dominated by a close-binding mother who was unhappy with her husband. She was affectionate toward D., in fact, much more so than toward D.'s younger sister (his only sibling, and his father's favorite). She would complain to D. about his father's drinking and prolonged absence from home, thus using her son as confidant and forming an alliance with him against the father. From early childhood until mid-adolescence (when D. himself put a stop to it) she would often take him to bed with her so that he could hug her and be physically close because she needed to be "consoled" by her son. D. reported that he did not find it sexually stimulating to be so physically close to his mother and that he definitely did not like it; he did it only to please his mother toward whom he felt great loyalty and love. Even up to his mid-twenties his mother would repeatedly beg him to get into bed with her despite his consistant refusals.

His relationship with his father was rather distant, although his father was not really hostile to D. However, D. hated and feared him, mostly because he would treat the mother badly, rather than D. himself, who was only occasionally the object of his father's anger. From childhood on, D. found himself sexually aroused whenever he saw his father's genitals. This happened rather frequently, since his father would go to the bathroom (past D.'s room) dressed only in a pajama-top. D. also found himself sexually attracted to a succession of young men with whom his mother would develop close friendships. Although he had homosexual "crushes" on various males whom he envied and admired, he never engaged in actual homosexual relations until he was about twenty-eight years old. Nor had he been consciously attracted to women, except in a social, nonsexual way. He would be at ease with a woman as long as he felt certain she had no sexual designs upon him. On a few occasions he became involved with aggressive women who tried to interest him in sex relations, but he panicked and fled in each such instance. He has remained slightly effeminate in manner.

D. expressed strong aversion for female genitalia as well as for female breasts. He always had a fairly cordial relationship with his sister and had thinly disguised incestuous dreams about her which caused him anxiety. His concept of sexual pleasure was that of something evil and dirty and this sexual attitude extended to homosexuality. Therefore it was his practice to avoid a sexual relationship with anyone he admired or was fond of, except for "one-night-stands" with such a partner. His most common practice was to pick up total strangers in bars, public toilets, and so forth; to have homosexual relationships that were transient and devoid of any meaningful, personal interchange. Although his preference was to be an anal insertee, he has indulged in all other homosexual acts at various times. There have been periods during which he has had a continuing homosexual relationship; he would invariably choose a selfish, inconsiderate, exploitative partner whom D. would try desperately to please in every possible way but without success. Usually it was the partner who broke off the relationship. In addition, he has had sustained relationships with partners with whom he has taken the role of insertor, usually in anal intercourse. This apparently was possible for D. only when he was far from home, for example, during vacations in a foreign country where he would set up a liaison with a much younger, submissive, uneducated, or mentally dull partner. With such a partner, D. would assume a patronizing, protective attitude, and would try to cater to his needs. It is likely that this type of partner was identified with his sister, and that the relationship involved the acting-out of sibling-hostility, reaction formations to it, and the covert satisfaction of unconscious incestuous wishes. On the other hand, the hostile exploitative partner appears to have been identified more specifically with his father. This type of identification involved maneuvers to control a fearsome male. The patient was especially attracted to a large penis, especially in erection. He became relatively inactive sexually after he began psychoanalysis, which he sought at age forty because of recurrent depressions and work inhibitions, but without any thought of "curing" his homosexuality.

EXCLUSIVE INSERTORS AND EXCLUSIVELY ANAL INSERTEES

Eleven of the 33 insertees preferred anal insertion to the exclusion of other homoerotic practices. Six additional insertees showed a strong preference for anal insertion and have only on rare occasions engaged in any other homoerotic activity; they have therefore been included in a group (totalling 17) of exclusively anal insertees. This group manifests a type of sexual behavior far removed from the cultural pattern of masculine practices. At the other extreme is a group of 16 of the 38 insertors who limit themselves exclusively to the use of the penis for insertion into the partners mouth or anus, while completely excluding their own bodily orifices from the sexual act.

Table IX-14 offers data on the homosexual relationships of the exclusive insertors and the exclusively anal insertees. All but 2 of

TABLE IX-14 *Exclusive Insertors and Anal Insertees: Characteristics of Desired Partners*

	Exclusive insertors (16)		Anal insertees (17)	
1. Identification of partner:				
male	50%	(8)	88%	(15)*
female	38%	(6)	0%	(0)**
Mixed identification: male-female	12%	(2)	12%	(2)
2. Seeks partner with large penis	56%	(9)	71%	(12)
3. Special interest in buttocks	44%	(7)	47%	(8)
4. Mother seductive and first homosexual experience before age 14	50%	(8)	29%	(5)

these 17 insertees sought a partner with masculine attributes but even the 2 who did not, nevertheless identified the partner with the father. On the other hand, 8 of the exclusive insertors identified their partners with their fathers or desired exclusively masculine traits in their partners; the rest identified the partner with a female figure (6) or made a combined masculine-feminine identification (2).

If we hypothesize that insertees are acting-out the fantasy of a "feminine" role, using the anus as "vagina," and that the insertors are acting-out their fantasy of a masculine role seeking a substitute "feminine" orifice, we would then expect the "passive" insertee to seek a "masculine" partner, while the "masculine-aggressive" insertor would seek a "feminine" partner. We found that 15 of the 17 anal insertees identified their partners with a masculine image. But a consistent pattern does not hold for the insertors, since the partner was identified with a feminine image in only 38 per cent of the cases, while another 50 per cent identified the partner with a masculine image. Obviously, other variables are operative aside from the criterion of sexual practice. We assume that the quest for a partner with male characteristics, especially by the insertor, represents defensive, reparative behavior oriented toward the resolution of problems related to cardinal male figures, particularly the father.

Considering the other items in Table IX-14, no significant differences were elicited regarding either a special interest in the partner's buttocks or the desire for a partner with a large penis. Item 4 indicates that in each instance where a patient had reported that he had begun his homosexual activity prior to the age of 14, he also reported that his mother had been seductive with him. In 4 of the insertor cases the patient had identified his partner with a feminine figure; in 3 cases the identification was masculine, and in 1 case the identification was a combined masculine and feminine image.

The items in Table IX-15 probe the parental relations of exclusive insertors and anal insertees. More insertees (77 per cent) were submissive to the father than were exclusive insertors (31 per cent). Of the 9 anal insertees who experienced contempt and/or humiliation from their fathers, 8 were submissive to their fathers, and all 9 feared them. On the other hand, of the 8 exclusive insertors whose fathers were contemptuous and/or humiliating toward them, only 2 were reported as submissive to their fathers. Among the anal insertees, in each of 6 instances in which a sister was the father's favorite, the patient was the child least-favored by the father and/or was shown contempt and humiliation by the father. Four anal insertees had brothers, none of whom was a favorite of the father's. Of the 8 exclusive insertors who had sisters favored by the father, 5 patients were least-favored by him or had experienced contempt or humiliation from him; and of the 10 exclusive insertors with male siblings, 4 had brothers who were the father's favorite. Hatred of the father was somewhat more common among the exclusive insertors. Respect for the father was reported by approximately one-third of each of these two groups.

The anal insertee's relationship with his mother is of especial

TABLE IX-15 *Exclusive Insertors and Anal Insertees: Relations with Parents*

		Exclusive insertors (16)		Anal insertees (17)	
1.	Son submissive to father	31%	(5)	77%	(13)**
2.	Son shown contempt/humiliation by father	50%	(8)	53%	(9)
3.	Son submissive to father and contempt/humiliation by father	13%	(2)	47%	(8)
4.	Father hated	63%	(10)	47%	(8)
5.	Father respected and/or admired	38%	(6)	29%	(5)
6.	Patient had sister(s)	81%	(13)	65%	(11)
7.	Sister was father's favorite	50%	(8)	35%	(6)
8.	Patient least-favored by father	44%	(7)	25%	(4)
9.	Patient least-favored and/or contempt/humiliation by father and sister was father's favorite	31%	(5)	35%	(6)
10.	Brother was father's favorite	25%	(4)	0%	
11.	Mother seductive	69%	(11)	65%	(11)
12.	Mother seductive and mother encouraged feminine activities and mother interfered with heterosexuality	19%	(3)	41%	(7)
13.	Mother seductive and mother interfered with heterosexuality in adolescence	25%	(4)	59%	(10)
14.	Mother seductive and much guilt about masturbation	25%	(4)	53%	(9)
15.	Mother interfered with heterosexuality	31%	(5)	77%	(13)*
16.	Much guilt about masturbation	25%	(4)	71%	(12)*
17.	Mother admired/respected	44%	(7)	77%	(13)
18.	Son frail/effeminate in childhood and much guilt about masturbation and mother seductive and mother interfered with heterosexuality	6%	(1)	47%	(8)

interest. Of 17 mothers whose sons were anal insertees, 11 (65 per cent) were seductive with their sons, and 10 of the 11 mothers had interfered with their sons' heterosexual strivings, including 7 mothers who had encouraged feminine activities. While 11 of the 16 exclusive insertors (69 per cent) had seductive mothers, only 4 of these 11 mothers had interfered with their sons' heterosexuality, but 3 of these 4 had encouraged feminine activities in their sons. Of the 11 anal insertees with seductive mothers, much guilt about masturbation was reported for 9 patients, but masturbatory guilt was reported for only 4 of the 11 exclusive insertors with seductive mothers. The anal insertee more commonly admired and/or respected his mother, compared to the exclusive insertor.

A constellation of the following four items was reported for 8 anal insertees: Frail or effeminate in childhood; much guilt about masturbation; mother seductive; mother interfered with heterosexuality. Only 1 exclusive insertor showed this cluster. The evidence in Table IX-15 indicates that the mothers of anal insertees, more often than among the exclusive insertors, had a relationship with their sons conducive to heterosexual arousal (seductiveness), and at the same time inhibited their assertive behavior, particularly heterosexual behavior. Submissive behavior toward a father who showed contempt or humiliation was more prevalent among the anal insertees than among the exclusive insertors, many of whom were not submissive to such fathers. In the 6 instances in which the anal insertee's father favored a sister, the son's submissive attitude may have involved a competitive attempt to please his father in order to win him over. The over-all picture of the anal insertee's relationship with his parents is that *both* parents exercised an inhibiting influence, and this occurred more frequently than it did among the exclusive insertors.

Concerning attitudes towards women (see Table IX-16), only 2 of 17 anal insertees were found to "idolize" women, yet neither patient admired the mother or a sister. In contrast, 5 of 16 exclusive insertors (31 per cent) "idolized" women, and 4 of these had admired their mothers and/or sisters. A feeling of rivalry with women was noted for 7 anal insertees (41 per cent), compared to 3 exclusive insertors (19 per cent), and 4 of these 7 insertees had a history of effeminacy in childhood, whereas only 1 exclusive insertor had been effeminate in childhood and he was not competitive with women. It is noteworthy that 4 anal insertees who had competitive problems with women, had sisters; in 2 cases the sisters were hated; 3 patients had a sister who was the father's favorite, and the fourth patient had a half-sister. In these cases, the patient's hatred for his sister appears to stem from rivalry with her for the father's affection, and the anal insertee sexual preference may be a symbolic striving to gain the father's love through sexual techniques. Thus, rivalry with women, and perhaps even childhood effeminacy, may be in some cases the consequences of rejection by a father who showed favoritism to a sister.

TABLE IX-16 *Exclusive Insertors and Anal Insertees: Relationships with Women*

	Exclusive insertors (16)		Anal insertees (17)	
1. Idolize women and admire mother/sister	25%	(4)	0%	
2. Rivalry with women and effeminate in childhood	0%		24%	(4)
3. Anxiety with sexual excitement	50%	(8)	77%	(13)
4. Anxiety with sexual excitement and fantasies of violence with sexual excitement	25%	(4)	41%	(7)
5. Much guilt about masturbation and punishment for sex-play with girls	0%		29%	(5)*
6. Bisexuals	31%	(5)	29%	(5)
7. Bisexuals with much guilt about masturbation	6%	(1)	29%	(5)

The more frequently noted sexual inhibition of the anal insertee (as compared to the exclusive insertor) in shown in items 3, 4 and 5 of Table IX-16. Of the anal insertees, 77 per cent developed anxiety when experiencing sexual excitement, as compared to 50 per cent of exclusive insertors. In 7 of the 13 insertee cases, the anxiety was associated with fantasies of violence, whereas there were 4 such instances among exclusive insertors. Of the 12 anal insertees who had reported marked guilt feelings about masturbation, 5 had also been threatened or punished for sexual play with girls during childhood, contrasted to 4 exclusive insertors for whom much guilt about masturbation had been reported and none of whom had been threatened or punished for sexual play with girls. There were 5 bisexuals among the exclusive insertors and an equal number among the anal insertees; however, only 1 of these bisexual exclusive insertors had much guilt about masturbation, whereas all 5 bisexual anal insertees had much masturbatory guilt. It is noteworthy that 13 anal insertees had mothers who had interfered with their heterosexuality while only 5 mothers among the exclusive insertors were reported to have done so (see Table IX-15).

After an extensive analysis of our data, we have found that few *significant* differences emerged between the exclusive insertors and the exclusively anal insertees—in the face of conventional expectations. Many items, however, consistently showed severe psychopathology to be proportionately more frequent among the 17 anal insertees than among the 16 exclusive insertors. The number of cases is small and therefore the results can only be suggestive. From our data, it cannot be said that insertors are more "heterosexual" and insertees less so. Each group is more like the other than either group is like the heterosexual comparison group.

SUMMARY

The homosexual patients were found to be wary and fearful of women where there was a possibility of *sexual* contact, yet a majority of homosexuals sought to maintain *social* relationships with them. Heterosexual interests were nevertheless frequently indicated. All but 28 of the 106 homosexuals in our sample had, at one time or another, successfully or unsuccessfully attempted heterosexual intercourse while 30 of the H-patients were bisexually adapted. Evidence of *covert* heterosexual interests was revealed in the manifest content of dreams.

Most of the homosexuals in our sample, in the judgment of their psychoanalysts, sought "masculine" qualities in partners, but a substantial minority sought "feminine" qualities. "Masculine" partners were usually identified with the father or a brother, while "feminine" partners were usually identified with the mother or a sister. In some cases both "masculine" and "feminine" attributes were sought in the partner.

Many homosexuals were attracted to a partner with a large penis, but this was not associated with a predilection for either "masculine" or "feminine" traits in the partner, nor with the sexual role taken by the homosexual. The desire for a large penis in the partner was more frequent among homosexuals who had aversion to female genitalia and among those who feared injury to their own genitalia. A special attraction for the buttocks of the partner was noted in about one-third of homosexuals, but no association could be demonstrated between this interest and the traits desired in the partner, nor with sexual-role preferences.

Many homosexuals showed a preference for inserting the penis into the partner's bodily orifices (insertors), and many others allowed their own bodily orifices to be used by the partner (insertees). The group of insertors included most homosexual patients who sought "feminine" partners; most of the insertees sought a "masculine" partner. Many homosexuals took any of a variety of sexual roles.

As a general trend, we noted: More insertees than insertors feared and were submissive to their fathers; fewer insertees consciously hated, or respected their fathers; more insertees admired their mothers and were their mothers' confidants; more insertees had seductive and overprotective mothers who had interfered with their sons' heterosexuality and had punished them for sexual play with girls during childhood; more insertees had much guilt about masturbation, anxiety with sexual excitement, and potency difficulties even in homosexual relationships.

Those insertees who preferred fellatio more frequently became heterosexual through psychoanalytic treatment than did anal insertees.

Bisexuals were found with equal frequency among insertors and insertees, and those homosexuals who became heterosexual during psychoanalytic treatment were about evenly divided between insertors and insertees.

Homosexual patients were found to be compulsively preoccupied with sexuality in general and with sexual practices in particular. In addition to providing sexual release and gratification, the homosexual relationship served to fulfill a range of *irrational defensive and reparative needs:* It is irrational to seek feminine qualities in a male sexual partner; it is irrational to endow a large penis with special value; it is irrational for a person restricted by sexual inhibitions to believe that inhibitions can be ameliorated by contact with a large penis; it is pathologic to endow a large penis with magical, symbolic power.

Many facts emerge to demonstrate strong heterosexual trends within the homosexual group set against inhibitory influences. We found strong fears of the father, yet about half of the homosexuals also unconsciously identified the partner with the father or a brother. We found many mothers who were consciously as well as unconsciously seductive and sexually stimulating, yet punished their sons for heterosexual play during childhood, interfered with heterosexual activities during adolescence, and banished sex from social recognition. These conflicting influences produced ambivalence in the homosexual relationship—derived on the one hand from deep-seated sexual inhibition linked with sexual fears of women, and on the other hand from fear, envy, and hostility toward men.

Although many homosexual relationships may be quite stable, continuity is unusual. Genital gratification is one goal in homosexual as in heterosexual relationships, but in both situations the relationship between the partners includes strong interpersonal elements, e.g., warmth, friendship, concern for the other's welfare and happiness, and so forth. However, in the homosexual pairing, hostile and competitive trends (overt and covert) often intrude to prevent a stable relationship with a partner. We found many homosexuals to be fearful, isolated, and anxious about masculinity and personal acceptability. Ambivalence leads to impermanence or transiency in most homosexual contacts. The inability to sustain a relationship frequently arises from an inability to bring social and sexual relations into a unity. This problem is well illustrated by the superficial and evanescent quality of social activities often carried on at bars and in "cruising." Warm interpersonal relations between individuals of the same sex do not become sexual unless there is inhibition of heterosexual expression. A man and woman may be warm, close friends without desire on the part of either for sexual activity with the other. This also holds for relationships between two women, or between two men. In fact, two homosexuals may have a friendly relationship without sexual interest in one another. We do not regard friendship relationships as necessarily homosexual even between two homosexuals.

When a homosexual tries to bring social and sexual components into a unity in one individual, he may be beset with the same difficulties he faces in his relations with women. Because the partner then becomes a highly valued love-object, intense anxiety is aroused, similar to the anxiety surrounding the sexual and possessive feelings toward a mother figure. Furthermore, fears around the thought of excluding another man (who might effectively retaliate) begin to mount.

Much in the homosexual relationship is destructive. Yet, there may exist positive aspects. There is some attempt to establish and preserve human contact and to develop and maintain meaningful relationships. It is *one* kind of adaptation in the face of crippling circumstances of growth and development; it is an attempt to participate in social living as much as is tolerable within the limitations of anxiety.

X

"Latent" Homosexuality

IT WILL BE recalled that the sole criterion for selecting comparison patients was active heterosexuality. These patients were exclusively heterosexual in that they had had no homosexual experiences in their adult lives although a few had had episodic homosexual experiences during childhood or adolescence. However, protocols of many of the comparison patients revealed that they feared homosexuals and homosexuality and that they had experienced homosexual fantasies and dreams. These data were examined to see whether they could contribute to further understanding of "latent" homosexuality. This phase of our study presented an opportunity to find out how such comparison patients systematically resembled, and differed from, homosexual patients.

Since the earliest days of psychoanalysis, "latent" or "unconscious" homosexuality has been employed as a diagnostic as well as a genetic concept. Freud's theory of bisexuality, which derived from mythological sources, histological data, and comparative biologic studies, postulated the existence of a constitutionally determined duality of the sexual instinct. Normal heterosexuality was considered to be necessarily dependent upon the capacity of the individual to repress and sublimate the homosexual component of the sexual instinct and the "passive-feminine" wishes deriving from the negative Oedipus complex. Thus, a universal homoeroticism is postulated which may or may not be held in abeyance depending on both instinctual and experiential factors that determine libidinal development. According to Freud, excessive pressure of pregenital libidinal components and failure of the defenses of repression and sublimation permit or threaten emergence into consciousness of homosexual impulses, which give rise to conflict manifested in the appearance of symptoms. These symptoms include fear of being homosexual, dreams with manifest and "latent" homosexual content, conscious homosexual fantasies and impulses, "homosexual panic," disturbances in heterosexual functioning, and "passive-submissive" responses to other males. Individuals in whom such symptoms appear are frequently referred to as "latent homosexuals." The Freudian position on "latent" homosexuality is summarized in the following quotation by Karl Abraham: "In normal individuals the homosexual component of the sexual instinct undergoes sublimation. Between men, feelings of unity and friendship become divested of all sexuality. The man of normal feeling is repelled by any physical contact implying tenderness with another of his own sex. . . . Alcohol suspends these feelings. When they are drinking, men will fall upon one another's necks and kiss each other . . . when sober, the same men will term such conduct effeminate. . . . The homosexual components which have been repressed and sublimated by the influence of education become unmistakably evident under the influence of alcohol."

Many writers have questioned the concept of "latent" homosexuality on theoretical and clinical grounds. Salzman, among the more recent critics, has pointed out that latency implies dormancy—the presence of fully developed and mature functions in an inactive state—and potentiality—the presence of possible but undeveloped functions. Further, the term as commonly used in clinical practice assumes psychological characteristics of the opposite sex, and is applied to tendencies, attitudes, and behavior involving difficulty with mature sexuality. The point is stressed that the term is not used to refer to the overt homosexual who attempts to suppress his homosexuality and tries to lead a heterosexual life; it applies only to heterosexuals. Difficulties in relating to the opposite sex and the superficial resemblance to commonly accepted characteristics of the opposite sex are viewed as insufficient evidence to establish the presence of a fully developed and mature dormant process (homosexuality), ready to emerge to a manifest state.

A somewhat different approach was taken by Rado in a critique of the theory of bisexuality. In substance, the theory "represents a constitutional and biological assumption that has been made into a psychological assumption." He pointed out that, biologically, maleness and femaleness cannot be determined from any single element (such as a gonad) or from relative percentages of male and female hormones; sex is determined only from the character of the reproductive system as a whole. "The zygote is not, in fact, bisexual but merely possesses a bipotentiality of differentiation. . . . Hormonal and genetic disturbances do not produce bisexuality but sexual crippling." On the basis of the bisexual theory, the classification of behavior as "masculine" and "feminine," made by many psychoanalysts, is arbitrary.

Approaching the problem from still another perspective, Szasz states, "The notion of 'homosexuality' has occupied an important position in the psychoanalytic literature of psychosis and in the explanations put forward to account for all types of withdrawal from the outside world. Although this notion is of some value, revisions and refinements are necessary, among them the need for clarification of that which this notion of 'homosexuality' creates—namely that the patient is sexually interested in another person who is of the same sex. Observation often shows that the patient is interested only in his own body. An ego orientation to the body might readily appear to be homosexual to the observer, particularly if it is in a manifestly projected form. What is meant by this is that the patient might treat another person—man or woman—as if this person were his body. If the person in question is of the same sex as the patient, the observer usually concludes that this is 'homosexuality.' . . . Or as has happened in psychoanalysis, the inner experience of the patient is correctly apprehended but is described by the rather obscure term of 'latent homosexuality.' In this way, phenomenologically overt heterosexuality is sometimes viewed by psychoanalysts as being 'in reality' a form of homosexuality."

Disagreement about the validity of "latent" homosexuality is not recent. Some believe that the category "latent" homosexuality has been a psychopathological wastebasket in which many types of pathology are included that bear little or no relationship to homosexuality. To test the "latency" concept we used as questionnaire items those criteria by which the "syndrome" is usually diagnosed:

1. Has the patient expressed fear of homosexuality?
2. Has the patient reported homosexual fantasies, dreams, ideas, or impulses?

3. How often have homosexual advances been made to the patient by known or suspected homosexuals? (Never, rarely, occasionally, frequently.)

4. How has the patient reacted to such homosexual advances? (Fear, anxiety, rage, disgust, horror, fascination, understanding, indifference, other.)

5. How has the patient reacted when in the presence of known homosexuals? (Fear, anxiety, rage, disgust, horror, fascination, understanding, indifference, other.)

6. Does the patient report dreams with erotic homosexual manifest content?

7. Did the patient report any early childhood experience in which he was erotically aroused by a male?

8. Were there homosexual contacts with male siblings?

9. Did the patient ever want to be a woman?

Each case was then scored for the number of affirmative answers and each question given equal weighting. In addition to the scores, descriptive data added by many of the reporting psychoanalysts and information obtained through personal communications with the psychoanalysts in some cases, permitted us to assign each comparison patient to one of the following four categories: No homosexual problem; mild homosexual problem; moderate homosexual problem; severe homosexual problem. Each of the protocols was evaluated independently by two members of the Committee. If they disagreed, the protocols were judged by the Committee as a whole. Complete data were available on 96 patients. Table X-1 presents these data.

TABLE X-1 *Classification of Homosexual Problems (in per cent)*

No problem	41
Mild problem	17
Moderate problem	15
Severe problem	27
	100

We were able to differentiate the homosexuals from the comparisons on the basis of the Six Developmental Score[1] and the Twenty

[1] See Chapter VII. The six questions tap preadolescent development; the answers to these questions significantly distinguished homosexuals from comparisons.

Questions Score.[2] It seemed reasonable to assume that if "latent" homosexuality and "overt" homosexuality were comparable entities, heterosexual patients who scored highest on severity would resemble the homosexual patients more closely than would patients with lower scores. In order to have two groups of heterosexual patients for purposes of comparison, we combined patients classified as having "no problem" and "mild problem" into a group of "Low Scorers" and patients classified as having "moderate problem" and "severe problem" into a group of "High Scorers." The Low Scorers consisted of 56 patients and the High Scorers consisted of 40 patients.

TABLE X-2 *Comparison Between Low and High Scorers on Six Developmental Items (in per cent)*

Six developmental score	High scorers N = 40	Low scorers 56
0-2	62.5	64
3-4	15.0	27
5-6	22.5	9
	100	100

Examination of Table X-2 reveals a striking fact. Of the High Scorers 77.5 per cent and of the Low Scorers 91 per cent fall into the low-to-borderline range on the scale of the Six Developmental Items whereas only 10 per cent of the homosexual patients fell into this range. It would appear that the childhood developmental pattern of even the High Scorers differs significantly from the homosexuals for these items.

Tables X-3 and X-4 refer to the ratings achieved by comparison patients on the Twenty Questions Score. In the main, this score reflects frequencies of close-binding intimate mothers and detached fathers. When we established a critical score of 11 above which 70 per cent of the homosexuals scored, only 40 per cent of the High Scorers had a comparable score. Only one significant difference occurs (Table X-3) between High and Low Scorers and that is the difference in the number who are found in the 14-20 range. A similar difference, al-

[2] The Twenty Questions Score was derived by giving equal weighting to the answers to 20 questions tapping parent-son relationships which most significantly differentiated the homosexual from the comparison sample (see Appendix B).

TABLE X-3 *Comparison Between Low and High Scorers on Twenty Questions Score (in per cent)*

Twenty questions score	High scorers N = 40	Low scorers 56
0-7	40.0	55
8-10	20.0	23
11-13	17.5	20
14-20	22.5*	2
	100	100

TABLE X-4 *Comparisons Between Heterosexuals and Homosexuals Scoring Over 11 on Twenty Questions Score (in per cent)*

Low scorers	21
High scorers	40
Homosexuals	70

though not significant, is noted in the 5-6 range of the Six Developmental Score (Table X-2). However, it was also observed that 10 High Scorers (25 per cent) had zero scores on the Six Developmental Score and 14 (35 per cent) High Scorers had zero on the Twenty Questions Score. In attempting to account for this apparent paradox, we found that High Scorers fell into two groups and that the heavy weighting in the 5-6 range of the Six Developmental Score and the 14-20 range of the Twenty Questions Score was accounted for by 9 patients. The scores achieved by this latter group on the two scales were indistinguishable from the scores of the majority of homosexuals. These patients will be discussed separately. For the remaining comparison patients there was no correlation between scores on the two scales and the severity of homosexual problems.

We then approached the data with the specific aim of determining which items revealed similarities between High Scorers and homosexuals. The only item appearing with comparable frequency of responses for High Scorers and homosexuals was the item for "Seductive mother." High scoring patients scored midway between the Low Scorers and homosexuals on the items "Excessive fear in childhood," "Avoided fights in childhood" and the "Feeling of having been babied by the mother." Differences among homosexuals and high and low scoring comparison patients on these four items are given in Table X-5. On all other items the Low Scorers were identical or nearly identical with the High Scorers.

TABLE X-5 *Comparison of Low Scorers, High Scorers, and Homosexuals in Which Highs Scored Equal to Homosexuals, or Between Low Scorers and Homosexuals* (*in per cent*)

	Low scorers	High scorers	Homosexuals
N =	56	40	106
Mother seductive	32	53	57
Excessively fearful in childhood	36	58	75
Avoided fights in childhood	48	65*	89
Felt mother babied him	36	48	61

If we separate the 9 exceptional cases (see p. 262) from the High Scorers, the differences diminish between Low Scorers and High Scorers on the items "Seductive mother" and "Excessive fearfulness in childhood." This is shown in Table X-6.

TABLE X-6 *Comparison of Low Scorers, High Scorers, and Homosexuals, as in Table X-5, with the 9 Exceptions Removed from the High Scoring Group* (*in per cent*)

	Low scorers	High scorers	Homosexuals
N =	56	31	106
Mother seductive	32	42	57
Excessively fearful in childhood	36	45*	75
Avoided fights in childhood	48	61*	89
Felt mother babied him	36	48	61

Another similarity between the High Scorers and homosexuals emerged when comparisons were made on the basis of parental profiles. Among the heterosexual patients, 32 had close-binding-intimate mothers. All three questionnaires were filled out on 30 of these 32 patients (many of the items relating to homosexual problems were in the Third Questionnaire). Of the 30 patients, 17 were found to be High Scorers. All 9 exceptional patients (see p. 262) were among the group of 17.

When this same comparison was made for the category of controlling-dominating mothers (the other large maternal category), a striking difference was found. There was a trend in this group toward a negative correlation between controlling-dominating mothers and High Scorers, although it did not reach a level of significance.

The fact that the CBI mothers of comparison patients had more sons among High Scorers suggests that these mothers were similar to the CBI mothers of homosexuals, and tended also to promote the sexual psychopathology related to homosexual problems.

The material presented thus far has illustrated the differences between the comparison patients having homosexual problems and the homosexuals on the basis of the Six Developmental and Twenty Questions Scores. In analyzing the individual components of the Six Developmental Score and comparing the relative scores of High Scorers and homosexuals, the parameters that indicate adaptive deviation in the preadolescent period revealed that the High Scorers were significantly differentiated from the homosexuals on 5 of the Six Developmental Items. Further, the High Scorers could not be significantly differentiated from the Low Scorers on any of these items. This obtained even though the 9 exceptional cases were included among the High Scorers (Table X-7). It is pertinent to the present study that High Scorers and Low Scorers resembled each other. Both groups tended to have the preadolescent development normative in our culture, unlike the majority of homosexuals whose preadolescence was deviant (Chapter VII). High Scorers were more frequently fearful than were Low Scorers, yet sociosexual development proceeded in congruence with the biocultural patterns of males. The psychopathologic factors noted in the preadolescence of High Scorers had not basically influenced the male sexual adaptation.

TABLE X-7 *Comparison of High Scoring Heterosexuals and Overt Homosexuals on the Six Developmental Items* (*in per cent*)

	High scorers	Homosexuals
N=	40	106
1. Excessively fearful of injury in childhood	58	75
2. Avoided fights in childhood	65*	89
3. Played primarily with girls	13*	33
4. Was "lone wolf"	35*	60
5. Involved in group competitive games	65**	17
6. Played baseball	58**	16

There were only 9 comparison cases who could not be readily distinguished from homosexuals in responses to questionnaire items. The charts of these patients were subjected to detailed scrutiny and individual psychoanalysts were personally interviewed. We were, in a sense, attempting to find out why these 9 patients were not homosexual since 7 of the 9 were rated as having severe homosexual problems. Of the 9, all had CBI mothers; 5 had the parental combination of CBI mothers and detached-hostile fathers, representing the most pathogenic parental pairing in our study (Table X-8).

TABLE X-8 *Parental Pairing of 9 Exceptional Comparison Cases*

1.	CBI Mothers—detached-hostile fathers	5
2.	CBI Mothers—not-detached-hostile fathers	2
3.	CBI Mothers—detached-indifferent fathers	1
4.	CBI Mothers—close-binding fathers	1
		9

Only 2 of the 9 exceptional cases had had homosexual experiences in childhood. One patient had had a homosexual experience when he was 26 years old. He was a passive participant in an incident involving him with a bunkmate while serving in the navy. The partner came in drunk one night and performed fellatio on the patient while he was presumably asleep.

Case histories of 5 of these 9 exceptional comparison patients follow.

PATIENT NO. 240

This patient entered analytic therapy at the age of seventeen, following an acute schizophrenic reaction characterized by paralyzing anxiety, confusion, withdrawal, and inability to continue either at school or on the job. He was preoccupied with fears of sexual inadequacy and fears of being homosexual. The manifest content of his dreams was homosexual and he responded with fear and rage when in the presence of homosexuals. He was obsessed with a need to have a heterosexual experience and ruminated continually over his past sexual failures.

The patient, the younger of two male children, was born at a time when the relationship between his parents was close to complete disintegration. The mother had married the father with the avowed purpose of changing him to suit herself. The father, an aggressive, hard-driving, competitive, labile-tempered man took pride in his capacity to throw himself into business activities and work very long hours. The mother considered him crude, unfeeling, and insensitive. She was expressly unhappy about her failure to mold him into a kindly, "sensitive" person. The father responded to her attempts at domination and control with towering rage, and there was perpetual conflict between the two. When the patient was born, the mother decided that this son was going to be the kind of man she had always wanted for herself and she set about deliberately to achieve this goal. She was with her son constantly, lavishing affection and concern upon him, and protecting him from all external frustrations. She succeeded in isolating him from his father. During the patient's early childhood and adolescence mother and son would often discuss the father's failings —his crudeness, insensitivity, and brutality. In addition to the smothering overprotection and physical affection, she utilized guilt provocations as a technique for achieving her purposes. The patient recounted many preadolescent memories of returning from school to find his mother in bed—depressed and moaning in pain. She would then detail all her frustrations and unhappiness, attributing them always to the father's insensitivity. In the course of these conversations, the patient would experience a painful sense of guilt, as if he were in some way inadequate since he felt unable to relieve his mother's distress. Until he began treatment, he was in perpetual torment over the idea that if he could only be the kind of person his mother wished him to be, she would then be "happy."

The mother engaged in excessive talk with the patient about sex under the guise of "educating" him. She involved herself constantly in his fantasies and preoccupations. During his adolescence they would discuss his dates as well as his sexual problems and activities. The mother encouraged his sexual activities and seemed to derive satisfaction from hearing about his sexual exploits as he matured. Even when the patient developed a gonorrheal infection when he was nineteen, she was remarkably unconcerned. When she discussed this incident during an interview with the psychoanalyst she seemed *pleased* about the sexual incident that resulted in the venereal infection. Even after repeated exhortations by the psychoanalyst over a period of several years, she continued to indulge in interminable discussions with the patient about his sexual life, a temptation he was unable to resist.

The father, a stern, detached man, had been isolated from the patient early in the boy's life, leaving him to his mother almost entirely. The father, on the surface, accepted this isolation from his son, and made no serious attempt either to interfere with the mother-son relationship or to establish himself as an effective father, although he was able to do this with his older son. The mother, however, did not make the same demands on her older son as she did on the patient. The father related to the patient only in terms of demands and setting standards. When the patient was an older adolescent, the father began to realize how disturbed his son was. Paternal "help" consisted of prodding the patient to be an aggressive, competitive, and responsible worker. Since the patient's only conscious feeling toward his father was hatred, paternal demands served only to increase the boy's antipathy. Verbally, the father encouraged sexual activity but this encouragement was accompanied by admonitions which tended to increase the boy's anxiety.

An additional factor influencing the patient was the mother's relationship with her older brother who was married and had children of his own. She expressed admiration and affection for the uncle, a rather mild and ineffectual man. The father was constantly compared to the uncle—always unfavorably—with the result that the uncle rather than the father was held up as a model for the patient. As a consequence, the patient developed a reasonably trusting relationship with his uncle; certainly, it was the best relationship he had formed with any male prior to the time he entered treatment with a male psychoanalyst.

Thus, in spite of the mother's seductiveness and her binding, symbiotic relationship to the son, her attitude toward his sexuality, albeit bizarre and ambivalent, was definitely in the direction of heterosexuality. She somehow communicated the feeling to her son that his *heterosexual* activity was of *value* to her. The father was also ambivalent toward his son's sexuality but, at least verbally, he encouraged heterosexual activity. The mother's relationship with the uncle provided the boy with a male, heterosexual model *acceptable to the mother*. Thus in the patient's life there were experiences and influences that promoted male identification and heterosexuality.

PATIENT NO. 260

This patient sought psychoanalytic therapy because of sexual impotence. An obsessive fear of homosexuality was revealed as one of his symptoms. His mother was possessive and binding. She dominated all family decisions and was openly contemptuous of the father, whom she regarded as inferior. The patient was greatly favored over his only sibling, a younger sister.

The mother was unusually seductive toward the patient throughout his childhood, adolescence, and early adult life. They would use the bathroom at the same time until the patient began psychoanalysis. Although the mother verbally expressed antisexual attitudes, there was no modesty in the home; all four members of the family were in the habit of appearing nude before one another. In the course of treatment, it became apparent that many of the patient's difficulties originated in the excessive sexual stimulation of an overtly seductive mother, undeterred by the father. At one point in the patient's psychoanalysis, he stated that his mother might even consciously wish to have sexual relations with him. In evaluating the mother's behavior, the psychoanalyst felt that the patient's statement was indeed closer to reality than to fantasy.

In the opinion of the patient's psychoanalyst, a notable characteristic of the mother was her respect, admiration, and envy of masculine men. She rationalized her contemptuous and derogatory attitudes toward her husband on the ground that he lacked "masculinity." The father, a conscientious and industrious man, was indeed passive, fearful, and unassertive. The patient recalled feelings of deprivation and disappointment when he compared his father to the fathers of some friends. The mother openly admired her own older brother who was more successful than her husband and who was an obviously virile and assertive male. The uncle's son, an older cousin of the patient, became a model of masculinity whom the patient strove to emulate with the active encouragement of the mother. She was extremely proud, indeed boastful, of the patient's superior intellectual and academic achievements. There was no evidence that the mother had at any time been feminizing or overprotective. The patient preferred to play with boys and engaged in competitive sports.

Thus, despite a close-binding-intimate, seductive mother and an indifferent, ineffective father, there were factors that fostered masculine development and identification. The mother consistently communicated the idea that a virile male was of value to her. Masculine figures—the uncle and cousin—were encouraged as models for the patient.

PATIENT NO. 249

This patient began psychoanalytic therapy at age twenty-six, because of premature ejaculation during sexual intercourse. The patient experienced conscious fears of homosexuality, and at age twenty-two had a fantasy of hugging a male. As a consequence, he developed constraint about urinating in public places. According to his psychoanalyst, during the preschool and school periods the patient was exposed to the vicissitudes of a "broken home." His mother was oversolicitous, overprotective, and made unreasonable demands especially in scholastic and social achievement. When he was ten he was further traumatized by the introduction of a stepfather who was alcoholic, indifferent, rejecting, dominating and overcritical. The patient was obsequious and submissive to his mother and intensely frightened of his stepfather. The boy, thin and frail himself, admired boys and men who were strong, muscular and healthy-looking. In his fantasies as an adult he saw himself as an athlete—strong, handsome and admired by all women at all times.

He was unable to maintain his relationships with women for any length of time and was fearful of a warm, heterosexual relationship. He demanded love, affection, and sexual gratification of women but was unable to be affectionate or loving with them. When he felt accepted by a woman his spirits were high; when his unreasonable demands were not satisfied, he felt rejected and thought little of himself.

He found it impossible to void in public toilets in the presence of other men. He felt that they would see he had a small penis and that his urinary stream was weak. To protect himself against exposing his "defects," he avoided situations where this could occur.

In contrast to his admiration for strong, romantic, athletic men, he would be overcome with feelings of fury in the presence of weak, thin, frail, effeminate, or homosexual men—according to his psychoanalyst. His anger was an expression of self-contempt, since such men resembled his own picture of himself—weak, submissive, and sexually inadequate. He would think he was a homosexual and feel guilty whenever he found himself admiring a man. Hostility toward men perceived as unmasculine also had the reparative effect of reinforcing his identification with heterosexuals.

When the psychoanalyst who treated the patient was closely questioned, it was discovered that although the mother fostered a close-binding relationship, she wanted the patient to be masculine, encouraged masculine attitudes, and reacted positively to his heterosexual activity. The patient's stepfather also clearly indicated that he expected the patient to be a strong, virile man.

PATIENT NO. 250

This patient entered psychoanalytic treatment at age thirty for symptoms of anxiety, impotence, and fear of homosexuality. His dreams contained homosexual material; his response to homosexual advances was one of fear, and when in the presence of a homosexual he felt anxiety and disgust.

Although the relationship between this patient's parents was one in which open demonstrations of affection sometimes occurred, there were frequent arguments. The father was dominant in family decisions, but in the event of any trouble it was the mother who took over the reins. The mother indicated to the patient that she had been forced to marry an inferior man because she had been in ill health and therefore could not get a better man. The psychoanalyst described the mother as a masochistic individual, and the father as a man who would go on periodic alcoholic sprees and beat his wife. The parents spent very little time together and had no similar interests. Whenever conflict between the parents occurred, the patient would ally himself with the mother. The patient revered his mother and felt that she protected him from his father.

There were three female siblings (eight years older, four years older, and six years younger). The patient was the mother's favorite. Despite the mother's demonstrations of affection, he did not feel accepted or admired by her, and he reported that she was often contemptuous of him. The mother demanded that she be the center of his attention and pre-empted much of his time. Masculine attitudes were discouraged and feminine attitudes and activities actively encouraged. Although there were three sisters in the family, the patient would do housework for his mother because he "felt sorry for her." Although she was seductive to the patient, he regarded her as frigid and puritanical. She openly preferred him to his father and formed an alliance with the patient against the father. The patient was afraid of the mother and because he feared that any assertive behavior on his part would aggravate her illness, he relied on techniques of submission and charm to cope with her.

The patient felt "babied" by his mother, who was overconcerned about his health and safety. She restricted his activities, directed his choice of friends, and insisted that he avoid fights. The mother slept with him whenever he was sick and indulged in intimate discussions with him about the father's "awful" sexual behavior with her. The patient reported that when he was an adolescent his mother informed him that the father performed cunnilingus upon her and that they engaged in coitus a tergo.

Although the mother expected him to have heterosexual interests, she was jealous, disapproving, and belittling of his girl friends and frequently warned him that some designing female would "wind him around her finger."

The patient's father preferred the youngest sister of all his children; the patient was the least favored by him. The father was physically cruel to him and ridiculed him as a "sissy." The patient reported that, during his childhood, whenever his father was home he was drunk and abusive. He consciously hated and feared his father, avoiding him whenever possible. The father was concerned about the patient's tendency toward effeminacy and although it cannot be said that the father "encouraged" the patient in any area, he promoted masculinity and tried to discourage feminine attitudes and behavior. When he became aware that the patient was repeatedly choosing girls who were ill or had physical defects he objected vociferously. (The mother, who proclaimed herself a sick person, was convinced she had heart disease and "back" trouble.) The patient reported a recurrent dream in which he was with a girl; everything proceeded smoothly, until the father walked in, evicted the patient, and had intercourse with the girl.

Like many patients who come from families with similar dynamics, the patient hated his three sisters who in turn hated the mother. They remained loyal to her because of guilt feelings. While the patient's sympathies were entirely with his mother, the sisters were partial to the father, feeling that he was the unlucky partner in the marriage. The patient felt he could compete with his sisters on a feminine level only; thus he attempted to win his mother's love by outdoing them in performing household chores which they refused to do. However, the patient displayed an active sexual interest in his youngest sister who would feign sleep while the patient fondled her breasts and masturbated. The patient reported a desire to perform cunnilingus on her.

According to the patient, he received no sexual information from either parent during childhood. He experienced much guilt about masturbation. His initial heterosexual contact was in the form of kissing and did not take place until he was twenty-two and in the army. He petted for the first time when he was twenty-four with a thirty-two-year-old woman who was the initiator. He first attempted intercourse at age twenty-six, again with an older woman who initiated it. This attempt proved unsuccessful. His first successful intercourse occurred one year later. Currently, the patient experiences intense anxiety when sexually aroused and is frequently impotent. He is terrified of his impotence and becomes enraged whenever a woman is hostile or rejecting.

His earliest memory of arousal by a female figure is reported as having occurred at age eight. He never experienced aversion to female genitalia, but was fearful that intercourse would lead to injury to his genitals. He recalled that he had had the desire to be a woman—a desire accompanied by the feeling that girls get a better break in life, are better loved by the father, and don't have to work. He has wanted to be a quiet, peaceful person, clean in habits and leading a respectable life. He has also wanted to be like his mother.

The patient's Six Developmental Items Score indicated that he experienced excessive fear of injury and avoided fights in childhood, did not participate in group games, and did not play baseball. However, he was not a lone wolf as a child, and did not play exclusively with girls. His high Twenty Questions Score illustrates the close-binding relationship with the mother and the fearful, hostile relationship with the father.

The patient reported several dreams with homosexual content, as follows: "I see a man's erection . . . I am terrified but I cannot take my eyes off it."—"I see one man mounting another." —"Young boys are fondling my genitals."

Of the entire group of 9 patients under consideration this patient resembles the homosexual most closely in family dynamics, behavior patterns, and psychodynamics. His conscious identification with his mother, his attempt to gain love by competing as a woman, his homosexual dreams, and his terror of homosexuality indicate the profound degree to which he has been damaged. His delayed sexual activity, his impotence and fear of women, clearly indicate the extent of injury to his sexual functioning. However, he reports no homosexual activity and no conscious *erotic* response to males.

The father maintained sufficient interest in the patient to fight against the feminizing influence of the mother. Even though this fight was expressed in a bizarre fashion at times, the patient was very much aware that his father valued male sexuality and masculinity in his son.

PATIENT NO. 211

This patient, a twenty-eight-year-old male, diagnosed as schizophrenic, entered psychoanalysis following the onset of an acute panic. Included among his symptoms were fears of homosexuality, anxiety in the presence of homosexuals, and conscious homosexual impulses. In addition, there was homosexuality in the manifest content of his dreams.

The relationship between the parents was described by the psychoanalyst as poor. There were frequent arguments and no open demonstrations of affection. The mother was the dominant member in the marriage, regarded the father as inferior, and was openly contemptuous of him.

The patient, an only child, had the same close-binding relatedness to the mother as did the other members of this group of patients. The mother was very affectionate to him, expressing it through frequent kissing and hugging. But her ambivalence was revealed by her alternating between acceptance and admiration, and contempt and humiliation. She demanded the patient's complete attention and intruded on his free time. She discouraged masculine activities and encouraged feminine activities. She was described as puritanical and sexually frigid. On the other hand, she was very seductive, and undressed frequently in front of the patient. She stimulated him genitally when she bathed him; she slept with him and would use the bathroom while he was present. In addition, she interfered with his adolescent sexual activity by belittling his girl friends and demonstrating her jealousy of them.

Although the patient consciously feared and hated his mother, encouraged by her, he has sided with her all his life. She also formed an alliance with him against the father. The mother was very overprotective, restricted his play as a child on the basis of an inordinate concern over his health and safety. In spite of this, the patient was aware that the *mother wanted him to grow up to be like the mother's father who was a virile and sexually potent male.*

The father spent very little time with the patient, never expressed affection toward him, was contemptuous, humiliating, and physically cruel. The patient could not recall ever feeling accepted or admired by his father. The latter, however, actively encouraged masculine attitudes and discouraged feminine attitudes, partly, according to the psychoanalyst, as a result of the father's own search for "supermasculinity." The patient regarded his father as puritanical although sexually potent. The patient felt that he could cope with his father more easily than with his mother. As a child he consciously wished to be like his father.

In childhood, the patient received no sexual information from his parents and recalled being threatened for sexual play with girls.

During adolescence, he engaged in frequent masturbation, experiencing considerable guilt. His first attempt at heterosexual intercourse took place at the age of nineteen. This attempt proved unsuccessful. His first successful intercourse occurred at the age of twenty-five. In psychoanalysis, he expressed fear and aversion to female genitalia. In regard to his own genitals, he felt they were too small; he was fearful of injury to them. When sexually aroused, he experienced much anxiety. During intercourse, he engaged in fantasies characterized by violent rage and, as might be expected, he was frequently impotent. In his current masturbatory fantasies, he sees himself ripping a woman apart with his penis.

This patient presents a familial and developmental profile similar to those of the homosexual patients, except that both parents, despite their ambivalent and irrational behavior, somehow communicated that the patient's sexual *maleness* was of value to them. The mother wished him to be like her own father who was a virile and potent man, while the father actively promoted masculine attitudes and activities in a way that allowed the patient to consciously identify with him, at least in some degree. Thus, we see a patient with severely damaged sexual function, but one whose sexual adaptation has been in the direction of heterosexuality since childhood.

Of the 9 patients who represented exceptions to the heterosexual patients, 5 cases have been described in some detail. To present the remaining group would be repetitive since they illustrate similar psychodynamic configurations, and reveal with almost monotonous regularity the same close-binding relationship with a seductive, overprotective mother. Each of the 9 patients was either an only child or, if there were other siblings, the mother's favorite. All the mothers regarded the father as inferior and were openly contemptuous of him, obviously preferring the son and establishing an alliance with him against the father. In every instance, there was the covert "romance" between mother and son, as evidenced by the seductiveness of the mother who, at the same time, professed puritanical attitudes.

All 9 patients were alienated from their fathers, who were characterized as indifferent or hostile. There was not one instance of an affectionate father. Each was hated by his son. An indication of the sexual difficulties among this group of patients was the pattern of delayed genital heterosexual activity, varying degrees of impotence, anxiety accompanying sexual arousal, and fears of homosexuality. All 9 exhibited homosexual content in their dreams; several had conscious homosexual impulses and fantasies. Family dynamics as reflected by our data were indistinguishable from those of the majority of homosexual patients. Our data indicated experiential differences between this group of patients and the homosexuals—differences that may be determining in sexual adaptation. The histories of these 9 patients revealed that one or both parents were able to communicate in one way or another that the son's heterosexuality was personally valued. This idea was often communicated in the devious and destructive ways associated with parental ambivalence. However, in each case, a model of a sexually potent male provided some encouragement for the patient to emulate and identify with that model.

We wish to emphasize, however, that we do not imply that parental valuation of the son's heterosexuality and the presence in the family of masculine figures on which the child may model himself are *necessarily* the determining factors in sexually adaptive outcome; nor do we imply that such factors are the only ones that explain why certain patients did not become homosexual. Special studies of similar cases may gather and evaluate the data that are necessary to answer such questions.

Summary

By our rating technique, and by the inclusion of items probing the major manifestations of "latent" homosexuality, we were able to delineate a group of 40 cases with homosexual problems. Of this group, 26 were classified as having "severe" homosexual problems and 14 as having "moderate" homosexual problems. On a continuum of hetero-homosexuality they appeared close to an adaptational shift to homosexuality. Yet, of the 26, only 9 could not be significantly differentiated from the homosexual group. The remaining 17 "severe" and 14 "moderate" patients could be distinguished from the homosexual group in items differentiating the homosexual from the comparison group at high levels of statistical significance. Whereas only 10 per cent of the homosexuals scored 0-2 on the Six Developmental Score, 65 per cent of the "severe" high scoring group and 62.5 per cent of the "moderate" group scored in this range. From these data we concluded that the High Scorers were heterogeneous and could be subdivided into two distinguishable groups of 9 and 31 patients, respectively.

The authors of this volume have not been able to validate the ubiquity of "latent" homosexuality. We have psychoanalyzed many males in whom we have been unable to observe any evidence of this "complex." In 40 per cent of the comparison group all items tapping this "complex" were answered in the negative. We accept the possibility that some psychoanalysts, owing to a subjective bias of one kind or another, do not observe "latent" homosexual manifestations, but we also accept the possibility that in many cases evidences of homosexuality do not, in fact, exist. The latter possibility is supported by the fact that in numerous instances the same responding psychoanalyst reported cases with and without homosexual problems.

The data included in this chapter tend to preclude simplistic, unidimensional interpretations. The heterogeneity of the High Scorers and the absence of both homosexual arousal and homosexual problems in many heterosexual patients point to a *complex* of experiential and adaptive factors. A constitutional inability to repress and sublimate a universal perverse impulse is a metapsychological hypothesis that our data cannot support.

XI

The Results of Treatment

April 9, 1935

Dear Mrs. ——

I gather from your letter that your son is a homosexual. . . . Homosexuality is assuredly no advantage, but it is nothing to be ashamed of, no vice, no degradation, it cannot be classified as an illness; we consider it to be a variation of the sexual function produced by a certain arrest of sexual development. . . .

By asking me if I can help, you mean, I suppose, if I can abolish homosexuality and make normal heterosexuality take its place. The answer is, in a general way, we cannot promise to achieve it. In a certain number of cases we succeed in developing the blighted germs of heterosexual tendencies which are present in every homosexual, in the majority of cases it is no more possible. It is a question of the quality and the age of the individual. The result of treatment cannot be predicted.

What analysis can do for your son runs in a different line. If he is unhappy, neurotic, torn by conflicts, inhibited in his social life, analysis may bring him harmony, peace of mind, full efficiency, whether he remains a homosexual or gets changed. . . .

Sincerely yours with kind wishes,
Freud[1]

Freud's views, succinctly stated, epitomize psychoanalytic opinion of what may be expected from the psychoanalysis of homosexuals. Other

[1] *American Journal of Psychiatry 107:*786, 1951. By permission.

investigators have held even less optimistic views. The recent report of the Wolfenden Committee, which surveyed the problem of homosexuality in Great Britain, asserted: "We were struck by the fact that none of our medical witnesses were able, when we saw them, to provide any reference in medical literature to a complete change. . . . Our evidence leads us to the conclusion that a total reorientation from complete homosexuality to complete heterosexuality is very unlikely indeed."

The 106 homosexual cases reported in this study have provided a unique opportunity to appraise the results of psychoanalytic treatment of homosexuality. Table XI-1 shows the H-patients' sexual status at the beginning of treatment and the status reported to the Research Committee by the responding psychoanalysts at the final follow-up inquiry in June, 1960. Of the total H-sample, 74 patients had terminated psychoanalysis while 32 had not as yet completed treatment; *29 patients had become exclusively heterosexual during the course of psychoanalytic treatment.* The shift from homosexuality to exclusive heterosexuality for 27 per cent of the H-patients is of outstanding importance since these are the most optimistic and promising results thus far reported.

TABLE XI-1 *Outcome of Treatment—Homosexual Patients*

Initial status		Status as of June, 1960[a]			
		Exclusively homosexual	Inactive	Bisexual	Exclusively heterosexual
Exclusively homosexual	72	42 (57%)	2 (3%)	14 (19%)	14 (19%)
Bisexual	30	0	2 (7%)	13 (43%)	15 (50%)
Inactive[b]	4	1 (25%)	2 (50%)	1 (25%)	0
Total	106	43 (41%)	6 (6%)	28 (26%)	29 (27%)

[a] Sexual status of 32 patients still in treatment at final follow-up, June, 1960: Exclusively heterosexual: 6; bisexual: 5; inactive: 1; exclusively homosexual: 20.

[b] These patients, though actively homosexual as adults, were sexually inactive at the beginning of treatment.

Of the 76 patients who were exclusively homosexual or inactive on beginning psychoanalysis, 14 (19 per cent) were exclusively heterosexual at last contact. In contrast, of 30 patients who were initially bisexual, 15 (50 per cent) became exclusively heterosexual. The difference in outcome between those who began treatment as exclusively homosexual and those who were initially bisexual *is significant at the .01 level.*

Improvement in areas other than sexual

Improvement which was not directly related to sexual problems was reported for 97 homosexuals and 94 comparison patients while no improvement of any kind was reported for only 7 H-patients and 2 C-patients (no answer: 2 H-patients; 4 C-patients). The responding psychoanalysts reported an improved occupational effectiveness for 85 H-patients and 84 C-patients; social relationships were improved for 86 H-patients and 87 C-patients; symptomatic improvement occurred in 86 H-patients and 88 C-patients. These statistics indicate that an equal proportion of homosexual and heterosexual males who undertake psychoanalysis are likely to experience improvement in certain nonsexual areas of behavior, though in cases of homosexuality an adaptational shift to heterosexuality may not occur.

Factors affecting the outcome of treatment

The patient's stated reasons for undertaking psychoanalysis are a primary consideration in evaluating outcome of treatment since motivational factors were positively correlated to change in sexual adaptation. Among the H-patients, 51 stated that they had undertaken psychoanalysis because of "sexual problems," while 52 offered a variety of reasons "other than sexual" for seeking therapy (no answer: 3 cases). Only 10 C-patients indicated a "sexual problem" as the primary reason for entering treatment, while 89 had "other than sexual" reasons (no answer: 2 cases). The category "sexual problem," includes homosexuality per se, as well as impotence, premature ejaculation, and similar difficulties not necessarily related to homosexuality. The "other than sexual problems" included a wide range of distressing symptoms: anxiety, depression, work and social inhibitions, psychosomatic disorders, and many others. Although slightly less than half (51) of the homosexuals offered a "sexual problem" as the primary reason for undertaking psychoanalysis, 64 H-patients specifically wanted to overcome homosexuality.

Table XI-2 compares the duration of treatment, as measured by the number of treatment sessions, for the homosexual patients who became exclusively heterosexual and the group which did not.

Of 28 H-patients who terminated analysis in fewer than 150 hours, 2 had become exclusively heterosexual after this relatively brief period of therapy. One of the 2 had died in an automobile accident while still in treatment, but was reported to have been heterosexual at the

TABLE XI-2 *Duration of Treatment—Homosexuals Only*

Total number of psychoanalytic sessions	N =	Became exclusively heterosexual 29	Did not become exclusively heterosexual 77	Total 106
Fewer than 150		2	26	28
150-349		9	31	40
350 or more		18	20	38

time of his death. The second patient was a 16-year-old adolescent who had discontinued treatment after having rapidly established heterosexual relationships. His psychoanalyst reported that this patient had remained exclusively heterosexual at a follow-up four years later.

Of the 40 patients whose analyses were of 150 to 349 hours duration, 9 (23 per cent) became heterosexual. Of the group who had 350 or more therapeutic sessions, 18 (47 per cent) achieved the shift to heterosexuality. These statistics are not necessarily final since 26 H-patients who had not become heterosexual were still in analysis at the time of the last follow-up report. Some patients in this group may yet become heterosexual as a result of continuing treatment. All such additional "terminated heterosexual" cases would necessarily fall into the "more than 350 hours" category and the 47 per cent rate for this category would rise.

The difference between the H-group that remained in psychoanalysis for fewer than 150 hours and terminated as heterosexual (2 of 28) and the H-group that remained in treatment for 150 hours or more and became heterosexual (27 of 78) is significant at the .01 level. Clearly, the homosexual who remains in treatment above 150 hours is much more likely to achieve a heterosexual adaptation.

Factors related to remaining in treatment

The duration of treatment appeared to be a crucial factor in a favorable outcome. Therefore, it was decided to compare the questionnaire responses of the H-group that remained in treatment for 150 hours or more with those who remained for fewer than 150 hours. This comparison was expected to yield information on the following: features that distinguished those who remained in therapy for an extended period from those whose treatment was abbreviated; factors related to the probability of remaining in therapy and, by implication, factors that might be favorable prognostic indicators. Table XI-3 lists the 16 questions which significantly distinguished the two H-groups. The first three questions in Table XI-3 are concerned with the mother-son relationship. Significantly more homosexuals who remained in treatment for at least 150 hours had (a) admired their mothers, (b) admired them currently, and (c) had mothers who took the patient's needs and desires into consideration. Taken together, these questions indicate that the H-patient who thought of his mother as admirable and considerate was more likely to remain in treatment than was the patient who felt his mother to be neither admirable nor considerate. The patient's belief that his mother was admirable and considerate, whether or not realistically based, points to an optimism and trust perhaps lacking in those who thought of their mothers as neither admirable nor considerate. Positive filial attitudes toward the mother appear to help motivate participation in a long-term, and sometimes arduous, reconstructive procedure.

The next item, "Time mother spent with father: very little," reflects serious disturbance in the interparental relationship. Detachment between husband and wife was significantly more frequent among the parents of patients who *did not* remain in therapy.

The fifth item, "Number of siblings: none," focuses on the 11 "only children" among the total homosexual sample. Of the 28 who dropped out of treatment early, 7 were "only children" while 4 were among 78 who remained in psychoanalytic treatment. This difference is significant at the .01 level. The numbers are so small, however, that no conclusions can be drawn.

For the question, "In childhood, was there a sense of rivalry or competition with male siblings?" the data were tabulated on the basis of the number of patients who had male siblings. Of those H-patients who reported sibling rivalry and competitiveness, a significantly greater number had more than 150 sessions. We must remember that affirmative answers do not indicate whether such competitiveness existed, but that rivalrous feelings were perceived and recognized as such. Since covert competitiveness was far more frequent than overt competitiveness among the H-patients, the greater frequency of perceived competitiveness in childhood among those who remained in treatment (.05 level of significance) suggests that the capacity to acknowledge and deal with rivalry is associated with greater likelihood of sustaining a therapeutic relationship, and hence indicates a better prognosis.

TABLE XI-3 *Comparison of Duration of Analysis of Homosexual Patients*

		Fewer than 150 hours N = 28	More than 150 hours N = 78	Significance level
1.	Did patient regard mother as admirable? *Yes	4 (19%)	45 (60%)	.01
2.	Does patient now regard mother as admirable? *Yes	1 (5%)	24 (32%)	.05
3.	Does patient feel mother took his needs and desires into consideration? *Yes	1 (5%)	23 (31%)	.05
4.	Time mother spent with father: very little	12 (43%)	10 (13%)	.05
5.	Number of siblings: none	7 (25%)	4 (5%)	.01
6.	In childhood did patient have sense of rivalry or competition with male siblings? (Based on no. of patients with male siblings.) **Yes	5 (33%)	38 (79%)	.05
7.	Age of first heterosexual experience involving physical contact* <16	0	15 (20%)	.05
	>16	14 (67%)	46 (61%)	
8.	Age of first homosexual experience* <16	14 (67%)	58 (77%)	
	>16	7 (33%)	17 (23%)	N.S.[a]
9.	Age of first heterosexual genital experience* <21	8 (38%)	25 (33%)	
	>21	2 (10%)	33 (44%)	.05
	never	12 (57%)	16 (21%)	.05
10.	Age at first attempt at heterosexual intercourse* <21	8 (38%)	21 (28%)	
	>21	2 (10%)	36 (48%)	.05
11.	Age of first successful heterosexual intercourse* <21	5 (24%)	15 (20%)	
	>21	2 (10%)	33 (44%)	.05
12.	Does patient have fantasies of violence accompanying sexual excitement? Yes	2 (7%)	30 (39%)	.05
13.	Was there improvement in occupational effectiveness? Yes	13 (46%)	73 (93%)	.01
14.	Was there improvement in social relationships? Yes	15 (54%)	72 (92%)	.01
15.	Was there symptomatic improvement? Yes	17 (61%)	71 (91%)	.05
16.	Was patient eager to conceal his homosexuality? Yes	18 (64%)	72 (92%)	.01

Questions with * N [<150] = 21, N [>150] = 75
Questions with ** N [<150] = 15, N [>150] = 48

[a] Not significant

Items 7 to 11 tap the ages at which certain sexual events first took place. It must be recalled that the group of patients who remained for over 150 sessions included: 27 of 29 patients who became heterosexual; 29 of 30 patients who were bisexual at the outset of treatment. Consequently, this group as a whole may be expected to show a larger proportion of heterosexual contacts in the items listed. In part, this larger proportion reflects the development of heterosexuality in those 14 patients who were exclusively homosexual at the outset and terminated as heterosexual. Additional details are revealed when the data are tabulated according to age.

Item 7 indicates that approximately the same proportion of each group made their first heterosexual physical contact after age 16. The significant finding is that *none* of those who dropped out early had made any heterosexual contact before age 16, while 15 of those who remained in analysis had made such early adolescent heterosexual contacts by age 16.

For item 8, which gives the corresponding data for the first homosexual physical contact, there is no significant difference between the groups. However, it is noteworthy that 67 per cent of those who dropped out early had already had *homosexual* contact by age 16, although none of these had yet had heterosexual contact. Since there is no significant difference in the distribution of first homosexual contacts before the age of 16, the occurrence of such contacts does not in itself indicate the likelihood of remaining in analysis.

Items 9 to 11 show that of those who dropped out early, only 2 H-patients had made their first heterosexual-genital contact, including heterosexual intercourse, after 21, while 33 H-patients, a significantly greater number, who had made such initial contact after 21, remained in analysis. Of the 96 H-patients for whom data was available, 12 of those patients who left treatment early (57 per cent) had *never* made heterosexual genital contact at any age. Only 16 of those who remained in analysis (21 per cent) had never had heterosexual genital contact. This significantly distinguishes the two groups on age-sex contact at the .05 level.

The data may be summarized as follows:

1. Homosexual experiences before age 16 do not give any clear indication of the likelihood of remaining in psychoanalysis.

2. Heterosexual experiences before age 16 suggest a greater likelihood of remaining in analysis.

3. Initial heterosexual genital contact between ages 16 and 21

does not give any indication of likelihood of remaining in treatment.

4. If no heterosexual attempt was made by age 21, the subsequent course is associated with whether or not a heterosexual attempt is made after 21. Failure to make such an attempt is associated with dropping out of analysis, while making such an attempt is associated with remaining in analysis, and suggests a better prognosis for shift in sexual adaptation.

5. Failure to make any attempt at heterosexual genital contact at any age is associated with dropping out of analysis, while making such an attempt is associated with remaining in analysis, and suggests a better prognosis for ultimate change in sexual adaptation.

Clinical experience has shown that the 16 to 21 age period is characterized by an increasing heterosexual drive. This conclusion is supported by a separate count from the individual protocols which shows that attempts at *heterosexual* contact were made by 33 (31 per cent) of the *homosexual* patients by age 21, with 29 (27 per cent) having made their first heterosexual contact between the ages of 16 and 21. In view of the prominence of heterosexual interests among homosexuals between the ages of 16 and 21, it is probable that patients may be more favorably influenced by analysis undertaken during this period. In this connection, of the 2 patients who were reported to have become exclusively heterosexual in fewer than 150 sessions, 1 was 16 years old when he started psychoanalysis.

Fantasies of violence accompanying sexual excitement occurred more frequently among those who remained longer in analysis. The meaning of this datum is uncertain. It may reflect the greater opportunity to report such fantasies by those who remain longer in analysis. It may also indicate a greater capacity to perceive and acknowledge aggression. This would be consistent with the capacity to perceive and acknowledge competitiveness with siblings as revealed in Item 6, Table XI-3.

Items 13, 14 and 15 deal with changes in nonsexual areas of functioning consequent to psychoanalytic treatment. About one-half of those who dropped out early achieved substantial improvement in nonsexual areas of personality and behavior. The proportion was significantly higher among those who remained in analysis for more than 150 sessions.

Item 16 shows that a greater proportion of those who remained longer in analysis were eager to conceal their homosexuality. This item is of special interest, since 90 patients of the total group of H-patients

(85 per cent) were eager to conceal their homosexuality and only 16 were not. More than one-half of these 16 patients were among the group who dropped out early in the course of treatment.

The correlation between the wish to conceal homosexuality and remaining in treatment for more than 150 hours is significant at the .01 level. In this connection, it is noteworthy that in the entire homosexual sample, there were only 2 patients who were markedly and openly effeminate. It appears that blatantly effeminate individuals who exhibit rather than conceal their homosexuality do not often seek psychoanalytic treatment. The desire to conceal homosexuality is a factor both in starting and then continuing psychoanalysis over an extended period of time.

Factors that distinguish homosexuals who became exclusively heterosexual

A comparison which would be of prognostic value required that we determine which questions significantly distinguished the homosexuals who became exclusively heterosexual from those who did not make such an adaptational shift. In order to extract the most meaningful information we decided to exclude (1) patients who were bisexual since they represented a "mixed" group and would tend to blunt differences, and (2) patients who had fewer than 150 hours of analysis since in all but two exceptional cases they were judged to have had insufficient analysis for profound changes in sexual behavior to have occurred. The data collected for individual items is presented in Table XI-4. This table compares the 26 patients who had 150 or more hours of analysis and remained exclusively homosexual with those 27 patients who had 150 or more hours and achieved an exclusively heterosexual adaptation.

We found that 78 per cent of the patients who became exclusively heterosexual had expressed the wish to overcome homosexuality at the outset of treatment while 42 per cent of the patients who remained homosexual had expressed this wish; the difference is significant at the .01 level. The 2 patients who had terminated as heterosexual in fewer than 150 hours of psychoanalysis also wished to become heterosexual. Thus, of the 29 patients who became heterosexual, 23 had consciously *wanted to change*. These data emphasize the importance of motivation in overcoming homosexuality. The wish to become heterosexual is a favorable prognostic indicator.

The next item is concerned with the mother of the H-patient.

TABLE XI-4 *Comparison of Patients Who Terminated Exclusively Heterosexual with Patients Who Terminated Exclusively Homosexual (150 or more hours)*

		Terminated homosexual	Terminated heterosexual	Significance level
	N =	26	27	
1. Patient wanted homosexuality cured		11 (42%)	21 (78%)	.01
2. Mother openly preferred patient to husband		18 (69%)	9 (33%)	.05
3. Mother envied men		2 (8%)	11 (41%)	.05
4. Did patient respect father? Yes		5 (19%)	13 (48%)	.05
5. Did patient regard father as an admirable person?				
In past: Yes		5 (19%)	9 (33%)	
At present: Yes		6 (23%)	15 (56%)	.05
6. Does father respect patient now? Yes		3 (12%)	12 (44%)	.05
7. Was father affectionate? Yes		3 (12%)	10 (37%)	.05
8. Father's reaction to women: liked them		8 (31%)	18 (67%)	.05
9. Patient's attitude toward women: idolize		5 (19%)	13 (48%)	.05
10. Did patient have effeminate voice or gestures in childhood? Yes		14 (54%)	2 (7%)	.01
11. Patient's reaction to stress: rage		6 (23%)	18 (67%)	.01
12. Age at beginning of analysis: <35		15 (58%)	24 (89%)	.05
>35		11 (42%)	3 (11%)	
13. Who initiated first heterosexual genital contact?[a]	Patient	5	15	.05
	Partner	3	5	
	Mutual	1	1	
	Never tried	13	0	.001
	No answer	3	5	
14. Currently does patient have anxiety in making major decisions? Yes		20 (77%)	11 (41%)	.05
15. Is there erotic heterosexual activity in manifest dream content? Yes		6 (23%)	19 (70%)	.01

[a] N (excl. Homosexuals) = 23; N (excl. Heterosexuals) = 22; based on number who answered question.

"Mother openly preferred patient to husband" is one of a number of items which revealed a CBI mother-son relationship. The H-patient was preferred to his father in 69 per cent of the cases who remained *homosexual* while those patients who became *heterosexual* were preferred to the father in only 33 per cent of these cases; the difference is significant at the .05 level.

Item 3 "Mother envied men" occurred significantly more often in those cases who moved to a heterosexual adaptation. Among the complex effects involved in the perception that the mother envies men, a positive effect may consist of the son's impression that heterosexual masculinity is of value.

Items 4 through 8 probed the father-son relationship and father's attitudes to women. Among the patients who terminated treatment as heterosexual, a significantly greater number respected their fathers in childhood. A finding which does not appear in this table but is nonetheless of considerable importance, is that only 11 homosexuals in the total sample both *respected and admired* their fathers. Of these 11 patients, 8 were included among the 29 who became heterosexual, as compared to the other 3 among the 77 who did not, significant at the .01 level. Admiration for the father in childhood does not statistically distinguish between those patients who became heterosexual and those who did not. However, significantly more patients who shifted to heterosexuality had been reported as respecting their fathers currently. This change in filial attitude toward the father noted among some patients may be a result of therapy. Clinical experience as well as data presented in Chapter III, point to maternal influences upon the H-patient's negative attitude toward his father which we assume was reinforced when the mother was CBI and she was dominating-minimizing to her husband. Psychoanalysis helps the patient to reassess his belief systems and to increase his capacity to cope with destructive attitudes in others. Both factors may have contributed to a more favorable view of fathers. Patients who became heterosexual significantly more often had fathers who had been affectionate.

Affirmative answers to the item, "Father liked women," occurred with greater frequency among the patients who became heterosexual, significant at the .05 level. This item suggests that the father's positive attitude towards women may have been communicated to the son and stimulated a similar attitude in him which eventually may have been a contributing factor in establishing a heterosexual relationship. Significantly more patients who became heterosexual were reported to "idolize" women (.05 level). This exaggerated attitude at least reflects a positive feeling towards women and may be included among those factors which during psychoanalysis militated toward establishing heterosexuality.

"Effeminate voice or gestures during childhood" occurred more frequently among those patients who remained exclusively homosexual. It has been previously noted that effeminate homosexuals are less inclined to undertake or remain in psychoanalysis. The more frequent occurrence of effeminate traits in childhood in the group which remained exclusively homosexual is consistent with the expectation that obvious effeminacy is unfavorable prognostically, although it does not preclude the possibility of change in sexual adaptation.

Patients who became heterosexual were more likely to react to stress situations with rage (item 11) and less likely to have anxiety in making major decisions (item 14). The more frequent occurrence of rage reactions suggests that the capacity for assertive emotional experience is associated with the greater likelihood of achieving heterosexuality. This is consistent with the greater frequency of awareness of competitiveness with siblings noted under Item 6 of Table XI-3.

Item 12 shows that 24 of the 27 patients who became exclusively heterosexual began analysis at the age of 35 or younger while 3 started psychoanalysis when over 35. In comparing these two groups the difference is significant at the .05 level. These data indicate that while change may occur beyond age 35, the prognosis is more favorable if analysis is undertaken before this age.

Item 13 probes "Who initiated first heterosexual genital contact?" and shows that among the group who became heterosexual it was the patient who most often took the initiative, significant at the .05 level. Among the group which remained exclusively homosexual, half the patients *never* tried to establish any heterosexual contact. Nine patients among those who remained homosexual had had some heterosexual genital contact, but the partner initiated the activity almost as often as the patient. These data suggest that failure to attempt any heterosexual genital contact is linked to an unfavorable prognosis. Initiative in establishing such contact, on the other hand, is favorable.

In order to further explore the prognostic significance of attempts at heterosexual contact, the age of first attempted intercourse and the age at which each patient undertook analysis was determined from the individual case protocols of all 29 patients who became heterosexual and for the 26 patients who remained exclusively homosexual. It was found that 23 of the 29 patients who became heterosexual had made such attempts *prior* to treatment. Of the 26 patients who had remained homosexual only 6 had made an attempt at heterosexual intercourse prior to treatment. The difference is significant beyond the .01 level, and indicates that a history of attempted heterosexual intercourse before entering analysis is prognostically favorable, although not necessarily an assurance of success in treatment. Conversely, a history of no such attempt is prognostically unfavorable.

Manifest erotic heterosexual content in dreams was more often reported for those who became heterosexual. The questionnaires did not record whether manifest heterosexual dreams had occurred prior to analysis, but it seems that the occurrence of such dreams prior to psychoanalysis would be a useful prognostic indicator. It is of interest that dreams with manifest incestuous erotic content were reported with equal frequency among those who became heterosexual and those who did not, and also occurred in approximately equal ratio among the homosexual group as a whole and the comparison patients. Manifest incestuous dreams do not seem to be directly related to the presence or absence of homosexuality, or to change as a result of treatment.

Parent-child constellations and interparental systems

Table XI-5 lists the categories for the mother-son relationship for the 29 patients who became heterosexual. (For a detailed discussion of the mother-son categories see Chapter III).

Although a majority of those who became heterosexual had CBI

TABLE XI-5 *Mother-Son Relationship*

N =		Terminated heterosexual 29	Total H-sample 106
Close-binding-intimate mother	(CBI)	17	(73)
Controlling-dominating mother	(CD)	2	(9)
Detached-hostile mother	(DH)	2	(4)
Not-detached, hostile mother	(NDH)	6	(8)**
Mother-surrogate	(MS)	1	(2)
Unclassifiable mother	(Unc.)	1	(3)
Detached-poorly related	(DPR)	0	(6)

** .01 level of significance

mothers (17 of 29), this statistic is proportionate to the 73 of 106 such mothers in the total H-sample. It appears that the CBI relationship, whose role in the genesis of homosexuality has been extensively discussed in preceding chapters, does not in itself preclude the possibility of overcoming homosexuality. Similarly, the number of controlling-dominating, detached-hostile, mother-surrogate, and unclassifiable mothers among the successful outcomes is proportionate to the frequency of these maternal types in the total H-sample. The actual numbers are too small, however, to permit any conclusions regarding favorable or unfavorable prognosis.

Not-detached, hostile mothers were overrepresented among the group where shift to a heterosexual adaptation occurred. Of 8 not-detached, hostile mothers in the total H-sample, 6 were among the mothers of 29 patients who became heterosexual, significant at the .01 level. Five H-sons of these 6 not-detached, hostile mothers were bisexual at the beginning of psychoanalysis while only 1 was exclusively homosexual. Of the 8 patients, 2 did not become heterosexual; 1 dropped out of analysis after 30 sessions and was listed among those who remained homosexual; the other patient was initially homosexual and became bisexual in the course of treatment, indicating a qualitative change in sexual behavior.

It is difficult to ascertain the precise reasons why the H-sons of not-detached, hostile mothers fared so well in psychoanalysis. It was found, however, that no case in this group achieved the maximum and "poorest" score of 6 on the Developmental Cumulative Score which we had referred to as the Six Score (see Chapter VII). One case scored 5; 4 cases scored 4 or lower. It might be supposed that these hostile mothers may have induced more active "fight" than "flight" in their sons but this must be regarded as speculative. The individual protocols of these 6 patients were carefully examined for information which might relate to their improvement:

CASE NO. 128

The interparental system was Class 3 (see Chapter VI). The father accepted and admired the patient, and did not show him contempt. The patient participated in competitive sports, played baseball, went to baseball games with his father, was not a "lone wolf," and had not played predominantly with girls. He respected his father, who, he believed, understood his needs. Despite the mother's rejecting behavior, her attachment to the patient was revealed by the fact that she made him her confidant. He was seventeen years old when he had his first heterosexual experience and he continued to have heterosexual contact. The patient was bisexual when he began treatment. He preferred the role of insertor in homosexual activities.

CASE NO. 137

The interparental system was Class 3. The father left home when the patient was about three years old, never to return. The mother remarried when the patient was ten years old. His relationship with the stepfather was excellent. Affection for the patient was often openly expressed in hugging and kissing. He felt accepted and admired by his stepfather who favored the boy over his brother, three years older and the only other sibling. When treatment was initiated the patient was bisexual; he preferred to be an oral insertee in homosexual relations. His first heterosexual intercourse had occurred when he was twenty-five years old. Patient was motivated toward change and was eager to overcome homosexuality.

CASE NO. 143

The interparental system was Class 3. The patient had one younger brother who, he believed, was preferred by both parents. Yet his father was more intimate with the patient, more ambitious for him, and respected him more than he did the younger boy. The father "wanted the patient to grow up to be like father." The patient was not excessively fearful of physical injury in childhood and he participated in competitive games with other boys though he was a "lone wolf." When he began psychoanalysis he was an exclusively homosexual insertor. He had his first homosexual experience when he was twenty-two years old. The patient wanted to become exclusively heterosexual.

CASE NO. 147

The interparental system was Class 2. The only positive features discernible in this case were that the father was the dominant spouse who did not minimize his wife, and the mother liked men. She "babied" and overprotected the patient while at the same time she was hostile and minimized him. The father was detached. This patient first had heterosexual intercourse at the age of twenty. He started psychoanalysis as a bisexual. In homosexual activities he preferred the role of insertor. The patient wanted to overcome homosexuality and this was one of the reasons given for entering psychoanalytic treatment.

CASE NO. 158

The interparental system was Class 3. The patient very much admired a brother seven years his senior whom he wanted to be like. He identified his homosexual partners with his brother. Among positive features noted were that the mother encouraged masculine activities, discouraged feminine activities, and openly indicated that she wished the patient to grow up to be a strong and virile man. He would side with his father against his mother when the parents had arguments and he found it easier to cope with his father than with his mother. The patient began heterosexual petting activities when he was twenty and first had intercourse when he was twenty-three years old. When he entered psychoanalysis he was bisexual; in homosexual activities he was the insertor. He wanted to overcome his homosexuality.

CASE NO. 160

The parents were in Class 1. The patient admired and wanted to be like his brother who was six years older; homosexual partners were identified with him. When the patient was fifteen his brother drowned; he had had an epileptic seizure while alone in the water. The patient respected his mother even though she "babied" him. He was exclusively homosexual when he began treatment and had engaged in mutual fellatio. He was motivated toward change in sexual adaptation.

Six mothers were classified as detached and poorly related. None of their 6 H-sons became heterosexual. The numbers are too small to permit any conclusions but a trend is indicated.

Table XI-6 lists the father-son categories for the 29 cases who became heterosexual. (For a detailed discussion of the father-son categories see Chapter IV.)

Only one category of fathers was significantly overrepresented in this group. There were 4 not-detached, ambivalent fathers of the total of 6 such fathers in the entire sample. The difference is significant at the .05 level. This type of father may be considered to have a more positive relationship to his son than a detached father or a not-[illegible]d but hostile father. We have already noted that the individual

TABLE XI-6 *Father-Son Relationship*

N =		Terminated heterosexual 29	Total H-sample 106
Detached-ambivalent father	(DA)	4	(14)
Detached-hostile father	(DH)	11	(44)
Detached-indifferent father	(DI)	4	(18)
Not-detached, ambivalent father	(NDA)	4	(6)*
Not-detached, hostile father	(NDH)	1	(4)
Not-detached, overprotective father	(NDO)	2	(3)[a]
Absent father	(Abs)	3	(12)
Detached-dominating-exploitative	(DDE)	0	(3)
Unclassified	(Unc)	0	(2)

* .05 level of significance
[a] Not statistically significant, but reveals a trend.

questions indicating positive, respecting, admiring, and affectionate features in the father-son relationship significantly distinguished the cases who became heterosexual from the exclusively homosexual cases. The not-detached ambivalent father may be considered to be the "best" or least damaging paternal type occurring in the H-sample. None of the fathers designated as not-detached warmly related were found among the 106 H-cases.

A second category of fathers, not-detached overprotective, was represented twice among those patients who became heterosexual out of a total of only 3 such fathers in the entire H-sample. The numbers are too small to be statistically significant but paternal overprotectiveness may be viewed as a positive prognostic indicator since overt paternal harshness, hostility, or detachment did not characterize these father-son relationships.

The five remaining father categories, including 11 detached-hostile fathers, are represented at a rate which is close to their proportion in the entire sample. Again, the numbers are small and do not permit any conclusions as to association with favorable or unfavorable prognosis.

Table XI-7 shows the parent-child constellations of the 29 cases who became heterosexual. (For a detailed discussion of parent-child constellations see Chapter VI.)

In Chapter VI the CBI/DH category was seen to be the numerically largest group in the H-sample. This parent-child constellation was

TABLE XI-7 *Mother-Son and Father-Son Relationships*

Mother/Father N =	Terminated heterosexual 29	Total H-sample 106
CBI/DA	3	(10)
CBI/DH	4	(30)*
CBI/DI	4	(13)
CBI/NDA	3	(5)
NDH/DH	3	(5)
Twelve parent pairs, one case each	12	

judged to be the most pathogenic combination for the development of homosexuality in the son. Only 4 patients who became heterosexual had CBI/DH parents as compared with 30 such parent-child relationships in the total H-sample. This difference, which is just short of significance at the .05 level, suggests a negative correlation between CBI/DH parents and heterosexual outcome.

Table XI-8 lists the parent-child constellations of each of the 29 patients who made a heterosexual adaptive shift distributed among the five interparental power-affect classes (see Chapter VI).

The distribution of the 29 cases among the interparental classes reveals no disproportionate representation. We note that 3 of the 4

TABLE XI-8. *Interparental Power System—Parental Pairings of Those Who Became Heterosexual*

Class 1 Husband dominant and minimizing	Class 2 Husband dominant	Class 3 Wife dominant and minimizing	Class 4 Wife dominant	Group 5 Mixed
Mother Father				
CBI/NDA	CBI/DA	CBI/DA	CBI/NDH	CBI/Abs
CBI/NDA	CBI/DH	CBI/DA	CBI/DI	CBI/Abs
CBI/DH	Unc./DH	CBI/DI	CD/DH	MS/DH
CBI/DH	NDH/DH	CBI/DI	DH/DH	
NDH/DH		CBI/DI		
DH/NDA		CBI/DH		
		CBI/NDA		
		NDH/DA		
		NDH/NDO		
		NDH/DH		
		NDH/Abs		
		CD/NDO		
TOTALS 6	4	12	4	3

cases having the parental combination CBI mother and detached-hostile father had fathers who were dominant in the marital relationship. In the fourth case the mother was a dominant and minimizing wife (Class 3). In the total H-sample there were 11 cases with the CBI/DH constellation where the mother was dominant and minimizing toward the husband. Only 1 of these, as just noted, became heterosexual. This represents a 9 per cent rate of shift for the CBI/DH Class 3 group as compared with a 27 per cent rate for the total H-sample.

Of the 12 patients listed as Class 3 in Table XI-8, only 2 had fathers who were judged as hostile. In the total H-sample 48 of 103 fathers were judged as hostile (3 fathers were absent during the patient's infancy). Thus, hostile fathers were underrepresented among the Class 3 patients who became heterosexual, significant at the .05 level. This may indicate that the relative absence of paternal hostility is not only a positive influence in the patient's background, but that it may counteract the deleterious effects of witnessing the father being minimized by a dominant wife. The mothers of these 12 H-patients were either CBI (8), or were NDH (4), closely related though overtly hostile to their H-sons.

Psychiatric diagnosis

A final consideration is the psychiatric diagnosis of patients who became exclusively heterosexual. For the total H-sample the responding psychoanalysts made the following diagnoses: *schizophrenia,* 28 patients; *psychoneurosis,* 33 patients; *character disorder,* 45 patients. Among those who became heterosexual, the diagnoses were: *schizophrenia,* 7 patients; *psychoneurosis,* 10 cases; *character disorder,* 12 cases. These statistics indicate that the three diagnostic categories are represented at a rate proportionate to occurrence in the total H-sample. They imply that the probability for change from homosexuality to heterosexuality is independent of the psychiatric diagnosis. More specifically, they indicate that within the H-sample, schizophrenia is not an additional handicap for an adaptational shift to heterosexuality.

Factors within the psychoanalytic process which may relate to change

The outcome of psychoanalytic treatment may be affected by factors which have to do with the treatment process itself, rather than with the characteristics of the case. Undoubtedly, there were many differences in procedure and in conceptual approach among the psychoanalysts who contributed to this study. The questionnaires were not designed to make any systematic inquiry into this issue. Variations in theoretical outlook among the responding psychoanalysts were subsumed under the headings "Freudian" and "Culturalist," and were discussed in Chapter II. The responding psychoanalysts of these two theoretical persuasions had approximately equal rates of success with homosexual patients. The sex of the psychoanalyst is a second variable which has been recorded and discussed in Chapter II. Although the number of participating female psychoanalysts was small, their rate of successful outcomes is approximately equal to that reported by the male psychoanalysts.

Three case histories follow; one patient became *exclusively heterosexual,* the second became *bisexual* after having been exclusively homosexual, and the third began and terminated treatment as *exclusively homosexual.*

CASE NO. 166

This case illustrates some of the favorable features which contributed to achieving an *exclusively heterosexual* adaptation. The patient undertook analysis at age twenty-eight because of feelings of depression, an abortive attempt at suicide, and an intense desire to give up homosexuality.

He came from a prosperous middle-class family in a small southern town. His parents were of different religious faiths. His mother, an "American Gothic" type, stern and forbidding, was cold and formal to her husband, children, and outsiders alike. The father, a successful business man, was strong and dominant, though often aloof. The parents had few interests in common, and were rarely openly affectionate to each other in the presence of the children.

In the patient's early childhood and preadolescence his mother had the more profound influence upon him. She was possessive and overprotective towards all her children—the patient, an older and a younger brother, and a younger sister. Her chief concern was, first, her children's health and, second, that they maintain the outward appearance of gentlemanly and ladylike deportment. Appearances and propriety preoccupied her and she paid little heed to the children's feelings, interests, and individual personalities. Of the four children, the patient believed himself to have been his mother's favorite and as a result he had more than his share of her controlling and binding attentions.

In the patient's early childhood his remote father had occasional episodes of anger and stern discipline in which he would be physically cruel and verbally humiliating toward the patient. The patient remembers hating as well as fearing his father on these occasions.

The patient feared and admired his older brother whom he considered to be like his father. He tried to please this brother and win a friendly response but was usually not successful. He admired his sister whom he felt to be somewhat like his mother but he resented it when his mother made him take his sister to the formal, boring school dances. The patient had few neighborhood or school friends; his mother placed restrictions on his socializing outside the family. He recalls that sex was a tabooed subject, except for the few instances when his mother made ominous and critical allusions to the dangers associated with sex.

As the patient grew into adolescence, certain changes seemed to occur subtly in the family interactions. He came to see his mother's binding and infantilizing behavior and began to feel less of the previous "guarded respect." Inwardly, at least, he became critical of her. At the same time, his father seemed to emerge as a warmer, more interested person; he began to spend more time with the patient, appeared to be closer to him than to his brothers, and interceded on the patient's behalf with the mother. The patient recalls exchanging confidences with his father and feeling that as the relationship between his parents worsened, his own relationship with his father improved.

In early adolescence, the patient engaged in his first homosexual experience, mutual masturbation with his older brother. These episodes were initiated by the brother, and the patient at first complied; he earnestly wanted the apparent warmth and acceptance of his revered older brother. As a young adult the patient felt himself to be inadequate compared to his peers. He believed his penis was smaller than normal and that dangers were associated with premarital sex. He drifted toward homosexuality, at first practicing mutual masturbation, repeating the pattern originally initiated by his brother. Later he came to prefer anal intercourse, always taking the role of insertor. His homosexual contacts were frequent, but always transient. Even before analysis, he had heterosexual erotic dreams and had conscious heterosexual impulses but he was usually too fearful to act upon them. He had occasional dates with girls, attempting little more than the most superficial intimacies. When he finally worked up the courage to attempt heterosexual intercourse, his advances were spurned and he felt "crushed and hopeless." He made an abortive suicidal attempt under the influence of this disappointment, but quickly came to recognize his need for help and made arrangements to begin psychoanalysis.

During the course of treatment he established a relationship with a girl who seemed to care very much for him. When he told her about his homosexual problem, she was kind and understanding, and encouraged and supported his initial faltering attempts at heterosexual intercourse, which increased in effectiveness as time went on. He finally was able to marry this girl. Before completing analysis, he had advanced to a high executive post in his firm.

At last follow-up, three years after completion of psychoanalysis, the patient reported that he was happily married, had a son in whom he took great pride, and that he has continued to do exceedingly well in his work.

This patient's history and background illustrate many of the features associated with homosexuality which have been discussed earlier in this volume. Furthermore, the case reveals several factors suggestive of a favorable therapeutic outcome. The positive relationship with his father during adolescence seems to have been of singular importance. There is also a history of attempts at heterosexual contact before analysis, and of manifest heterosexual dream content, particularly during adolescence.

In discussing the case, the responding male psychoanalyst stressed (a) the duration of treatment and the frequency of sessions—three times per week for over four years; (b) his own optimistic outlook and positive feelings about the patient's prospects; (c) the fact that the patient was able to relate to a girl who was accepting, supportive, and understanding.

Once established, the heterosexual adaptation proved to be stable and enduring for this patient. In other instances of change there may be a period following a shift to heterosexuality which is occasionally interrupted by a homosexual experience. Patients who were functioning at this level at the time of the last report have been classified as bisexual, as illustrated by the following case:

CASE NO. 183

This patient came for psychoanalysis at age twenty-six, complaining of impotence and wishing to change his homosexual behavior. He was somewhat effeminate in manner and appearance, although not conspicuously so. He had come to New York City following his military service, having failed in several jobs which had been obtained for him in his home city.

The patient was raised in a middle-class family in a large city. His mother was an extremely anxious person who had undergone many years of psychotherapy, but had never required psychiatric hospitalization. She was a "highly emotional" woman, given to showing affection and rage with equal ease. His father was a successful business man who tried to maintain a controlling hand over all phases of family activity. Although the father was clearly the dominant figure in the family, the mother maintained an active struggle against his domination.

The patient had an older sister who fought openly with the mother, but was the father's favorite. The patient himself was his mother's favorite and she clearly preferred him to his father. His mother made him a confidant, freely discussing intimate aspects of her life with the father, and engaging her son's allegiance in her struggle against her husband's domination. The patient felt that he was the most important person in his mother's life. They spent a great deal of time together, and she lavished affection upon him though there were times, during tantrums, when she became verbally humiliating towards him. At other times, she openly "babied" him and was overly concerned about his health. She tried to manipulate his teachers and school authorities in order to assure him favorable treatment. A prominent feature of the mother-son relationship was the mother's seductiveness. She dressed and undressed in the patient's presence until he reached late adolescence and they both often used the bathroom simultaneously.

The patient saw his father as a powerful, successful, and fearsome individual. He could not help but envy his father's virility, aggressiveness, and masculinity; he himself felt neither admired nor respected by his father. The mother, too, admired the father's strength, and wanted her son "to be like him, plus . . ." The psychoanalyst judged that the mother envied men, including her husband, but she also valued masculinity, and liked men. The patient took his father as a model whom he hoped to be like, but felt generally inadequate to the task. He believed that he lacked the masculinity required to emulate and compete with aggressive males like his father.

The patient's earliest memory of specific sexual arousal by a male was around the age of ten, when he found some pornographic literature belonging to his father. Another memory occurring at about the same age involved an incident at a beach. His father had placed the patient's head between his legs. The patient believes his father had an erection. The first definite homosexual contact was at the age of thirteen and consisted of mutual masturbation with another boy of the same age. Some time later, he became engaged in fellatio as insertor. These late adolescent homosexual contacts were always transient. When he was twenty years old he made his first attempt at heterosexual contact. It consisted of kissing and fondling, but he carefully avoided the girl's genitals, towards which he felt a distinct aversion. At twenty-four, he attempted intercourse, but was impotent. At twenty-six, he began psychoanalysis. His first successful heterosexual intercourse was at age thirty while he was still in analysis. During his early heterosexual contacts, he had fantasies of homosexual experiences. During masturbation he had voyeuristic homosexual fantasies in which he imagined himself as exciting many men sexually and then refusing their advances. He had dreams with manifest erotic homosexual, heterosexual, and incestuous content.

This patient was seen three times per week for a total of more than 600 sessions. He maintained a successful heterosexual relationship for an extended period and seemed to have resolved his homosexual problems. At the time of the final follow-up (June, 1960) the psychoanalyst reported that the patient was still in analysis, and had had two recent homosexual experiences. In addition to the fluctuating sexual adaptation there was improvement in nonsexual areas, specifically in his occupation and in his social life. He remained in New York City, separated from his parents; his relationship with them had improved.

The favorable aspects in these two cases may be compared with the following case who *remained homosexual.*

CASE NO. 177

This patient began psychoanalysis at age thirty-two. His stated reason for seeking treatment was to obtain relief from anxiety. He appeared frail and somewhat effeminate in appearance, manner, and gesture. Although concerned about exposure of his homosexuality, he was not particularly eager to conceal it. He expressed no desire to become heterosexual.

The parental relationship was described as "fair," but the parents did not share similar interests, and engaged in frequent quarrels. The mother was dominant in the family and openly minimized the father. The patient's older sister had been the father's favorite.

The patient was his mother's favorite. She openly preferred him to his father, allied with the boy against her husband, and made her son her confidant. She "showered" him with affection; in turn, he felt accepted and respected by her. At the same time, she restricted his play and was unduly concerned with protecting him from physical injury. Although he respected his mother, he also hated and feared her. She discouraged masculine attitudes and activities, and encouraged those that were feminine. The patient felt that she resented men. He considered her frigid and puritanical.

The father spent very little time with the patient and when he did he was hostile and contemptuous of the patient. The patient did not view his father as a virile male; he saw him rather as weak, puritanical, and resentful toward women. The patient had neither affection nor respect for his father, who was indifferent, withdrawn, overtly hostile, and minimizing.

The earliest memory of a specific sexual arousal by a male was at age fourteen, upon seeing another boy's genitals. At fifteen, he engaged in mutual masturbation with a boy his own age. Later he came to prefer anal intercourse, in which he was the insertee. He sought warmth from his partner and tended to prefer permanent relationships. When he was sixteen he had one episode of kissing and necking with a girl of fifteen. He derived no pleasure from the experience and did not repeat it. Heterosexual intercourse was never attempted. The manifest dream content was exclusively homosexual. He reported no fantasies during homosexual relationships.

The patient was treated twice a week for a total of 240 sessions. He remained exclusively homosexual with no tendencies toward heterosexuality. General symptomatic improvement was noted, however, and there was some increase in occupational effectiveness, but there was no improvement in the anxiety he felt in his social relationships. He had moved away from the parental home at the age of twenty-eight and continued to feel dissatisfied and antagonistic toward his parents on the infrequent occasions when he visited them.

This patient showed many features which indicated a poor outlook for a shift toward heterosexuality. Clearly, motivation for such a change was poor at the outset. Treatment was neither frequent nor of long duration. There was some improvement in nonsexual areas although the patient retained many symptoms. In comparing this patient's early life experiences with those of Case No. 183, we note that the father in the latter instance was a strong male who was recognized and valued as such. Although the son's masculine attitudes and activities were discouraged, the father did provide a model for the male role, and the mother supported the patient's competitive attempt to emulate and even surpass his father. In contrast, the father of Case No. 177, just described, was ineffective, detached-hostile, and was held in contempt by a wife who allied against him with their son. Identification with the father was not encouraged, nor did the father provide any basis for a positive identification. A homosexual adaptation was far more entrenched than in the other two cases described, and heterosexual contacts had been almost completely avoided.

Outcome of treatment of homosexuality compared with results reported by others

Woodward reported on a total of 113 homosexuals who were referred to the Portman Clinic in London by courts and other agencies. After diagnostic evaluation, 15 were considered to be exclusively homosexual, the remainder being "attracted by both sexes." Treatment was recommended for 92 cases, but only 81 came for treatment. Only 1 case was listed as having had between 130-169 sessions over a period of 3 years. Four cases had between 90 and 129 sessions. Sixteen cases were seen for over 2 years, and an additional 24 were seen for between 1 and 2 years. A satisfactory result was defined as "no homosexual impulse, increased heterosexual interest." On the basis of this criterion, 7 cases achieved a satisfactory result. None of these 7 cases was exclusively homosexual at the outset.

Curran and Parr reported on 100 cases seen in private practice, on referral from various sources. Treatment was sporadic; only 3 out of 38 exclusively homosexual cases were reported to show "change towards heterosexuality."

Knight compiled the results of psychoanalytic treatment from several psychoanalytic institutes in the United States and Europe. He listed a total of 952 cases of whom 12 were treated for homosexuality. Two of the 12 homosexuals were judged to have been cured.

The 27 per cent rate reported in the present study argues in favor of a more optimistic outlook than is held by these and other investigators.

SUMMARY

1. Of 106 homosexuals who undertook psychoanalysis, either as exclusively homosexual or bisexual, 29 (27 per cent) became exclusively heterosexual:
   (a) Of the 72 H-patients who began treatment as exclusively homosexual, 14 (19 per cent) became heterosexual.
   (b) Of the 30 H-patients who began treatment as bisexual, 15 (50 per cent) became heterosexual.
2. The results of treatment as related to duration were as follows:
   (a) Only 2 patients of 28 (7 per cent) who had fewer than 150 hours became heterosexual.
   (b) Nine of 40 (23 per cent) of those patients who had 150-349 hours of analysis became heterosexual.
   (c) Eighteen of 38 (47 per cent) of patients who had 350 or more hours of analysis became heterosexual.
3. Factors which increase the probability that the homosexual will sustain the therapeutic relationship:
   (a) Patient's mother was thought of as an admirable person and considerate of his needs.
   (b) Patient was not an only child.
   (c) Patient acknowledged a sense of rivalry or competition with his brothers.
   (d) Patient made his first heterosexual contact by age 16.
   (e) Patient wanted to conceal his homosexuality.
4. Factors which increase the probability that the homosexual will discontinue analysis at an early date:
   (a) Patient's parents spent very little time together.
   (b) Patient was an only child.
   (c) Patient had homesexual physical contact but no heterosexual contact before age 16.
   (d) Patient had never attempted heterosexual genital contact.
   (e) Patient did not care to conceal his homosexuality.
5. *Favorable prognostic indicators* which increase the probability that the homosexual will achieve an exclusively heterosexual adaptation:
   (a) Patient was bisexual at the beginning of analysis.
   (b) Patient began analysis before age 35.
   (c) Patient continued in analysis for at least 150 hours, preferably 350 hours or more.

(d) Patient was motivated to become heterosexual.

(e) Patient had a not-detached, and at least an "ambivalent," father.

(f) Patient's father respected and/or admired the patient, was affectionate, was more intimate with patient than with other male siblings, and liked women.

(g) Patient "idolizes" women.

(h) Patient had tried heterosexual genital contact at some time.

(i) Patient had erotic heterosexual activity in the manifest content of his dreams.

6. *Unfavorable prognostic indicators* which increase the probability that the homosexual will fail to achieve a heterosexual adaptation:

(a) Patient was exclusively homosexual at the beginning of analysis and had never attempted heterosexual genital contact.

(b) Patient began analysis at 35 years or older.

(c) Patient undertook analysis for a reason other than the desire to alter his sexual pattern.

(d) Patient drops out of analysis in fewer than 150 hours.

(e) Patient had a close-binding intimate mother and a detached-hostile father.

(f) Patient's mother openly preferred patient to father.

(g) Patient had effeminate voice and gestures during childhood.

7. *Factors which appeared unrelated to prognosis or change:*

(a) Psychiatric diagnosis: Patients with the diagnosis of schizophrenia, psychoneurosis, and character disorder achieved an exclusively heterosexual orientation in numbers proportionate to their number in the total sample.

(b) Theoretical orientation of the psychoanalyst: "Freudian" and "Culturalist" psychoanalysts were equally successful in effecting change in sexual behavior.

(c) Sex of the psychoanalyst: Male and female psychoanalysts were equally successful in effecting change in sexual adaptation.

XII

Conclusions

THIS STUDY PROVIDES convincing support for a fundamental contribution by Rado on the subject of male homosexuality: A homosexual adaptation is a result of "hidden but incapacitating fears of the opposite sex."

A considerable amount of data supporting Rado's assumption has been presented as evidence that fear of heterosexuality underlies homosexuality, e.g., the frequent fear of disease or injury to the genitals, significantly associated with fear and aversion to female genitalia; the frequency and depth of anxiety accompanying actual or contemplated heterosexual behavior.

We have described the specific types of disturbed parent-child relationships which have promoted fear of heterosexuality (discussed in psychodynamic detail later on) and we have emphasized throughout these chapters the role of parents in the homosexual outcome. The data have also demonstrated that many of the homosexuals in our sample showed evidences of heterosexual interest and desire manifested in dreams, fantasies, and attempts at heterosexual activity.

The capacity to adapt homosexually is, in a sense, a tribute to man's biosocial resources in the face of thwarted heterosexual goal-achievement. Sexual gratification is not renounced; instead, fears and inhibitions associated with heterosexuality are circumvented and sexual responsivity with pleasure and excitement to a member of the same sex develops as a pathologic alternative.

Any adaptation which is basically an accommodation to unrealistic fear is necessarily pathologic; in the adult homosexual continued fear of heterosexuality is inappropriate to his current reality. We differ with other investigators who have taken the position that homosexuality is a kind of variant of "normal" sexual behavior.

Kinsey *et al.* did not regard homosexuality as pathologic but rather as the expression of an inherent capacity for indiscriminate sexual response. In support of this assumption the authors referred to the high frequency of homosexual experiences in the preadolescence of American males. Thus, an assumption of normalcy is based on the argument of frequency though, in fact, frequency as a phenomenon is not necessarily related to absence of pathology. For example, most people in New York will contract a cold during a given period of time. This expectancy will show a normal probability distribution but respiratory infections are patently pathologic conditions.

Kinsey *et al.* also stated that the personality disturbances associated with homosexuality derive from the expectation of adverse social reactions. Although most H-patients in our study were apprehensive about being exposed as homosexuals, these were secondary responses to a primary disorder. Further, anxiety about social acceptance would not account for the many significant differences between homosexuals and heterosexuals which were found among the large number of items tapped; in particular, hostility to the H-father, to brothers rather than to sisters, the close relationship with the mother, and so forth. Moreover, some patients had no apparent problems about social acceptance. Without minimizing its importance, the emphasis upon fears of censure and rejection as promotive of the personality disorders associated with homosexuality seems to be a quite superficial analysis of this complex disorder.

Ford and Beach, in accord with Kinsey *et al.,* also imply that homosexuality is not pathologic but that "the basic mammalian capacity for sexual inversion tends to be obscured in societies like our own which forbid such behavior and classify it as unnatural." The authors compare the sporadic and indiscriminate "homosexual" behavior frequently observed among infrahuman species (though heterosexual behavior is not extinguished in hardly any instances and is reinstated with no apparent change), with human homosexual behavior where cognitive and highly complex patterns are involved and where, at least in our society, fear of heterosexuality is salient. Based on the frequency of homosexual phenomena, the authors state, "The cross-cultural and cross-species comparisons presented . . . combine to suggest that a biological tendency for inversion of sexual behavior is inherent in most if not all mammals including the human species." Following their logic, one might assume that any frequently occurring sexual aberration may be explained by postulating an inherent tendency. A pathologic formation, i.e., homosexuality, viewed as an inherent tendency points to a confusion between the concept of adaptational potential and that of inborn tendency.

Ford and Beach do not distinguish between *capacity* and *tendency. Capacity* is a neutral term connoting *potentiality* whereas *tendency* implies the probability of action in a specific direction. In our view, the human has a capacity for homosexuality but a tendency toward heterosexuality. The capacity for responsivity to heterosexual excitation is inborn. Courtship behavior and copulatory technique is learned. Homosexuality, on the other hand, is acquired and discovered as a circumventive adaptation for coping with fear of heterosexuality. As we evaluate the maturational processes, a homosexual phase is not an integral part of sexual development. At any age, homosexuality is a symptom of fear and inhibition of heterosexual expression. We do not hold with the now popular thesis that in all adult males there are repressed homosexual wishes. In fact, most adult heterosexual males no longer have the potential for a homosexual adaptation. In the comparison sample one-fourth of the cases revealed no evidence of homosexual propensities—conscious or unconscious. If we assume that homosexuality is a pathological condition, and our data strongly support this assumption, we would no more expect latent homosexuality to be inevitable among well-integrated heterosexuals than we would expect latent peptic ulcer to be inevitable among all members of a healthy population.

Another approach to the question of homosexuality as behavior within a normal range is found in Hooker's work (see page 17, Chapter I). In this investigation projective techniques were utilized to determine whether homosexuality and homosexual adjustment could be distinguished from that of heterosexuals. It was found that the differences sought between the two populations could not be reliably distinguished. The conclusion was that "homosexuality may be a deviation in sexual pattern which is within the normal range psychologically." Since the tests and adjustment ratings were performed by competent workers and the implication of the findings and conclusions are at marked variance with those of our own and other studies, we suspect that the tests themselves or the current methods of interpretation and evaluation are inadequate to the task of discriminating between homosexuals and heterosexuals.

Still another type of argument is that homosexuality in certain individuals is related to genetic factors. In Kallman's twin studies, homosexuality among monozygotic twins was investigated (see page 13, Chapter I). Each sibling of forty pairs was found to be homosexual. Kallman placed enormous emphasis on genetic factors; yet, he contradicted his own position by stating that the sexual impulse is easily dislocated by experiential factors. Even assuming a genetic determination, it cannot be strongly operative if sexuality responds so sensitively to nongenetic influences. We propose that the study should have included psychoanalytic treatment for at least some of the pairs studied. Had a shift to heterosexuality occurred in the course of treatment, as it had in one-fourth of the homosexuals in our sample, the reversibility would have cast doubt on the significance of genetic determinants in homosexuality. Though reversibility in itself is not a sufficient argument against the genetic position, there is so much evidence on the side of the nurture hypothesis and so little on the side of the nature hypothesis, that the reliance upon genetic or constitutional determinants to account for the homosexual adaptation is ill founded.

A point of view which has gained some acceptance in psychoanalytic circles is that homosexuality is a defense against schizophrenia; that is to say, if the H-patients had not become homosexual they would have become schizophrenic. Our findings do not support this hypothesis. One-fourth of the homosexual cases were diagnosed as schizophrenic; thus, homosexuality obviously had not defended these homosexuals against schizophrenia. Further, there were no schizophrenic sequelae among those H-patients who became exclusively heterosexual.

The idea that paranoia is a defense against homosexuality goes back to Freud's early analysis of the Schreber case. According to anecdotal data offered by E. A. Weinstein[1] homosexual content was absent in the delusional systems during the acute paranoid states of native Virgin Islanders. We propose that schizophrenia and homosexuality represent two distinct types of personality maladaptation which may or may not coexist.

---

[1] United States Public Health Psychiatrist to the Virgin Islands, 1958-1960.

An analysis of the data obtained on the schizophrenic homosexual and comparison cases was made. The analysis was not presented in this volume since it was not central to our study. We did find, however, that with certain item clusters, those patients who were diagnosed as schizophrenic in the H-sample were more like the schizophrenic heterosexuals than like the other nonschizophrenic homosexuals. On other item clusters, however, the schizophrenic homosexuals resembled other H-patients more than they did heterosexual schizophrenics. For example, on item clusters tapping father-son relationships, the schizophrenic patients in both samples were significantly more fearful, more distrustful, and had fewer friendly, accepting, and respectful relationships with significantly more frequently hostile and unsympathetic fathers than was noted among the nonschizophrenic H- and C-patients. But on the Six Developmental Items and on the item tapping aversion to female genitalia, the responses converged according to sexual adaptation, e.g., schizophrenic and nonschizophrenic homosexuals resembled each other more than they did schizophrenic and nonschizophrenic comparison patients whose responses also converged on these items.

The differences in psychopathology between the homosexuals and schizophrenics suggest that the time in life when predisposing influences became effective may have occurred earlier among schizophrenics. The nonschizophrenic homosexuals may not have been exposed to as severe pathogenic influences until the appearance of behavior construed by parents as heterosexual; this usually occurs in the early phase of the Oedipus Complex.

Freud's formulations on so-called "narcissistic" love object choice are supported by our findings in the Adolescent Study (Chapter VIII). Reciprocal identifications and love for an exchanged self-image were noted among the adolescents.

Freud postulated that castration anxiety, which he deemed to be a major factor in homosexuality, was strongly reinforced in the male child upon his shocked discovery of the absence of a penis in the female. Our study does not provide data directly bearing upon this hypothesis although our findings permit us to make certain inferences. Fear of and aversion to the female genitalia were reported for approximately three-fourths of the homosexual patients in contrast to only one-third of the heterosexuals. If the assumed anxiety reaction in the young male goes beyond a transitory childhood experience so as to become a determining force in masculine psychosexual development, we could expect a much higher frequency of fear and aversion to female genitalia among heterosexuals. Such was not the case among the heterosexual patient sample. We conclude that the male child's reaction to the observed absence of a penis in the female may be an important determinant of anxiety but only when reinforced by other determinants of anxiety related to sexuality. The significant association between fear and aversion with other items of the questionnaire indicates to us that the aversion is a defense against fear of heterosexuality.

Our findings are replete with evidence of a close mother-son relationship and confirm the observations of Freud and other investigators that "mother fixation" is related to homosexuality. The data also provide convincing evidence of the importance of the Oedipus Complex in the etiology of homosexuality. Our material highlights the parental distortions of this phase of child development, as noted in the overcloseness and seductiveness of the H-mother and the hostility of the H-father.

The data on identification of the homosexual partner with family members support two other of Rado's assumptions: (1) heterosexual impulses may be acted-out in the homosexual act or homosexual relationship; (2) the homosexual adaptation frequently includes attempts to solve problems involving the father.

The identification of the homosexual partner with the mother and sisters, which occurred in some patients of our sample, suggests that heterosexual strivings were being acted-out in these homosexual relationships. On the other hand, the identification of the homosexual partner with a father or brothers who were hated and feared suggests that these patients were making reparative attempts to solve relationship problems originating with the father and/or brothers.

Rado had also stated that two other determinants of homosexual behavior are "temporary expedience" and "a desire for surplus variation." We are in disagreement with these views. We do not base our differences on material derived from our study since our sample was composed of patients who were not "sporadic" homosexuals, and they had well established homosexual patterns—but rather upon psychiatric reports on military personnel during World War II. Lewis and Engel have abstracted the major psychiatric papers published during the war years; none referred to expedient homosexual behavior despite the deprivation of women for millions of men. Further, a member of the Research Committee who had had the opportunity to observe all homosexuals apprehended for homosexual activity in a particular Theater of Operations did not clinically observe patients with the motivations Rado has proposed. Homosexual behavior was relatively uncommon in the armed forces of Great Britain and the United States. It occurred in individuals with premilitary homosexuality, or occasionally in individuals under the influence of alcohol as might occur in civilian life.

The assumption of "surplus variation" could apply to any aberrant sexual activity. Clinical experience has shown that aberrant behavior is always pathologically motivated. The "doing-it-for-kicks" assumption does not adequately explain aberrant sexuality. We are committed to Rado's own proposition that homosexuality is an adaptation to fear of heterosexuality, and we extend this proposition to account for all homosexual behavior.

Theories which postulate that homosexuality is a coincidental phenomenon in a more comprehensive psychopathologic process are given minimal support by our data. The construct proposed by Ovesey differentiates *actual* (acted-out) homosexuality from *pseudo*homosexuality ("latent" or unconscious). Dependency and inhibited assertion are assumed to be the basic psychodynamics underlying pseudohomosexuality so that homosexual preoccupation, fear, panic, and so forth, are viewed merely as symbolic representations of more fundamental pathologic formations. We have found pathologic dependency to be a characteristic of the majority of homosexuals but we have also identified it in most heterosexual patients. According to our formulation, pathologic dependency forms part of the psychodynamic constellation of homosexuality, but, as pointed out in Chapter VII, pathologic dependency appears as a secondary process. In our view, dependency and inhibited assertiveness are the *consequences* of psychologic injury and not the *causes* of it. The patients' symbolization of dependency in homosexual terms does not dispose of homosexuality as a central problem since when such symbolizations occur in dreams, fantasies, and obsessions, a homosexual *solution* is being contemplated (consciously or unconsciously) and an adaptive shift may be potential at those times.

Our findings support those of Kolb and Johnson in their emphasis upon the parental role in promoting homosexuality; those of Sullivan as to the importance of peer group relationships; those of Thompson in that heterosexuality is biologically more congenial; those of West who asserted that the participation of both parents in the molding of a male homosexual was essential. Lang found an overrepresentation of homosexual siblings in the homosexual sample he studied which is in accord with our data.

Psychodynamics

Our study has helped us refine and extend certain concepts relevant to the etiology of male homosexuality. Certainly, the role of the parents emerged with great clarity in many detailed aspects. Severe psychopathology in the H-parent-child relationships was ubiquitous, and similar psychodynamics, attitudes, and behavioral constellations prevailed throughout most of the families of the homosexuals—which differed significantly from the C-sample. Among the H-patients who lived with a set of natural parents up to adulthood—and this was so for the entire H-sample except for fourteen cases—neither parent had a relationship with the H-son one could reasonably construe as "normal." The triangular systems were characterized by disturbed and psychopathic interactions; all H-parents apparently had severe emotional problems. Unconscious mechanisms operating in the selection of mates may bring together this combination of parents. When, through unconscious determinants, or by chance, two such individuals marry, they tend to elicit and reinforce in each other those potentials which increase the likelihood that a homosexual son will result from the union. The homosexual son becomes entrapped in the parental conflict in a role determined by the parents' unresolved problems and transferences.

Each parent had a specific type of relationship with the homosexual son which generally did not occur with other siblings. *The H-son emerged as the interactional focal point upon whom the most profound parental psychopathology was concentrated.* Hypotheses for the choice of this particular child as "victim" are offered later in this discussion.

The father played an essential and determining role in the homosexual outcome of his son. In the majority of instances the father was explicitly detached and hostile. In only a minority of cases was paternal destructiveness effected through indifference or default.

A fatherless child is deprived of the important paternal contribution to normal development; however, only few homosexuals in our sample had been fatherless children. Relative absence of the father, necessitated by occupational demands or unusual exigencies, is not in itself pathogenic. A good father-son relationship and a mother who is an affectionate, admiring wife, provide the son with the basis for a positive image of the father during periods of separation. We have come to the conclusion that a constructive, supportive, warmly related father *precludes* the possibility of a homosexual son; he acts as a neutralizing, protective agent should the mother make seductive or close-binding attempts.

The foundations of personality and psychopathology are set within the nuclear family; more specifically, within the triangular system. Parental attitudes toward a particular child are often well defined by the first year of life and after the fourth year are well established. Parental attitudes in most instances undergo little fundamental change so that the child is exposed to a continuity of relatively unchanging parental influences. When these influences are pathogenic, they create and then maintain psychopathology in the child.

In important ways, sibling relationships and parent-sibling relationships also contribute to personality formation and to psychodynamic mechanisms operant in interpersonal affairs. Siblings may "tip the scales" one way or the other; they do not set the tenuous balance. However, a good sibling relationship—in particular, one with an older male sibling—may to some extent compensate for a poor one with the parents; it may even reinforce a heterosexual adaptation in a child who might otherwise have become homosexual. A rivalrous, disturbed sibling relationship, or sibling behavior outside the family which is traumatic to the child even when not directed at him, may be the "final straw" to precipitate homosexuality. But again, it is the parents who determine the family atmosphere and the relationships that transpire within the family setting. Other events are relatively of secondary importance.

We believe that sexual development (and its vicissitudes) is a cornerstone in homosexual adaptation. We do not regard homosexuality as a nonspecific manifestation of a generalized personality disorder. Therefore we shall outline a formulation of sexual development relevant to male homosexuality.

The first manifestations of sexuality occur as an integral part of the total growth process. Intricate and complex attitudes, behavior patterns and interpersonal relationships have already evolved before significant sexual development begins. All that has preceded sexual organization plays some part in determining its course. Conversely, the sexual process will itself condition the totality of pre-existing personality attributes, interpersonal relationships, and behavior patterns.

The initial stage of heterosexual responsivity occurs between the third and sixth years of life. Differentiated reactions toward males and females are observable at this period. These reactive differences are determined by a beginning capacity to respond to sexual stimuli from heterosexual objects in the environment—parents and siblings included. The young male child not only develops the capacity to respond sexually to females but he becomes capable of exciting such responses in females, including his mother. Bieber has advanced the hypothesis that olfaction plays an important part in the initial organization of the capacity for heterosexual responsivity and differentiation; the male takes on the odor characteristic of males sometime between the third and fifth year of life. Sexual responsivity in the young male stimulates a wish to be physically close to females and, as culturally patterned, to kiss, hug, and so forth. Rivalrous feelings toward males, particularly toward the father, generally accompany the developing capacity for heterosexual responsivity. The sexual response to the mother and rivalrous feelings to the father constitute the fundamentals of the Oedipus Complex.

Sexual reactions to the mother constitute one manifestation of the male child's developing capacity for heterosexual responses. The profound relationship established with the mother during infancy and into the pre-Oedipal years becomes integrated with the emerging heterosexual responsivity toward the mother as the most prominent and accessible female in the immediate environment. The nature of the child's sexual response in no way differs from that felt toward any comparably accessible female though the singular attachment of son to mother includes the earlier infantile dependence upon her which begins to articulate with his developing heterosexual interests. It is at this point that the incest taboo is first communicated from parent to child. Because of anxiety connected with incest, the mother will suppress her son's heterosexual responses to her. Sexual repression in concert with filial rivalry toward the father results in the son's repression of incestuous wishes.

Parental responses to the child's emerging heterosexuality are not ordinarily emphasized in a discussion of the Oedipus Complex, yet these responses are crucial in determining the fate of the Oedipus Complex. Developmental processes in children, sexual and other, form part of a reverberating stimulus-response system with the parents. Every maturational phase of development in the child stimulates responses in the parents which, in turn, condition the original stimuli and fundamentally determine the nature of development of that specific maturational phase. We refer to the interactional response patterns involved in bowel training, walking, talking, early masturbation, and so forth.

A mother who is pleased by her son's masculinity and is comfortably related to his sexual curiosity and heterosexual responsiveness to her and other females, encourages and reinforces a masculine identification. A father who is warmly related to his son, who supports assertiveness and effectiveness, and who is not sexually competitive, provides the reality testing necessary for the resolution of the son's irrational sexual competitiveness. This type of parental behavior fosters heterosexual development which in adult life is characterized by the ability to sustain a gratifying love relationship. Parents who are capable of sexually constructive attitudes to a child usually are individuals who are capable of a love relationship with each other and provide a stable and affectionate atmosphere in the home. In the context of sexual development, a positive parental relationship provides no basis in reality for expectations of exclusive possession of the mother. Where the marital relationship is unsatisfactory, the parents may make attempts to fulfill frustrated romantic wishes through a child. In the case of the mother the child chosen for this role is usually a son. Thus, in part, she fulfills the son's unconscious incestuous wishes and she intensifies his rivalry with and fear of the father. She alienates son from father who, in turn, becomes hostile to both wife and son.

The majority of H-parents in our study had poor marital relationships. Almost half the H-mothers were dominant wives who minimized their husbands. The large majority of H-mothers had a close-binding-intimate relationship with the H-son. In most cases, this son had been his mother's favorite though in a few instances an underlying CBI relationship had been concealed by a screen of maternal minimization and superficial rejection. Most H-mothers were explicitly seductive, and even where they were not, the closeness of the bond with the son appeared to be in itself sexually provocative. In about two-thirds of the cases, the mother openly preferred her H-son to her husband and allied with son against the husband. In about half the cases, the patient was the mother's confidant.

These data point to maternal attempts to fulfill frustrated marital gratifications with the homosexual son. A "romantic" attachment, short of actual physical contact (specifically, genital contact), was often acted-out.

We assume that the unusually close mother-son relationship and the maternal seductiveness explicit in over half the cases had the effect of over-stimulating the sons sexually. We further assume that sexual over-stimulation promoted sexual activity rather than sexual patterns characterized by total inhibition as seen in apparent asexuality or impotence. The combination of sexual over-stimulation and intense guilt and anxiety about heterosexual behavior promote precocious and compulsive sexual activity, as was noted among H-patients. In support of these assumptions we found that homosexuals as a group began their sexual activity earlier than did the heterosexuals; the H-patients were more active sexually in preadolescence than were C-patients. The preoccupation with sexuality and sexual organs frequently observed among homosexuals appears to emerge out of an intensity of sexual urges pounding against extensive impairment of heterosexual functioning. Sexual over-stimulation together with heterosexual impairment, promotes compulsive homosexual activity. Reparative mechanisms, usually unconscious and irrational, operate to restore heterosexuality. A reparative mechanism noted among the H-patients included the selection of homosexual lovers who were quite masculine—the "large penis" type. Such a maneuver involves an attempt to identify with a powerful male through symbolic incorporation usually expressed in oral sexual practices. Not infrequently the homosexual lover is perceived as a potent rival or as the most likely threat to heterosexual goals. The reparative aim is to divert the partner's interest from women, thus symbolically "castrating" him in the homosexual act—an irrational and magical attempt to achieve heterosexuality by eliminating an obstructive, threatening rival.

Earlier, we pointed out that one son was chosen for a particular role. Certain kinds of parental psychopathology are acted-out with this son and eventuate in his becoming homosexual. We propose that the mother chooses a son whom she unconsciously identifies with her father or with a brother who has great emotional value to her—usually he is an older brother. Such an identification may be made on the basis of physical traits or other cues to which the mother reacts transferentially but which, in a fundamental sense, evolve from her wish to possess a male like her father, or both. Since the H-son is the instrument which the mother uses to act-out her own anxiety-laden incestuous wishes, she is especially alert to any sexual behavior her son may express to her. Lest his behavior expose her own feelings, she suppresses all such manifestations in her son who soon learns that any act which includes an element of sexuality and virile masculinity is unwelcome to her. If her anxiety is severe enough, she attempts to demasculinize her son and will even encourage effeminate attitudes.

Most H-mothers were possessive of their sons. Because they apparently could not tolerate a romantic relationship with their own husbands, they appeared to be insecure about their ability to maintain ties with a male perceived as "valuable"; as compensation, they clung tenaciously to the H-son. In general, demasculinization by the mother serves to insure her son's continued presence; his extinguished heterosexuality then protects her against abandonment for another woman. Demasculinizing maternal behavior may also occur in those women who have been rejected by their own mothers who had preferred a male sibling. Such H-mothers have a need to dominate and control males and to hinder their effectiveness in an irrational attempt to deter further deprivation of feminine love—a female homosexual dynamic. Again, psychoanalytic experience with this type of woman leads us to hypothesize that many such mothers are burdened by deep-going homosexual problems.

It is self-evident that a man who enters into a poor marriage, and then remains in it, has serious problems. The father who is detached, hostile, and rejecting to his son in most instances is in an unsatisfactory marriage, as our data have shown. Hence, such men have a double-pronged psychopathologic interpersonal involvement—with the wife on the one hand, and with the H-son on the other. These fathers, not unlike their wives, are unable to maintain a love relationship with a spouse. Some such men attempt to fulfill those emotional goals by acting-out with a daughter as their wives are acting-out with a son. These fathers tend to be unusually hostile to men perceived as sexual rivals. Rejected by their wives in favor of the H-son (many of whom were openly preferred and more highly esteemed), the already existing competitive attitudes the fathers had toward males were intensified with the H-sons. Thus paternal competitive attitudes are expressed in overt hostility and rejection or in indifference. As for the son, he accurately interprets his father's behavior as sexually competitive. Fear of attack from the father coupled with the wish for his love is indeed a potent combination; it disturbs the son's own developing masculine sexuality which, he senses, is offensive to the father. Paternal preference for a daughter with expressions of love for her, which the son witnesses and envies, fosters in him the wish to be a woman; further, it interferes with a masculine identification and a heterosexual adaptation.

Much of the data of this study document the importance of the father in his son's sexual outcome. The role-fulfilling father shares supportive, organizing, and orienting behaviors with the mother. Where a father has been devaluated by a wife's contempt while the son has been elevated to a position of preference, and where the father's potentially supportive role is undermined, a highly unrealistic and anxiety-laden grandiosity is promoted in the son. To be treated as superior to the father deprives the child of having the paternal leadership he craves and the support he requires.

In the father's specific contribution to his son's psychosexual development, the father should be a male model with whom the son can identify in forming masculine patterns in a specific cultural milieu. An affectionate father through his warmth and support provides a reality denial for any retaliatory expectations the son may have for harboring sexually competitive attitudes. The father who promotes an identification with him will ordinarily intercede between his son and a wife who may be CBI, thus protecting the boy from demasculinization. Such a father does not default his paternal role out of submissiveness to his wife. Our data record only one such supportive, affectionate H-father—he was a stepfather who came upon the scene when the patient was already ten years old. This patient became exclusively heterosexual in psychoanalytic treatment.

The father who is underprotective or who singles out one or several sons for the expression of hostile attitudes and behavior is usually acting-out a transference problem, generally based on difficulties had with his own father and/or a male sibling. Such a father tends to derogate his H-son and to show contempt at his failures in peer groups.

By the time the H-son has reached the preadolescent period, he has suffered a diffuse personality disorder. Maternal over-anxiety about health and injury, restriction of activities normative for the son's age and potential, interference with assertive behavior, demasculinizing attitudes, and interference with sexuality—interpenetrating with paternal rejection, hostility, and lack of support—produce an excessively fearful child, pathologically dependent upon his mother and beset by feelings of inadequacy, impotence, and self-contempt. He is reluctant to participate in boyhood activities thought to be potentially physically injurious—usually grossly overestimated. His peer group responds with humiliating name-calling and often with physical attack which timidity tends to invite among children. His fear and shame of self, made worse by the derisive reactions of other boys, only drives him further away. Thus, he is deprived of important empathic interactions which peer groups provide. The "esprit de corps" of boyhood gang-life is missed. Having no neighborhood gang to which to belong only accentuates the feeling of difference and alienation. More than half our H-sample were for the most part, isolates in preadolescence and adolescence, and about one-third played predominantly with girls.

Failure in the peer group, and anxieties about a masculine, heterosexual presentation of self, pave the way for the prehomosexual's initiation into the less threatening atmosphere of homosexual society, its values, and way of life. As a group, homosexuals constitute a kind of subculture with unique institutions, value systems, and communication techniques in idiom, dress, and gestures. The tendency to gravitate to large cities may also be extended to residence in particular locales and to "hangouts." Often there is a sense of identification with a minority group which has been discriminated against. Homosexual society, however, in which membership is attained through individual psychopathology, is neither "healthy" nor happy. Life within this society tends to reinforce, fixate, and add new disturbing elements to the entrenched psychopathology of its members. Although the emotional need of humans to socialize with other humans keeps many homosexuals within groups, some find the life style incompatible with other held values so that in some cases they come to prefer relative isolation.

Some homosexuals tend to seek out a single relationship, hoping to gratify all emotional needs within a one-to-one exclusive relationship. Such twosomes are usually based on unrealistic expectations, often accompanied by inordinate demands; in most instances, these pairs are caught up in a turbulent, abrasive attachment. These liaisons are characterized by initial excitement which may include exaltation and confidence in the discovery of a great love which soon alternates with anxiety, rage, and depression as magical expectations are inevitably frustrated. Gratification of magical wishes is symbolically sought in homosexual activity which is intense in the early phase of a new "affair." These relationships are generally disrupted after a period of several months to a year or so; they are generally sought anew with another partner and the cycle starts again. The depressions accompanying the dissolution of a homosexual bond and the despondency brought about by developing insight into the futility of such relationships are often precipitating circumstances motivating the undertaking of psychiatric or psychoanalytic therapy. Chronic underlying depressive states, a frequent characteristic of homosexuals, are often masked by a façade of gaiety.

A detailed study of the etiology of homosexuality in the atypical cases must await a special study of larger numbers of these sub-groups than was available in the present investigation. In several instances, mothers were detached and hostile and several were detached and indifferent. Some fathers were not detached and a few were overprotective. Some homosexuals were not excessively fearful and some did not flinch from fighting; some even sought fights. Though they differed from the majority of H-patients in these aspects, they still had in common with the others highly pathologic relationships with parents and had come to fear a sustained heterosexual love relationship.

In about one-fourth of the comparison patients, evidence of severe homosexual problems was noted. None, however, had actually participated in homosexual activity in adolescence or adult life. We infer that a fragmentary homosexual adaptation had been organized and that the possibility of a homosexual shift had been considered on either a conscious or unconscious level at some time. Since a homosexual integration takes place only where there is severe anxiety regarding heterosexuality, some of these heterosexual patients were apparently tempted to escape from their fears by a flight into homosexuality. This kind of alternative to anxiety usually produces added and even more intense anxiety, since the renunciation of heterosexuality represents a serious loss to perceived self-interest; it is, in a sense, a type of castration. Secondarily, the homosexual solution is socially unacceptable and confronts the individual with unforeseen pitfalls in a new way of life. Certain heterosexuals are thus caught between the anxiety experienced in a sexual bond with a woman, and the panic and fear associated with homosexuality. We view such individuals as potentially homosexual. Only those men who have such problems are considered by us to be "latent" homosexuals, but since the concept of homosexual latency is one that assumes a universal tendency present in all men, we prefer to discard the term entirely and refer to *homosexual problems* in those patients among whom such difficulties can be identified.

The therapeutic results of our study provide reason for an optimistic outlook. Many homosexuals became exclusively heterosexual in psychoanalytic treatment. Although this change may be more easily accomplished by some than by others, in our judgment a heterosexual shift is a possibility for all homosexuals who are strongly motivated to change.

We assume that heterosexuality is the *biologic* norm and that unless interfered with all individuals are heterosexual. Homosexuals do not bypass heterosexual developmental phases and all remain potentially heterosexual.

Our findings are optimistic guideposts not only for homosexuals but for the psychoanalysts who treat them. We are firmly convinced that psychoanalysts may well orient themselves to a heterosexual objective in treating homosexual patients rather than "adjust" even the more recalcitrant patient to a homosexual destiny. A conviction based on scientific fact that a heterosexual goal is achievable helps both patient and psychoanalyst to take in stride the inevitable setbacks during psychoanalysis.

We have learned a great deal about male homosexuality, yet we are under no illusion that this is a final statement on the subject. We hope that our work will stimulate other investigators to find answers to the many questions still unanswered.

APPENDIX A

Homosexuality Questionnaire

Analyst's Name: **Patient's Initials:** **Year of Birth:**

Homosexual: **Control:** **(Check appropriate item)**

		H	C
I. Relation between parents.	Good	5	14
A. Can the relations between parents be described as:	Fair	41	34
	Poor	60	52
B. Were there open demonstrations of affection between parents?	Yes	22	19
	No	80	81
	NA	4	0
C. Were there frequent arguments between parents?	Yes	68	65
	No	34	35
	NA	4	0
D. Which parent was dominant in family decisions?	Mother	61	55
	Father	42	39
	Neither	1	5
	NA	2	1
E. 1. Was contempt by one parent for the other a prominent part of parental relationship?	Yes	62	51
	No	41	48
	NA	3	1
2. Which parent showed contempt?	Mo	46	28
	Fa	11	18
	Reciprocal	5	5
	Neither	41	49
	NA	3	0
F. 1. Was one parent regarded as inferior by the other?	Yes	66	55
	No	37	44
	NA	3	1

			H	C
	2. Which one?	Mother	18	21
		Father	46	29
		Neither	37	45
		Both	2	5
		NA	3	0
G.	1. Does analyst believe that either or both parents suffered gross psychiatric aberration? Which?	Mother	22	21
		Father	11	13
		Neither	58	43
		Both	11	19
		NA	4	4
*H.	1. How much time did mother spend with father?	Great deal	1	13
		Average	44	49
		Little	37	24
		Very little	22	13
		NA	2	1
	2. Did they share similar interests?	Yes	21	37
		No	82	61
		NA	3	2
*I.	Did family usually eat evening meal together?	Yes	73	73
		No	29	27
		NA	4	0
**J.	Describe any changes in the patient's life history:			
	1. Infancy:			
	Sickness or death of parent or sibling		5	0
	Separation or divorce of parents		7	6
	Separation of child from parents		3	1
	Change in economic status		2	7
	Serious illness		4	10
	2. Childhood:			
	Sickness or death of parent or sibling		5	5
	Separation or divorce of parents		6	13
	Separation of child from parents		6	5
	Change in economic status		9	9
	Serious illness		3	10
	3. Adolescence:			
	Sickness or death of parent or sibling		5	7
	Separation or divorce of parents		4	8
	Separation of child from parents		4	11
	Change in economic status		7	4
	Serious illness		6	5
**K.	With which parent did patient side in arguments?			
	1. Childhood:	Mother	64	52
		Father	7	22

* Second Questionnaire

** Third Questionnaire—96H—96C

		H	C
	Mixed	2	1
	No side	10	8
	NA	13	13
2. Adolescence:	Mother	62	50
	Father	11	24
	Mixed	3	1
	No side	7	5
	NA	13	16
3. Currently:	Mother	25	16
	Father	12	19
	Mixed	3	5
	No side	10	8
	NA	46	48
4. Either childhood or adolescence:	Mother	67	53
**L. 1. Does the patient feel his mother protected him from father?	Yes	42	31
	No	48	59
	NA	6	6
2. Does patient feel his father protected him from mother?	Yes	7	14
	No	83	78
	NA	6	4
**M. 1. Which parent does the patient feel he could cope with more easily?	Mo	61	46
	Fa	20	38
	Neither	6	7
	NA	9	5
2. What techniques did patient use to handle or cope with each parent? Mother:	Submission	59	55
	Detachment	10	11
	Rebellion	9	22
	Charm	30	19
	Other	22	25
	NA	3	
Father:	Submission	55	51
	Detachment	28	16
	Rebellion	8	19
	Charm	15	12
	Other	17	3
	NA	10	6
II. Relation between patient and mother:			
A. 1. Was patient mother's favorite?	Yes	63	39
	No	30	38
	No sibs	11	22
	NA	2	1
2. If not, was another sibling the favorite? Which?	Bro	18	15
	Sis	7	7
3. Was patient least favored sibling?	Yes	14	14
Least favored by both parents		9	8
Favorite of both parents		2	11

		H	C
Favorite of mother and least favored by father		29	10
B. 1. Did mother express affection for patient?	Yes	80	70
	No	24	28
	NA	2	2
2. In physical acts such as kissing and hugging?	Yes	55	41
	No	49	55
	NA	2	4
C. 1. Did patient feel accepted by mother?	Yes	74	61
	No	32	39
	NA		
2. Did patient feel admired by mother?	Yes	52	45
	No	49	55
	NA	5	0
D. 1. Did mother express contempt for patient?	Yes	27	23
	No	77	77
	NA	2	0
2. Did mother humiliate patient?	Yes	40	34
	No	63	66
	NA	3	0
Either/or 1. and 2.	Yes	43	38
E. Was mother physically cruel to patient?	Yes	12	8
	No	92	92
	NA	2	0
F. 1. Did mother demand she be prime center of patient's attention?	Yes	65	36
	No	37	64
	NA	4	0
2. Was she dominating?	Yes	86	65
	No	18	32
	NA	2	3
3. Does the analyst consider that the mother was seductive in her activities with the patient?	Yes	60	34
	No	46	66
	NA	3	1
Was there: Talk about sex	Yes	17	9
Dressing or undressing with patient	Yes	22	17
Common use of bathroom	Yes	12	6
Genital stimulation by mother	Yes	7	4
Sensuous kissing or fondling by mother	Yes	14	12
Frequent enemas	Yes	14	4
Patient sleeping with mother	Yes	13	7
Patient sleeping in parental bedroom.	Yes	10	7
G. Amount of time spent between mother and patient?	Great deal	59	27
	Average	21	53
	Little	16	11
	Very little	8	9
	Absent	2	0

			H	C
H.	1. Did mother encourage masculine attitudes and activities?	Yes	18	47
		No	85	47
		NA	3	6
	2. Did mother discourage masculine attitudes and activities?	Yes	39	16
		No	61	76
		NA	6	8
	3. Did mother encourage feminine attitudes and activities?	Yes	37	11
		No	65	84
		NA	4	5
	4. Did mother discourage feminine attitudes and activities?	Yes	14	24
		No	82	64
		NA	10	12
I.	1. Was mother considered puritanical?	Yes	66	48
		No	35	47
		NA	5	5
	2. Was mother considered sexually frigid?	Yes	68	47
		No	27	37
		NA	11	16
		Both 1 and 2	53	36
		Either	82	55
J.	1. Was mother knowingly hated by patient?	Yes	31	31
		No	73	69
		NA	2	0
	2. Was mother knowingly feared by patient?	Yes	45	44
		No	59	56
		NA	2	0
		Both 1 and 2	20	21
*K.	Did patient consciously fear physical injury from mother?	Yes	13	16
		No	91	83
		NA	2	1
*L.	Did mother try to ally with son against father?	Yes	66	40
		No	38	60
		NA	2	0
*M.	Did mother openly prefer patient to husband?	Yes	62	38
		No	43	62
		NA	1	0
N.	1. Did mother want patient to grow to be like some particular individual?	Yes	28	27
	2. If yes, who?			
	Mother		6	0
	Father		5	5
	Male sib.		4	2
	Female sib.		3	1
	Other male		10	19
	Other female		0	0
	None		65	68
	NA		13	5

Question	Response	H	C
3. If male, was he a virile male?	Yes	10	21
	No	15	2
	NA	81	77

There was no question O in Part II.

Question	Response	H	C
*P. 1. Did or does the mother definitely know patient is homosexual?	Yes	22	
2. If yes, what were mother's reactions? (check one or more)	Tolerant	4	
	Accepting	7	
	Understanding	3	
	Indifferent	1	
	Hostile	7	
	Repelled	3	
	Despairing	3	
	Eager for change	7	
	Others	3	
3. If no, did patient suspect mother knew?	Yes	18	
*Q. 1. How many families had other male siblings?	Yes	64	63
	No	42	37
2. If yes, how was mother to patient as compared to other male siblings:			
A. Intimate with patient	More	36	18
	Less	13	16
	Not with any	5	8
	Equally	3	18
	NA	7	3
B. Ambitious for success of patient	More	20	19
	Less	12	10
	Not with any	7	5
	Equally	11	24
	NA	14	5
C. Respect for patient	More	17	17
	Less	15	16
	Not with any	5	4
	Equally	14	20
	NA	13	6
D. Encouraging of masculine traits in patient	More	0	6
	Less	20	11
	Not with any	10	10
	Equally	22	28
	NA	12	8
*R. 1. Did patient believe mother interfered with heterosexual activity during adolescence and after?	Yes	39	25
	No	65	74
	NA	2	1
2. Does analyst believe mother interfered?	Yes	62	35
	No	42	63
	NA	2	2

			H	C
*S.	1. Was patient the mother's confidant?	Yes	55	36
		No	50	63
		NA	1	1
	2. Was mother patient's confidante?	Yes	41	23
		No	64	77
		NA	1	1
*T.	1. Did the patient repulse mother's physical demonstrations of affection	Yes	20	15
		No	77	78
		NA	9	7
	2. Did patient respect mother?	Yes	64	56
		No	37	44
		NA	5	0
**U.	1. In childhood was patient's mother *unduly* concerned about his health	Yes	55	44
		No	35	52
		NA	6	0
	2. Was she *unduly* concerned with protecting him from physical injury?	Yes	56	37
		No	33	54
		NA	7	5
	3. Did mother's concern about health or injury cause her to interfere with or restrict his play, social or other activities?	Yes	47	25
		No	44	66
		NA	5	5
	4. Does the patient consider his mother to have been overprotective?	Yes	59	44
		No	35	51
		NA	2	1
	5. Does analyst consider patient's mother to have been overprotective?	Yes	64	41
		No	30	54
		NA	2	1
**V.	In childhood was the patient *excessively* fearful that *his* assertiveness or nonconformity might:			
	1. Hurt mother	Yes	34	33
	2. Anger mother	Yes	54	54
	3. Disappoint mother	Yes	35	28
	4. Make mother sick	Yes	23	27
	5. Lose mother's love	Yes	49	40
		NA	16	17
**W.	1. In childhood was the patient *excessively* dependent on his mother for advice or direction in making decisions?	Yes	61	40
		No	32	56
		NA	3	0
	2. Currently does the patient have anxiety in making major decisions?	Yes	69	68
		No	25	28
		NA	2	0
**X.	1. Did the patient feel that he was used by his mother to satisfy her needs?	Yes	68	59
		No	25	32
		NA	3	5

		H	C
2. Which of mother's needs was patient used to satisfy?			
3. Did the patient feel his mother understood and accepted his needs and feelings?	Yes	17	22
	No	75	72
	NA	4	2
4. Does the patient feel that his mother was insensitive to his needs?	Yes	66	68
	No	28	25
	NA	2	3
5. Does patient feel that his mother took his needs and desires into consideration in decisions and activities involving patient? (i.e., choice of friends, hobbies, vocation, use of patient's free time, others)	Yes	24	27
	No	66	65
	NA	6	4
6. Does patient feel his mother "babied" him?	Yes	59	39
	No	33	55
	NA	4	2
**Y. 1. Did patient have temper tantrums or other expressions of rage towards mother?	Yes	43	40
	No	49	54
	NA	4	2
2. Were such expressions of rage generally successful in achieving his purpose?	Yes	20	21
	No	33	25
	NA	43	50
**Z. Currently does the patient consider his mother jealous, disapproving or belittling of his female friends?	Yes	32	31
	No	37	40
	NA	27	25
**AA. Currently does patient feel respected as an adult by his mother?	Yes	32	43
	No	48	31
	NA	16	22
**BB. Does patient feel his mother:			
1. Understood men	Yes	4	11
2. Liked men	Yes	18	30
3. Resented men	Yes	61	58
4. Envied men	Yes	29	31
Either 3 and/or 4		68	61
	NA	14	13
**CC. 1. Did patient regard his mother as an admirable person?	Yes	61	43
	No	31	51
	NA	4	2
2. Does he now regard her as such?	Yes	25	33
	No	67	61
	NA	4	2
III. Relation between patient and father.			
A. 1. Was patient father's favorite?	Yes	7	22
	No	84	53
	No Siblings	11	22
	NA	4	3
2. If not, was another sibling the	Bro.	25	11

		H	C
favorite? Which?	Sis.	31	17
3. Was patient least favored sibling?	Yes	42	19
B. 1. Did father express affection for patient?	Yes	27	51
	No	76	48
	NA	3	1
2. In physical acts such as kissing or hugging?	Yes	12	8
	No	86	84
	NA	8	8
C. 1. Did patient feel accepted by father?	Yes	24	47
	No	79	50
	NA	3	3
2. Did patient feel admired by father?	Yes	8	14
	No	94	83
	NA	4	3
D. 1. Did father express contempt for patient?	Yes	42	27
	No	60	73
	NA	4	0
2. Did father humiliate patient?	Yes	47	40
	No	54	59
	NA	5	1
Either 1. or 2.	Yes	52	45
Neither 1. or 2.	Yes	54	55
E. Was father physically cruel to patient?	Yes	20	17
	No	82	83
	NA	4	0
F. 1. Did father demand that he be prime center of patient's attention?	Yes	14	11
	No	89	87
	NA	3	2
2. Was he dominating?	Yes	42	42
	No	60	57
	NA	4	1
3. Does the analyst consider that the father was seductive in his activities with the patient?	Yes	3	2
	No	98	95
	NA	5	3
Was there: Talk about sex?	Yes	1	3
Dressing or undressing with patient	Yes	4	1
Common use of bathroom	Yes	4	1
Genital stimulation by father	Yes	0	0
Sensuous kissing or fondling by father	Yes	1	1
Frequent enemas	Yes	1	0
Patient sleeping with father	Yes	4	0
Patient sleeping in parental bedroom	Yes	10	7
G. Amount of time spent between father and patient?	Great deal	3	3
	Average	11	37
	Little	35	30
	Very little	45	26

		H	C
	Absent	12	4
H. 1. Did father encourage masculine attitudes and activities?	Yes	48	60
	No	53	38
	NA	5	2
2. Did father discourage masculine attitudes and activities?	Yes	4	5
	No	91	90
	NA	4	5
3. Did father encourage feminine attitudes and activities?	Yes	1	3
	No	96	92
	NA	9	5
4. Did father discourage feminine attitudes and activities?	Yes	34	37
	No	60	53
	NA	12	10
I. 1. Was father considered puritanical?	Yes	39	34
	No	59	64
	NA	8	2
2. Was father considered sexually potent?	Yes	78	74
	No	13	16
	NA	15	10
J. 1. Was father knowingly hated by patient?	Yes	63	37
	No	40	62
	NA	3	1
2. Was father knowingly feared by patient?	Yes	70	54
	No	33	46
	NA	3	0
Both 1 and 2		60	31
*K. Did patient consciously fear physical injury from father?	Yes	59	43
	No	44	57
	NA	3	0
*L. Did father try to ally with son against mother?	Yes	8	14
	No	94	85
	NA	4	1
*M. Did father openly prefer patient to mother?	Yes	10	11
	No	94	87
	NA	2	2
*N. 1. Did father want patient to grow up to be like some particular person?	Yes	28	19
2. If yes, who?			
Father		21	10
Mother		0	0
Male sib.		4	2
Female sib.		0	0
Other male		3	6
Other female		0	1
None		62	73
NA		16	8
3. If male, was he a virile male?	Yes	26	17

		H	C
*O. 1. Did patient feel accepted by father?	Yes	24	47
	No	79	50
	NA	3	3
2. Did patient accept father?	Yes	21	50
	No	80	49
	NA	5	1
*P. 1. Did or does father know patient is homosexual?	Yes	18	
	No	84	
	NA	4	
2. If yes, what were father's reactions? (check one or more)	Tolerant	3	
	Accepting	3	
	Understanding	2	
	Indifferent	3	
	Hostile	2	
	Repelled	5	
	Despairing	3	
	Eager for change	7	
	Others	2	
3. If no, did patient suspect father knew?	Yes	3	
*Q. 1. How many families had other male siblings?	Yes	64	63
	No	42	37
2. If yes, how was father to patient as compared to other male siblings:			
A. Intimate with patient	More	5	17
	Less	21	16
	Not with any	15	8
	Equally	11	16
	NA	12	6
B. Ambitious for success of patient	More	1	8
	Less	20	10
	Not with any	15	14
	Equally	17	23
	NA	11	8
C. Respect for patient	More	3	9
	Less	27	12
	Not with any	10	9
	Equally	15	25
	NA	9	8
D. Encouraging of masculine traits in patient	More	2	8
	Less	17	9
	Not with any	14	14
	Equally	21	18
	NA	10	14
*R. 1. Did patient believe father interfered with heterosexual activity during adolescence and after?	Yes	16	14
	No	87	85
	NA	3	1

			H	C
	2. Does analyst believe father interfered?	Yes	17	12
		No	84	86
		NA	5	2
	3. Either and/or 1 and 2	Yes	22	16
*S.	1. Was patient father's confidant?	Yes	5	5
		No	98	94
		NA	3	1
	2. Was father patient's confidant?	Yes	3	5
		No	99	95
		NA	4	0
*T.	1. Did patient repulse father's physical demonstrations of affection before adolescence?	Yes	19	10
		No	68	59
		NA	19	31
	2. Did patient respect father?	Yes	30	48
		No	70	50
		NA	6	2
**U.	1. In childhood was the patient's father *unduly* concerned about patient's health?	Yes	4	5
		No	85	91
		NA	7	0
	2. Was father *unduly* concerned with protecting him from physical injury?	Yes	5	5
		No	84	91
		NA	7	0
	3. Did father's concern about health or injury cause him to interfere with or restrict his play, social, or other activities?	Yes	4	4
		No	66	78
		NA	26	14
	4. Does patient consider his father to have been overprotective?	Yes	5	5
		No	85	90
		NA	6	1
	5. Does analyst consider patient's father to have been overprotective?	Yes	4	7
		No	85	86
		NA	7	3
**V.	In childhood was patient *excessively* fearful that *his* assertiveness or nonconformity might:			
	1. Hurt father	Yes	7	17
	2. Anger father	Yes	73	53
	3. Disappoint father	Yes	19	29
	4. Make father sick	Yes	4	4
	5. Lose father's love	Yes	29	29
		None	12	0
		NA	7	25
**W.	1. In childhood was the patient *excessively* dependent on his father for advice or direction in making decisions?	Yes	7	18
		No	84	76
		NA	5	2
	2. Currently does patient have anxiety in making major decisions?	Yes	61	67
		No	30	27
		NA	5	2

Question	Response	H	C
**X. 1. Did the patient feel that he was used by his father to satisfy his needs?	Yes	16	26
	No	73	69
	NA	7	1
2. Which of father's needs was the patient used to satisfy?			
3. Did patient feel that his father understood and accepted his needs and feelings?	Yes	6	19
	No	85	75
	NA	5	2
4. Does patient feel that his father was insensitive to his needs?	Yes	76	75
	No	13	20
	NA	7	1
5. Does patient feel that his father took his needs and desires into consideration in decisions and activities involving patient? (i.e., choice of friends, hobbies, vocation, use of patient's free time, other)	Yes	6	19
	No	81	75
	NA	9	2
6. Does patient feel his father "babied" him?	Yes	7	7
	No	84	88
	NA	5	1
**Y. 1. Did patient have temper tantrums or other expressions of rage towards father?	Yes	26	31
	No	63	63
	NA	7	2
2. Were such expressions of rage generally successful in achieving his purpose?	Yes	5	8
	No	35	26
	NA	56	62
**Z. Currently does patient consider his father jealous, disapproving, or belittling of his female friends?	Yes	7	13
	No	46	62
	NA	43	21
**AA. Currently does patient feel respected as an adult by his father?	Yes	29	48
	No	36	25
	NA	31	23
**BB. Does patient feel his father:			
1. Understood women	Yes	4	11
2. Liked women	Yes	39	48
3. Resented women	Yes	40	35
4. Envied women	Yes	1	8
	NA	22	22
**CC. 1. Did patient regard his father as an admirable person?	Yes	15	40
	No	75	54
	NA	6	2
2. Does he now regard him as such?	Yes	28	37
	No	55	55
	NA	13	4
IV. Relation of patient to siblings. (Note: identify sibling by sex and age)	No sibling	11	22
A. 1. Was any sibling hated?	Older brother	23	15
	Older sister	7	9

		H	C
	Younger brother	12	7
	Younger sister	8	5
	None	44	42
	NA	1	0
2. Was any sibling feared?	Older brother	19	18
	Older sister	7	7
	Younger brother	4	2
	Younger sister	3	3
	None	60	48
	NA	2	0
3. Was any sibling admired?	Older brother	19	23
	Older sister	22	9
	Younger brother	6	9
	Younger sister	7	4
	None	40	29
	NA	1	4
B. Were any siblings homosexual? Which?	Older brother	4	1
	Younger brother	4	0
	Older brother	0	2
	Younger sister	1	0
	None	84	74
	NA	2	1
C. How many siblings were there?	None	11	22
	One	42	33
	Two	20	22
	Three	24	11
	Four	4	9
	Five	4	3
	Six	1	0
D. 1. Any gross psychiatric aberrations in siblings?	Yes	33	26
	No	62	52
2. Which sibling?	Older brother	13	10
	Older sister	9	5
	Younger brother	6	10
	Younger sister	9	4
	None	62	52
3. Aberration?	Psychosis	4	7
	Celibacy	4	1
	Eccentricities	5	1
	Severe neurosis	20	16
E. 1. Was there homosexual contact with siblings?	Yes	17	3
2. Which one?	Older brother	8	3
	Younger brother	9	0

V. Sexual development
and current functioning.

Part (a). The following questions apply to homosexual and comparison cases.

Question	Response	H	C
A. 1. Was sexual information obtained from mother?	Much	1	3
	Some	4	5
	Little	21	10
	None	78	79
	NA	2	3
2. Was sexual information obtained from father?	Much	0	0
	Some	3	6
	Little	16	23
	None	85	70
	NA	2	1
B. Guilt feeling about masturbation?	Much	56	48
	Some	29	35
	Little	13	11
	None	8	5
	NA	0	7
C. 1. Age of first homosexual activity?			
2. Type of activity?	See Part c, X 1.		
3. Age of partner?			
D. 1. Age of first heterosexual activity?			
2. Type of activity?	See Part c, Y 1.		
3. Age of partner?			
E. Frequency of sexual activity			
1. Childhood	Great deal	17	5
	Some	26	29
	Little	24	31
	None	33	31
	NA	6	4
2. Preadolescent	Great deal	17	5
	Some	38	37
	Little	29	36
	None	17	19
	NA	5	3
3. Puberty	Great deal	35	21
	Some	41	44
	Little	15	26
	None	10	8
	NA	5	1
4. Early adulthood	Great deal	46	30
	Some	40	52
	Little	15	13
	None	3	5
	NA	2	0
5. Present	Great deal	40	31
	Some	42	50
	Little	19	11

		H	C
	None	3	1
	NA	2	7
F. 1. Is sexual excitement accompanied by: Anxiety?	Yes	66	49
	No	40	50
	NA	0	1
2. Violence?	Yes	12	4
	No	87	92
	NA	7	4
3. Fantasies of violence?	Yes	32	22
	No	71	77
	NA	3	1
*G. Has patient expressed any fear or aversion to female genitalia?	Yes	74	34
	No	32	66
*H. Has patient expressed fear of physical injury or disease of his genitals?	Yes	57	43
	No	49	57
*I. 1. Does patient feel his genitals are smaller than normal?	Yes	40	28
	No	62	69
	NA	4	3
*2. Smaller than he desires?	Yes	46	35
	No	52	56
	NA	8	9
*J. Does patient recall threats or punishment for sexual play with girls during childhood?	Yes	34	24
	No	71	73
	NA	1	3
*K. Was there an extended period during childhood or adolescence when contemporary heterosexual objects were not accessible for social relationship?	Yes	19	16
	No	87	82
	NA	0	2
*L. Was patient in childhood seduced by an adult male homosexual?	Yes	24	7
	No	80	92
	NA	2	1
*M. 1. Does patient often have potency difficulties in: Heterosexual intercourse?	Yes	47	34
	No	27	61
	Never had	28	0
	NA	4	5
2. Homosexual relations?	Yes	19	
	No	81	
*N. 1. Does patient have fantasies during sexual intercourse? In homosexual intercourse?	Yes	25	
	No	60	
	NA	21	
2. In heterosexual intercourse?	Yes	21	31
	No	35	52
	Never had	28	0
	NA	22	17
3. Describe characteristic fantasy.			
*O. 1. Does patient have fantasies during masturbation?	Yes	61	46
	No	31	33

			H	C
		NA	14	21
	2. Describe characteristic fantasy.			
*P.	1. Has patient ever had erotic heterosexual activity in the *manifest* content of his dreams?	Yes	50	87
		No	54	12
		NA	2	1
	2. Erotic homosexual activity?	Yes	92	25
		No	11	65
		NA	3	10
	3. Incestuous activity?	Yes	35	38
		No	70	56
		NA	1	6
	Part (b). The following questions apply to homosexuals only.			
*Q.	Is patient concerned about exposure of his homosexuality?	Yes	96	
		No	10	
*R.	In homosexual activity does patient prefer to insert penis into an orifice?	Yes	38	
		No	64	
		NA	4	
*S.	In homosexual activity does patient prefer to have penis inserted into one of his orifices?	Yes	33	
		No	61	
		NA	12	
	Which orifice?	Mouth	2	
	Insertors:	Anus	8	
		No preferences	28	
	Insertees:	Mouth	18	
		Anus	15	
	Takes role of insertor or insertee without preference for either		25	
*T.	Does patient practice mutual ("69")?	Yes	28	
		No	65	
		NA	13	
*U.	Is estimated duration of actual intercourse (time between insertion and orgasm) in homosexual act a matter of seconds minutes			
*V.	1. Does patient give warmth in homosexual relationship?	Yes	51	
		No	53	
		NA	2	
	2. Does patient receive warmth from homosexual partner?	Yes	54	
		No	50	
		NA	2	
*W.	1. Does patient believe himself to be a warm, sensitive person?	Yes	84	
		No	19	
		NA	3	
	2. Does patient believe homosexual partner is a warm, sensitive person?	Yes	36	
	In permanent relationship?	No	33	
	In transitory relationship?	Yes	27	
		No	62	

		H	C
Part (c). The following questions apply to both homosexual and comparison cases.			
**X. 1. At what age did the patient have his first homosexual relationship which involved either his own or his partner's genitals?	0-10	29	11
	11-14	29	8
	15-18	24	0
	19-24	11	2
	25+	3	1
2. What was the specific activity?	Mutual masturbation	56	0
	Oral	23	7
	Anal	6	3
	Other	7	4
	NA	4	72
3. What was the age of the partner?	Younger	1	0
	Same	54	14
	Older	30	8
	NA	11	74
4. Who initiated this activity?	Patient	19	1
	Partner	52	14
	Mutual	14	5
	NA	11	76
5. Was the patient seduced?	Yes	42	8
	No	48	11
	NA	10	77
6. Any unusual circumstances surrounding this event?			
**Y. 1. At what age did the patient have his first homosexual relationship which involved either his own or his partner's orifice? Specify orifice.	0-10	7	0
	11-14	13	6
	15-18	26	0
	19-24	26	2
	25+	9	1
	NA	25	11
	Oral	25	3
	Anal	58	9
	Both	3	0
	NA	10	85
2. What was the specific activity?			
3. What was the age of the partner?	3-9 yrs. younger	4	0
	Same	38	6
	3-9 yrs. older	17	2
	10+ yrs. older	17	3
	NA	20	85
4. Who initiated this activity?	Patient	24	0
	Partner	45	9
	Mutual	8	2
	NA	19	85

			H	C
	5. Was the patient seduced?	Yes	30	5
		No	52	7
		NA	14	84
	6. Any unusual circumstances surrounding this event?			
**Z.	1. At what age did patient have his first heterosexual experience involving physical contact with his partner?			
	2. What was the specific activity?	Kissing	53	66
		Necking	28	48
		Petting	23	24
		Intercourse	12	9
		Attempted intercourse	0	2
		Oral	1	0
		Never	16	0
		Other	5	5
		NA	10	11
	3. What was the age of the partner?	3-9 yrs. younger	6	3
		Same	53	72
		3-9 yrs. Older	5	3
		10+ Older	7	2
		NA	25	16
	4. Who initiated this activity?	Patient	43	48
		Partner	20	17
		Mutual	5	6
		NA	28	24
	5. Any unusual circumstances surrounding this event?			
**AA.	1. At what age did patient have his first heterosexual experience involving his own or his partner's genitals?	0-14	4	7
		15-18	10	28
		19-24	37	43
		25-29	5	4
		30-39	10	2
		40+	2	0
		Never	28	0
	2. What was the specific activity?	Kissing	15	15
		Necking	16	14
		Petting	22	40
		Intercourse	38	38
		Attempted intercourse	3	6
		Oral	1	3
		Other	4	3
		Never	27	1
		NA	8	20

			H	C
	3. What was the age of the partner?	10 yrs. younger	1	0
		3-9 yrs. younger	5	4
		Same	39	54
		3-9 yrs. older	10	12
		10+ yrs. older	4	3
		NA	37	23
	4. Who initiated this activity?	Patient	37	49
		Partner	16	18
		Both	4	5
	5. Any unusual circumstances surrounding this event?			
**BB.	1. What was the age of the patient at the first attempt at heterosexual intercourse?	0-14	1	1
		15-18	9	28
		19-20	19	22
		21-24	19	32
		25-29	8	7
		30-39	8	3
		40+	3	0
		Never tried	28	
		NA	1	3
	2. Age of partner?	10+ yrs. younger	1	0
		3-9 yrs. younger	6	4
		Same	33	59
		3-9 years older	13	10
		10+ yrs. older	4	4
		NA	39	19
	3. Who initiated this activity?	Patient	38	54
		Partner	15	21
		Both	5	5
		NA	38	16
	4. Was this attempt successful?	Yes	37	65
		No	24	16
	5. What was patient's age at time of first successful intercourse?	Under 25 yrs.	39	
		Over 25 yrs.	16	
**CC.	1. Did the patient have an early memory of sexual arousal involving a male figure?	Yes	75	16
		No	1	36
		NA	20	44
	Specify earliest age and stimulus	0-10	31	7
		11-14	34	5
		15-18	7	2
		19-24	2	0
		25+	1	3

		H	C
2. Did patient have an early memory of sexual arousal involving a female figure?	Yes	52	65
	No	17	0
	NA	27	31
Specify earliest age and stimulus	0-10	22	43
	11-14	11	22
	15-18	8	0
	19-24	4	
	25+	7	
VI. Developmental			
A. Was patient excessively fearful of of physical injury in childhood?	Yes	80	46
	No	26	54
	NA	0	0
B. 1. Did patient avoid physical fights?	Yes	94	55
	No	11	43
	NA	1	2
2. Did patient seek physical fights?	Yes	6	13
	No	96	81
	NA	4	6
C. Was play activity before puberty predominantly with girls?	Yes	35	10
	No	69	89
	NA	2	1
D. Was patient "lone wolf" in childhood?	Yes	64	27
	No	41	72
	NA	1	1
E. Did patient participate in competitive group games?	Yes	18	63
	No	87	36
	NA	1	1
F. 1. Did patient play baseball?	Yes	17	62
	No	87	35
	NA	2	3
2. Is he today a baseball fan?	Yes	6	29
	No	96	65
	NA	4	6
*G. Whom did patient want to be like?	Mother	18	1
	Father	12	20
	Brother	12	5
	Sister	6	1
	Other male	12	17
	Other female	1	0
	No one	10	14
	NA	35	42
*H. Did patient ever want to be a woman?	Yes	41	8
	No	61	64
	NA	4	28
**I. 1. Describe the patient's physical make-up in childhood.	Frail	47	20
	Clumsy	22	10
	Athletic	12	39
	Well-coördinated	12	49
	Overweight	15	9
	Effeminate	26	2

		H	C
	Artistic	29	11
	None	7	5
	NA	2	0
2. Describe same currently.	Frail	17	9
	Clumsy	5	3
	Athletic	17	37
	Well-coördinated	12	37
	Overweight	8	5
	Effeminate	26	4
	Other	13	14
	None	12	8
	NA	12	13
3. Effeminate in childhood or currently		33	
**J. 1. Was patient a clinging child?	Yes	48	25
	No	42	68
	NA	6	3
2. Was patient reluctant to start school?	Yes	41	22
	No	42	71
	NA	13	3
Did patient frequently turn to either mother or father for protection? Specify to whom.	Mother	52	29
	Father	2	2
	Both	2	3
	Neither	33	58
	NA	7	4
**K. 1. In childhood did patient feel a sense of rivalry or competitiveness with mother, father or any sibling? Specify	Mother	8	6
	Father	24	30
	Male sib.	43	39
	Female sib.	23	18
	None	21	24
	NA	4	3
2. Was this competitiveness acted-out by patient in a specific area?	Scholastic attainments	33	38
	Athletics	7	19
	Earning power	6	13
	Work	2	8
	Masculinity	1	10
	Status	7	15
	Artistic ability	29	11
	Other	6	6
	None	22	26
	NA	15	14
3. Is there evidence that patient was covertly competitive?	Yes	78	80
	No	12	11
	NA	6	5
4. Does the analyst feel patient was:			
(a) Overtly competitive?	Yes	30	40
(b) Covertly competitive?	Yes	75	76
	Neither	6	3

			H	C
		NA	3	0
	5. Was either parent openly competitive with patient or with another sibling? Specify	Mother	8	7
		Father	14	20
		Sib	5	2
		None	59	59
		NA	13	8
	6. Was any sibling openly competitive with patient?	Yes	35	33
		No	33	41
		NA	28	22
	7. In current functioning is patient openly competitive with:	Family members	22	30
		Friends	15	13
		Authority	22	30
		Peers	33	27
		Subordinates	6	6
		None	34	46
		NA	8	0
	8. Is patient covertly competitive in current functioning?	Yes	66	54
		No	10	25
		NA	20	17
**L.	1. Is patient now living at home?	Yes	14	13
		No	79	83
		NA	3	0
	2. (a) If not, at what age did he leave home?			
	(b) Mother's and father's reaction to his leaving home? (approval, hostility, indifference, etc.)			
	(c) What are patient's current feelings when returning to parental home?			
	3. (a) If still living at home, does he fear disapproval from mother or father if he does leave home? Specify.			
	(b) Does he have any other reason to fear leaving home?			
	4. Before analysis, was patient contributing to the financial support of parents? Regularly or irregularly?			
	5. Currently is patient contributing to parent's financial support?	Yes	15	22
		No	69	69
		NA	12	5
VII. Choice of homosexual partner				
A.	1. Does patient identify partner with family members?	Yes	35	
		No	69	
		NA	2	
	2. Which member or members?	Mother	9	
		Father	21	

		H	C
	Sister	4	
	Brother	11	
	None	15	
	NA	4	
B. 1. Does analyst see identification of partners with family members?	Yes	65	
	No	36	
	NA	5	
2. Which ones?	Father	31	
	Brother	7	
	Father & brother	8	
	Mother	6	
	Sister	1	
	Mother & sister	4	
	Mother & father	5	
	Father, mother & brother	1	
	Father, mother & sister	1	
	Brother & sister	1	
C. 1. Does patient seek predominantly masculine qualities in partners?	Yes	73	
	No	32	
	NA	1	
2. Does patient seek predominantly feminine qualities?	Yes	22	
	No	79	
	NA	5	
D. Is patient eager to conceal his homosexuality?	Yes	90	
	No	16	
E. Does patient seek partners for:			
1. Warmth?	Yes	45	
2. Contact?	Yes	63	
3. Friendliness?	Yes	47	
4. Permissiveness?	Yes	25	
	NA	5	
F. 1. Does patient seek for large penis?	Yes	60	
	No	37	
	NA	9	
2. Special interest in buttocks?	Yes	36	
	No	62	
	NA	8	
VIII. Relation to women			
A. Does patient have any or some of the following attitudes to women?			
1. Idolize	Yes	31	33
2. Rivalry	Yes	36	29
3. Fear	Yes	73	52

		H	C
4. Contempt	Yes	36	33
	NA	7	20
B. Many male homosexuals, consciously or otherwise, seek out social contacts with women so that they manage not to be away from such contacts for any length of time. Is this true for this patient?	Yes	70	
	No	33	
	NA	3	
IX. Adaptational response			
A. Are any or some of the following responses dominant patterns in reaction to stress situations?			
1. Withdrawal	Yes	67	49
2. Anxiety	Yes	89	76
3. Depression	Yes	63	57
4. Sulking	Yes	39	27
5. Assertiveness	Yes	11	18
6. Rage	Yes	42	41
7. Submissiveness	Yes	42	58
	NA	1	0
X. Psychosomatic			
A. Is general health	Excellent	23	25
	Good	66	60
	Fair	16	12
	Poor	1	1
	NA	0	2
B. Does patient have gastrointestinal difficulties?	Yes	36	31
	No	70	65
	NA	0	4
1. Peptic ulcer	Yes	6	4
2. Hemorrhoids	Yes	10	6
3. Functional gastrointestinal symptoms	Yes	27	25
4. Other	Yes	11	5
	NA	59	62
C. Any other dominant system involvement?	Yes	26	25
	No	76	69
	NA	4	6
**XI. Latent homosexuality. The following questions apply only to the comparison group.			
A. Has patient expressed fear of homosexuality?	Yes		59
	No		37
B. Has patient had overtly homosexual fantasies, dreams, ideas or impulses? Specify.	Yes		51
	No		39
	NA		6
C. How often have homosexual advances been made to patient by known or suspected overt homosexuals?	Never		41
	Rarely		42
	Occasionally		7
	Frequently		2

		H	C
	NA		4
D. How has patient reacted to homosexual advances made to him?	Fear		18
	Anxiety		24
	Rage		8
	Disgust		9
	Horror		2
	Fascination		5
	Understanding		16
	Indifference		9
	Other		7
	Never approached		23
	NA		17
E. How has patient reacted when in the presence of or upon casually seeing known homosexuals?	Fear		9
	Anxiety		25
	Rage		6
	Disgust		14
	Horror		1
	Fascination		5
	Understanding		29
	Indifference		30
	Other		8
	Never approached		10
**XII. General question			
Did analyst feel questionnaire explored the fundamental dynamics of his patient?	Yes	28	29
	No	23	23
	NA	55	48
If not, formulate current dynamic and genetic factors currently used in this patient's case. Specifically, the relationship of parents or siblings to the genesis of his homosexuality, the role of the homosexual partner, and the meaning of the homosexual act.			
*XIII. Diagnosis and therapy			
A. What is clinical psychiatric diagnosis of patient?			
1. Schizophrenia		28	18
2. Manic depressive		0	2
3. Psychoneurosis		31	42
4. Character disorder		44	36
5. Other		2	2
	NA	1	0
B. Date of initiation of treatment with you.	1950 or before	19	17
	1951-6	83	81
	NA	4	2
C. 1. Number of sessions per week	1	15	10
	2	53	47
	3	34	40
	4	3	3
	5	1	0

		H	C
2. Number of sessions at time First Questionnaire was answered	0-150	46	23
	151-450	46	63
	451+	8	13
	NA	6	1
(a) Number of sessions to 1961 follow-up	0-150	28	
	151-350	40	
	351+	38	
3. Date of termination, if terminated			
D. What was the patient's stated reason for coming into treatment?			
1. Sex problem		51	10
2. Other than sex problem		52	88
	NA	3	2
E. Did patient want his homosexuality cured?	Yes	64	
	No	32	
	NA	10	
F. Patient's sexual status: Beginning therapy.			
1. Exclusively homosexual		72	0
2. Bisexual		30	0
3. Exclusively heterosexual		0	100
4. Inactive		4	0
5. Married		8	51
Patient's sexual status: Last contact.			
1. Exclusively homosexual		43	0
2. Bisexual		28	0
3. Exclusively heterosexual		29	100
4. Inactive		6	0
5. Married		15	57
G. Has there been a shift to a more masculine role in homosexual activity?	Yes	41	
	No	54	
H. Were there evidences of improvement in areas other than sexual?	Yes	97	94
	No	7	2
	NA	2	4
1. Increased occupational effectiveness?	Yes	85	84
	No	15	10
	NA	5	6
2. Improved social relationships?	Yes	87	87
	No	16	9
	NA	3	4
3. Symptomatic improvement?	Yes	86	88
	No	11	6
	NA	9	6
I. Any previous treatment?			
1. Psychoanalytic?	Yes	31	26
(a) Duration?	No	70	67
	NA	6	7

		H	C
2. Sex of therapist	Male	18	19
	Female	7	4
3. Shock treatment	Yes	4	6
(a) Number of treatments			
(b) Number of courses of treatment			
4. Other			

APPENDIX B

Inferential Estimates and Cumulative Scores

THREE MAJOR Inferential Assessments were made in this study: one for categorizing the mothers (see Chapter III); one for fathers (see Chapter IV); and the third for evaluating the severity of homosexual problems where present among the comparison patients (see Chapter X). The techniques employed were identical in all three instances. Careful study of each individual case protocol and of the statistical data directed the choice of categories into which the data could be most appropriately ordered. Questionnaire items relevant to each category were clustered. Two members of the Committee were assigned to judge each protocol for classification into the designated categories. The judges could use the relevant item clusters as a guide but they were free to make independent judgments based on their clinical impressions and the frequent volunteered comments of the responding psychoanalysts in the case protocols. In those instances where the judges disagreed, the cases were examined and categorized according to the consensual decision of the entire Research Committee. Two additional inferential assessments describing parental attitudes were made: "feminizing"; "minimizing." The same procedure was followed as already described. The questionnaire item clusters for each assessment follow below.

Three cumulative scores which appear in this report are the Developmental Six Score (Chapter VII); the Excessive Fearfulness of Physical Injury in Childhood Score (Chapter VII), and the Twenty Questions Score (Chapter X). The Twenty Questions Score assembles 20 items relating interparental and parent-child relationships which distinguished the H- and C- samples at high levels of statistical significance. The item clusters for each of these three scores are given below.

The following number-letter combinations refer to the specific questions in Appendix A.

I. Parent Feminizing
   II and III H2; H3; N; Q4—less or no; VI H

II. Parent Minimizing
II and III A3; B *no;* D1; D2; Q 3—less or not; X6; AA—no

III. Developmental Six Score
VI A; VI B1; VI C; VI D; VI E; VI F1

IV. Excessive Fear of Physical Injury in Childhood
II U1; U2; U3; V2; V5; X6
III D2; J1; J2

V. Twenty Questions
1. Relation between parents
   I H1; I H2
2. Relation between patient and mother
   II F1; II F3; II H2 and 3; II I1; II I2; II L; II M; II O; II R1; II S1
3. Relation between patient and father
   III A1; III C1; III G; III H1; III J1; III K; III O2; III T2

Bibliography

ABRAHAM, KARL (1948). Sexuality and Alcoholism. In *Selected Papers on Psycho-analysis.* 3rd Ed. London: Hogarth Press.

ACKERMAN, NATHAN W. (1958). *The Psychodynamics of Family Life.* New York: Basic Books.

BANCROFT, J., AXWORTH, D., AND RATCLIFFE, S. (1982). The personality and psychosexual development of boys with 47 XXY chromosome constitution. *Journal of Child Psychology and Psychiatry and Allied Disciplines* 23:169–180.

BATESON, GREGORY, JACKSON D. D., HALEY, J., AND WEAKLAND, J. (1956). Toward a Theory of Schizophrenia. *Behavioral Science* 1:251–264.

BAUER, J. (1940). Homosexuality as an Endocrinological, Psychological, and Genetic Problem. *Journal of Criminal Pathology* 2:188–197.

BELL, A. P., WEINBERG, M. S., AND HAMMERSMITH, S. K. (1981). *Sexual Preference: Its Development in Men and Women.* Bloomington, IN: Indiana University Press.

BERG, C., AND ALLEN, C. (1958). *The Problem of Homosexuality.* New York: Citadel Press.

BERGLER, EDMUND (1957). *Homosexuality: Disease or Way of Life.* New York: Hill and Wang.

BIEBER, IRVING (1953). The Meaning of Masochism. *American Journal of Psychotherapy* 7: 433–448.

_____ (1959). Olfaction in sexual development and adult sexual organization. *American Journal of Psychotherapy* 13:851–859.

_____ (1975). Sexual arousal mechanisms in male homosexuals. In *Sexual Behavior—Pharmacology and Biochemistry,* ed. M. Sandler and G. I. Gesa, New York: Raven Press.

_____ (1977). Pathogenicity of parental preference. *Journal of the American Academy of Psychoanalysis.* New York: John Wiley & Sons.

_____ (1980). Disorders of the work function. In: *Cognitive Psychoanalysis,* I. Bieber, New York: Jason Aronson.

BIEBER, I., AND BIEBER, T. B. (1979). Male homosexuality. *Canadian Journal of Psychiatry* 24:409–421.

BIEBER, I., DAIN, H., DINCE, P., DRELLICH, M., GRAND, H., GUNDLACH, R., KREMER, M., RIFKIN, A.,

WILBUR, C., AND BIEBER, T. B. (1962). *Homosexuality: A Psychoanalytic Study of Male Homosexuals.* New York: Basic Books.

BIEBER, T. B. (1971). Group therapy with homosexuals. In *Comprehensive Group Psychotherapy,* ed. H. I. Kaplan and B. S. Sadock. Baltimore: Williams and Wilkins.

BYCHOWSKI, G. (1954). The Structure of Homosexual Acting Out. *Psychoanalytic Quarterly* 23:48–61.

CARPENTER, EDWARD (1912). *The Intermediate Sex.* New York: M. Kennerly.

CHANG, JUDY, AND BLOCH, J. (1960). A Study of Identification in Male Homosexuals. *Journal of Consulting Psychology* 24:307–310.

CURRAN, DESMOND, AND PARR, DENIS (1957). Homosexuality: An Analysis of 100 Male Cases Seen in Private Practice. *British Medical Journal* 797–801.

DAVIDS, A., JOELSON, M., AND MC ARTHUR, C. (1956). Rorschach and TAT Indices of Homosexuality in Overt Homosexuals, Neurotics, and Normal Males. *Journal of Abnormal and Social Psychology* 53:161–172.

DOIDGE, W. T., AND HOLTZMAN, W. H. (1960). Implications of Homosexuality Among Air Force Trainees. *Journal of Consulting Psychchology* 24:9–13.

EVANS, R. B. (1969). Childhood parental relations of homosexual men. *Journal of Consulting Clinical Psychology* 33:129–135.

ELLIS, ALBERT (1951). Study of 300 Sex Offenders. *International Journal of Sexology* 4:127–134.

FORD, CLELLAN S., AND BEACH, FRANK A. (1951). *Patterns of Sexual Behavior.* New York: Harper.

FREUD, ANNA (1951). Clinical Observations on the Treatment of Male Homosexuality. *Psychiatric Quarterly* 20:337–338 (abstract).

FREUD, SIGMUND (1911). Psychoanalytic Notes Upon an Autobiographical Account of a Case of Paranoia. *Journal of British Psychoanalytic Psychopathology* 3:9–68.

_____ (1938). Three Contributions to the Theory of Sex. In *The Basic Writings of Sigmund Freud,* ed. A. A. Brill. New York: Modern Library.

_____ *Three Essays on the Theory of Sexuality. Standard Edition*, 17.

GLOVER, B. H. (1951). Homosexuality in University Students. *Journal of Nervous and Mental Disease* 113:377–387.

GREEN, R. (1987). *The "Sissy Boy" Syndrome and the Development of Homosexuality.* New Haven: Yale University Press.

HIRSCHFELD, M. (1938). *Sexual Anomalies and Perversion.* London: Encyclopaedic Press.

HOOKER, EVELYN (1956). A Preliminary Analysis of Group Behavior of Homosexuals. *Journal of Psychology* 42:217–225.

_____ (1957). The Adjustment of the Male Overt Homosexual. *J. Proj. Tech.* 21:18–31.

_____ (1958). Male Homosexuality in the Rorschach. *J. Proj. Tech.* 22:33–54.

HORNEY, KAREN (1937). *The Neurotic Personality of Our Time.* New York: Norton.

_____ (1945). *Our Inner Conflicts.* New York: Norton.

JACKLIN, C. N., MACCOBY, E. E., AND DOERING, C. H. (1983). Neonatal sex steroid hormones and timidity in 6-18-month-old boys and girls. *Developmental Psychobiology* 16:163–168.

JONES, ERNEST (1912). *Papers on Psycho-analysis.* London: Baillière, Tindall & Cox.

KALLMAN, FRANZ (1952). Comparative Twin Studies on the Genetic Aspects of Male Homosexuality. *Journal of Nervous and Mental Disease* 115:283–298.

KALOGERAKIS, M. (1963). The role of olfaction in sexual development. *Psychosomatic Medicine* 25:420–432.

KARDINER, A. (1939). *The Individual and His Society.* New York: Columbia University Press.

_____ (1949). Discussion in *Psychosexual Development in Health and Disease,* ed. Paul Hoch and Joseph Zubin. New York: Grune & Stratton.

KINSEY, ALFRED, POMEROY, W. B., AND GEBHARD, P. H. (1948). *Sexual Behavior in the Human Male.* Philadelphia: Saunders.

KLEIN, M. (1932). *The Psychoanalysis of Children.* London: Hogarth Press.

KLEIN, M., HEIMANN, PAULA, ISAACS, SUSAN, AND RIVIERE, JOAN (1952). *Developments in Psycho-analysis.* London: Hogarth Press.

KNIGHT, R. P. (1941). Evaluation of the Results of Psychoanalytic Therapy. *American Journal of Psychiatry* 98:434–436.

KOLB, L.C., AND JOHNSON, A. M. (1955). Etiology and Therapy of Overt Homosexuality. *Psychoanalytic Quarterly* 24:506–515.

KRAFFT-EBING, R. (1934). *Psychopathia Sexualis.* Rev. Ed. Brooklyn: Physicians & Surgeons Book Co.

THE LADDER (1960). Daughters of Bilitis. Sept.

LANG, T. (1940). Studies on the Genetic Determination of Homosexuality. *Journal of Nervous and Mental Disease* 92:55–64.

LITTEN, E. M., GRIFFIN, M. E., AND JOHNSON, A. M. (1956). Parental Influence in Unusual Sexual Behavior in Children. *Psychoanalytic Quarterly* 25:1–15.

LOMBROSO, CESARE (1895). *Criminal Anthropology.* New York: The Forum.

MAIER, N. R. F. (1960). Maier's Law. *American Psychology* 15:208–212.

MAINLAND, D., HARRERA, L., AND SUTCLIFFE, M. I. (1956). *Statistical Tables for Use with Binomial Samples—Contingency Tests, Confidence Limits, and Sample Size Estimates.* New York: New York University College of Medicine.

MANTEGAZZA, PAOLO (1932). *Anthropological Studies of Sexual Relations of Mankind.* New York: Anthropological Press.

MASSERMAN, J. (1951). Some Current Concepts of Sexual Behavior. *Psychiatry* 14:61–62.

MAYER-GROSS, W., SLATER, E., AND ROTH, M. (1954). *Clinical Psychiatry.* London: Cassell & Co.

MILLER, PAUL R. (1958). The Effeminate Passive Obligatory Homosexual. *American Medical Association Archives of Neurology and Psychology* 80:612–618.

MONEY, J., HAMPSON, J. G., AND HAMPSON, J.I. (1959). An Examination of Some Basic Concepts: The Evidence of Human Hermaphroditism. *Bulletin of the Johns Hopkins Hospital* 97:284–310.

OVESEY, LIONEL (1954). The Homosexual Conflict. *Psychiatry* 17:243–250.

_____ (1955). The Pseudohomosexual Anxiety. *Psychiatry* 18:17–25.

PARÉ, C. M. B. (1956). Homosexuality and Chromosomal Sex. *Journal of Psychosomatic Research* 1:247–251.

PARSONS, TALCOTT, AND BALES, ROBERT F. (1955). *Family Socialization and Interaction Process.* Glencoe, Ill.: Free Press.

PETERSON, R. E., IMPERATO-MC GINLEY, J., GUATIER, T., AND STURLA, E. (1977). Male pseudohermaphroditism due to steroid 5 alpha reductase deficiency. *American Journal of Medicine* 62: 170.

RABOCH, J., AND NIDOMA, K. (1958). Sex Chromatin and Sexual Behavior. *Psychosomatic Medicine* 20:55–59.

RADO, SANDOR (1940). A Critical Examination of the Theory of Bisexuality. *Psychosomatic Medicine* 2:459–467.

_____ (1949). An Adaptational View of Sexual Behavior. In *Psychosexual Development in Health and Disease,* ed. Paul Hoch and Joseph Zubin. New York: Grune & Stratton.

Report of the Committee on Homosexual Offences and Prostitution (1957) (Wolfenden Report). London: H. M. S. O.

SAWYER, G. I. (1954). Homosexuality: The Endocrinological Aspects. *Practitioner* 172:374–377.

SILVERBERG, W. V. (1952). *Childhood Experiences and Personal Destiny*. New York: Springer.

STOLLER, R. J. (1987). *Presentations of Gender*. New Haven: Yale University Press.

SULLIVAN, HARRY STACK (1953). *The Interpersonal Theory of Psychiatry*, ed. Helen Swick Perry and Mary Ladd Garvel. New York: Norton.

SZASZ, THOMAS (1957). *Pain and Pleasure*. New York: Basic Books.

THOMPSON, CLARA (1947). Changing Concepts of Homosexuality in Psychoanalysis. *Psychiatry* 10:2–13.

TRITES, DAVID K. (1957). Graphic Determination of Significance of 2×2 Contingency Tables. *Psychological Bulletin* 54:140–144.

WEST, D. J. (1959). Parental Figures in the Genesis of Male Homosexuality. *International Journal of Social Psychology* 5:85–97.

WESTWOOD, GORDON (1960). *A Minority—A Report on the Life of the Male Homosexual in Great Britain*. London: Longmans, Green.

WITSCHLI, E., AND MENGART, W. F. (1942). Endocrine Studies on Human Hermaphrodites and Their Bearing on Interpretation of Homosexuality. *Journal of Clinical Endocrinology* 2:279–286.

WOLFENDEN REPORT. See *Report of the Committee on Homosexual Offences and Prostitution.*

WOODWARD, MARY (1958). The Diagnosis and Treatment of Homosexual Offenders. *British Journal of Delinquency* 9:44–58.

Index